Lecture Notes in Computer Science 6411

Commenced Publication in 1973
Founding and Former Series Editors:
Gerhard Goos, Juris Hartmanis, and Jan van Leeuwen

Editorial Board

David Hutchison
Lancaster University, UK

Takeo Kanade
Carnegie Mellon University, Pittsburgh, PA, USA

Josef Kittler
University of Surrey, Guildford, UK

Jon M. Kleinberg
Cornell University, Ithaca, NY, USA

Alfred Kobsa
University of California, Irvine, CA, USA

Friedemann Mattern
ETH Zurich, Switzerland

John C. Mitchell
Stanford University, CA, USA

Moni Naor
Weizmann Institute of Science, Rehovot, Israel

Oscar Nierstrasz
University of Bern, Switzerland

C. Pandu Rangan
Indian Institute of Technology, Madras, India

Bernhard Steffen
TU Dortmund University, Germany

Madhu Sudan
Microsoft Research, Cambridge, MA, USA

Demetri Terzopoulos
University of California, Los Angeles, CA, USA

Doug Tygar
University of California, Berkeley, CA, USA

Gerhard Weikum
Max Planck Institute for Informatics, Saarbruecken, Germany

Rajkumar Kannan   Frederic Andres (Eds.)

Data Engineering and Management

Second International Conference, ICDEM 2010
Tiruchirappalli, India, July 29-31, 2010
Revised Selected Papers

 Springer

Volume Editors

Rajkumar Kannan
Bishop Heber College (Autonomous)
Tiruchirappalli 620017, India
E-mail: rajkumar@bhc.edu.in

Frederic Andres
National Institute of Informatics (NII)
Tokyo, 101-8430, Japan
E-mail: andres@nii.ac.jp

ISSN 0302-9743   e-ISSN 1611-3349
ISBN 978-3-642-27871-6   e-ISBN 978-3-642-27872-3
DOI 10.1007/978-3-642-27872-3
Springer Heidelberg Dordrecht London New York

Library of Congress Control Number: 2011944847

CR Subject Classification (1998): F.3, D.2.4, D.2, D.3, I.2, F.4.1

LNCS Sublibrary: SL 2 – Programming and Software Engineering

© Springer-Verlag Berlin Heidelberg 2012
This work is subject to copyright. All rights are reserved, whether the whole or part of the material is
concerned, specifically the rights of translation, reprinting, re-use of illustrations, recitation, broadcasting,
reproduction on microfilms or in any other way, and storage in data banks. Duplication of this publication
or parts thereof is permitted only under the provisions of the German Copyright Law of September 9, 1965,
in its current version, and permission for use must always be obtained from Springer. Violations are liable
to prosecution under the German Copyright Law.
The use of general descriptive names, registered names, trademarks, etc. in this publication does not imply,
even in the absence of a specific statement, that such names are exempt from the relevant protective laws
and regulations and therefore free for general use.

Typesetting: Camera-ready by author, data conversion by Scientific Publishing Services, Chennai, India

Printed on acid-free paper

Springer is part of Springer Science+Business Media (www.springer.com)

Preface

Data engineering and data management practices are key for digital libraries, knowledge management and Mulselmedia. Many research efforts have been made in related areas. Recent advances in computing, networking, storage, and information technology have enabled the collection and distribution of vast amounts of data including multimedia and mulsemedia in a variety of applications such as education, culture, digital government, data security, and health.

The proliferation of multimedia data and its rich semantics from these applications have created the need for advanced data engineering and management functionalities for in-depth data processing, analysis, indexing, learning, searching, retrieval, mining and management. Our International Conference on Data Engineering and Management (ICDEM) series addresses these research issues annually.

The Second ICDEM was held during July 29–31, 2010 at Bishop Heber College (Autonomous) in Tiruchirappalli, India. The conference program included research contributions, tutorials, keynote talks, and a co-located Workshop on Data Mining with Graphs and Matrices (WDGM 2010).

The keynote talks were offered by Shailly Goyal (TCS, India) on "Semantic Information Retrieval from Enterprise Data" and by George Ghinea (Brunel University, UK) on What About Mulsemedia—Challenges and Opportunities?"

The sponsoring organization and the Organizing Committee deserve praise for the support they provided. A number of individuals contributed to the success of the conference. We thank C. Sathish Kumar, E. Samuel Roy, J. Sam Charles Pinto, A.S. Sathis Kumar, S. Sophia and Thirupathi for providing continuous support and encouragement.

We would like to thank the members of the Program Committee for their support and all authors who submitted their papers to ICDEM 2010.

We would like to express our gratitude to M. Marcus Diepen Boominathan, Principal of Bishop Heber College, for supporting the initial idea of ICDEM 2010. Many thanks also to the faculty members at the college for their cooperation and support.

July 2010   Rajkumar Kannan
                                                                                                    Frederic Andres

Table of Contents

Data Management and Knowledge Extraction

Digital Library

Knowledge and Mulsemedia

Data Management

Digital Library

Knowledge and Mulsemedia

Knowledge and Mulsemedia

Data Processing and knowledge Extraction

Natural Language Processing

Workshop on Data Mining with Graphs and Matrices

Semantic Collation of Enterprise Data for Effective Information Retrieval

C. Anantaram and Shailly Goyal

Innovation Labs, Tata Consultancy Services Ltd
249 D&E, Udyog Vihar Ph. IV, Gurgaon, India
{c.anantaram,shailly.goyal}@tcs.com

Abstract. In this work we present a technical architecture to enable semantic information retrieval from enterprise data that is spread across data sources and applications each having their own data. In order to search and query on such enterprise data effectively, the different applications and data sources that contain relevant data will need to be semantically tagged and their semantic cross-relationship identified. We present a 3-tier ontology based architecture to semantically collate the information from disparate data sources in an enterprise.

1 Introduction

Retrieving or querying relevant data from enterprise systems can be difficult especially if the data is spread across various systems, and the user is interacting at a level where parts of the required data require semantic composition from different enterprise systems. Data warehouse applications address part of the task but miss out on semantic compositionality, application of domain rules and context-driven relevant information retrieval [1]. In order to search and query on such enterprise data effectively, the different applications and data sources that contain relevant data will need to be semantically tagged and their semantic cross-relationship identified. In this work we present a 3-tier ontology based methodology to semantically collate the information in various data sources of an enterprise.

In our architecture, the data from the disparate data sources in an enterprise, along with their metadata, is iteratively refined and composed to create semantically meaningful entities for easy query and retrieval. This is done by a step-by-step process, where the basic data is first converted into a standard data format with semantic labels (such as RDF) from its relational data store. This forms the first level of Ontology (Level 1) that is subsequently refined. This data is then semantically merged through a Composite Mapper to determine the Composite entities and relations between them. This forms the second level of the Ontology (Level 2) that has a composed view of the disparate data that was ingested from the enterprise systems. However, this by itself is not enough considering that end-users tend to interact at even higher levels with abstract concepts that need to be mapped or composed from the Level 2 entities. Thus,

R. Kannan and F. Andres (Eds.): ICDEM 2010, LNCS 6411, pp. 1–8, 2012.
© Springer-Verlag Berlin Heidelberg 2012

we process and generate a Level 3 ontology that may be created from Level 2 entities through constraints and rules applied on the entities. It is the Level 3 Ontology (which we call as the Domain Ontology) that will form the basic backbone for the enterprise semantic information search and query operations.

2   Related Work

Most of the works towards semantic collation of diverse data sources focus on 2-layer schema [2,3,4]. First layer ('wrapper') represents the underlying data and the second layer ('mediator') mediates between the different wrappers to provide a global view. Although this approach identifies the relations between the different data sources, it is not able to capture the end-application specific semantic schema. Caragea et al [5] presents a system for knowledge acquisition from various data sources by enabling application to view a collection of data sources as a collection of tables structured according to an ontology supplied by the user. The limitation of this system is that it assumes each data source as a single table, not as a set of inter-related tables.

3   Levels of Ontology

In order to structure the various data sources in an enterprise, we propose to structure the ontology into three levels. Level-1 Ontology would transform the data in each data source into a Common Data Format (RDF) with each field of each row being expanded into a RDF triple. The common data will then be semantically merged through a Composite Mapper to determine the Composite entities and relations between them. The Composite Mapper will map the various entities using an Ontology and apply the rules for mapping. The rules itself can be defined in a rulebase in the OWL schema. This will create the Level-2 Ontology. We propose to further enhance the Level-2 Ontology with the semantic schemas of the Knowledge Management application and its domain specific rules. This will create the Level-3 Ontology that will form the basic backbone for the Search and Query operations. Figure 1 gives an overview of the 3-level ontology merging.

3.1   Semantic Mapping: Level-1 Ontology

For level 1 ontology, the data source (i.e. the database of the business application) forms a part of the domain terms and their relationships in the ontology. This helps forms the main concepts of the domain and their relationships with a ⟨subject-predicate-object⟩ structure for each of the concepts. The Seed Ontology describes the basic relations that are applicable in the domain. The system has the flexibility of incorporating domain rules (applicable on the data source) therefore enriching the ontology. The Level-1 rules along with Seed Ontology1 and the data from a data source is given to the Ontology Generator, which creates the appropriate RDF file (RDF_i). This is done for all data sources that are going

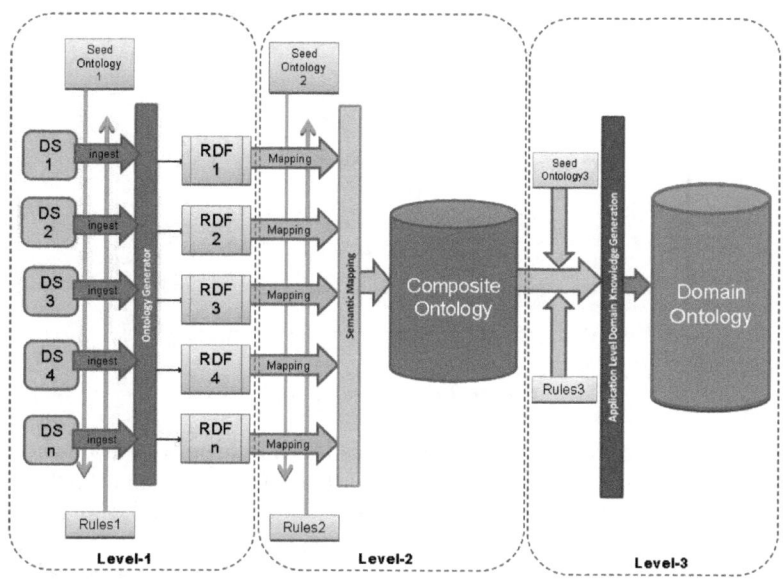

Fig. 1. Ontology Levels

to ingest data and meta-data into the Ontology for the retrieval purpose. Figure 2 describes the ontology generation for a data source.

For illustration, examples of Level-1 Ontology for skill management system and HR system of an organization are indicated below using N3 notation.

```
RDF1: Skill management system        RDF2: HR system
a:employee  c:has  a:name            b:emp  c:has  b:emp_name
a:employee  c:has  a:eid             b:emp  c:has  b:emp_id
a:employee  c:has  s:skill           b:emp  c:has  b:age
s:skill  c:has  s:competency         b:emp  c:has  p:past_exp
s:skill  c:has  s:prof_level         p:past_exp  c:has  p:company
s:skill  c:has  s:certification      p:past_exp  c:has  p:duration
                                     p:past_exp  c:has  p:technologies
```

3.2   Identifying Composite Entities: Level-2 Ontology

In this level of ontology generation, each RDF (RDF_i) acts as the data source. The abstract concepts if any are explicitly specified in Seed Ontology2. These abstract concepts describe the composite entities which may be present in the varied RDF's, created in the previous level. The RDFs will then be semantically merged through a Composite Mapper to determine the Composite entities and relations between them. The Composite Mapper will map the various entities using an Ontology and apply the rules for mapping. Semantic mapping between various sub-classes as well as between the individuals are defined using some ontology generator tool like Protégé. Further the Ontology also aids in setting up the properties and defining the relationships between various sub classes and

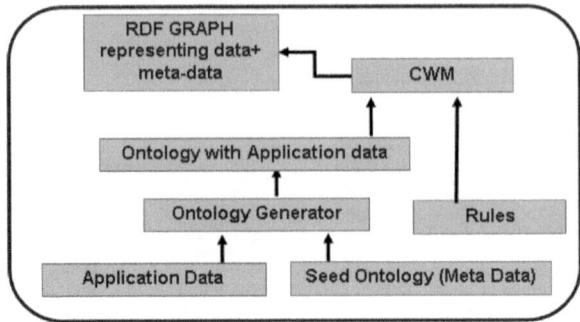

Fig. 2. Ontology Creation

the various individual concepts. Again at this level, in order to enrich the domain knowledge, one could specify rules on the abstract concepts. The RDF obtained from previous level along with seed ontology and rules, is given to ontology generation tool to obtain the Composite Ontology.

As an example, for the ontologies given in Section 3.1, we may have the following Seed Ontology2 and thus would generate the composite ontology as shown below.

```
Level 2 Seed ontology
a:employee    c:same_as    b:emp
a:name        c:same_as    b:emp_name
a:eid         c:same_as    b:emp_id

Composite Ontology:

a:employee    c:has    a:name
a:employee    c:has    a:eid
a:employee    c:has    s:skill
s:skill       c:has    s:competency
s:skill       c:has    s:prof_level
s:skill       c:has    s:certification
a:employee    c:has    b:age
a:employee    c:has    p:past_exp
p:past_exp    c:has    p:company
p:past_exp    c:has    p:duration
p:past_exp    c:has    p:technologies
```

3.3   Enhancing the Ontology: Level-3 Ontology

In this level, the Ontology generated in Level2 is enriched with the semantic schemas of the enterprise knowledge management application and its domain specific rules. Thus the Seed Ontology3 contains concepts that are important from an enterprise search level, and would contain the mapping of these concepts to the various composite entities in Level2. For example, one may have a concept of a *Multi-unit employee* as one who has job responsibilities in various units of the company. Before an employee is marked as a *Multi-unit employee* the Level2 entities would be checked to determine if the constraints imposed by the Level3 concept is met. The rules specified at this level contribute towards the application level knowledge and semantics. These are then fed to the ontology generation tool to obtain the Domain Ontology.

The Domain Ontology is the enriched data source containing the application data along with the semantic knowledge of the domain concepts and their mapping in the RDF format. This forms part of the data on which the query engine works to extract the relevant answer.

For an example, a level 3 rule can be "IF employee has a skill with proficiency level more than L4 and has experience more than 3 yrs on the competency THEN `a:employee c:expert s:skill`". With such rules, the domain ontology will be

```
Domain ontology

a:employee      c:has        a:name
a:employee      c:has        a:eid
a:employee      c:has        s:skill
s:skill         c:has        s:competency
s:skill         c:has        s:prof_level
s:skill         c:has        s:certification
a:employee      c:has        b:age
a:employee      c:has        p:past_exp
p:past_exp      c:has        p:company
p:past_exp      c:has        p:duration
p:past_exp      c:has        p:technologies
a:employee      c:expert     s:skill
```

4   Information Retrieval

Effective, efficient and correct retrieval of data from the domain ontology is critical for the system. We propose a hybrid querying model for the system under consideration. The user can query the system either via natural language or through the flexible menu based querying mechanism. Figure 3 gives the architecture of the proposed information retrieval approach.

4.1   Natural Language Based Querying

Processing natural language questions to obtain relevant information from a database has long been an area of research in artificial intelligence [6,7,8]. For a robust natural language question answering system to business applications, query interpretation is a crucial and complicated task. Goyal et al [9] discuss an approach to analyse and chunk the natural language queries to have correct

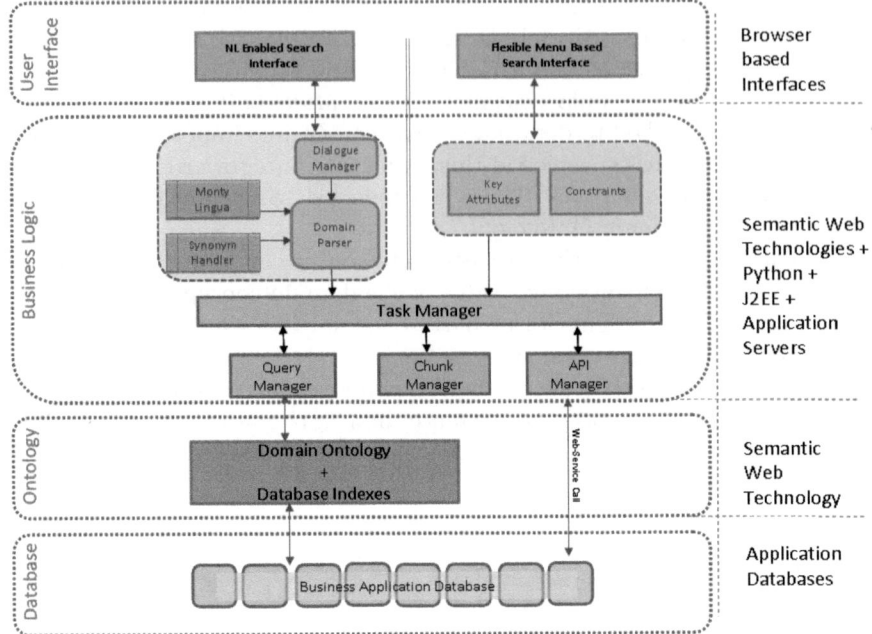

Fig. 3. Querying Architecture

formal query generation and answer extraction from a single database. They view an NL query as consisting of a set of *unknown predicates* whose values need to be determined based on the *constraints* imposed by the rest of the query. Further, semantically valid chunks (SVC) set for the given question using the domain ontology and the syntactic structure of the question are obtained. Similar approach can be used to determine the SVC set for a question in case of multiple data sources, provided a common ontology (Level-3 ontology) is available.

The semantic chunks of the SVC set will be processed by the QueryManager which will generate a formal query is generated on-the-fly. Since the domain ontology is in RDF format, queries will be generated in SPARQL[1], a query language for RDF. The SPARQL queries will be generated iteratively, starting from the semantic chunks not containing any sub-chunk. The unknown predicate of the semantic chunk forms the 'SELECT' clause, and the constraints form a part of the 'WHERE' clause.

4.2   Menu Based Querying

Menu based query interface shall have 'Key Attribute' and 'Constraint' information. Key attribute will specify the attributes for which corresponding value needs to be extracted from the system and Constraints specify the conditions

---

[1] http://dev.w3.org/cvsweb/2004/PythonLib-IH/Doc/sparqlDesc.html?rev=1.11

on the key attribute. Since the *'unknown predicate'* and *'Constraints'* are identified by the virtue of this interface, only remaining task, i.e. query formulation will be similar to the query formulation in case of natural language based query interface.

4.3   An Example

For illustration, such systems can obtain information like "`List all the Java experts below 35 years age`". Using the domain ontology, the system will be able to identify that the user wants '`employees`' with '`age < 35 years`' and '`expert in Java`'. The SPARQL query for the same will be obtained as:

```
Select=("?x")
Where = GraphPattern([]);
Where.addConstraint(lambda binding: ["?y"] < 35)
Where.addPatterns([
                    ("?x"    "expert"       "?a")
                    ("?a"    "skill"        "?b")
                    ("?b"    "comp_name"    "java")
                    ("?x"    "age"          "?y")
                  ])

Result=sparqlGr.query(Select,Where)
```

5   Conclusion

Enterprises today have multiple data sources for various applications. Usually these data sources are not designed for integration and interoperability. Users should be able to access this data without bothering about the data location. In this work we have described an approach to collate independent data sources by converting them to a rich common format. Our three level ontology based architecture aids in the capture of the semantic relations between the data sources, and effectively incorporating them to obtain semantically meaningful entities for querying and retrieval.

References

1. Ziegler, P., Dittrich, K.R.: Three decades of data integration - all problems solved? In: Jacquart, R. (ed.) 18th IFIP World Computer Congress (WCC 2004), Building the Information Society. IFIP International Federation for Information Processing, vol. 156, pp. 3–12. Kluwer, Toulouse (2004)
2. Wang, J., Lu, J., Zhang, Y., Miao, Z., Zhou, B.: Integrating heterogeneous data source using ontology. Journal of Software 4(8), 843–850 (2009)
3. Munir, K., Odeh, M., McClatchey, R., Khan, S., Habib, I.: Semantic information retrieval from distributed heterogeneous data sources. CoRR abs/0707.0745 (2007)

4. Verschelde, J.L., dos Santos, M.C., Deray, T., Smith, B., Ceusters, W.: Ontology- assisted database integration to support natural language processing and biomedical data-mining. Journal of Integrative Bioinformatics 1(1) (2004)
5. Caragea, D., Pathak, J., Bao, J., Silvescu, A., Andorf, C., Dobbs, D., Honavar, V.: Information Integration and Knowledge Acquisition from Semantically Heterogeneous Biological Data Sources. In: Ludäscher, B., Raschid, L. (eds.) DILS 2005. LNCS (LNBI), vol. 3615, pp. 175–190. Springer, Heidelberg (2005)
6. Androutsopoulos, I., Ritchie, G., Thanisch, P.: Natural language interfaces to databases - an introduction. Natural Language Engineering 1(1), 29–81 (1995)
7. Lopez, V., Motta, E., Uren, V., Sabou, M.: State of the art on semantic question answering - a literature review. Technical report, KMI (May 2007)
8. Bhat, S., Anantaram, C., Jain, H.: Framework for Text-Based Conversational User-Interface for Business Applications. In: Zhang, Z., Siekmann, J.H. (eds.) KSEM 2007. LNCS (LNAI), vol. 4798, pp. 301–312. Springer, Heidelberg (2007)
9. Goyal, S., Bhat, S., Gulati, S., Anantaram, C.: Ontology-driven approach to obtain semantically valid chunks for natural language enabled business applications. Research in Computing Science. Special Issue: Natural Language Processing and Its Applications 46(1), 105–116 (2010)

Beyond Knowledge Management:
Knowledge Services Innovation

Asanee Kawtrakul

Uknow, Kasetsart University, Bangkok, Thailand
asanee_naist@yahoo.com

Abstract. Knowledge Management is driven by the needs and requirement of new knowledge-driven economy. Its functions are how it be acquired, represented, exchanged, integrated and converted into useful knowledge. The intelligent use of knowledge and knowledge services are driven by the needs and requirement of creative-and-service-driven economy. The key functionalities of innovational services are how to provide personalized knowledge service and satisfy the individual demand. CyberBrain, a digital ecosystem for the execution of knowledge management and knowledge services innovation, is aimed to be a collaborative knowledge space interconnecting knowledge resources, organization and community best practices with the heterogenous expression. Domain specific ontologies and standard metadata are the basic elements through which Cyber Brain can deploy for integrating and aggregating the scattered knowledge sources. Moreover, Cyber Brain paid more attentions to provide one stop service and ubiquitous personalized knowledge service. This paper overviews some key technologies and methodologies emerging in knowledge engineering, ontology engineering, language engineering, including knowledge processing and utilizing model which meet the consumers' knowledge demand of mobility and personality.

Keywords: Knowledge Management, Knowledge Services, Ecosystem, Knowledge engineering, Language Engineering, Ubiquitous services, Personalized knowledge services, one-stop-shop knowledge accessibility.

1   Introduction

Main issues to be faced by new knowledgedriven economy are the management and exploitation of knowledge sources. Knowledge sources are divided into two different categories: Tacit knowledge and Explicit knowledge. Tacit knowledge, which is hard to be utilized and transfered, has been defined as the knowledge embedded in the people and organizations such as direct experience and action, lesson-learned, and know-how. Explicit knowledge corresponds to any knowledge that can be articulated, codified, and store, such as reports, articles, patents and thesis. With the development of the Internet and the World Wide Web, the enormous amount of explicit knowledge resources is distributed over several websites among various kinds of sources in heteroeneous

R. Kannan and F. Andres (Eds.): ICDEM 2010, LNCS 6411, pp. 9–15, 2012.
© Springer-Verlag Berlin Heidelberg 2012

expressions and unstructured format. Knowledge Management is, then, driven by the needs and requirement of knowledge economy. The targets of both tacit and explicit knowledge management are collecting and distribution knowledge through organizations. Its functions are acquired, represented, exchanged, maintained, integrated and converted into useful knowledge.

However, most organizations have access to and use plenty of knowledge but neither effectively nor efficiently. To achieve more ambitious goals, beyond knowledge management, the intelligent use of knowledge and knowledge services are driven by the needs and requirement of creative-and-service- driven economy that provides the value added to any product such as manufacturing, and agricultural including information, knowledge, and software, as a service or anything as a service. The key functionalities of innovational services are how to provide personalized service and satisfy the individual demand.

CyberBrain, a digital ecosystem for the execution of knowledge management and knowledge services innovation, is aimed to be a collaborative knowledge space interconnecting knowledge resources, organization and community best practices with the heterogenous expression. Domain specific ontologies and standard metadata are the basic elements through which Cyber Brain can deploy for integrating and aggregating the scattered knowledge sources. Moreover, Cyber Brain paid more attentions to provide one-stop-shop knowledge with knowledge fusion and ubiquitous personalized knowledge service.

This paper describes some key technologies and methodologies emerging in knowledge engineering, ontology engineering, language engineering, including knowledge processing and utilizing model which meet the consumers' knowledge demand of mobility and personality. Section 2 describes the issues in knowledge management and CyberBrain. Section 3 reviews the ontology-based knowledge fusion which is the process by which heterogeneous information from multiple sources is extracted and aggregated to create knowledge that is more complete to provide one-stop-shop knowledge accessing services. Section 4 describes the methodologies of question and answering for WH-questions. Section 5 conclude and discuss the next step and challenges.

2   Issues in Knowledge Management and Cyberbrain

The focus of this paper is primarily on our research into two main issues of knowledge management that need some keys technologies and methodologies for enabling the efficiently and effectively knowledge accessing and exploiting.

2.1   Scattered and Heterogeneous Knowledge

The knowledge applicable to an intended problem solving consists of data items and/or information that are organized and processed to convey understanding, experience, accumulated learning and expertise. However, sources of these data are scattered across several locations and websites with heterogeneous expressions or different vocabularies (which may differ for linguistic and/or cultural reasons). Consequently, collecting the valuable knowledge from scattered resources is very difficult since the semantic relations among those resources are not directly stated. More over, to access these scattered knowledge consume a lot of time and power.

2.2   Knowledge Overloaded

With the emergence of Web 2.0, the ontology-based *knowledge portal,* that is a central point of semantic access of organizational or thematic knowledge has become a key resource to facilitate access to volumes of organizational knowledge and to systems that were previously accessible only through separate entry points. However, knowledge portal often fail to provide adequate support to knowledge workers in situations requiring highly domain-specific and time critical information.

Since Ontology not only acts as a powerful tool for aggregating knowledge based on different expressions but for deducing or navigating the concept characteristics or properties that should be extracted. Accordingly, the ontology-based one-stop-shop knowledge accessibility would enable scattered and heterogeneous knowledge to be exploited fully. The properties of concept acts as a template to extract the data.

To develop automated knowledge digestion is to draw on information extraction techniques that need both Language Engineering and Knowledge Engineering.

2.3   Cyberbrain: An Ecosystem Platform of Knowledge Collection and Services

Cyberbrain[1] has been designed as an ecosystem platform of knowledge collection and services to handle a diversity of resources, viewpoints, users, etc. We summarize a number of key points here, focusing on technologies, tools and toolkits categorized by interacted person: Knowledge owners, Knowledge brokers and Knowledge consumers.

3   Knowledge Fusions and Information Extraction

Knowledge fusion, is defined as the process by which heterogeneous information from multiple sources is merged to create knowledge portal that is more complete, and less access time. Knowledge fusion can also involve annotating the content with automatic meta-data extraction.

Our approach to developing automated knowledge fusion also includes a set of rules to extract necessary information based on information extraction techniques. Language Engineering is also applied making the knowledge service system understand users' query more comprehensive and provide more digestive knowledge.

A key feature of knowledge service innovation is . the content for service, power of knowledge elicitation,   the process of service and satisfying the individual demand. We are drawing on a range of existing formal techniques in knowledge extraction, reasoning and fusion for handling aggregation, heterogeneity and time.

One case study is BioCaster – an information mining data source for infectious diseases based on a pre-defined set of 50 diseases and 2,000 regions (captured in the dedicated BioCaster ontology) that are monitored in a pre-set collection of RSS data feeds .

4   Knowledge Service with Q&A System

We focus on the "", ""and ""queries. For examples, "what is the disease name when symptoms are given as a question", "Why the leaf has spots like diamond shaped with gray-white centers and brown to red- brown margins?" and "How to control the outbreak of Leaf-spots event?". annotation guidelines to model the semantics of those queries and ""in texts based on semantic roles will be described. It will be shown that annotation is a useful method to identify the different components (arguments, adjuncts, temporal adverbs that will be used to characterize the matching between the question and the answer. On top of these, inference rules are developed since, in most cases, questions do not have direct responses which can be immediately found in the texts. Finally, we show, with some examples, how these annotations and inference rules contribute to the generalization of the matching system over semantic categories in order to have a large scale question-answering system.

In natural, the question can be asked with different form, for examples:

Q:2.1 How to control Rice Blast?
Q:2.2 Blast Control
Q:2.3 Method of   Blast Prevention.

The answer can be returned as a descriptive answer with a set of events, as the following

A2.1: To prevent the Rice Blast: for the places that we often found the disease, use the disease-resistant rice variety. Don't sow the rice seed too densely. Don't use too much Nitrogen. If it is severe outbreak and it is the state of young plant, plow and sow again. If it was the epidemic state, use Fungus-Removal chemical as Carbendasim.

A2.2: Brown spot may be reduced by balanced fertilization, crop rotation, and the use of high quality planting seed. Seed treatment fungicides reduce the incidence and severity of seedling blight caused by this fungus.

The examples above show that it is considerable that using verb with/without question word or noun phrase can be represented the same meaning of question sentence. Moreover, there is non-correspondent clue word between Q and A.

4.1   Dealing with Texts: The Document Indexing Level

Texts are initially indexed based on the main terms they contain which are relevant w.r.t. Questions given in the corpus. Our representation is similar to a frame approach, but it is more flexible since there is no predefined structure to represent indexes. This is more in accordance with the variety of texts in terms of contents. Indexes basically are formed from:

Top level terms that structure the domain: for example, concepts like symptom, spreading, treatment, time, place, effect, etc. where predicative (action terms) terms as well as entities are found,

Relatively generic terms, found in the questions and structured in the domain ontology: water, clean, control, eradicate, etc., which are organized w.r.t. The top concepts above,

Named entities, typed as: disease names, location names, chemical product names, bacteria names, etc.

In our representation, those generic terms (and near synonyms) are represented as predicates, while arguments, represented as attribute-value pairs (or attributes alone), include typed names entities and any kind of terms besides the generic terms. Indexes are associated with texts in the text database. Indexes must remain general so that indexing is fast and as reliable as possible. The idea is that when a question is uttered, a small number of texts is first selected on the basis of the indexes for further analysis. An example is the following:

Index: Disease-name (Rice Blast), symptoms (disease: Rice Blast), origin (disease: Rice Blast, place: X, date: Y), spreading (disease: Rice Blast, period: a month after planting, medium: [soil, water]),   treatment (disease: Rice Blast, product).

Symptoms of Rice Blast first appear about a month after planting. Infected seedlings appear to be.....

The most effective means to **treat** *this disease is the use of non-infested seed. Also,......... Field trials indicate that a seed treatment with sodium....*

4.2   Matching Selected Texts with Questions with Examples

Our major concern, in this paper, is to develop a method for annotators so that a large number of texts can be tagged homogeneously and also so that the technique can be reproduced for other technical areas. Finally, in terms of response identification, the goal is to define a metric that defines the best match and selects the text fragment(s) that best respond(s) to the question among several potential candidates.

LET US FIRST CONSIDER A SIMPLE EXAMPLE. GIVEN THE QUESTION:
HOW TO ERADICATE RICE BLAST?
WITH THE FOLLOWING REPRESENTATION:
<QUESTION TYPE="OR SQE"FOCUS "BLAST"> HOW TO <ACTION> ERADICATE <THEME> BLAST </THEME> </ACTION> ? </QUESTION>

The main terms of the question are ''and ''. The text above is therefore selected on the basis of its indexes, because ''is a closely related term (in, terms of semantic relation: 'to realize an event') of ''in the domain ontology.

Then, the question terms are then searched in the selected text and the sentences that contain them are annotated using semantic roles: For example, the following sentence is a candidate:

THE MOST EFFECTIVE MEANS TO TREAT THIS DISEASE IS THE USE OF UNINFECTED SEEDS. IT IS TAGGED AS:

<ACTION> TREAT <THEME> THIS DISEASE </THEME> <INSTRUMENT> UNINFECTED SEEDS </INSTRUMENT> </ACTION> .

The answer is that sentence and the text fragment that follows (introduced by the connector also) since the response is of type procedure:

The most effective means to treat this disease is the use of uninfected seed. Also, when possible, burning plant residues with known infection in fall may help limit the disease.

This structure is annotated as a single instructional compound, which is the fundamental unit in a procedural text. This is the structure that is typically returned to users.

Let us present here another illustrative example of a text fragment where the response is annotated together with the required related reasoning elements:

Q: HOW CAN THRIPS DESTROY THE RICE ?
annotation:
<QUESTION TYPE=""FOCUS = ""> HOW CAN <AGENT> THRIPS </AGENT> <ACTION> DESTROY <THEME>   THE RICE </THEME>   </ACTION>   ? </QUESTION>
The text fragment that corresponds to the answer is annotated as follows:
<response> <agent> The rice thrips <action> sucks the sap <source>   from the young plant. </source> </action> </response>

To match the action "in the question with the text portion from which the response is extracted, it is then necessary to identify the inference:

<lex_inference> <action> Suck sap of X </action> <entail> <modality> probably
    </modality> <action> destroy X </action> </entail> ,
  <type> X : plant </type>
  <part-of> sap : X </part-of >   </lex inference>

The example above shows that (a) in the question and in the answer, annotations are used to identify the different components, arguments, adjuncts, but also some other components (e.g. temporal adverbs), and (b) the annotation developed to characterize the matching steps and inferential components (either lexical or domain knowledge) between the question and the answer. This latter form of annotation, which is quite time consuming to develop, is the means we use to induce and develop domain dependent forms of lexical inference (or other phenomena like synonymy, lexical equivalence, etc.) and relevant domain knowledge. The introduced types and lexical functions are then used in the process of induction of generalizations over some semantic categories (plants, products, etc.), and verb classes. This way of annotating knowledge and inferences is obviously a simple bottom-up process, with well-known limitations, but we feel it may have some advantages for inducing an upper organization of knowledge, in conjunction, and as a complement to the domain ontology. It is also simple and accessible to annotators. Obviously this remains to be evaluated.

5   Discussion and Conclusions

At this level, the inferences that may be drawn are directly attached to the terms that are tagged. This is obviously too limited. We are now experimenting different generalization strategies in order to tune lexical inference rules. This process involves:

(1) Developing various generic generalization principles over different types and categories (via the domain ontology), and;
(2) A set of principles that limit these generalizations via, for example, the taking into account of the semantics restrictions imposed by lexical items, in particular verbs.

The tuning of the level of these generalizations is obviously one main parameter of our project. It has several conceptual dimensions that we explore and may also be domain dependent.

Moreover, the matching problem between questions and documents to retrieve answers in question-answering systems in concrete applicative contexts is often a difficult problem. This matching procedure often requires very accurate domain knowledge, besides ontological descriptions (hierarchy of concepts together with their basic properties). It is not always easy to access to this knowledge in a structured or to extract it from texts. The present contribution, still experimental and in an early stage of development, is an attempt, via annotations at resolving this problem following a simple and clear methodology.

Finally, this approach, and the principles we have briefly outlined, allow us to introduce a working method for the development of question-answering systems for concrete applications, for non-factoid questions, an area which is still not very much developed in spite of its obvious usefulness. One of the reasons that is non-factoid questions require a language processing technology, analysis methods, reasoning aspects and a conceptual approach which are substantially different from what is used for factoid questions.

Reference

[1] Kawtrakul, A., Pechsiri, C., Rajbhandari, S., Andres, F.: Problems-Solving Map Extraction with Collective Intelligence Analysis and Language Engineering. In: Prince, V., Roche, M. (eds.) Information Retrieval in Biomedicine: Natural Language Processing for Knowledge Integration, University of Montpellier and LIRMM-CNRS, France, pp. 325–343. IGI Book (2009) ISBN 978-1-60566-274-9

Ontology Driven Data Management with Topic Maps

Frederic Andres[1] and Rajkumar Kannan[2]

[1] National Institute of Informatics, Tokyo, Japan
[2] Department of Computer Science
Bishop Heber College(Autonomous), Tiruchirappalli, India
andres@nii.ac.jp, rajkumar@bhc.edu.in

Abstract. Our study involves associating a context with semantic indexes and descriptors based on topic maps for efficient ontology-driven data managelent (e.g. blogs, cooperative platforms, digital libraries, document versioning tools, etc.). We believe that supporting contextual semantics can add a set of properties that vary according to the use of ontological topic maps (TM). Their use is beneficial for users who intend to exchange semantic knowledge in an application domain. Existing semantic layers in current systems are not yet capable of supporting relevant contextual semantic description. In this paper, we aim at extending the many-sorted algebra formalizing the topic maps layer in order to support 5W1H contexts (What, Why, Where, Who, When and How) using TMBLOG system as case study.

Keywords: Ontology engineering, Data management, Topic maps.

1   Introduction

In order to retrieve relevant information, internal search engines are commonly used to navigate through index databases of posting management systems (PMS: blogs, cooperative platforms, digital libraries, document versioning tools, etc.). Retrieval methods vary from one engine to another but are mainly related to the attributes defined in each application even if the PMS being searched is based on a simple index database (related to the posted data), augmented (index with hierarchical metadata) database, or multiple/integrated index databases. For instance, in library indexing (e.g. Bliss, Dewey, Goettingen, LC, Ranganathan, Riders, etc.), classifications are done by librarians without necessarily understanding the resource (books, documents, reports, etc.) contents. The used indexes are based on standard library attributes and methodologies; consequently, information retrieval is restricted because it is limited to attributes without considering the content. Inspired by the model proposed in [8], our goal is to integrate topic maps (TM) into the retrieval process in order to provide relevant and richer results by allowing the user to search outside the known and/or predefined attributes and norms of classifications by including document content. In this paper, we study two issues. The first issue is related to TM creation from documents and management of this creation in a collaborative environment by integrating six contextual parameters. The second issue is connected to the improvement of

R. Kannan and F. Andres (Eds.): ICDEM 2010, LNCS 6411, pp. 16–23, 2012.
© Springer-Verlag Berlin Heidelberg 2012

information retrieval in TMs. We typify the related problems with concrete examples in the following sections.

The rest of this paper is organized as follows. Section 2 describes the related work on TMs and information retrieval. Section 3 presents our approach and management of topic maps for semantic augmented information. It also shows our architecture to improve semantic management using TMs. Section 4 describes a case study regarding contextual semantic management. Section 5 concludes this study and discusses ongoing work.

2   Related Work

Several studies exist on multimedia[1,2] data management and retrieval. For instance, the search engine NIX (NASA Image eXchange: http://nix.nasa.gov) allows users to search NASA's online image and photo collections over the web. Retrieval is done on texts associated to images by using Boolean operators. Other famous search engines (like Google, Altavista, Yahoo!, Amore, and MSN) use similar methods to search the multimedia content of web pages. The main differences between these engines are in how they automatically locate textual descriptors in the web pages according to their position and importance to the image to be described. The drawbacks of using traditional textual-based methods for multimedia retrieval have been identified by the scientific community and other users. In fact, there are several directions of research attempting to extend current methods with ontologies and taxonomies to rewrite user queries and improve application results. Nevertheless, to the best of our knowledge, none of the existing methods can utilize topic maps for semantic augmented information search and retrieval. The major benefit for end-users of being able to do so would be access to seamless knowledge under ISO standard 13250.

Several studies have used topic maps to visualize, adapt, and otherwise represent information to the user. For instance, the ENWiC (EduNuggets Wiki Crawler) project [1] for students provides an interface to wikis "*in order to take advantage of the large information repositories*". It represents the structure of a wiki as a topic map (automatic creation of instances, associations, and topic) but it only makes use of TMs for adaptation of existing databases. Krötzsch et al.'s work [2] on Wikipedia claimed that information searching in Wikipedia was primitive. Although their solution used semantic technology, it goes without saying that imposing semantic technology on an already existing information base will not achieve much without initially considering the underlying information. An approach to annotation of the Wikipedia website is provided in reference [13]. It consists of creating a layer of information on the existing information that does not directly affect the structure or content of the existing information. In a related work, the KendraBase project [14] was conceived to

---

[1] In this section, we cite examples from information management in multimedia databases, blogs, and wikis because this sort of information management is comparable to information management using topic maps (i.e., we are not attempting to draw a border line between these terminologies).

[2] We use the word multimedia to describe documents including several data types such as text, audio, video, and image.

enable people with diverse ideas to collaborate for knowledge creation. The project was intended to be "a semantic wiki / database with auto form generation for data input and queries". The Edunuggets project [5] considered how to provide a personalized knowledge repository in a learning environment.. In references [1, 8], the overall objective was to support on-line teaching and learning by: (a) providing a means to evaluate and annotate available information, (b) providing a context for the organization of the available information, and (c) supporting learners' access. Their work was a way of reorganizing and "repacking" existing information. The approach of the System for Universal Media Searching (SUMS) is not just limited to the organization of the information base; it extends to "reorganization" of the information base according to the user's knowledge. SUMS is a tool for finding, retrieving, and organizing material on the Internet aiming at linking personal local collections of facts with the external electronic world [10]. In "Towards a Semantic Web for Culture", Prof. Kim Veltman asserted that "Culture is about both objects and the commentaries on them; about a cumulative body of knowledge; about collective memory and heritage. ... In this context, the science of meaning (semantics) is necessarily much more complex than semantic primitives".

For all these reasons and for efficient enhanced information retrieval, we believe that there is need to combine information creation and information search for a specific objective in a collaborative environment.

3   Semantics Augmented Information Management

The usage of TMBLOG [8] has pointed out an innovative layer based on topic maps to enrich multimedia postings with metadata and to extract semantic spatial-temporal semantics from those postings. Topic maps provide a new kind of semantic structure for spatial-temporal postings storage, navigation, and visualization. However, the topic map management including contextual semantic support influences the efficiency of the retrieved information. Let us review the related issues.

3.1   Topic Maps Management Issues

Two issues need to be considered in order to manage semantic augmented information efficiently in topic maps:

- The automatic creation phase of topic maps according to the documents' structure and content;
- The enhancement of topic maps toward their usages as topic maps are sets of subject proxies;

The basis of *enhanced* information retrieval in topic maps is the creator point of view regarding the target documents. Table 1 introduces a possible search scenario associated with the type of information that can be derived in TMs. The scenario assumes that there is no subclass in the three parameters. In essence, we want to show that the analysis of information built on three parameters will necessarily entail inter-parameter, intra-parameter and subclass analysis to improve the search using topic maps. Let us consider the following example wherein N employees create a topic map on D documents in an institution over a period of T years. Suppose first that a user produces only one topic map per year from only one document. Over the period of five years (T=5), the user will have created five topic maps and thus the N employees will have 5xN topic maps. In contrast, if all the employees can make one topic map on each of 1000 documents per year, there will be (5x1000) x N topic maps after five years. Now, if the topic maps are not restrained by the number of times, by the number of creators, or by the number of documents involved, the situation becomes very complex (NxTxD potential topics maps) particularly when all these parameters values are high. The problem that readily comes to mind is how to manage the large number of topic maps.

Table 1. Scenario of information search in a Topic Map

Context of information search	Fixed parameters			Representation	Value range Where u=user,d=document,t=time]
	User	Document	Time		
(1) Topic map of all users of all documents irrespective of time				$\iiint dU dD dT$	[0≤u<∞, 0≤d<∞, 0≤t<∞]
(2) Topic map of all users of all documents at a specific time			X	$T\iint dU dD$	[0≤u<∞,0≤d<∞]
(3) Topic map of all users of a document at all times		X		$D\iint dU dT$	[0≤u<∞,0≤t<∞]
(4) Topic map of all users of a document at a specific time		X	X	$DT\int dU$	[0≤u<∞]
(5) Topic map on all documents used by a user all the time	X			$U\iint dD dT$	[0≤u<∞,0≤d<∞]
(6) Topic map on all documents used at a specific time by a user	X		X	$UT\int dD$	[0≤d<∞]
(5) Topic map on a document used by a user any time	X	X		$UD\int dT$	[0≤t<∞]
(6) Topic map by a user of a document at a specific time	X	X	X	UDT	[u=1,d=1,t=1]

The basis of *enhanced* information retrieval in topic maps is the creator point of view regarding the target documents. Table 1 introduces a possible search scenario associated with the type of information that can be derived in TMs. The scenario assumes that there is no subclass in the three parameters. In essence, we want to show that the analysis of information built on three parameters will necessarily entail inter-parameter, intra-parameter and subclass analysis to improve the search using topic maps. Let us consider the following example wherein a topic map on *D* documents is created in an institution by *N* employees over a period of *T* years. Suppose first that a user produces only one topic map per year from only one document. Over the period of five years (T=5), the user will have created five topic maps and thus the N employees will have 5xN topic maps. In contrast, if all the employees can make one topic map on each of 1000 documents per year, there will be (5x1000) x N topic maps after five years. Now, if the topic maps are not restrained by the number of times, by the number of creators, or by the number of documents involved, the situation becomes very complex (NxTxD potential topics maps) particularly when all these parameters values are high. The problem that readily comes to mind is how to manage the large number of topic maps.

Having presented the key issues associated with the creation and management of topic maps, we now present our approach regarding contextual topic maps and our related architecture to handle them.

3.2   Architecture and Contextual Topic Maps Issues

Our approach consists of integrating several parameters that will reflect not just the organization of information but the content to permit comprehensive access to information in contextual topic maps. The analysis proposed in reference [9] is still possible in the context of TM usage. Figure 1 presents an overview of the interactions of the constituents involved in topic map creation and subsequent topic–related information searches. The information system consists of documents, topic maps, and semantic databases. Below, we will not discuss the content of these databases but only their relative usage. The functional architecture is composed of two tasks:

- The creation task.
- The topic maps search task.

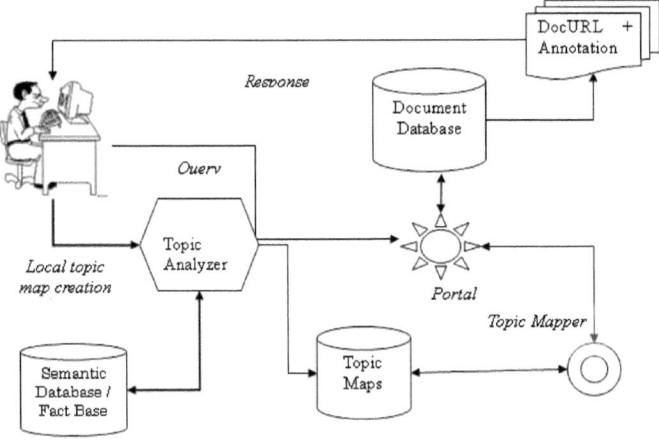

Fig. 1. Functional Architecture

In the first task, the user creates a topic map from a document. The retrieved document can include topic maps previously created from other documents. The retrieved documents' content becomes the subjects of the user's topic maps. The topics are analyzed by the topic analyzer shown in Figure 1. When this is done, the local topic maps are sent to the topic maps storage with references to the semantic database ["with reference to the semantic database" is grammatical but I'm not sure what it refers to in the sentence. For instance, "When this is done with reference to the semantic database", "the local topic maps with reference to the semantic database", "are sent with reference to the semantic database", or "the topic maps storage with reference to the semantic database."]. The semantic database itself may be a creation from previous topic map sessions. Note that the user's topic maps must fulfill all the contextual parameters (detailed in the following sections). Users must also supply one or more descriptive subjects to each of these parameters.

The topic mapper directly relates the search terms of the users within the topic maps. Users can search using any of the concepts they are familiar with from the list coming from the topic maps.

4   Case Study of TMBLOG

The resource algebra enables various users to share their documents as part of a colla- borative platform such as a blog. Resource semantic type and functions in the TMs are directly represented using the appropriate data type and functions supported by the resource algebra. This algebra has two targets. First, it is a semantic interface between scientists who are able to reduce the semantic gap and to strength the metadata bridg- ing them. Second, it facilitates a "collaborative intersection" of scientists using TMs integrating high-level semantics.

Let us recall the notion of many sorted algebra [5]. Such algebra consists of several sets of values and a set of operations (functions) between these sets. It consists of two sets of symbols called sorts (e.g. topic, pdf, rtf, lsi_sm) and operators (e.g. tm_transcribe, semantic_similarity); the function sections constitute the signature of the algebra. The second order signature is based on two coupled many-sorted signa- tures where the top-level signature provides kinds (set of types) as sorts (e.g. DATA, RESOURCE, SEMANTIC_DATA) and type constructors as operators (e.g. set). To illustrate the approach, we assume the following simplified many-sorted algebra:

```
Kinds DATA, RESOURCE, SEMANTIC_DATA, TOPIC_MAPS, SET
Type constructor
  -> DATA        topic
  -> RESOURCE pdf,rdt,htm,xml,cvs,jpeg,tiff
        //resource document type
  -> SEMANTIC_DATA lsi_sm, mpeg7_sm, dc_sm, vra_sm,
  cdwa_sm, ecai_sm, objectid_sm
        // Semantic and metadata vectors
  -> TM tm(topic maps)
TM ->SET Set
```

Unary Operations:
```
∀resource in RESOURCE,
    resource → sm: SEMANTIC_DATA,tm  tm_transcribe
∀ sm in SEMANTIC_DATA   sm → set(tm)semantic_similarity
```

Binary Operations:

$\forall$ tm in TOPIC_MAPS, (tm)$^{+}$ → tm   **topicmaps_merging**

$\forall$ sm in SEMANTIC_DATA , $\forall$ tm in TOPIC_MAPS,
      sm,tm tm → tm   **semantic_merging**

$\forall$ topic in DATA, $\forall$tm in TOPIC_MAPS,
      set(tm) x (topic → bool) → set(tm)   **select**

The semantic merging operation takes two or more operands that are all TM values. The select statement takes an operand type set (tm) and a predicate of the type topic as input and returns a subset of the operand set fulfilling the predicate. From the implementation point of view, the resource algebra is an extensible library package providing a collection of resource data types and operations for domain-oriented resource computation (e.g. cultural field).

The most important concepts in blog management according to [6] are postings access and postings management. Although postings management has been regarded as organizing postings "constituents" (such as information types), we believe that an organization of postings content can facilitate retrieval. Postings searches can be based on one algorithm or the other. The applicability of algorithms used for postings searches depends on the content of the information base or on the organization of the underlying information base.

5   Conclusion

The above proposal can greatly improve the specificity of information creation and information research and thereby improve the access rate. We showed how a topic map can be created bearing in mind its usage in "enhanced information retrieval". We proposed a contextual query methodology based on topic maps. The next step of this work is on combining TMBLOG with a collaborative research project on a semantic tracking platform [15].

Acknowledgments. The research presented in this paper would not have been possible without the support and advise of respected professors and colleagues at the National Institute of Informatics (Japan). The authors would like to thank NII for providing the necessary resources to carry out this research.

References

1. Espiritu, C., Stroulia, E., Tirapat, T.: ENWiC: Visualizing WIKI semantics as Topic Maps: An automated topic discovery and visualization tool. In: Proceedings of the 8th International Conference on Enterprise Information Systems, Paphos, pp. 35–42 (May 23-27, 2006), http://www.cs.ualberta.ca/stroulia/EduNuggets/enwic-iceis2006.pdf
2. Krötzsch, M., Vrandečic, D., Völkel, M.: Wikipedia and the Semantic Web: The missing Links. In: Proceedings of Wikimania, Frankfurt, Germany (2005), http://www.aifb.uni-karlsruhe.de/WBS/mak/pub/wikimania.pdf

3. Güting, R.H.: Gral: an extensible relational database system for geometric applications. In: Proceedings of the 15th International Conference on Very Large Data Bases, pp. 33–44. Morgan Kaufmann Publishers, San Francisco (1989)
4. Haase, K.: Context for semantic metadata. In: Proceedings of the 12th Annual ACM International Conference on Multimedia, MULTIMEDIA 2004, October 10-16, pp. 204–211. ACM Press, New York (2004)
5. Jari, K., Stroulia, E.: EduNuggets: an intelligent environment for managing and delivering multimedia education content. In: Proceedings of the 8th International Conference on Intelligent User Interfaces, Miami, Florida, USA, pp. 303–306. ACM Press (2003) ISBN:1-58113-586-6
6. Le Grand, B., Soto, M.: Visualisation of the Semantic Web: Topic Maps Visualisation. In: Proceedings of 6th International Conference on Information Visualisation (IV 2002) (2002)
7. Naito, M., Andrès, F.: Application Framework Based on Topic Maps. In: Maicher, L., Park, J. (eds.) TMRA 2005. LNCS (LNAI), vol. 3873, pp. 42–52. Springer, Heidelberg (2006), http://dx.doi.org/10.1007/11676904_4, doi:10.1007/11676904_4
8. Rajbhandari, S., Andres, F., Naito, M., Wuwongse, V.: Semantic-Augmented Support in Spatial-Temporal Multimedia Blog Management. In: Maicher, L., Sigel, A., Garshol, L.M. (eds.) TMRA 2006. LNCS (LNAI), vol. 4438, pp. 215–226. Springer, Heidelberg (2007) ISSN 0302-9743, ISBN 978-3-540-71944-1
9. Rath Holger, H.: The Topic Maps Handbook, Empolis Arvato Knowledge Management, Gütersloh, Germany (2003)
10. Veltman Kim, H.: Towards a Semantic Web for Culture. Journal of Digital Information 4(4) (2004)
11. Veltman Kim, H.: Electronic Media in the Study of Alberti, Congrès International Leon Battista Alberti, Paris (1995), http://www.mmi.unimaas.nl/people/Veltman/veltmanarticles/1995%20Electronic%20Media%20in%20the%20Study%20of%20Alberti.pdf
12. Topic Maps, http://www.topicmaps.org/xtm/
13. Semantic Wiki Wiki Web, http://www.c2.com/cgi/wiki?SemanticWikiWikiWeb
14. KendraBase, http://www.kendra.org.uk/wiki/wiki.pl?KendraBase
15. Kawtrakul, A., Yingsaeree, C., Andres, F.: A Framework of NLP Based Information Tracking and Related Knowledge Organizing with Topic Maps. In: Kedad, Z., Lammari, N., Métais, E., Meziane, F., Rezgui, Y. (eds.) NLDB 2007. LNCS, vol. 4592, pp. 272–283. Springer, Heidelberg (2007) ISBN 978-3-540-73350-8
16. Kannan, R., Andres, F., Guetl, C.: DanVideo: an MPEG-7 authoring and retrieval system for dance videos. In: Multimedia Tools and Applications, pp. 545–572. Springer, Netherlands (2009) ISSN 1380-7501, doi:10.1007/s11042-009-0388-3

Web Access Pattern Mining – A Survey

A. Rajimol[1] and G. Raju[2]

[1] School of Computer Science, Mahatma Gandhi University, Kottayam, Kerala, India
[2] Department of IT, Kannur University , Kannur , Kerala, India
kurupgraju@rediffmail.com

Abstract. This article provides a survey of different Web Access Pattern Tree (WAP-tree) based methods for Web Access Pattern Mining. Web Access Pattern Mining mines complete set of patterns that satisfy the given support threshold from a given Web Access Sequence Database. A brief discussion of basic theory and terminologies related to web access pattern mining are Presented. A comparison of the different methods is also given.

Keywords: Web Access Pattern Mining, Pre-order Linked Web Access Pattern Mining, First-Occurrence Linked Pattern Tree mining, First-Occurrence Forest Mining, Conditional Sequence Mining.

1   Introduction

Web mining is the extraction of interesting and useful knowledge and implicit information from activity related to the WWW. The web data is typically unlabelled, distributed, heterogeneous, semi-structured, time varying and high dimensional [2].

Web usage mining, also known as Web log mining, discover interesting and frequent user access patterns from the web browsing details stored in server web logs, proxy server logs or browser logs [1]. Web log mining has become very critical for effective web site management, creating adaptive Web sites, business and support services, personalization and so on [2].

Sequential pattern mining is an important data mining tool used for web log mining. Sequential pattern mining that discover frequent pattern in a Web Access Sequence Data Base (WASD) was first introduced by Agarwal and Srikant in [3]: Given a set of sequences, where each sequence consists of a list of elements and each element consists of a set of items, and given a user-specified minimum support threshold, sequential pattern mining is to find all frequent subsequences. A web log is a sequence of pairs: user-id and access information. For the purpose of study of sequential pattern mining, preprocessing [6] is applied to the original log file and WASD is generated.

Let E be a set of events. A Web Access Sequence (WAS), $S = e_1 e_2 .....e_n$ for $(1 \leq i \leq n)$, is a sequence of events where events can be repeated; n is the length of access sequence. $S' = e_1' e_2' .....e_n'$ is subsequence of Access Sequence (AS) $S = e_1 e_2 .....e_n$ and S is a super sequence of S', if and only if $1 \leq i_1 \leq i_2 \leq .. \leq i_n \leq n$ such that $E'_j = Ej$ for $1 \leq j \leq n$ [7]. In $S = e_1 e_2 ....e_k e_{k+1}....e_n$, if subsequence $S_{suffix} = e_{k+1}...e_n$ is a super sequence of pattern $P = e_1' e_2' ...e_l'$, and $e_{k+1} = e_1'$, the subsequence of S, S prefix $= e_1 e_2...e_k$, is called the prefix of S with respect to pattern P [1]. Support of a pattern S in WASD is

R. Kannan and F. Andres (Eds.): ICDEM 2010, LNCS 6411, pp. 24–31, 2012.
© Springer-Verlag Berlin Heidelberg 2012

the number of sequences S_i in WASD, which contain the subsequence P, divided by the number of transactions in the database. An access sequence S is said to be an access pattern of WASD, if support of S in WAS, supWAS(S), is greater than or equal to the given threshold. Given a WASD and a support threshold ξ, Web Access Pattern Mining mines the complete set of ξ patterns of WAS [7]. In the succeeding sections, we review the WAP-tree structure and some selected WAP-tree based mining algorithms and in the last section we give a comparison of their performance.

2   WAP-Mine Algorithm

Pei et al. in [7] proposed a compressed data structure known as Web Access Pattern Tree (WAP-tree) and WAP-Mine (Web Access Pattern tree Mining) algorithm for mining web access patterns efficiently from web logs. WAP-Mine, the recursive mining algorithm used to generate access patterns from the WAP-tree, is based on the suffix heuristic: if a is a frequent event in the set of prefixes of sequences in WAS with respect to pattern P, then sequence aP is an access pattern of WAS. WAP-tree registers all access sequences and corresponding count very compactly and maintains linkages for traversing prefixes with respect to the same suffix pattern.

2.1   Construction of WAP-Tree and Mining of WAP-Tree

Only frequent 1-sequences are considered for constructing WAP-tree, as they only are useful in generating k-sequences where $k>1$. Common prefixes are shared in the WAP-tree to save space. WAP-tree registers two pieces of information, label and count. The root of the tree is a special virtual node with an empty label and count 0.

The construction of WAP-tree is done as follows: for each access sequence, frequent subsequence is entered into the tree, starting from the root node. While inserting the first event e, if the current node has already a child e, then the count of the child node with event e is incremented by 1, otherwise a new child with label e and count 1 is created. Then recursively insert the rest of the subsequence to the sub tree rooted at the current e node. All nodes with same label e are linked by shared label linkages into a queue, called event-queue. Event queue for e_i is called e_i-queue. Head of each event-queue is registered in a header table H.

A simple web access sequence database obtained after preprocessing, with the set of access events $E = \{a, b, c, d, e, f\}$ is shown in Table 1 [1] and WAP-tree with linkage header for the WASD is given in Fig. 1.

Table 1. A database of web access sequences

User ID	web access sequence	frequent sub- sequence
100	abdac	abac
200	eaebcac	abcac
300	babfaec	babac
400	afbacfc	abacc

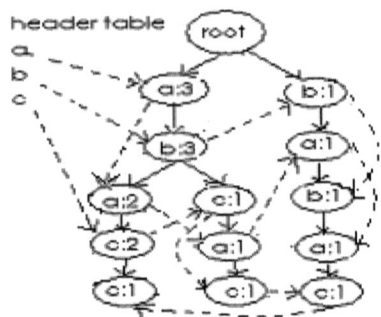

Fig. 1. WAP-tree with linkage (*dotted line*) for the frequent sub-sequences in Table 1

All pattern information related to a frequent event e_i can be accessed by following all the branches in WAP-tree linked by e_i-queue only once. All nodes in the path from root of the tree to node e_i (excluded) form a prefix sequence of e_i and the count of this node is the count of the prefix sequence. Let G and H be two prefix sequences of e_i and G is also formed by the sub-path from root that H is formed by, H is called a super-prefix sequence of G, and G is a sub-prefix sequence of H. For a prefix sequence of e_i without any super-prefix sequences, the un-subsumed count is the count of it. For a prefix sequence of e_i with some super-prefix sequences, the un-subsumed count is the count of that sequence minus un-subsumed counts of all its super-prefix sequences. Access patterns with same suffix are now used for searching all web access patterns.

Mining is done as follows: For each event e_i in the header list, conditional sequence base is found. The conditional sequence list of a suffix event is got by following the header link of the event and reading the path from the root to each node (excluding the node). The count of the prefix sequence is same as the count of the node. For each prefix sequence inserted into the conditional sequence base with count c, all its sub-prefix sequences are inserted with $-c$ as count, to get the un-subsumed count. Then the set of conditional frequent events is found. If it is not empty, recursive mining is done on the conditional WAP-tree of each frequent event. When there is only one branch in the conditional WAP-tree, all unique combinations of nodes in that branch are generated as patterns.

3   PLWAP-Mine Algorithm

Y. Lu, and C. I. Ezeife propose Pre-Order Linked WAP-Tree Mining (PLWAP) and a method of assigning binary position code to tree nodes in [8]. PLWAP algorithm based on WAP-tree avoids recursive re-construction of intermediate WAP-trees by using binary position codes to the nodes of the tree to determine the suffix trees of any frequent pattern prefix under consideration by comparison.

The position code is assigned to the nodes on the binary tree equivalent of the tree using the Huffman coding idea. Given a WAP-tree with some nodes, the position code of each node is assigned following the rule that the root has null position code, and the leftmost child of the root has a code of 1, but the code of any other node is derived by appending 1 to the position code of its parent, if this node is the leftmost child, or appending 10 to the position code of the parent if this node is the second leftmost child, the third leftmost child has 100 appended, etc. A node α is an ancestor of another node β if and only if the position code of α with "1" appended to its end, equals the first x number of bits in the position code of β, where x is the number of bits in the position code of $\alpha + 1$.

Building of PLWAP-tree is done as follows: Root node is created with position code NULL and count 0. Tree and header table is generated from access sequences as in the creation of WAP-tree [7]. The Constructed tree is traversed in pre-order and each node e_i is attached to the corresponding e_i-queue and head of each queue is registered in corresponding header table entry. Major difference in the construction of a PLWAP-tree and a WAP-tree is in the generation of binary code for nodes along with tree creation and in the generation of the pre-order linkages.

PLWAP-Mine starts by finding the frequent 1-sequence $\{a, b, c\}$. Then for every frequent event and the suffix trees of current conditional PLWAP-tree being mined, it finds the first occurrence of this frequent event in every suffix tree being mined by following the pre-order linkage of this event, and adds the support count of all first occurrences of this frequent event. If the count is greater than the minimum support threshold, then this event is concatenated to the previous list of frequent sequence, F. Now, the suffix trees of these first occurrence events in the previously mined conditional suffix PLWAP-trees are used for mining the next event.

4   CS-Mine

In [9] B.Y. Zhou et al. propose a method CS-Mine (Conditional Sequence Mining) based on WAP-tree structure [7]. CS-Mine involves Constructing Initial Conditional Sequence Base (CSB), Constructing Event Queues (EQ) for CSB, Single Sequence Testing for CSB, Constructing Sub-CSB, and Recursive Mining for Sub-CSB.

The conditional sequence base of event e_i based on suffix sequence S_{suffix}, is the set of all long prefix sequences of e_i in sequences of a database. If Ssuffix is empty, the conditional sequence base is the frequent sub-sequence set of the given database. Otherwise, it is the conditional sequence base $CSB(S_{\text{suffix}})$.

CS-mine starts by constructing the initial CSB by mining WAP-tree. For each frequent event e_i in the given WAP-tree, all the prefix sequences of all the nodes in the e_i-queue form the Initial CSB of e_i, Init-CSB(e_i). The count of related suffix node in the e_i-queue is the count of each prefix sequence. To avoid duplicate counting, for each prefix sequence of e_i with count n, all of its sub-prefix sequences are also inserted into Init-CSB(e_i) with minus count, $-n$. To construct event queues for each $CSB(S_c)$ ($S_c = e_i$ for Init-CSB), conditional frequent events, events in $CSB(S_c)$ that satisfy minimum support are found first. Header table is created with all the conditional frequent events. Then, for each conditional frequent event e_i, a linked-list structure called e_i–queue, connecting the last item labelled ei in the sequences of CSB (S_c), is created. The head pointer of each event queue is recorded in the Header Table. Finally, all non-frequent events in sequences in CSB (S_c) are discarded.

CSB(e_i+S_{suffix}) is called the sub-conditional sequence base of CSB(S_{suffix}), if e_i is not null. The Construct-SubCSB algorithm is used for constructing CSB(e_i+S_c) based on CSB(S_c) for each event e_i in the Header Table of CSB(S_c). Single Sequence Test checks whether all sequences in CSB(S_c) can be combined into a single sequence. If so, the mining of CSB(S_c) will be stopped. Otherwise, Sub-CSB for each event in the Header Table based on CSB(S_c) is found and recursive mining is done.

5   FLWAP-Mine

Peiyi Tang et al. introduce First-occurrence Linked WAP-tree and present a pattern mining algorithm FLWAP-Mine based on that in [10]. They also present the theory of conditional searching on which their pattern-growth mining algorithms are based.

Given a web access sequence S and a symbol a, from the set of symbols Σ such that a is in S, the a-prefix of S is the prefix of S from the first symbol to the first occurrence of a inclusive. The a-projection of S is what is left after the a-prefix is deleted. Given the database D and a symbol a in Σ, the a-projection database D_a of D is the multi-set of a-projections of the web access sequences in D that support a. D_a is used to grow frequent patterns by using symbols from Σ. It is sufficient to use the sub-trees rooted at the children of the first-occurrences of a, to represent projection database D_a, ignoring possible empty sequences. Since first-occurrences play a central role in finding the support of a symbol and its projection database, all pattern-growth mining algorithms based on aggregate trees [10] try to find them efficiently.

Given a symbol a, from Σ and database D, the support of pattern p in the a-projection database D_a of D is equal to the support of pattern $a.p$ in the original database D. And support of empty pattern is $\left| D_a \right|$. That is,

$$\mathrm{Sup}_D(a) = \left| D_a \right|. \tag{1}$$

Let $F(D, \eta)$ be the set of frequent patterns in D with respect to η and $F'(a.D \ \eta)$ be the set of non-empty frequent patterns in D that start with symbol a, then $F'(a.D, \eta)$ is equal to a. $F(Da, \eta)$. Thus

$$F(D,\eta) = \emptyset \qquad\qquad \text{if } \left| D \right| < \eta \quad \text{and} \tag{2}$$
$$F(D,\eta) = \{\varepsilon\} \cup \cup \ a \in \Sigma \ a \ F(Da, \eta) \quad \text{if } \left| D \right| \geq \eta$$

The equations (1) and (2) are the base of the FLWAP-Mining algorithm.

5.1   Mining with FLWAP-Tree

A node is a first-occurrence, if none of its ancestors has the same label. The count of first-occurrence of a node with label a, is the number of sequences in D that share the common a-prefix represented by the path from the root node to this. The sum of the counts of all the first-occurrences of a symbol, is the number of sequences in D that contain at least one occurrence of a, i.e. the support of a in D, $Sup_D (a)$.

To build FLWAP-tree, sequences are entered into the tree as in the base WAP-tree. Then the first-Occurrences of each symbol are linked to form the First-occurrence Linked WAP-tree (FLWAP-tree). The first-occurrences can be found by the pre-order traversal of a portion of the base WAP-tree. Once the FLWAP-tree is constructed, it is mined to generate all patterns using the FLWAP-mine algorithm. The algorithm works as follows. For each frequent event a, follow the first-occurrence link to find its first-occurrences. If the sum of the counts of first-occurrences is greater than absolute threshold, a is concatenated to the previous pattern and added to the set of patterns. Now the set of the sub-trees rooted at the children of the first-occurrences is found, FLWAP-tree for Da is built and recursively mined.

Difference of FLWAP-Mine algorithm from PLWAP-Mine is in finding first-occurrences and in building intermediate tree for the projection database. To find the first-occurrences of a symbol, PLWAP attach a position code to each node and link all the nodes of the same label in a pre-order traversal of the tree whereas in FLWAP this is done by traversing a portion in pre-order and the algorithm is available in [11].

6   FOF-Mine

In [11], the authors present a modification to FLWAP mining method in [10]. Forest of First-Occurrence sub-trees (FOF structure) are the basic data structure for representing projection database instead of the concept of linked trees. Given a symbol a, each sub tree rooted at a first-occurrence of a, is the first-occurrence sub-tree of a. A list of pointers to the first-occurrences of a in the aggregate tree is the forest of first-occurrence sub-trees of a symbol.

In First-Occurrence Forest-Mine (FOF-Mine), the aggregate tree is extended to make the root node represent the empty symbol ε. The count of the root node is the total number of sequences in the database. The count of first-occurrences of a node with label a, is the number of sequences in that share the common a-prefix. The sub-trees rooted at the children of first-occurrences of symbol a, represent all the non-empty a-projections of the sequences sharing this common a-prefix.The sum of the counts of the root nodes of the first-occurrence sub-trees of a gives $Sup_D (a)$. As all the nodes already exist in the original aggregate tree of the database to be mined, the memory cost of the forest of first-occurrences sub-trees is only the list of pointers.

Recursive FOF-Mine algorithm is used for mining FOF structure. The initial FOF structure based on aggregate tree is passed on to the mining function. The sub-trees rooted at the children of the first occurrence nodes represent the current database to be mined. The FOF structure for the projection database is established by repeatedly calling a function Find-First-Occurrences. In FOF-Mine, for each frequent event a, the projection database of the current database is build. If the sum of the counts of the root nodes of all the sub-trees is greater than the absolute threshold, a is appended to the previous pattern and added to the set of pattern. Now, the new database is recursively mined to generate all patterns starting with the current event.

7   Comparison of the Methods

WAP-Mine introduced in [7] is quite different from the apriori methods like Apriori, Apriori All, Apriori Some [4], GSP (Generalized Sequential Pattern mining) [5], PSP (Prefix Tree for Sequential Patterns) that are based on generate and test methods. WAP-Mine uses a very compact WAP-tree structure to store access sequences. Sharing of common prefixes by branches makes support counting and mining easier. Moreover, the conditional searching improves the efficiency. Experimental studies proved WAP-Mine to better than GSP. Both GSP and WAP-Mine exhibit linear scalability, but WAP-Mine outperforms GSP [7].

Recursive reconstruction of intermediate WAP-trees during mining in WAP-Mine, in order to compute frequent prefix subsequences of every suffix sequences is very time consuming. PLWAP-Mine [8] modify base WAP-tree to Pre Order Linked WAP-tree that link similar nodes in a pre-order fashion. PLWAP algorithm identifies the suffix trees or forest of any frequent pattern prefix under consideration by comparing the binary codes of nodes. Experiments show that PLWAP outperforms both GSP and WAP-Mine when the number of frequent patterns increases and the minimum support threshold is low. Performance of PLWAP degrades when the length of sequence is more than 20 because of the increase in the size of position codes as the depth of tree increases [12].

Use of the original PLWAP-tree for the entire mining forces it to go through the nodes that are not in the projection databases to find the first-occurrences though the memory requirement is reduced. The FLWAP-tree algorithm [10] links the first occurrences of each symbol. Since all the non-empty sequences in the a-projection database D_a of database D are included in the sub-trees rooted at the children of the first occurrences of a symbol a, the FLWAP-tree for D_a can be built from these sub-trees. Though the building of new trees for projection databases use more memory, reduction in the sizes of projection databases reduces the processing complexity. That is, FLWAP-tree mining is a trade-off memory for high performance. During experiments FLWAP-tree mining outperforms the PLWAP-tree mining consistently as the average length of sequence increases. The speed up of FLWAP also increases linearly as the average length of sequence increases [10].

The FLWAP-tree algorithm rebuilds every projection database, and thus, uses a lot of memory. Both the PLWAP-tree [8] and FLWAP-tree algorithms [10] are based on the concept of the linked tree. FOF algorithm [11] outperforms both PLWAP and FLWAP. Memory usage is very high for FLWAP as the latter creates intermediate projection trees. Due to the increase in size of the tree nodes in PLWAP, the FOF algorithm outperforms even the PLWAP-tree algorithm in memory usage, even though it does not create additional projection databases [11].

CS-Mine also is based on WAP-tree, but it uses WAP-tree only for generating conditional sequence base. Experimental results have shown that the CS-mine algorithm performs much more efficient than the WAP-mine algorithm, especially when the support threshold becomes small and the number of web access sequences gets larger [9].

8   Conclusion

Though the literature for Web Access Pattern Tree based methods includes a good number of papers, due to the space constraint only a set of important and basic methods of web access pattern mining are selected and presented in this review. Basic terminologies, theory and performance are highlighted. Finally a comparison of the different methods is given. With the exponential growth of WWW, there is imperative need for more efficient Web Access Pattern Mining algorithms.

References

1. Kosala, R., Blockeel, H.: Web Mining Research: A Survey. ACM SIGKDD Explorations 2, 1–15 (2000)
2. Srivastava, J., Cooley, R., Deshpande, M., Tan, P.N.: Web Usage Mining: Discovery and Applications of Usage Patterns from Web Data. ACM SIGKDD Explorations 1, 12–23 (2000)
3. Agrawal, R., Srikant, R.: Fast algorithms for mining association rules in large databases. In: 20th International Conference on Very Large Databases, Santiago, Chile, pp. 487–499 (1994)
4. Agrawal, R., Srikant, R.: Mining Sequential Patterns. In: 11th International Conference on Data Engineering, Taipei, Taiwan, pp. 3–14 (1995)
5. Srikant, R., Agrawal, R.: Mining Sequential Patterns: Generalizations and Performance improvements. In: Apers, P.M.G., Bouzeghoub, M., Gardarin, G. (eds.) EDBT 1996. LNCS, vol. 1057, pp. 3–17. Springer, Heidelberg (1996)
6. Cooley, R., Mobasher, B., Srivastava, J.: Data Preparation for Mining World Wide Web Browsing Patterns. J. Knowledge and Information Systems 1, 5–32 (1999)
7. Pei, J., Han, J., Mortazavi-asl, B., Zhu, H.: Mining Access Patterns Efficiently from Web Logs. In: Terano, T., Chen, A.L.P. (eds.) PAKDD 2000. LNCS, vol. 1805, pp. 396–407. Springer, Heidelberg (2000)
8. Lu, Y., Ezeife, C.I.: Position Coded Pre-order Linked WAP-Tree for Web Log Sequential Pattern Mining. In: Whang, K.-Y., Jeon, J., Shim, K., Srivastava, J. (eds.) PAKDD 2003. LNCS (LNAI), vol. 2637, pp. 337–349. Springer, Heidelberg (2003)
9. Zhou, B.Y., Hui, S.C., Fong, A.C.M.: CS-Mine: An Efficient WAP-Tree Mining for Web Access Patterns. In: Yu, J.X., Lin, X., Lu, H., Zhang, Y. (eds.) APWeb 2004. LNCS, vol. 3007, pp. 523–532. Springer, Heidelberg (2004)
10. Tang, P., Turkia, M.P., Gallivan, K.A.: Mining web access patterns with first-occurrence linked WAP-trees. In: 16th International Conference on Software Engineering and Data Engineering (SEDE 2007), Las Vegas, USA, pp. 247–252 (2007)
11. Pearson, E.A., Tang, P.: Mining Frequent Sequential Patterns with First-Occurrence Forests. In: 46th ACM Southeastern Conference (ACMSE), Auburn, Alabama, pp. 34–39 (2008)
12. Lu, Y., Ezeife, C.I.: PLWAP sequential Mining: open source code. In: First International Workshop on Open Source Data Mining: Frequent Patterns Mining Implementation, Chicago, Illinois, pp. 26–35 (2005)

Graph Based Single Document Summarization

Nandhini Kumaresh and Balasundaram Sadhu Ramakrishnan

Department of Computer Applications,
National Institute of Technology,Trichirappalli,
Tamil Nadu, India
{405108052,blsundar}@nitt.edu

Abstract. E-Learning aims at defining education to be made as anytime, any-where and anybody entity. Usability can be increased by incorporating summa-rization in E-learning context. The aim of the text summarization is to select the most important information from an abundance of text. This paper investigates a new approach for single document summarization based on graph traversal technique with constraint to improve cohesion. The selection of features plays a vital role in the sentence extraction. By considering both the structured and the unstructured features, better summary can be generated.

Keywords: Sentence Scoring Technique, Extractive Summarization, Single Document Summarization, Graph Based Approach, Statistical Sentence Extraction.

1   Introduction

According to a survey most of the e-Learning contents are not used frequently by the users because of having more textual information than audio and video components. Learners may not be having patience to go through all the text to get an idea about whether it is relevant or interesting or useful for their requirements. The text can be summarized which gives a brief idea about the entire document, so that the reader can decide to read the content fully to get an idea or to skip. An e-Learning material con-sists of multilevel structure. A simple graph based approach can be further extended to hierarchical text summarization. Preview through summarization is a key to im-prove the cognition of the user in large set of heterogeneous resources [8]. In terms of usability, the summarization approach will enable the readers to skip the content or to proceed with existing content.

1.1   Extractive Summarization

Document summarization is the concept of condensing a source document into a shorter version preserving its information content. According to Radev & Hovy [6], a summary is a text that is produced out of one or more texts, that contains some information of the original text, and that is no longer than half of the original text. An extractive summary consists of sentences extracted from the document while an

R. Kannan and F. Andres (Eds.): ICDEM 2010, LNCS 6411, pp. 32–35, 2012.
© Springer-Verlag Berlin Heidelberg 2012

abstractive summary may contain words and phrases that may not appear in the original document. People can explore and analyze entire document collections just by looking at their summaries [1]. It aims to reduce documents in length and complexity while preserving some of their essential information [3]. Heuristically motivated features allow producing very precise and language independent extracts. Selection of features plays a vital role in summarization.

1.2   Related Works

For the past six decades there were extensive work done in the area of Extractive summarization. Luhn proposed that the frequency of a particular word in an article provides a useful measure of its significance [2]. Edmundson technique was based on assigning numerical weights to text sentences based on four basic characteristics such as cue, key, title and location [3]. Kupiec shows an extraction based summarization which extracts roughly 20% of original text through a Naïve Bayes classifier [4]. Baxendale demonstrated that sentences located at the beginning and end of paragraphs are likely to be good summary sentences [5]. Mann and Thompson introduced structured feature, where a rhetorical tree structure is built to represent rhetorical relations between sentence segments of the documents [7]. Very few works were done in graph based summarization using ranking algorithm such as HITRATE and PAGERANK algorithms [9].

The major drawback of extractive summarization based on sentence scoring is that, the summary generated may be disfluent due to extraction of the sentences with higher score sentences dispersed in the document. This paper focuses on graph based extractive summarization for generic, single document and fluent nature, by considering both structured and unstructured features to score the sentences and the cohesion can be increased by applying sentence similarity metric while selecting higher score sentence from the input document.

2   Methodology

For any document to be summarized, it must be preprocessed. The preprocessing involves segmentation, tokenization, removal of stop words and stemming. After preprocessing, group of terms in every sentence form the individual node of the graph. The nodes are scored based on structured and non structured features. The similarity metric helps in traversing the graph in a significant way. Finally the summarized document is evaluated using intrinsic and extrinsic measures. The preprocessing steps are as follows:

Sentence segmentation- the first step in preprocessing is to segment the sentences in the document. The string tokenization is used to separate the sentence segment of previous phase into tokens. During sentence scoring stop, words are not considered. Figure 1. shows the steps involved in summarization process. Stemming has the secondary effect of reducing the number of terms used for the representation of documents. In this context the Porter algorithm is used for stemming.

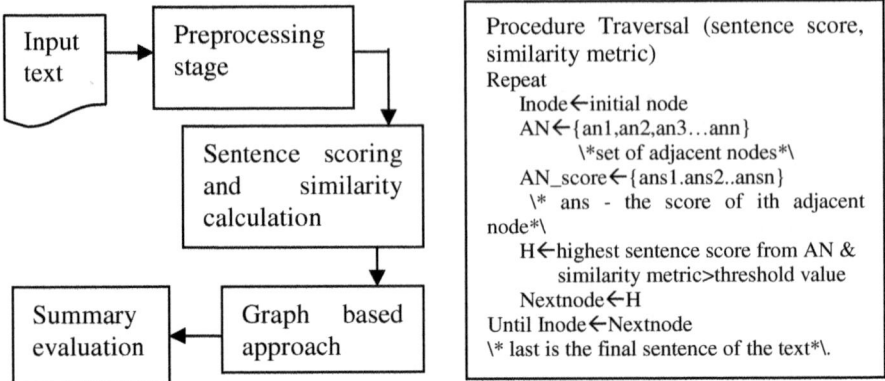

Fig. 1. Summarization Process   **Fig. 2.** Graph traversal algorithm

The selection of features plays an important role in determining the type of sentence selected as a part of summary. The sentence can be scored using the following structured feature such as rhetorical relations and unstructured features such as Term frequency, Sentence Location in the paragraph, Title keyword similarity, Cue phrases, Sentence relative length, Keyword occurrences and Cardinality.

2.1   Graph Theoretic Approach and Evaluation

Sentences in the document are represented as nodes in an undirected graph. There is a node for every sentence in the text. Two sentences are connected with an edge, if the two sentences share some common words. Every node is connected to its next node because it is assumed that there is a flow between the sentences. The graph traversal algorithm is given in Figure 2.

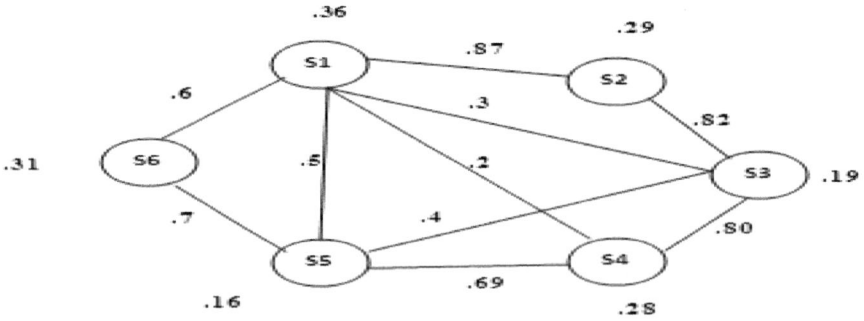

Fig. 3. Graph Representation of Sample Document

The graph representation of a sample document with its sentence score and similarity metric is shown in Figure 3. The nodes with high cardinality are important sentences that should be given higher preferences. Usually extractive summary generated by statistical techniques lacks cohesion, which can be improved by incorporating similarity metric above the threshold value and considering rhetorical structure of the document while extracting the summary from it. Sentence recall and precision are used in evaluating extracted summary. The number of sentences extracted from the document for summary depends on the compression ratio.

3   Conclusion

In this paper, a simple approach is proposed that extracts sentences based on graph traversal technique which will enable the learners of E-learning context to decide whether the document is relevant or irrelevant. This approach focuses mainly on simple text as input, which has to be further extended by considering shallow NLP features to improve the cohesion of the summary.

References

1. Chuang, T.W., Yang, J.: Text Summarization by Sentence Segment Extraction Using Machine Learning Algorithms. In: Proceedings of the ACL 2004 Workshop, Barcelona (2004)
2. Luhn: The Automatic Creation of Literature Abstracts. IBM Journal of R& D (2) (1958)
3. Edmundson, H.P.: New Methods in Automatic Abstraction. ACM Journal (1969)
4. Kupiec, J., Pederson, J., Chen, F.: A Trainable Document Summarizer. In: Proceedings of the 18 th Annual International ACM SIGIR Conference on R&D in Information Retrieval, Seattle, Washington, pp. 68–73 (1995)
5. Baxendale, P.B.: Machine-Made index for Technical Literature: An Experiment. IBM Journal of R&D 2(4) (1958)
6. Radev, D.R., Hovy, E., Mckeown, K.: Introduction to the Special Issue on Summarization. Computational Linguistics 28(4), 399–408 (2002)
7. Mann, W.C., Thompson, S.A.: Rhetorical Structure Theory: A Theory of Text Organization. Technical Report ISI/RS-87-190 (1987)
8. Ficher, G., Stevens, C.: Information Access in Complex, Poorly Structure Information Spaces. In: CHI 1991: Proceedings of the SIGCHI Conference on Human Factors in Computing Systems, pp. 63–70. ACM (1991)
9. Mihalcea, R.: Graph-Based Ranking Algorithms for Sentence Extraction, Applied to Text Summarization. In: Proceedings of the ACL 2004 (2004)

A Novel Text – Mining System for Generating Abstract from Extracted Summaries Using Anaphora Resolution

Ayyalu Hariharan Nandhu Kishore[1] and Mohan Saravanan[2]

[1] Department of Computer Science and Engineering,
Madurai Institute of Engineering and Technology (MIET), Madurai, Tamil Nadu, India
`ahnandhume@yahoo.co.in`
[2] Chennai, Tamil Nadu, India
`msdess@gmail.com`

Abstract. The amount of information available varies in length from one document to another. It becomes difficult and time-consuming activity to browse the information completely. It is essential to provide the information in a condensed form expressing the central idea of the document. Automatic text summarization is used for generating the summary for the document. This paper presents a novel Abstract Generation System (AGS) to generate an abstract from the extracted summary of an English language text document. The pronominal Anaphora Resolution (AR) Algorithm has been designed and used in AGS for scrutinizing and resolving the anaphors, the referring expressions present in the extract to make the summary more readable. AGS finally generates a fine-tuned summary for the given document. The experiments are conducted using a test set taken from the trained corpus, in AGS and other existing Anaphora Resolution Systems (ARS). The results are compared with the model summary written by human beings. The standard metric of Information Extraction (IE) systems namely the success rate has been used to measure and study the performance of AGS.

Keywords: Natural Language Processing (NLP), Text Summarization, Abstract Generation System, Anaphora Resolution, Dangling anaphora.

1   Introduction

The amount of data available nowadays is enormous. In a survey, it has been estimated that the total amount of information produced each year has been estimated to be more than 240 terabytes. Almost 10% of this information is textual [1]. Finding the facts of interest will be as tedious as finding a needle in the haystack. One of the intelligent IE tools namely the *automatic text summarization* [2] [3] is used for précising the document. Most of the existing auto summarizers follow *shallow approach*, which leads to *text extraction*. An *extract* is a summary that identifies most important information from a document and present it in a shorter form based on the percentage level of summarization provided to the summarizer. The extract contains sentences that are exactly present in the original document. The sentences that are selected for extract

R. Kannan and F. Andres (Eds.): ICDEM 2010, LNCS 6411, pp. 36–43, 2012.
© Springer-Verlag Berlin Heidelberg 2012

may have link with some other sentences in the document but they may not be available in the summary. This breakage of interconnection between the sentences results in loss of coherency and readability of the summary [4]. This is because, the anaphors present in the summary are not treated properly [5]. An alternate method called *deep approach* has to be followed which leads to *text abstraction*. An *abstract* is a summary, which contains some material that is not present exactly in the original document. It is highly complex to generate an abstract as a fully synthesized text for a given document, which is still under investigation. However, the abstract can be derived by fine-tuning the extract by applying *Anaphora Resolution (AR)* technique to that extract [6] [7].

Anaphora resolution forms one of the highly researchable areas of computational linguistics. The term 'anaphora' refers to a previously mentioned entity in the text, most often with the help of a pronoun or a different name. The process of finding and fixing the proper antecedent for each anaphor in the text is termed as *Anaphora Resolution* [8]. The correct interpretation and resolving of anaphors is vital for Natural Language Processing [9].

The previous work of anaphora resolution systems prescribes various approaches and outstanding issues for resolving the anaphors. The foremost methodology applied for anaphora resolution is knowledge-based approach. It emphasizes more on the use of syntactic and semantic knowledge of every individual word in the document. It utilizes a parser for analyzing and resolving the anaphors. A public reference implementation namely JAVA Resolution of Anaphora Procedure (JAVA RAP) has been designed under this approach [10]. One of the disadvantages of this approach is that it is a labor-intensive and time-consuming activity.

An alternate technique namely the knowledge-limited approach makes use of a POS tagger and simple noun phrase rules for anaphora resolution. An online anaphora resolution engine namely Mitkov's Anaphora Resolution System (MARS) has been designed under this approach [11].

In spite of the recent progress in Anaphora Resolution Systems (ARS), still there are a few outstanding issues related to the efficiency of the systems that remain unsolved or need further attention. A real-world anaphora resolution system vitally depends on the efficiency of the pre-processing tools, which analyzes the input before feeding it to the resolution algorithm. The system has to select an appropriate antecedent for an anaphor by taking the constraint sources such as number, gender, animacy, recency etc. into account. It should be able to resolve and distinguish the anaphoric and non-anaphoric 'it'. It should also handle the resolution of dangling anaphors present in the extract. The performance of the ARS relies on the metrics that are used for evaluation. Any implementation may lack in concentrating some of these issues [8] [11].

Hence a novel text-mining framework namely the Abstract Generation System is designed by implementing the pronominal anaphora resolution algorithm to rectify the above studied problems. One of the standard metrics of the IE systems namely the success rate [11] is used to measure the performance of the system which reflects the overall performance of the system. The success rate is defined as per the equation 1.

$$\text{Success Rate} = \frac{\text{Number of successfully resolved anaphors}}{\text{Number of all anaphors present in the summary}} \tag{1}$$

The following section illustrates the generation of extract and pre-processing of input text, which is carried out using the existing tools. The outputs of these activities will be fed as inputs to our system, which will be discussed in section 3.

2   Extract Generation and Text Pre-processing

The abstract generation process initially involves three phases. The phase1 is the generation of extract summary for a single input document using an existing auto summarizer namely MEAD [12] as shown in Fig 1.

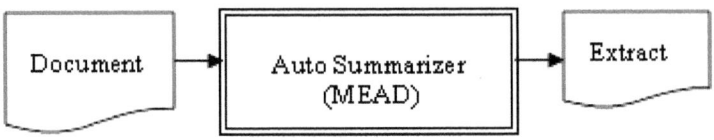

Fig. 1. Generation of Extract using MEAD

The phase2 deals with pre-processing the document using a text pre-processor tool namely General Architecture for Text Engineering (GATE) [13]. A POS tagged intermediate text file is obtained as a result of this process as shown in Fig 2.

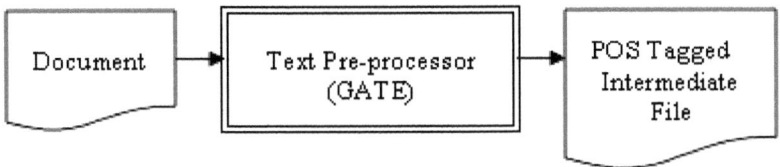

Fig. 2. Text Pre-processing Using GATE

The text pre-processing involves three sub-components namely the segmentation module, Tokenization module, Parts of Speech (POS) tagging module. These three components are tied together as a pipeline using a plug-in of GATE called A Nearly New Information Extraction system (ANNIE) [13]. Before executing this pipeline, the documents are trained well in advance for named-entities based on gender and their POS tag, by entering them manually in a text file called 'Lexicon' provided by this plug-in. Once the named-entities are trained, GATE guarantees for generating correct POS tag for a token. The result of execution of pipeline is saved as a text file named as POS tagged intermediate file of the document.

The phase 3 is the abstract generation phase, which intakes the output of phase 1 and 2, resolves the anaphors and produces the fine-tuned abstract summary. This phase is explained in detail in the following section.

3   The Framework of Abstract Generation System

The fig 3. illustrates the entire framework of AGS implemented with the pronominal anaphora resolution algorithm. The algorithm is implemented based on knowledge-limited approach for resolution of anaphors.

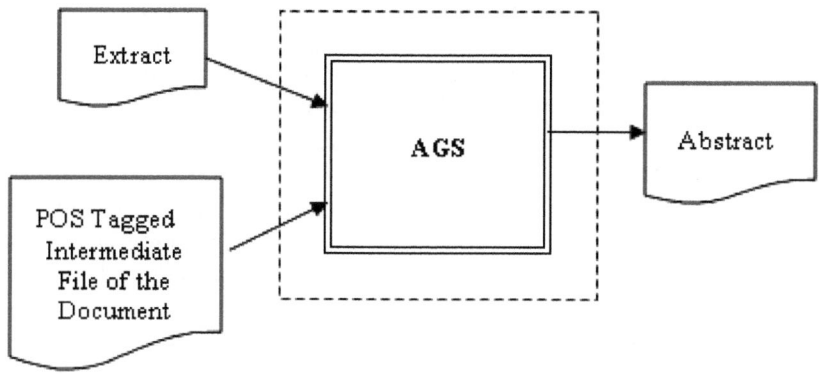

Fig. 3.   Text-mining Framework of AGS

The extracted information and the POS tagged intermediate file of the document obtained are fed to AGS. As a result of execution of AGS, the abstract for the given document is acquired after resolving the anaphors present in the extracted summary, which is carried out by the pronominal AR algorithm as discussed below,

3.1   The Pronominal Anaphora Resolution Algorithm

Input: The extract summary and POS tagged intermediate file of the document *Function*: To resolve the anaphors present in the extract by replacing them with their recent antecedent and to generate the final abstract summary.

Output: Anaphor resolved abstract summary.

Assumptions: Only the following categories of pronouns have been considered for resolution. The algorithm can be extended easily for other pronouns also.

Personal pronouns	–	he, she, it, him, her
Possessive pronouns	–	his, her
Pleonastic pronoun	–	it
Reflexive pronouns	–	himself, herself, itself

The algorithm takes care in resolving the above said pronouns as well as the dangling anaphors, i.e., the broken anaphoric reference that is created when extracting the summary of the document using the automatic text summarizer. Before carrying out the resolving process, a summary validation text file has to be constructed by comparing both the extract as well as the intermediate file of the document to check whether the extract belongs to the corresponding document.

3.1.1 Construction of Summary Validation File

Step 1: Fetch each sentence from summary. Fix the context with the first line in the intermediate file.

Step 2: Compare the summary line with the line in the intermediate file (context).

Step 2.1: If they get matched, place a mach tag <sum (Line No.) > Y </sum (Line No.), where Line No. is the count of summary lines that got matched with that of the document

Step 2.2: If no match occurred, a no match tag 'N' is placed. Move to the next line of the document.

Step 2.3: Write the corresponding sentence, the token set containing each word of the sentence along with its POS tag until </split> in the intermediate file and a <Linenum_> tag including the previous line number and current line number information to the summary validation file used for backtracking while resolving the anaphors.

Step 2.4: For each summary line, write the result of step 2.1 to step 2.3 in an output text file namely the summary validation file.

Step 2.5: Increment the count of summary line number. Fetch the next line of the summary and go to step 2.

Step 3: If summary line count is zero, then assert the user as file mismatch has occurred between the summary and the document. Else proceed for pronominal resolution with extract and validation file.

3.1.2 Pronominal Resolution of He, His, Him and Himself

The steps in resolution of male pronouns are,

Step 1: Fix the context in summary validation file. Scan it for the presence of the male pronouns.

Step 2: Identify the first occurrence of the POS tag namely the Male Antecedent (MAN) tag in that context. Read the string corresponding to the tag, which represents the candidate antecedent for that anaphor.

Step 3: Replace the male pronoun(s) with the candidate antecedent. Write the corresponding changes in the output text file (Abstract summary file).

Step 4: If the antecedent for an anaphor is not obtained within the current line (it is a dangling anaphor), then backtrack to the previous line, identify and replace the anaphor with candidate antecedent.

3.1.3 Pronominal Resolution of She, Her and Herself

The POS tag category of the string namely the Female Antecedent (FAN) tag is searched in summary validation file for the female pronouns. The corresponding string is selected and replaced for those pronouns present in the summary.

3.1.4 Pronominal Resolution of It, Its, Itself

The context is selected and searched for It Antecedent (IAN) tag. The corresponding string is selected and replaced for those pronoun(s).

3.1.5 Reporting the Presence of Pleonastic It

If the category of 'it' in summary validation file is Pleonastic Pronoun (PPN) and the IAN tag is not encountered within the given context, then the occurrence of pleonastic 'it' (Non Anaphoric 'it') pronoun is reported.

3.1.6 Dangling Anaphora Resolution Process

This process is carried out internally in the resolution of pronouns in the steps 3.1.2 to 3.1.4. Since the antecedents are scanned only from the original document and not with the summary, the pronouns will be replaced only with the recent antecedents taken from the document. Hence the loss of interconnectivity among the sentences due to dangling anaphors in the summary has overcome with AGS.

For Instance:

Sentences of Document	*Sentences of Model Summary*
1. Sachin was the opening bats man.	1. Sachin was the opening bats-man.
2. He scored a half-century.	2. He scored a half-century.
3. Ganguly hit a century.	3. He got man of the match award.
4. He got man of the match award.	

When the summary is read, the anaphor 'He' in the third sentence of the summary refers to Sachin. But it actually refers to Ganguly, which is evident from sentence 3 in the document. The anaphor 'He' in the extract is confirmed as dangling anaphor. From sentence 4, it is backtracked to third one in the document. Ganguly is taken as candidate antecedent and it is replaced with anaphor. The abstract summary is written as,

Anaphor Resolved Abstract Summary

1. Sachin was the opening batsman.
2. < Sachin > scored a half-century.
3. < *Ganguly* > got man of the match award.

4   Results and Discussions

The documents belonging to domains like sports, newspapers texts etc have been processed and experimented in AGS and other existing AR systems. The success rate of the systems is calculated using the formula as mentioned in section 1. Table 1 shows the comparison of success rates attained by the AGS and other ARSs. The performance of AGS reached 87% in success rate. Our system works in semi-automatic mode where as, MARS and JAVA RAP are online AR systems which are working in fully automatic mode. Hence the results are not directly comparable to show the effectiveness of our system.

Table 1. Evaluation Results of ARSs

S.No.	Name of ARS	Success Rate %
1.	MARS	47
2.	JAVARAP	47
3.	AGS	87

The performance chart is plotted using the success rate achieved by the summary sets that are tested in the ARSs as shown in fig 4.

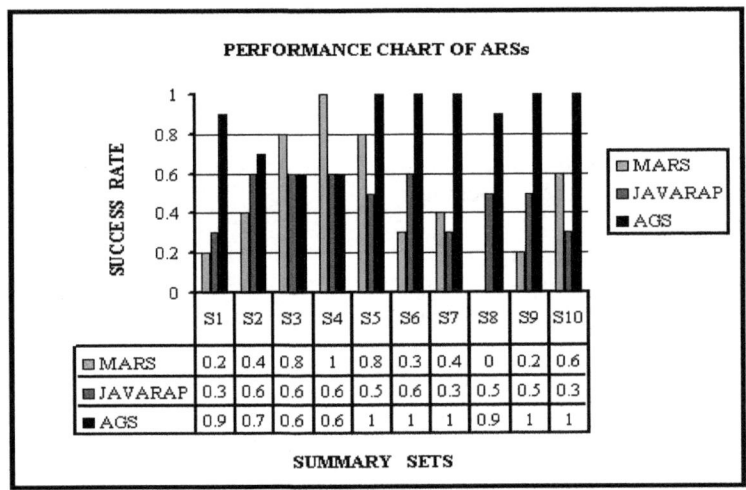

Fig. 4. Performance Chart of ARSs using Success Rate

It is obvious from the above bar chart that the success rate of AGS has reached to more than 0.6 for many domain sets because the system has mostly resolved the anaphors with appropriate antecedents by taking care of the constraint sources. It resolved and distinguished the anaphoric and non-anaphoric 'it'. It resolved the dangling anaphors in the extract, which could not be done by online ARSs.

5   Conclusion

The AGS framework designed with the pronominal AR algorithm has rectified most of the problems in summarization and anaphora resolution. The system performed well for pre-analyzed texts and resolved the anaphors in the extract efficiently and generated the coherent and readable summary for the document. The system has to be extended for synthesizing multi-document abstracts by running it in a fully automatic mode, which is scope for the future enhancement.

References

1. Marin, D., Kalina, B., Hamish, C., Diana, M.: A Light – Weight Approach to Coreference Resolution for Named Entities in text. In: MSc Thesis, University of Sofia, Bulgaria (2002)
2. Meru, B., Yllias, C., Christopher, J.P.: Text summarization using lexical chains. In: First Document Understanding Conference (DUC 2001), New Orleans, Louisiana, USA, September 13 – 14 (2001)
3. Patricia, N.G., Lucia, R., Renata, V.: Summarizing and referring: towards cohesive extracts. In: Eighth ACM Symposium on Document Engineering, Sao Paulo, Brazil, September 16-19, pp. 235–236 (2008)
4. Allaoua, R.: A Modular Architecture for Anaphora Resolution. The Journal of Computer Science 3(4), 199–203 (2007)
5. Saravanan, M., Reghu Raj, P.C., Raman, S.: Summarization and Categorization of Text Data in High Level Data Cleaning for Information Retrieval. In: First International Workshop on Data Cleaning and Preprocessing, Maebashi City, Japan, December 9-12, pp. 119–130 (2002)
6. Nandhu Kishore, A.H., Saravanan, M.: Anaphoric Resolution for Extracted Summaries on Different domains. In: International Conference on Advanced Computing and Communication (ICACC 2007), Madurai, Tamil Nadu, India, February 9-10, pp. 201–204 (2007)
7. Josef, S., Massimo, P., Mijail, A., Kabadjov, K.J.: Two Uses of Anaphora Resolution in Summarization. Information Processing and Management: an International Journal 43(6), 1663–1680 (2007)
8. Mitkov, R.: Outstanding issues in Anaphora Resolution. In: Second International Conference on Computational Linguistics and Intelligent Text Processing, Mexico, February 18-24, pp. 110–120 (2001)
9. Anna, K., Teruko, M., Benjamin, V.D., Eric, N.: Pronominal Anaphora Resolution for Unrestricted Text. In: International Conference on Language Resources and Evaluation (LREC), Lisbon, Portugal, May 24-30, pp. 1495–1498 (2004)
10. Qiu, L., Kan, M.Y., Chua, T.S.: A public Reference Implementation of the RAP Anaphora Resolution Algorithm. In: Language Resources and Evaluation Conference 2004 (LREC 2004), Lisbon, Portugal, May 26-28 (2004),
http://www-appn.comp.nus.edu.sg/%7Erpnlpir/cgi-bin/JavaRAP/JavaRAPdemo.html
11. Mitkov, R.: Towards a more consistent and comprehensive evaluation of anaphora resolution algorithms and systems. In: Discourse, Anaphora and Reference Resolution Conference (DAARC 2000), Lancaster, United Kingdom, pp. 96–107 (2000),
http://clg.wlv.ac.uk/demos/MARS/index.php
12. MEAD Summarizer, http://www.cnts.ua.ac.be/~iris/sumdemo.html
13. GATE's User Guide, http://gate.ac.uk/sale/tao/

Materialized Views Selection for Answering Queries

T.V. Vijay Kumar and Mohammad Haider

School of Computer and Systems Sciences,
Jawaharlal Nehru University,
New Delhi-110067, India

Abstract. A data warehouse stores historical data to support analytical query processing. These analytical queries are long and complex and processing these against a large data warehouse consumes a lot of time. As a result, the query response time is high. One way to reduce this time is by selecting views that are likely to answer a large number of future queries and storing them in a data warehouse. This problem is referred to as view selection. Several view selection algorithms have been proposed with most of these being focused around HRUA. HRUA considers the size of the views to select the most beneficial view for materialization. The views selected using HRUA, though beneficial with respect to size, may be unable to account for large numbers of queries and thus making them an unnecessary overhead. The algorithm proposed in this paper attempts to address this problem by considering query frequency, along with the size, of the view to select Top-K views for materialization. The proposed algorithm, in each iteration, computes the profit, defined in terms of size and query frequency, and then selects the most profitable view for materialization. As a result, the views selected are beneficial with respect to size and have the ability to answer future queries. Further, experimental results show that the proposed algorithm, in comparison to HRUA, is able to select views capable of answering larger number of queries against a slight increase in the total cost of evaluating all the views. This in turn would result in efficient decision making.

Keywords: Materialized View Selection, Greedy Algorithm.

1   Introduction

Historical data has been used by industries to lay out business strategies in order to be competitive in the market. Data warehouse [8] stores such historical data, upon which analytical queries are posed for strategic decision making. The size of the data warehouse, which continuously grows with time, and the nature of analytical queries, which are long and complex, leads to high query response time. This query response time needs to be reduced in order to make decision making more efficient. One way to address this problem is by answering queries using materialized views [11], which are pre-computed and summarized information stored in a data warehouse with the aim to reduce the response time for analytical queries.

The number of possible views is exponential in the number of dimensions [7, 10]. All of these cannot be materialized due to limitations of available storage space for materialization. Thus there is a need to select a subset of views, from among all

R. Kannan and F. Andres (Eds.): ICDEM 2010, LNCS 6411, pp. 44–51, 2012.
© Springer-Verlag Berlin Heidelberg 2012

possible views, that improves the query response time. Materialized views cannot be arbitrarily selected as they need to contain information that helps in answering future queries in a reduced response time. The selection of an optimal subset of views is shown to be NP-Complete [7]. Alternatively, the views can be selected empirically or heuristically. Empirically, the views are selected based on past query patterns [4, 9, 15, 17]. The heuristic based view selection is carried out by pruning the search space greedily [7] or in an evolutionary manner [20]. This paper focuses on the greedy based selection of materialized views.

The greedy based view selection algorithms, in each iteration, select the most beneficial views for materialization [7]. Several such algorithms have been proposed in literature [1, 2 , 3, 4, 5, 6, 7, 10, 12, 13, 14, 16, 17, 18, 19], most of which are focused around the algorithm in [7], which will hereafter be referred to as HRUA in this paper. HRUA, in each iteration, computes the benefit of each view, using its size, and then selects the most beneficial view for materialization. The selected views may be beneficial with respect to size but may not be capable of providing answers to large number of queries. As an example, consider a three dimensional lattice shown in Fig. 1(a). The size of the view in million (M) rows, and the query frequency (QF) of each view, is given alongside the view. Selection of Top-3 views using HRUA is shown in Fig. 1(b).

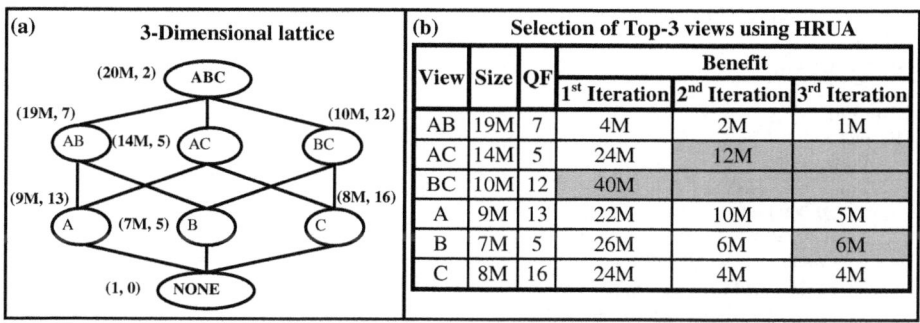

Fig. 1. Selection of Top-3 views using HRUA

HRUA assumes the root view to be materialized as queries on it are unlikely to be answered by any other views in the lattice. HRUA selects BC, AC and B as the Top-3 views. These selected views result in a Total View Evaluation Cost (TVEC) of 102 million rows. Considering the query frequency of each view, the Total Queries Answered (TQA) by the selected views is 22 queries, from among 60 queries. There is a need to select views that can provide answers to more number of queries i.e. select views having higher TQA value. The algorithm presented in this paper attempts to improve the TQA value by considering both the size, and the query answering ability of the view specified by its query frequency, to select the Top-k profitable views for materialization. The proposed algorithm aims to select views that are profitable with respect to size and also provide answers to large number of queries.

The paper is organized as follows: The proposed algorithm is given in section 2 followed by examples based on it in section 3. The experimental results are given in section 4. Section 5 is the conclusion.

2   Proposed Algorithm

As discussed above, the views selected using HRUA though beneficial with respect to size may not account for large number of queries. As a result, query response time may become high. The algorithm proposed in this paper attempts to address this problem by considering query frequency, along with the size, of the view to select the most profitable views for materialization. The proposed algorithm assumes past queries as useful indicators of queries likely to be posed in future. These queries are used to determine the query frequency of each view. The proposed algorithm, as given in Fig. 2, takes the lattice of views, with size and query frequency of each view, as input and produces the Top-K views as output.

```
INPUT: A Lattice of Views L with Size and Query Frequency of each view
OUTPUT: Top-K Views
METHOD:
Let
          V_R = Root view in the lattice L, MV = Set of materialized views, S(V) = Size of view V,
          QF(V) = Query Frequency of view V, QFS(V) = Query Frequency Sum of view V,
          CQF(V) = Cumulative Query Frequency of view V, D(V) = Set of descendents of view V
          in the Lattice, SMA(V) = Smallest Materialized Ancestor of View V in the Lattice,
          SB(V) = Benefit of view V with respect to its size, Profit(V) = Profit of view V,
          Profit_M = Maximum Profit, V_P = View with maximum profit
MV = { }
For each view V ∈ L
     SMA(V) = V_R
End For
Repeat
     Profit_M = 0
     For V ∈ L – MV ∪{V_R}
          QFS(V) = 0
          B (V) = 0
          For W ∈ Desc(V)
               If  (S(SMA(W)) – S(V)) > 0
                    QFS(V) = QFS(V) + QF(V)
                    SB(V) = SB(V)  + (S(SMA(W)) – S(V))
               End If
          End For
          Profit(V) = SB(V) × (CQF(SMA(V)) - QFS(V))
          If   Profit_M < Profit(V)
               Profit_M = Profit(V)
               V_P = V
          End If
     End For
     MV = MV ∪ {V_P}
     For V ∈ L – MV ∪{V_R}
          If V ∈ D(V_P) ∧ (S(V_P) < Size(SMA(V)))
               SMA(V) = V_P
          End If
     End For
Until |MV| = K
Return MV
```

Fig. 2. Proposed Algorithm

The proposed algorithm, in each iteration, computes the profit of each, as yet unselected, view. This profit is computed as the product of the size benefit of the view SB(V), as computed in [7], and the difference between the cumulative query frequency of the smallest materialized ancestor view, denoting the total number of queries that can be answered by it, and the query frequency sum of the view, denoting the total number of queries that can be answered by the view, which cannot be answered by previously selected views. This difference is computed as (CQF(SMA(V)) – QFS(V)). The most profitable view is then selected for materialization. The algorithm continues to select views, until the pre-defined K number of views is selected for materialization. The profit computation heuristic lays emphasis on the query frequency of each view, besides the size of the view. This would result in selection of views that are not only profitable with respect to size but can also provide answers to large number of queries. To illustrate this, examples are given next.

3   Examples

Consider the selection of Top-3 views, from the 3-dimensional lattice shown in Fig. 1(a), using the proposed algorithm. These selections are shown in Fig. 3.

View	Size	QF	Profit		
			1st Iteration	2nd Iteration	3rd Iteration
AB	19M	7	140M	80M	80M
AC	14M	5	624M	468M	504M
BC	10M	12	1080M	640M	
A	9M	13	1034M	517M	517M
B	7M	5	1430M		
C	8M	16	1056M	528M	34M

Fig. 3. Selection of Top-3 views using PA

The Proposed Algorithm (PA) selects B, BC and A as the Top-3 views. These selected views are able to account for 30 queries i.e. have a TQA of 30, which is more than the TQA of 22 achieved by HRUA. This implies that views selected using PA are able to account for more queries as compared to views selected using HRUA. TVEC due to views selected using PA is 103, which is slightly inferior to the TVEC of 102 due to views selected using HRUA. That is, the views selected using PA are able to account for more number of queries at the cost of slight increase in the TVEC value.

PA need not always select views with higher TVEC. As an example consider the 3-dimensional lattice shown in Fig. 4(a). Top-3 views selection using HRUA and PA are shown in Fig. 4(b) and Fig. 4(c) respectively. HRUA selects AC, BC and A as the Top-3 views as against A, B and AC selected by PA. The TVEC due to views selected using PA is 101 which is less than TVEC of 120 achieved by views selected using HRUA. Further, the TQA value of views selected using PA is 55 which is more than the TQA value 38 due to views selected using HRUA. This shows that the views selected using PA not only achieve better TQA but can also achieve better TVEC than the views selected using HRUA.

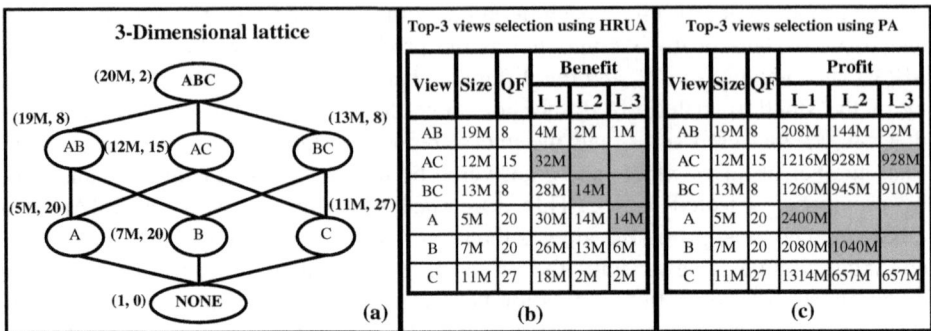

Fig. 4. Selection of Top-3 views using HRUA and PA

Thus, it can be said that PA, in comparison to HRUA, is able to select fairly good quality views capable of answering relatively more number of queries.

In order to compare the performance of PA with HRUA, both the algorithms were implemented and run on data sets with varying dimensions. The experimental based comparisons of PA and HRUA are given next.

4   Experimental Results

The algorithm PA and HRUA were implemented using JDK 1.6 in a Windows-XP environment. The experiments were performed on an Intel based 2 GHz PC having 1 GB RAM. The comparisons were carried out based on parameters like TVEC and TQA.

First, a graph was plotted to compare PA and HRUA algorithms on TQA against the number of dimensions for selecting Top-25 views for materialization. The graph is shown in Fig. 5

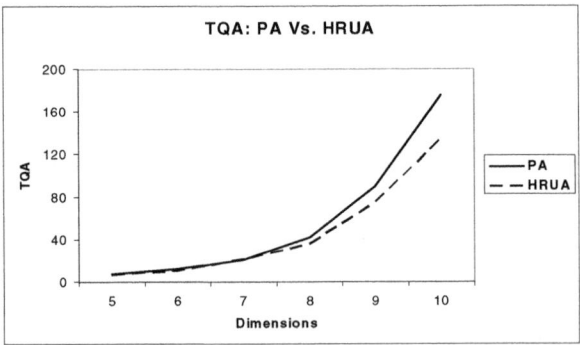

Fig. 5. TQA - PA Vs. HRUA

It is observed from the above graph that the increase in TQA value, with respect to number of dimensions, is more for PA vis-à-vis HRUA. This increase becomes significant for dimensions 8, 9 and 10. This shows that the views selected using PA perform relatively well with respect to answering greater number of queries.

Further, graphs were plotted to compare TQA for selecting Top-10 views from 8 and 10 dimensional data sets using PA and HRUA. These graphs are shown in Fig. 6.

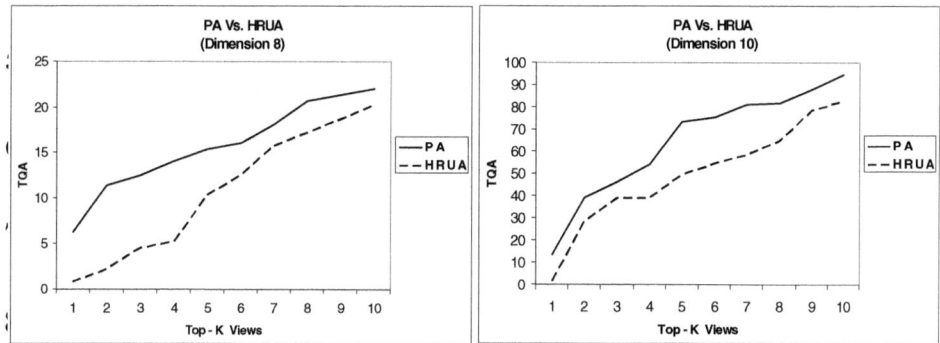

Fig. 6. PA Vs. HRUA - TQA Vs. Top-K Views for Dimensions 8 and 10

It is observed from the graph that the TQA due to views selected using PA remains relatively higher than those selected using HRUA with every view selection. This implies that the top views selected using PA are able to answer comparatively greater number of queries than those selected using HRUA.

In order to study the impact of higher TQA achieved by Top-25 views selected using PA on the TVEC, a graph for TVEC versus Dimensions is plotted as shown in Fig. 7.

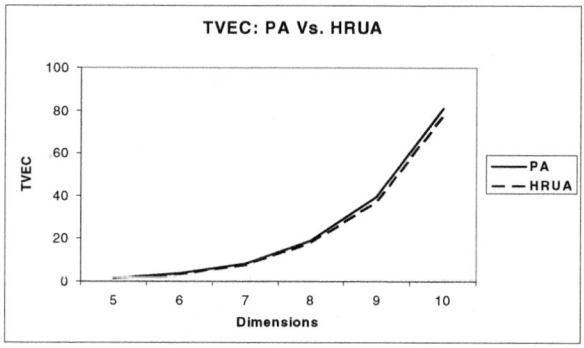

Fig. 7. TVEC - PA Vs. HRUA

It is observed from the above graph that, with increase in the number of dimensions, the increase in TVEC value is slightly higher for views selected using PA vis-à-vis those selected using HRUA. This shows that HRUA has a slight edge over PA with respect to the total cost of evaluating all the views.

Further, graphs comparing TVEC for selecting Top-10 views from 8 and 10 dimensional data sets using PA and HRUA is plotted as shown in Fig. 8. The graphs show that as views are selected, the TVEC for views selected using PA is slightly higher than those selected using HRUA. This implies that the top views selected using PA incurs a slightly higher total cost of evaluating all the views than those selected using HRUA.

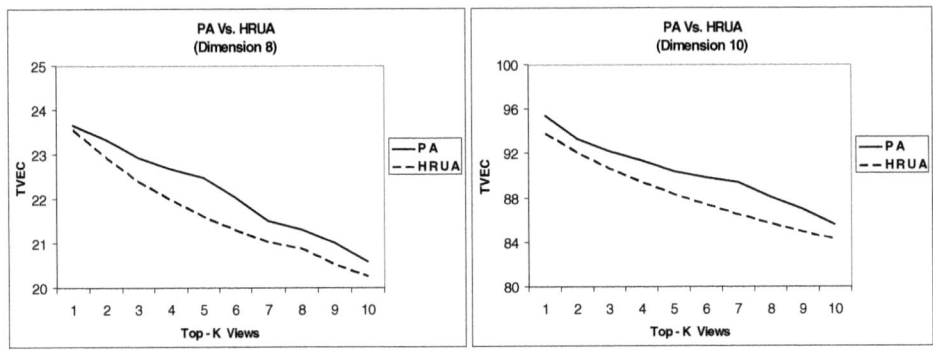

Fig. 8. PA Vs. HRUA - TVEC Vs. Top-K Views for Dimensions 8 and 10

It can be reasonably inferred from the above graphs that PA, in comparison to HRUA, trades significant improvement in TQA with a slight increase in TVEC of views selected for materialization.

5   Conclusion

In this paper, an algorithm is proposed that greedily selects Top-k views by considering query frequency along with the size of views. The proposed algorithm, in each iteration, computes the profit of each view defined in terms of its size and query frequency. This is followed by selecting the most profitable view for materialization. The selected views, which are profitable with respect to size and query frequency, are capable of answering large number of future queries leading to better average query response time.

Further, experiment based comparison of the proposed algorithm with HRUA showed that the views selected using the proposed algorithm were able to answer relatively higher number of queries against a slight increase in the total cost of evaluating all the views. This shows that the proposed algorithm trades a greater improvement in TQA for a slight increase in TVEC. The improved TQA would make decision making more efficient.

References

1. Agarwal, S., Chaudhuri, S., Narasayya, V.: Automated Selection of materialized views and indexes for SQL Databases. In: Proceedings Of VLDB, pp. 496–505 (2000)
2. Aouiche, K., Jouve, P.-E., Darmont, J.: Clustering-Based Materialized View Selection in Data Warehouses. In: Manolopoulos, Y., Pokorný, J., Sellis, T.K. (eds.) ADBIS 2006. LNCS, vol. 4152, pp. 81–95. Springer, Heidelberg (2006)
3. Aouiche, K., Darmont, J.: Data mining-based materialized view and index selection in data warehouse. Journal of Intelligent Information Systems, 65–93 (2009)
4. Baralis, E., Paraboschi, S., Teniente, E.: Materialized View Selection in a Multidimensional Database. In: Proceedings of VLDB 1997, pp. 156–165. Morgan Kaufmann Publishers, San Francisco (1997)
5. Gupta, H., Harinarayan, V., Rajaraman, A., Ullman, J.: Index Selection in OLAP. In: Proceedings ICDE 1997, pp. 208–219. IEEE Computer Society (1997)
6. Gupta, H., Mumick, I.: Selection of Views to Materialize in a Data Warehouse. IEEE Transactions on Knowledge and Data Engineering 17(1), 24–43 (2005)
7. Harinarayan, V., Rajaraman, A., Ullman, J.: Implementing Data Cubes Efficiently. In: Proceedings of SIGMOD, pp. 205–216. ACM Press (1996)
8. Inmon, W.H.: Building the Data Warehouse, 3rd edn. Wiley Dreamtech (2003)
9. Lehner, R., Ruf, T., Teschke, M.: Improving Query Response Time in Scientific Databases Using Data Aggregation. In: Proceedings of 7th International Conference and Workshop on Databases and Expert System Applications, pp. 9–13 (September 1996)
10. Nadeau, T.P., Teorey, T.J.: Achieving scalability in OLAP materialized view selection. In: Proceedings of DOLAP 2002, pp. 28–34. ACM Press (2002)
11. Roussopoulos, N.: Materialized Views and Data Warehouse. In: 4th Workshop KRDB 1997, Athens, Greece (August 1997)
12. Serna-Encinas, M.T., Hoya-Montano, J.A.: Algorithm for selection of materialized views: based on a costs model. In: Proceeding of Eighth International Conference on Current Trends in Computer Science, pp. 18–24 (2007)
13. Shah, B., Ramachandran, K., Raghavan, V.: A Hybrid Approach for Data Warehouse View Selection. International Journal of Data Warehousing and Mining 2(2), 1–37 (2006)
14. Shukla, A., Deshpande, P., Naughton, J.: Materialized View Selection for Multidimensional Datasets. In: Proceedings of VLDB 1998, pp. 488–499. Morgan Kaufmann Publishers (1998)
15. Teschke, M., Ulbrich, A.: Using Materialized Views to Speed Up Data Warehousing, Technical Report, IMMD 6. Universität Erlangen-Nürnberg (1997)
16. Theodoratos, D., Bouzeghoub, M.: A general framework for the view selection problem for data warehouse design and evolution. In: Proceedings of DOLAP, pp. 1–8 (2000)
17. Uchiyama, H., Ranapongsa, K., Teorey, T.J.: A Progressive View Materialization Algorithm. In: Proceeding of 2nd ACM International Workshop on Data Warehousing and OLAP, Kansas City Missouri, USA, pp. 36–41 (1999)
18. Vijay Kumar, T.V., Ghoshal, A.: A reduced lattice greedy algorithm for selecting materialized views. In: Prasad, S.K., Routray, S., Khurana, R., Sahni, S. (eds.) ICISTM 2009. CCIS, vol. 31, pp. 6–18. Springer, Heidelberg (2009)
19. Vijay Kumar, T.V., Haider, M., Kumar, S.: Proposing candidate views for materialization. In: Prasad, S.K., Vin, H.M., Sahni, S., Jaiswal, M.P., Thipakorn, B. (eds.) ICISTM 2010. CCIS, vol. 54, pp. 89–98. Springer, Heidelberg (2010)
20. Zhang, C., Yao, X., Yang, J.: An Evolutionary Approach to Materialized Views Selection in a Data Warehouse Environment. IEEE Transactions on Systems, Man and Cybernatics, 282–294 (2001)

Integration of XML Databases by Schema Restructuring

R. Kanchana, Aishwarya Rajagopal, S. Kaavya, and R. Bakiyalakshmi

Department of Computer Science and Engineering
SSN College of Engineering
Anna University – Chennai, India
rkanch@ssn.edu.in,
{icecoolgal,kaavya89,bakiya.dimple}@gmail.com

Abstract. Querying XML databases and their integration is an emerging area in applications related to database management systems. XML documents having similar data may differ in their organization. Hence a single query may not produce uniform results in all the documents. Different queries have to be generated for each of these hierarchies. To avoid this overhead, it is proposed to restructure and integrate different schemas by transforming all the XML schemas to a unique schema. We propose an algorithm to generate a unified query to extract results from this unique schema. Our work is demonstrated using an application of Primary Health Care (PHC) data maintenance system.

Keywords: XML, Databases, XQuery, Data Integration, Schema.

1 Introduction

XML stands for eXtensible Markup Language. XML's design goals emphasize simplicity, generality, and usability over the internet. Due to these reasons, XML is now becoming an efficient form of data storage. Considering the hierarchical organization of XML documents, data under a particular domain may be organized in more than one hierarchy. In such cases a particular query may fail to produce the desired result in all the hierarchies. As a solution to this problem, we perform restructuring of schemas by "closest relationship tracking" technique [2] and transform all the XML schemas to a unique structure [3]. Now a single query is adequate for this final schema to retrieve the required results from any of the input schemas. The data available in different input databases are integrated according to the restructured schemas so that queries can be answered without knowing the original schema. The authors of [1] assume that the same data is organized according to different formats and perform re-structuring. Our software works for different data organized according to different schemas.

2 Proposed Framework

A case study in the domain of Primary Health Care (PHC) has been considered to demonstrate this work. In India, the PHC system organizes its records in different

R. Kannan and F. Andres (Eds.): ICDEM 2010, LNCS 6411, pp. 52–56, 2012.
© Springer-Verlag Berlin Heidelberg 2012

hierarchies at the state level. The states may organize their records based on categories such as department, healthcare schemes, gender, schemes for children and adults, and location. Our system has been designed as shown in Fig. 1 to query and compare the Health care data of different states in India. To start with the user logs into the portal and enters his requirements. The users are employees of the department of PHC and are required to have a basic knowledge about the classification of schemes in the department. From the requirements, a context node is selected. The sequence of nodes closest to the context code are generated using closest node locater algorithm [4] applied on different schemas of all states. Then the tag name conflicts in different schemas are resolved using vocabulary control technology. The resulting schemas are transformed into a uniform structure using polymorphic restructuring algorithm [3], so that a single query works on all the schemas. If the user input requires comparison of data available in two or more states, the data of the corresponding states are integrated into a new XML document. After obtaining the final XML document, a query is generated automatically. Aggregate functions have been used for comparison between the retrieved results. The generated query is executed in eXist XML [5] database and the results are displayed on the portal.

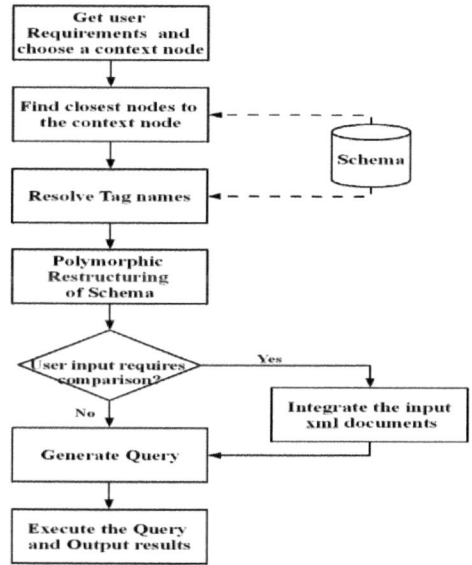

Fig. 1. XML Schema Restructuring and Integration

A novel algorithm for automatically generating a query in XQuery [6] form for the unified schema is shown in Fig. 2. The input parameters to the algorithm are XML file(s), context nodes along with input values, and the required output nodes. A snapshot of the initial user interface in our Primary Health Care portal is shown in Fig. 3. Sample query generated from query generation algorithm for selection of single state is given below. This query retrieves the schemes introduced by the Government of Tamil Nadu under a particular department "hds" and the result is shown in Fig. 4.

for $b in doc("tamilnadu.xml")/tamilnadu/dept[@name="hds"]/disease/scheme return $b.

```
Query (states, cn, val,adv, advval, ret)
  begin
        path;                    // list of paths for context nodes
        query;                   //list of all queries
        height;                  //context node height
        parse (states);          // parse input file using DOM
        for every c in adv.size
              list = get occurances of n from file;
              while  (p != rootNode)
                    path += "/" + n;
                    n = parent of n;
                    path = n;
                    height = No. Of '/' in path + 1
              max  = find Maximum of Height
              path = findPath (Max, path, cn)
              for every p in path
                    for every c in cn.attributes
                          query += c
                          for every r in ret
                                for every q in query
                                      append "and"+ ret[i] to query
  end
  findPath (max, path, cn)
  begin
        qpath;                   //contains the query path without duplicates
        for every path in path
              if path.height = max
                    for every c in cn
                          if path contains c
                                count = count +1;
                          add to qpath;
        return qpath
  end
```

Fig. 2. Query generation algorithm

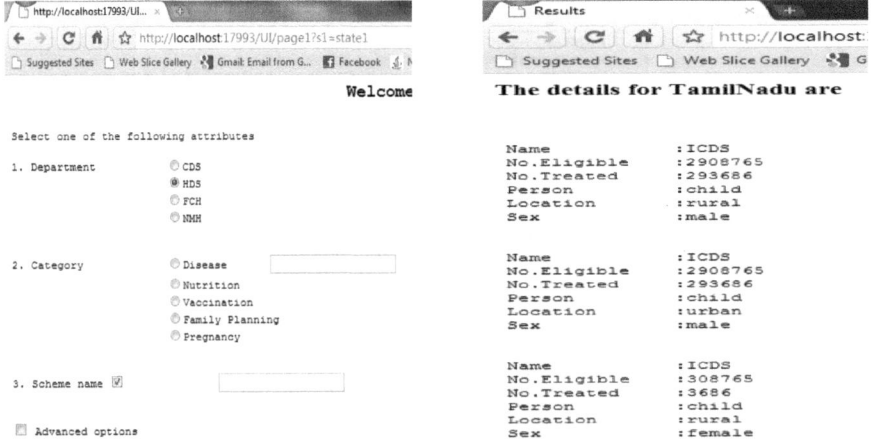

Fig. 3. User interface portal   **Fig. 4.** List of schemes in Tamil Nadu

3   Analysis

A detailed time response analysis has been performed as shown in Fig. 5 to analyze how the position of context node influences the execution time of the polymorphic restructuring algorithm. It is observed from the analysis that the schemas containing context node at higher levels (closer to the root node) take lesser time. It is also evident that the response time increases with the size of the schema.

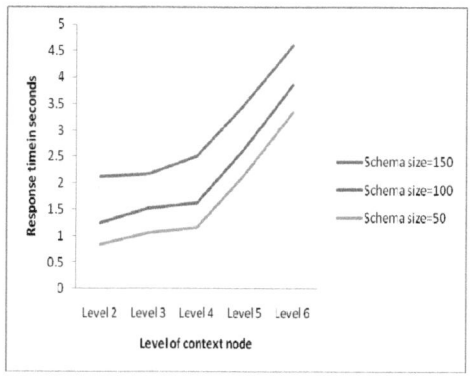
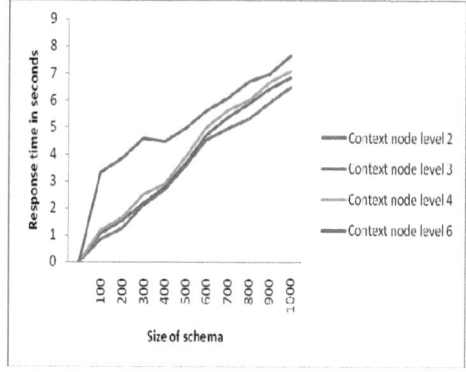

a. Level of context node (vs) Response time   b. Size of schema (vs) Response time

Fig. 5. Time response analysis for polymorphic restructuring algorithm

4   Conclusion

XML schemas organized in different hierarchies have been restructured to avoid generating a separate query for each state level schema. A query is automatically generated to extract the results from this unified database. The data from different XML databases are integrated to facilitate comparison of healthcare data in different states. However, this work does not integrate data from different domains. As a future work, the application domain can be expanded and advanced querying options can be used. In addition, instead of obtaining the databases of different states at the location of query, the databases can be accessed from heterogeneous sources.

References

1. Zhang, S., Dyreson, C.: The Benefits of Utilizing Closeness in XML. In: 19th IEEE International Conference on Database and Expert Systems Application (2008)
2. Leonardi, E., Bhowmick, S., Ng, Z., Dyreson, C.: Towards Evaluation of Symmetric XPath Axis in Tree-Unaware RDBMS. Technical Report, International World Wide Web Conference Committee (IW3C2). Nanyang Technological University, Singapore (2008)

3. Zhang, S., Dyreson, C.: Polymorphic XML Restructuring. In: Proceedings of IIWeb, WWW Workshop, International World Wide Web Conference Committee, IW3C2 (2006)
4. Bonifati, A., Cuzzocrea, A.: Synopsis Data Structures for XML Databases: Models, Issues, and Research Perspectives. In: 18th IEEE International Workshop on Database and Expert Systems Applications (2007)
5. XML Database, http://exist-db.org/quickstart.html
6. XQuery Help, http://www.w3schools.com/xquery/xquery_flwor.asp

Dynamic Materialized View Selection Algorithm: A Clustering Approach

Manoj S. Chaudhari and Chandrashekhar Dhote

CSE Dept., PRMIT & R, Badnera, India
manojchaudhary2@gmail.com

Abstract. A data warehouse can be seen as a set of materialized views defined over remote base relation. When the query is posed, it is evaluated locally using the materialized view without accessing the original database. The paper proposes clustering based dynamic materialized view selection algorithm. The base of the paper is to propose similarity function, clustering materialized view and then dynamically adjusting the materialized view.

Keywords: Data Warehousing, Views, Similarity function, Materialization, View Selection, View- Maintenance, Query processing cost.

1 Introduction

Data warehouse can be considered as a repository of an organization's electronically stored data. Data warehouses are designed to facilitate reporting and analysis of data, focuses on data storage. The data warehouse is intended to provide decisions support services for large volumes of data. So how to rapidly respond to query request is much great challenge in data warehouse.

When request is posed by a query, the data or the result of query has to be find out from the large data warehouse. Hence the query response time is very large and the performance response is much poor. If the similar query is requested again then the entire data warehouse has to be searched again to find the same result. Hence the approach of the paper is, it selects the dynamic materialized views and then clusters the queries. Dynamic materialized views only materialize the most frequently accessed rows. One or more control tables are associated with the view and define which rows are currently materialized. The set of materialized rows can be changed dynamically.

In a data warehouse, a materialized view relates to SQL statement. Generally materialized view corresponds to the result of SQL statement execution. So the materialized view can be transformed into a corresponding SQL statement. Hence the paper transforms clustering materialized view into clustering corresponding SQL statement. The paper aims to clusters queries and builds materialized views that can resolve multiple similar queries belonging to the same cluster so as to give good response performance for random query.

R. Kannan and F. Andres (Eds.): ICDEM 2010, LNCS 6411, pp. 57–66, 2012.
© Springer-Verlag Berlin Heidelberg 2012

2   Related Work

[1] Propose a framework for materialized view selection that exploits a data mining technique (clustering), in order to determine clusters of similar queries. It also proposes a view merging algorithm that builds a set of candidate views. [2] Presents an automatic strategy for the selection of XML materialized views that exploit a data mining technique, more precisely the clustering of the query workload. To validate the strategy, they implemented an XML warehouse modeled along the Cube specifications. [3] Has developed a theoretical framework for the general problem of selection of views in a data warehouse. Paper present polynomial time heuristics for a selection of views to optimize total query response time under a disk-space constraint, for some important special cases of the general data warehouse scenario. [4] Has developed a framework, for the selection of views to materialize, for a given storage space constraints, which intends to achieve the best combination of good query response, low query processing cost and low view maintenance cost.[5]Presents a heuristics approach for the selection of materialized view. The paper also presents the views that should be materialized in order to make the sum of the query performance and view maintenance cost minimum. [6] Proposes the clustering based dynamic materialized view selection algorithm. It firstly clusters materialized views and then dynamically adjusts materialized view set. This paper proposes a solution which firstly clusters materialized view, and then dynamically adjusts materialized view set.

3   Strategy of Materialized View Selection

➢ Extraction of set of queries resolved by the system.
➢ Extraction of the representation attributes from the set of queries.
➢ Application of the clustering algorithm to create cluster of queries.
➢ Generation of set of candidate views.
➢ Selection of the final view configuration.
➢ Materialization of the views.

Thus the paper is divided into two parts: First part consist of the clustering algorithm based on similarity function and second part elaborates the different algorithms for materialized views selection approaches that considers all the cost metrics associated with the materialized views such as the system's storage space constraints, view maintenance cost, query frequency, query access cost and base-relation update frequency.

3.1   Clustering Algorithm Based on Similarity Function

The paper proceeds by clustering the materialized view. First the similarity between two SQL statements is computed using some predefined criteria. The similarity function between two SQL statements is judged using the following criteria.

(1) Determine whether there is the same or contained base table set.
(2) Determine whether there is the same complete equivalence connectivity condition.

(3) Determine whether there is equal or contained scope equivalence condition.
(4) Determine whether there is equal or other kind of equivalence condition.
(5) Determine whether there is the same or contained output column.

The above five criteria are not equally important,   whose weights are different, (1) maximal, (5) minimal, and (2), (3), (4) the same weight which is between (1) and (5). That is in the calculation of the similarity of the SQL statement, the contribution of behind condition is less than front condition because if the base table sets of the two statements are not same or contained each other, the results of the two statements will not be too similar definitely. So, the weight of front condition is bigger.

3.2 Clustering Materialized View Set

Using the above similarity criteria, clustering algorithm is given below.

Input: Materialized view set Mv = {V1, V2,..., Vn} , similarity threshold β for similarity of queries.
Output: Materialized view set M' which is marked clustering category
(1)Take a sample from materialized view set, such as V1 and make V1 as the first category center, So, C1=V1.
(2)Then take Vi (i=2, 3, …, N) in turn, calculate the similarity between C1 and Vi.
(3)If Similarity > β , then determine that Vi belongs to class C1 and its center is V1.
(4)If Similarity ≤ β , then make Vi as a new class, and its center is also Vi.
(5)Then calculate similarity between remaining samples and C1 and between remaining samples and C2, respectively.
(6)If the bigger calculated similarity is bigger than or equal to similarity threshold β , then determine that Vi belongs to the class which has bigger similarity.
(7)Otherwise, make Vi as a new class and its center is Vi.
(8)So continue, until completely process all samples.

The characteristic of this algorithm is that it does not need to determine the number of clustering and the number of class that will be produced gradually in the clustering process in advance.

4   Different Cost Effective Approaches for Selection of Materialized Views

In this section we are explaining the different algorithms required for the clustering of queries and comparing the queries using conditional clauses and calculating different parameters of the query processing like preservation of existing materialized view, query access frequency ,query access cost etc. Again it explains the cost effective approach for materialized view selection. The proposed approach exploits all the cost metrics associated with the materialized views such as base relation update frequency, query frequency, query access cost and view maintenance cost.

The materialized view selection problem can be described as follows: Given a set of queries Q and maintenance time MT and existing materialized views Mv, the view selection problem is to select a set of views M to be materialized, that minimizes total cost associated with materialized views under storage space and maintenance cost constraints. The memory constraint is the space, which should not be exceeded by materializing the views. The maintenance cost is the total time, which should not be exceeded while maintaining the materialized views. The framework retains existing materialized views periodically by removing views with low access frequency and high storage space. The queries with high access frequencies are selected for the view selection problem. Then the query access cost and maintenance cost of selected views are calculated. The total cost of each view is calculated and views with optimum cost under the maintenance and space Constraints are selected for materialization. The proposed framework is discussed in detail in the following sections.

4.1 Retaining Existing Materialized Views

This section details the preservation of the existing materialized views. Before selecting new views for materialization, the existing materialized views are sustained based on their access frequency and storage space. The algorithm given below removes the materialized views with low access frequency and high storage space for the materialization of new views. The steps are given in Algorithm A.

Assumptions
V_M → Vector of materialized views
N → Total no of materialized views
MS → Memory size of materialized views
Thres → Threshold value
AF → Access frequency of materialized views
Algorithm A

   for each Materialized View in V_M

       W = 2 log (AF) - log (MS)

       if (W < Thres) then

           Remove current materialized view;

           end if

   end for

The above algorithm removes the materialized views with low access frequency and high storage space for the materialization of new views.

4.2 View Selection Using Weights

This section gives the initial selection of views based on their weightage in the given query set and storage space. Instead of selecting all the queries, the queries which have high access frequency are selected for the view selection problem. The queries are selected from the given query set using Algorithm B.

Assumptions:

Q → Given Set of Queries
Q_{AF} → Access Frequency of Queries
Φ → Threshold value
SQ → Vector of selected queries

Algorithm B

　　for each query in Q

　　　　　if $(Q_{AF} > \Phi)$ then

　　　　　Add query to vector SQ;

　　　　　end if

end for

The queries having access frequency greater than the threshold value Φ are selected for materialized view selection problem. After that the conditional clauses in each query are represented using Algorithm C.

Assumptions

SQ → Selected set of Queries
Q_C → 2D Array of conditional clauses
Q_{SV} → 2D Array of integer values of QC

Algorithm C

　　for each query in SQ

　　if the query has conditional clauses then

　　　　　Q [i] = Conditional Clause (Q_C)

　　　　　end if

end for

Each distinct conditional clause in Q_C is mapped to an integer value and the count of each distinct clause is calculated using the algorithm D.

Assumptions

DCC → Distinct conditional clauses
CC →Count of conditional clause

Algorithm D

The conditional clauses in each query are represented in 2-D format through previous algorithm. This 2-D representation is converted into 1-D representation and their counts are taken simultaneously for further processing. The algorithm for the above is as follows:
Set index = 0;

for each(i) row   in Qc

for each(j) conditional clause Cc in row

if ((DCC ∩ CC) == Φ)

DCC << C

CC << 1;

else

index = DCC[Cc];

CC[index] = CC[index] +1;

end if

end for

end for

4.3   View Selection Using Weights

Then the views are selected based on their weightage in the given query set and storage space using this algorithm. Then views with weightage greater than a threshold value α are selected for further process.

Assumptions

M_U → Vector of Storage space needed to store result of conditional clause

M_{Tot} → Total storage space needed

CC_{Tot} → Total Count

SV → Selected set of views

Algorithm E

    for each conditional clause in DCC
        $F1 = CC / CC_{Tot}$;
        $F2 = (1- (MU /M_{Tot}))$;
        $W = 2 \log (F1) + \log (F2)$;
            If $(W > \alpha)$;
        add current conditional clause based view to SV for further process;
        end if
end for

Then the views are selected based on their weightage in the given query set and storage space using Algorithm E. Then views with weightage greater than a threshold value α are selected for further process.

4.4 Query Processing Cost

The cost of query processing is query frequency multiplied by the cost of query access from the materialized views. The query processing cost of each view from SV is calculated using the following formula.

$$QP_{COST} =1/ \Sigma N \ Freq* Ca (V)$$

Where N is the total no of queries, Freq is the frequency of query and Ca (V) is the cost of access for query q using view V.

4.5 View Maintenance Cost

View maintenance is the process of updating precomputed views when the base table is updated. The maintenance   cost for materialized view is the cost used for refreshing this view whenever a change is made to the base table. The maintenance cost is calculated using update frequency and the priority value of the base table. A priority value in the range 1 – 10 is assigned for each base table based on its importance. The maintenance cost is calculated using Algorithm F.

Assumptions

P → Priority of Base tables
UF → Update frequency of Base tables

Algorithm F

    for each view in SV
        for each base table
        $VM_{COST} [i] = 1/(P[i]* (1/UF[i])$
        end for
    end for

4.6 Materialized View Selection

The total cost of each view is calculated by summing the query processing cost and maintenance cost. Then the views are sorted in ascending order based on their total cost.

$$TotCost = QP_{COST} + VM_{COST};$$

Then the views with minimal cost whose maintenance time and storage space falls within the given constraints are selected for materialization.

5 Experimental Results

In this section, we present the results of our experimental analysis. We have implemented all the algorithms   in Matlab 7.1 .The Algorithm A has successfully removed the existing materialized views with low access frequency and high storage space and thus freed the space for the materialization of new views. The Algorithm B has successfully selected the queries with high access frequencies for the view-selection problem. The conditional clauses from each selected query were extracted by Algorithm C. From the available views, some views were initially selected based on Algorithm E. We assume similarity threshold $\beta = 0.7$. Obtain initial materialized view set through the clustering algorithm as explained in section 3.2 . Figure 1 shows the clustering of the materialized views initially according to query set.

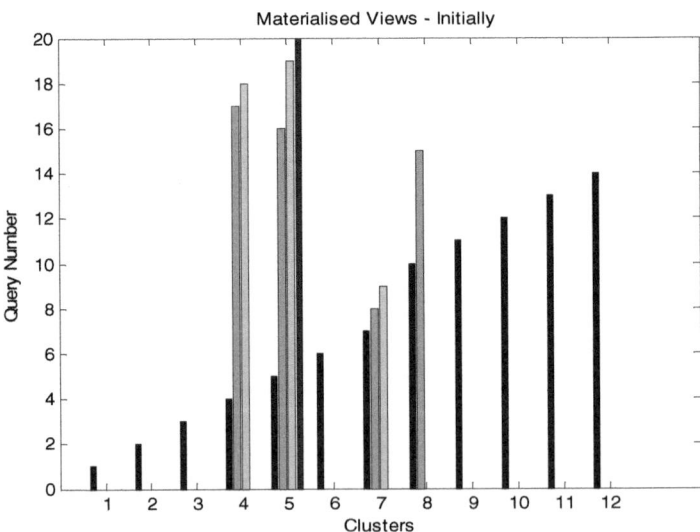

Fig. 1. Initial representation of Materialized Views

Figure2 shows the updated materialized view according to the new queries fired to query set.

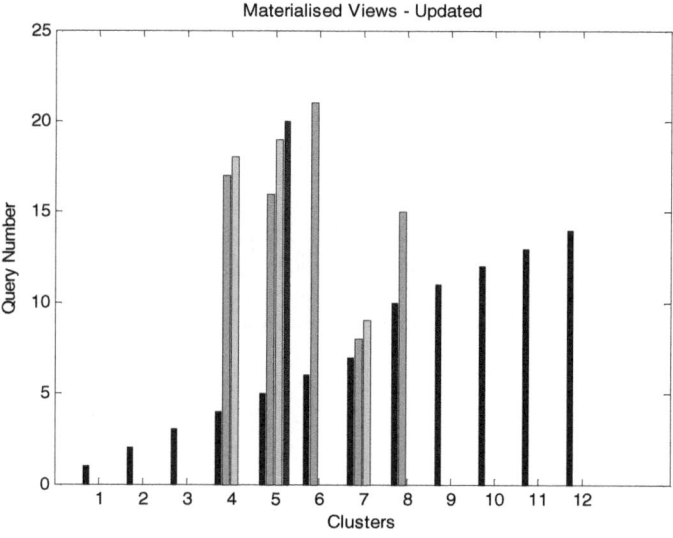

Fig. 2. Updated representation of Materialized Views

6 Conclusion

The proposed paper firstly selects the dynamic   materialized view by using above mentioned dynamic materialized   view selection algorithm. Then by clustering the queries, there is the search of the cluster for new queries by using similarity function and if the query is present in cluster the precomputed result is returned. Hence the approach of paper is to reduce the latency time means the time for computation as well as complexity to reduce time for number of operations by using the precompiled results of dynamic view as compared to the techniques already available. Again the view selection problem has been addressed in this paper by means of taking into account the essential constraints: maintenance cost and memory space. We have presented a approach for selecting views to materialize so as to achieve the best combination of good query response and low query processing cost .The presented approach considers all the cost metrics   associated with materialized views such as query execution frequencies, base-relation update frequencies, query access costs and view maintenance costs The most cost effective views have been selected for materialization by the framework and the maintenance, storage and query processing cost of the views have been optimized.

References

[1] Aouiche, K., Emmanuel Jouve, P., Darmont, J.: Clustering-Based Materialized View Selection in Data Warehouses. Technical Report, University of Lyon 2 (2007)
[2] Mahboubi, H., Aouiche, K., Darmont, J.: Materialized View Selection by Query Clustering in XML Data Warehouses. In: Fourth International Conference on Computer Science and Information Technology, Jordan
[3] Gupta, H., Mummick, I.S.: Selection of Views to Materialize in a Data Warehouse. IEEE Transaction on Knowledge and Data Engineering 17, 24–43 (2005)
[4] Ashadevi, B., Balasubramaniam, R.: Optimized Cost effective Approach for Materialized View Selection in Data Warehousing. CST&V 9(1), 21–26 (2009)
[5] Dhote, C.A., Ali, M.S.: Materialized View Selection Algorithm in Data Warehouse. In: International Conference on Information Technology (ITNG 2007) (2007)
[6] Gong, A., Zhao, W.: Clustering-based Dynamic Materialized View Selection Algorithm. In: Proceedings of Fifth International Conference on Fuzzy Systems and Knowledge Discovery, China, pp. 391–395 (2008)

Quality of Forecasting Based on Compressed High Frequency Time Series

Jerzy Korczak and Krzysztof Drelczuk

Wrocław University of Economics, Wrocław, Poland
jerzy.korczak@ue.wroc.pl, kdrelczuk@hotmail.com

Abstract. In this paper the general compression method of time series will be presented and adapted to financial time series analysis where dimensionality reduction is crucial. It will be shown that a double compression using Daubechies 4 wavelet does not significantly affect the quality of information carried by a time series. The reduction of dimensionality significantly affects the algorithmic complexity and improves its quality of prediction. In order to verify this hypothesis the highly frequent time series will be evaluated in terms of forecasting quality where future value is predicted only on the basis of the past quotations. In this project as a predictive algorithm ARAR will be applied due to its good results in forecasting of the real financial time series.

Keywords: wavelets, Daubechies 4, discrete wavelet transform, time series Analysis.

1 Introduction

Empirical evidence shows that the dimensionality reduction not only significantly affects the computing time of the classifiers, but also the quality of classification results, whereas in Euclidean space increasing the number of dimensions diminishes the distance between vectors. This has particularly important impact on the process of clustering. The space of solutions that is divided into clusters has the same dimensionality as entering vectors. With a large number of dimensions of difference between the nearest and farthest neighbour it becomes less important and it is a serious obstacle to partition the space into the significant clusters [2]. Too many dimensions can also cause overlapping multidimensional clusters impeding effective classification.

This hypothesis sets out to prove that double compression by Daubechies 4 wavelet does not significantly affect the quality of information carried by a time series in comparison to the original, raw time series. In other words, the double wavelet compression does not influence the deterioration of the time series, as the information source. In the case of clustering where the computational complexity is exponential, proving such an assumption has a significant impact on the usefulness of the clustering algorithms. Taking also into account the reduction of distance between clusters in the Euclidean space with increasing dimensionality, this demonstration would positively influence the quality of the prediction of time series.

In this work the authors made use of discrete wavelet transform for lossless compression of time series; lossless in the sense of preservation of the same quality of information as an untreated time series. In various systems of time series analysis,

R. Kannan and F. Andres (Eds.): ICDEM 2010, LNCS 6411, pp. 67–74, 2012.
© Springer-Verlag Berlin Heidelberg 2012

such as predictive systems, classification systems, archiving systems, the possibility to assure the lossless compression is of great importance.

2 ARAR and Discrete Wavelet Transform

The chosen prediction algorithm ARAR is a modification of previous algorithm ARARMA [8]. Its characteristic is the application of *memory-shortening* transformation for each time series, and then fitting with a model ARMA [3].

Wavelets are basis functions used in representing data or other functions. Wavelet algorithms process data at different scales or resolutions in contrast with discrete Fourier transform where only frequency components are considered. The origin of wavelets used in this paper can be can be traced to the work [5].

Daubechies wavelets are a family of orthogonal wavelets labelled D2-D20 (only the even index denotes nonzero coefficients of the scaling functions), are very often used, inter alia, because of very low computational complexity, that is $O(n)$. Comparatively, a widely used Fast Fourier Transformation (FFT) has the computational complexity $O(n \cdot \log n)$. In our project, the applied wavelet is D4 wavelet with four coefficients of scaling function.

Discrete wavelet transform, first described in [7], is very often applied in preliminary data analysis. With it one can reduce the number of dimensions of input vector to the target system, such as the classifier or predictive system, as well as remove some of the information considered as noise or data redundancies, in terms of Shannon's lossless data compression [9]. Below the source code of the compression algorithm (Discrete Wavelet Transform) is presented to show its simplicity and low algorithmic complexity.

Extract from the source code of discrete wavelet transformation

```
public static double[] D4Transform(double[] input, int approximation-
Size)
{
        double h0 = (1 + Math.Sqrt(3)) / 4 * Math.Sqrt(2);
        double h1 = (3 + Math.Sqrt(3)) / 4 * Math.Sqrt(2);
        double h2 = (3 - Math.Sqrt(3)) / 4 * Math.Sqrt(2);
        double h3 = (1 - Math.Sqrt(3)) / 4 * Math.Sqrt(2);
        double g0 = h3;
        double g1 = -h2;
        double g2 = h1;
        double g3 = -h0;
        int i = 0, j = 0;
        int half = approximationSize >> 1;
        double[] tmp = new double[approximationSize << 1];
        for (j = 0; j < approximationSize - 3; j = j + 2)
        {
            tmp[i] = a[j]*h0+a[j+1]*h1+a[j+2]*h2+a[j+3]*h3;
            tmp[i+half] =a[j]*g0+a[j+1]*g1+a[j+2]*g2+a[j+3]*g3;
            i++;
        }
        tmp[i] = a[n-2]*h0+a[n-1]*h1+a[0]*h2+a[1]*h3;
        tmp[i+half] = a[n-2]*g0+a[n-1]*g1+a[0]*g2+a[1]*g3;
        return tmp;
}
```

Input parameters are the input vector to be subjected to transformation (with a length which is the power of two) and the number of approximation coefficients which are to be created from it (which is also the power of two). The result is an array of approximation and details. For example, if we introduce a time series $S_{0,0}, S_{0,1}, S_{0,2}, S_{0,3}, S_{0,4}, S_{0,5}, S_{0,6}, S_{0,7}$, and the second parameter 4, then the result will be a table of four approximations and four details: $S_{1,0}, S_{1,1}, S_{1,2}, S_{1,3}, T_{1,0}, T_{1,1}, T_{1,2}, T_{1,3}$.

The wavelet D4 has been chosen because of its high-speed (low computational complexity) and the simplicity of implementation. In addition, it has been well studied in the literature from the viewpoint of its usefulness in the pre-processing efficiency of highly frequent time series.

3 Experiments

The tests have been carried out in two stages. In the first stage a single, randomly selected, financial time series was examined, extracted from the period of first four months from 2009 and first four months in 2010. The aim was to examine the different behaviour of financial time series. In the second stage, one financial time series was selected corresponding to 12 hours of quotations divided into equal size parts using sliding windows. The goal was to discover changes in time series. This study of the impact of wavelet compression on the time series information using wavelets Daubechies 4 was carried out on the currency market FOREX. According to statistics published in 2008 [1], most transactions concerned the pairs: EUR/USD 27%, USD/JPY 13%, and GBP/USD 12%.

Given these observations the authors have chosen the time series describing historical transactions for these three pairs of currencies. The selection of samples for the testing were purely random. The intervals (the first day and the last day of the month) were generated randomly using the pseudo-generator. The generated values indicate days of the time series to evaluate. To ensure the objectivity of research, we have drawn five time series of four consecutive months for the same days (if the number indicated the day when the FOREX is close the next closest date was taken on which the transactions take place), and all pairs (EUR/USD, USD/JPY, GBP/USD) have been selected from those days. Time series of the length of 256 have been created from the aggregated data to one minute; the first value represents the aggregated transactions within the first minute of the day (0:01), the last transactions 256 minutes later (at 4:17). The time series were grouped within the pairs of currencies. So the result was three sets of data, three sets of the average relative errors (computed for a single currency).

The test consisted of two phases. In the first, we have examined the amount of information in time series, evaluating the effectiveness of the prediction algorithm ARAR. Each of the selected series was divided into two series of length of 128. The first 128 values served as a learning set, and 20 consecutive values (the first 20 values from the second series) were treated as a validation set. Then, the mean relative error (*MRE*) for each of the quotes (from 1 to 20) was calculated according to the formula:

$$RE = \frac{\Delta x}{x} = \frac{x_0 - x}{x} = \frac{x_0}{x} - 1, \tag{1}$$

where x_0 is an expected value, x is a real value. *MRE* was obtained by dividing *RE* into a number of samples.

The second stage was to demonstrate if the quantity and quality of information afforded by the compressed time series significantly differed from the uncompressed one. To achieve this a series of length 256 was compressed by the discrete transform wavelet. The resulting series of length 128 (twice the compression) was divided into two series of length of 64. Values of the first series have been used as a learning set, and a set of next 20 values (the first 20 values from the second row) as a validation set. The last step was the calculation of the average relative errors (*MRE*) for each of the quotes using the same formula as for the series of the first stage.

As a result, three groups of the test series were performed, which included the values of the average relative errors ranked according to the period. Recall that the objective of this study was to demonstrate that the double wavelet compression did not significantly worsen the average prediction error. Such a result confirmed the hypothesis put at the beginning of the work that the double compression using wavelet Daubechies 4 does not affect significantly the quality of information carried by a time series in comparison with the original ones. To validate the hypothesis the compatibility the Kolmogorov–Smirnov test was applied. The test confirmed that the two populations had the same distribution, which is equivalent to saying that the two samples come from the same population.

In this project the algorithm ARAR for time series prediction and the authoring program to compress the time series were applied. In the experiments, the randomly selected quotes from January 8, 12, 16, 19, 20, 26 February 9, 12, 16, 17, 20, 21, March 8, 12, 16, 19, 20, 26 and April 8, 13, 18, 21, 27 were tested for 2010. For the second study, the quotes come from January, February, March and April 27 for 2009 year and from 5 January, February, March and April for 2010 year.

The average relative errors for the original and transformed time series are presented in Figures 1-3. The differences are practically negligible. Comparison of the cumulative average of errors is shown in Figures 4-6. The solid lines represent the values for the transformed time series, while the dashed lines illustrate original ones. Values are almost similar; only in case of USD/GBP the difference is greater. When comparing the maximum and minimum values we have noticed that in some cases better prediction results were achieved using the transformed time series, and in some, when predicting based on the original time series. Although in these cases the differences were small (except the USD/GBP where the wavelet compression significantly improved the least effective prediction).

The goodness-of-fit Kolmogorov–Smirnov test was also carried out. Null hypothesis was assumed that the distributions of the average relative prediction error in the original and compressed time series were the same. To validate the hypothesis the following statistic has been used

$$\lambda_n = \sqrt{n} \cdot \sup \left| F_{n_1}(x) - F_{n_2}(x) \right|, \tag{2}$$

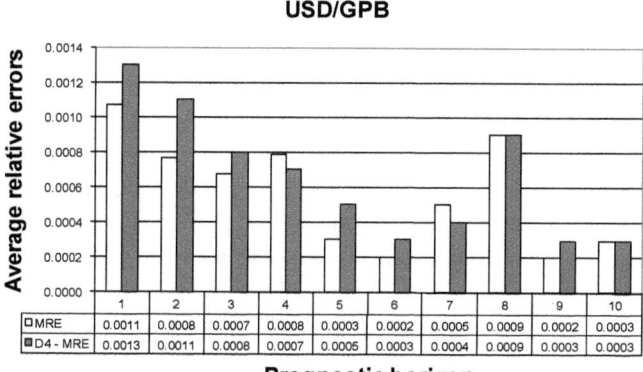

Fig. 1. Comparison of average relative errors for original and compressed time series. Pair USD/GBP.

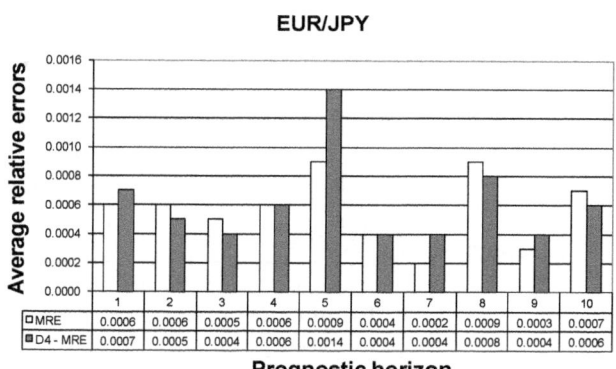

Fig. 2. Comparison of average relative errors for original and compressed time series. Pair USD/JPY.

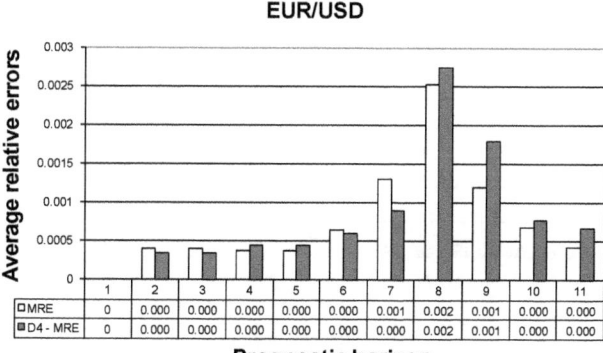

Fig. 3. Comparison of average relative errors for original and compressed time series. Pair EUR/USD

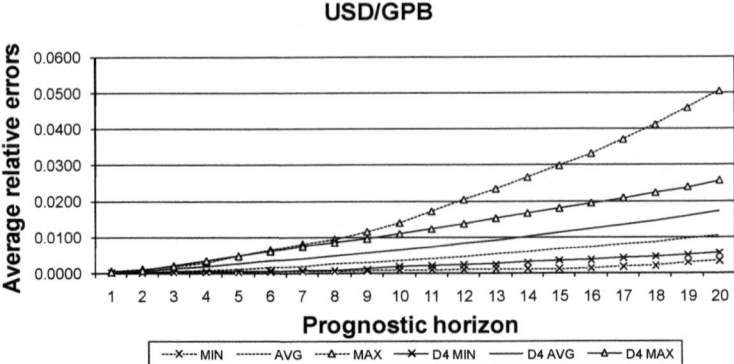

Fig. 4. Comparison of average cumulative errors (max, min and average) for original and compressed time series. Pair USD/GBP.

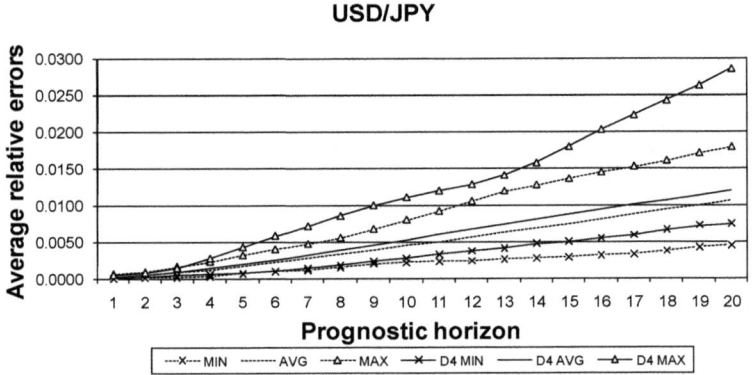

Fig. 5. Comparison of average cumulative errors (max, min and average) for original and compressed time series. Pair USD/JPY.

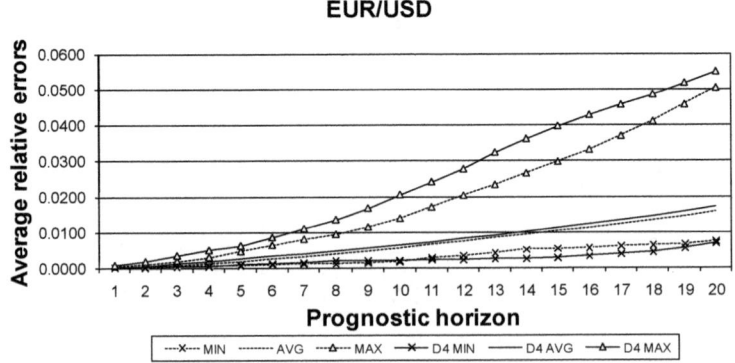

Fig. 6. Comparison of average cumulative errors (max, min and average) for original and compressed time series. Pair EUR/USD.

where

$$n = \frac{n_1 \cdot n_2}{n_1 + n_2} \tag{3}$$

and $F_{n_1}(x), F_{n_2}(x)$ are the empirical distribution functions computed on the basis of samples. Graphical presentation of the distribution is shown in Fig. 7.

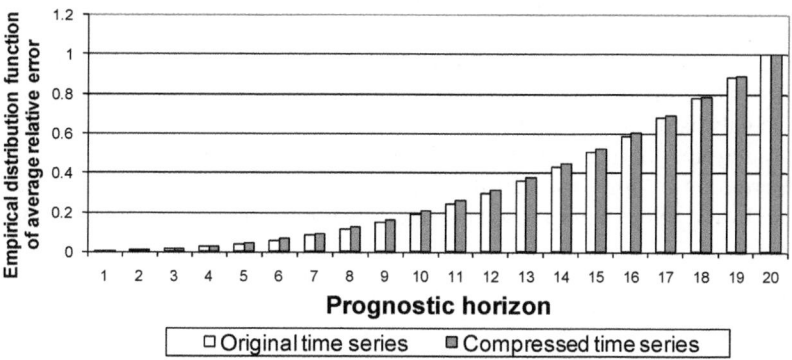

Fig. 7. Comparison of average error distributions for original and compressed time series

Values n_1, n_2 mean the sum of averages of relative errors of predictions. The value of empirical statistic was computed and it was equal to 0.014821. The limit λ-Kołmogorov distribution at the confidence level $\alpha = 0.01$ is equal to 1.61. So, based on the relation $\lambda_e < \lambda_\alpha$, so there is no reason to reject the null hypothesis. So, we say with 99% probability that the average error distributions are the same in the case of time series transformed by Daubechies 4 wavelet and as the raw time series.

In the second experiment, the differences were less noticeable for the average and minimum values. However, in all three cases the results were better for compressed time series than the uncompressed one. More details can be found in [6].

Taking into consideration that the predictions were made on double-compressed time series, it can be stated that the result was very encouraging. Not only was the computing time reduced, but also the prediction accuracy was improved.

4 Conclusions and Future Works

The results of this research have confirmed the hypothesis established at the beginning of the work that the information carried by uncompressed time series is qualitatively identical to the information carried by double-compressed time series using Daubechies 4 wavelet. The consequences are important. Colloquially speaking, it makes no sense to use the original time series since the use of a time series of two times shorter (after compressing by D4) assures the same results. Given the computing complexity of the classification algorithms, it is of utmost importance. It should be also noted that in the case of a long time series (covering 12-hours period) wavelet compression improved the quality of prediction. This would mean that, at least for these three examined time series, noise and redundant information have been eliminated by the compression process.

To determine the usefulness of wavelet compression in financial time series in general, it would be recommended to test them on significantly greater empirical material coming from various stock markets. One can also consider trying other wavelets of the Daubechies family. In the paper, we were focused on the computational complexity and its reduction in the context of prediction systems. It should be mentioned here that the wavelet D1 has lesser complexity than the D4, which could make it more useful for larger data sets or in real time systems. But one must have in mind that D1 is less sensitive to subtle, local changes in the original time series, and it is less efficient in analysis of highly frequent time series.

Summing up, although we have indicated that further research is required, the use of compression is fully justified if we are interested to reduce the multidimensional space and we do not want to lose any significant information contained in the original time series.

References

1. Bank for International Settlements, Triennial Central Bank Survey (2007),
   http://www.bis.org/publ/rpfxf07t.pdf
2. Beyer, K., Goldstein, J., Ramakrishnan, R., Shaft, U.: When is Nearest Neighbor Meaningful? In: Beeri, C., Bruneman, P. (eds.) ICDT 1999. LNCS, vol. 1540, pp. 217–235. Springer, Heidelberg (1998)
3. Brockwell, P.J., Davis, R.A.: Introduction to Time Series and Forecasting. Springer, New York (2002)
4. Burrus, C.S.: Introduction to Wavelets and Wavelet Transform. Prentice Hall, New York (2001)
5. Daubechies, I.: Ten Lectures on Wavelets. Society for Industrial and Applied Mathematics, Philadelphia (1992)
6. Drelczuk, K.: Wyszukiwanie wzorców kupna-sprzedaży w finansowych szeregach czasowych za pomocą teorii falek i gazów neuronowych, MSc Thesis, University of Economics, Wrocław (2008)
7. Mallat, S.G.: A Theory for Multiresolution Signal Decomposition: The Wavelet Representation. IEEE Transactions on Pattern Analysis and Machine Intelligence, Newark 11(7), 647–693 (1989)
8. Newton, H.J., Parzen, E.: Forecasting and Time Series Model Types of 111 Economic Time Series. In: Makridakis, S., et al. (eds.) The Forecasting Accuracy of Major Time Series Methods. John Wiley and Sons, New York (1984)
9. Shannon, A.: A Mathematical Theory of Communication. Bell System Technical Journal 27(3), 379–423 & 623-656 (1948)

Reduct and Variance Based Clustering of High Dimensional Dataset

Dharmveer Singh Rajput, P.K. Singh, and M. Bhattacharya

ABV – Indian Institute of Information Technology and Management,
Morena Link Road, Gwalior – 474010, Madhya Pradesh, India

Abstract. In high dimensional data, general performance of the traditional clustering algorithms decreases. As some dimensions are likely to be irrelevant or contain noisy data and randomly selected initial centre of the clusters converge the clustering to local minima. In this paper, we propose a framework for clustering high dimensional data with attribute subset selection and efficient cluster centre initialization. It uses rough set theory to determine the relevant attributes (dimensions) in first phase. In second phase, maximum variance dimension is used to determine the optimal initial centres of the clusters. The k-means clustering algorithm is applied with these initial cluster centres, in phase three, to find optimal clustering of data set. It improves efficiency of the clustering process tremendously and our experiment on test data set shows that accuracy of the results has improved considerably.

Keywords: Feature selection, Subspace, Rough set, K-Means, High dimensional data.

1 Introduction

Clustering is the process of discovering groups (clusters) of objects such that objects in one cluster are more similar to each other than to objects in another cluster [1]. Similarity between a pair of data objects is due to different features. If similarity is distance-based then for a pair of data objects in a cluster there exists at least a few features on which the objects are close to each other. Most clustering methods assume all features to be equally important for clustering. This is one of the reasons why most clustering algorithms may not perform well in the face of high-dimensional data. Another reason of the poor performance is the inherent sparsity of data in high-dimensional space [7], [12]. In reality different features have varying effects on clustering. Feature Selection is a process of determining and selecting the dimensions (features) that are most relevant to the data clustering. Subspace Clustering techniques seek to find clusters in a dataset by selecting the most relevant dimensions for each cluster separately [11]. Generally initial cluster centers are selected randomly and different initializations of clusters center can lead to different final clustering that's why partitioning algorithms only converges to local minima [6].

In this paper, we proposed a framework for clustering high dimensional data that select relevant dimensions as well as efficient cluster center initialization. It improves the efficiency of clustering process.

R. Kannan and F. Andres (Eds.): ICDEM 2010, LNCS 6411, pp. 75–79, 2012.
© Springer-Verlag Berlin Heidelberg 2012

Rest of the paper is organized as follows. Section 2 summarizes the previous relevant work. Afterwards the proposed methodology is presented in Section 3. We analyze performance of the proposed algorithm and compare the results with standard k-means algorithm in Section 4. Finally, Section 5 summarizes the conclusion and further scope of the work.

2   Literature Review

Clustering is one of the major considered areas mentioned in various literatures, e.g., [8], [1]. Agarwal, Yu [4], and Parsons et al. [7] particularly deal with subspace clustering. ISC proposed by Jahirabadkar and Kulkarni [11] to make use of identity based clustering which are embedded in higher dimensional in finding subspace clusters. To solve the problem of automatic subspace clustering, Niu et al. [3] have proposed a relation function to calculate the relevance of every two attributes. Kriegel et al. [12] proposed a novel filter refinement subspace clustering algorithm FIRES to efficiently compute maximum dimensional cluster approximate from ID cluster and then refined to obtain the true clusters. Arai and Barakbah [6] utilize all the clustering results of K-means in certain times even though some of them reach the local optima. To determine the initial centroids for K-means, they transform the result by combining with hierarchical algorithm. Ali Ridho [5] proposed a Pillar based approach which designates positions of initial centroids by using the farthest accumulated distance between them. M. Emre [2] investigates the performance of k-means as a colour quantization with different initialization scheme.

3   Proposed Methodology

We proposed a framework for clustering that select relevant dimensions as well as efficient initial clusters centres from high dimensional data. In this we use rough set theory [9] and k-means algorithm [8]. Our proposed algorithm is a combination of reduct and variance based K-Means algorithm. Reduct and Variance based K – Means Algorithm works as follows:

1. Create Discernibility matrix of n x n from given n x d data sets. (Here n denotes the number of objects and d is denotes the dimensions).
2. Calculate Discernibility function and find out the reduct.
3. Compute the variance of each dimension (column) of reduct. And select the column which has maximum variance (*cvmax*).
4. Divide the data points of *cvmax* into K partitions; here K is the desired number of clusters. And calculate the Medians of each partition.
5. Use the corresponding values of other dimensions of reduct. All such data points (vectors) are initial cluster centers (centroid).
6. Assign all points to the closest centroid.
7. Recomputed the centroid of each cluster.
8. Repeat steps 6 and 7 until the centroids don't change (or change very little).

First two steps in the algorithm uses rough set theory as attribute subset selection method and removes the irrelevant attributes. Further in step 3-5, algorithm finds the initial cluster center by using maximum variance column. Then in step 6-8, it uses standard k-means algorithm to obtain optimal clusters.

4 Experimental Results

In this Section, we present the experimental results of basic K-Means algorithm and our proposed algorithm. We used the test dataset which contains 25 objects and five dimensions [10]. First, we obtain the results using standard K-Means algorithm. As we desire to obtain four clusters we choose K = 4 and start with first four objects of the dataset as the initial centroids of the clusters. The K-Means algorithm converge the clusters in 12 iterations. The centroids of the four clusters are as follows: C_1 = (81.28, 7.42, 6.71, 4.14 and 1), C_2 = (68.33, 9.5, 17.5, 3 and 1.33), C_3 = (45.5, 10.5, 38.5, 0.5 and 0.5), and C_4 = (88.3, 2.6, 2.7, 5.6 and 0.4) and objects contained in these clusters are (O_8, O_9, O_{10}, O_{11}, O_{14}, O_{16}, O_{17}), (O_{18}, O_{19}, O_{20}, O_{21}, O_{22}, O_{23}), (O_{24}, O_{25}), and (O_1, O_2, O_3, O_4, O_5, O_6, O_7, O_{12}, O_{13}, O_{15}) respectively.

Afterwards, we solve the problem using proposed framework. In first phase, the reduct is used to determine the relevant dimensions by removing noisy or irrelevant dimensions from the high dimensional data set. Here, we denote the attributes by a_1, a_2, a_3, a_4 and a_5 for simplicity. First, we compute the discernibility matrix which yields discernibility function and solving the discernibility function we obtain $F(A)$ = $a_2 a_3$, i.e., the minimal subset of discernibility function is the attributes $a_2 a_3$. It renders that a_1, a_4 and a_5 are irrelevant attributes which are not useful in the clustering of data set. Hence, only reduct attributes a_2, a_3 are applied in the next steps of the method.

In second phase, the a_3 dimension has maximum variance and calls it *cvmax*. After that sort the *cvmax* in ascending order and divide the *cvmax* into the number of K partition. So the partitions are (1, 1, 2, 2, 3 and 3), (3, 3, 4, 5, 5 and 6), (6, 6, 7, 8, 9 and 13) and (13, 18, 20, 20, 21, 35 and 42). After that find the medians of each partition which are (2, 4.5, 7.5 and 20) for C1, C2, C3 and C4 respectively. Use the corresponding data objects of a_2 for each median to initialize the cluster centers. In our case initial centers of C_1, C_2, C_3 and C_4 are (3.5, 2), (4, 4.5), (6.5, 7.5) and (11, 20) respectively. Then in the third phase, initial cluster centers apply on the k-means to find optimal clustering of data set. Then it takes five iterations for convergence. The centroids of the final clusters are as follows: C_1 = (2.6, 2.7), C_2 = (7.16, 6.33), C_3 = (8.5, 13.25) and C_4 = (10.6, 27.6). The objects contained in these clusters are (O_1, O_2, O_3, O_4, O_5, O_6, O_7, O_{12}, O_{13}, O_{15}), (O_8, O_9, O_{10}, O_{11}, O_{14}, O_{16}), (O_{17}, O_{18}, O_{19}, O_{20}) and (O_{21}, O_{22}, O_{23}, O_{24}, O_{25}) respectively.

After that, we apply validity measures, which are defined below, to determine the quality of results obtained by both the methods. The obtained quality measures are shown table 1.

Dunn index: The index D is based on the ratio between the minimal intra cluster distances to maximal inter cluster distance. The Dunn index is limited to the interval [0, 1] and should be maximized.

Davies-Bouldin index: The small value of measure corresponds to clusters that are compact, and whose centers are far away from each other.

Jagota index: It measures the tightness or homogeneity of the objects within the cluster. It is small if (on average) the data objects in each cluster are close.

Siddheswar Index: It defines the *validity* measure as the ratio between intra cluster distances and inter cluster distance. Therefore, the minimum value of the measure indicates good quality clusters.

Table 1. Comparison of Results

Methods	Dunn Index	Davies-Bouldin Index	Jagota Index	Validity Measure
K-Means	0.55	0.23	13.87	0.33
Proposed Technique	0.60	0.11	11.74	0.18

5 Conclusions

High-dimensional data clustering are suffered from curse of dimensionality and randomly initialization of centers of clusters. In this paper, we proposed a framework for clustering high dimensional data by selecting relevant dimensions with efficient cluster center initialization. The framework improves efficiency of the clustering process tremendously and our experiment on test data set shows that accuracy of the results has improved considerably.

References

1. Jain, A.K., Murty, M.N., Flynn, P.J.: Data clustering: a review. ACM Computing Surveys (CSUR) 31(3), 264–323 (1999)
2. Celebi, M.E.: Effective Initialization of k-means for color quantization. In: IEEE International Conference on Image Processing (ICIP) (2009)
3. Niu, K., Zhang, S., Chen, J.: Subspace clustering through attribute clustering. Front. Electr. Electron. Eng. China 3(1), 44–48 (2008)
4. Aggarwal, C.C., Yu, P.S.: Finding generalized projected clusters in high dimensional spaces. In: International Conference on Management of Data, pp. 70–81 (2000)
5. Barakbah, A.R., Kiyoki, Y.: A pillar algorithm for k-means optimization by distance maximization for initial Centroid designation. IEEE (2009)
6. Arai, K., Barakbah, A. R.: Hierarchical K-means: an algorithm for centroids initialization for K-means. Reports of the Faculty of Science and Engineering 36(1) (2007)
7. Parsons, L., Haque, E., Liu, H.: Subspace Clustering for High Dimensional Data: A Review. Supported in Part by Grants from Prop 301 and CEINT (2004)
8. Jain, A.K.: Data Clustering: 50 Years Beyond K-Means. To Appear in Pattern Recognition Letters (2009)
9. Skowron, A., Pawlak, Z., Komorowski, J., Polkowski, L.: A Rough set perspective on data and knowledge. In: Handbook of Data Mining and Knowledge Discovery, pp. 134–149. Oxford University Press (2002)

10. http://www.uni-koeln.de/themen/statistik/data/cluster/milk.dat
11. Jahirabadkar, S., Kulkarni, P.: ISC – Intelligent Subspace Clustering, A Density based Clustering approach for High Dimensional Dataset. World Academy of Science, Engineering and Technology 55 (2009)
12. Kriegel, H.P., Krger, P., Renz, M., Wurst, S.: A Generic Framework for Efficient Subspace Clustering of High-Dimensional Data. In: Proc. 5th IEEE International Conference of Data Mining (ICDM), Houston, TX (2005)

Peer-to-Peer Network Classification Using *nu*-Maximal Margin Spherical Structured Multiclass Support Vector Machine

Santosh Kumar, Sukumar Nandi, and Santosh Biswas

Department of CSE, IIT Guwahati, India
{santosh.kr,sukumar,santosh_biswas}@iitg.ernet.in

Abstract. In this paper we propose a P2P network traffic classification method using nu-Maximal Margin Spherical Structured Multiclass Support Vector Machine (nu-MSMSVM) classifier. The P2P network traffic is classified into different classes based on four applications namely, Bit Torrent, PPLive, Skype and MSN. The concept of Hypersphere based classifiers being able to minimize the effect of outliers has been adapted in this work. The experimental results show low false positive and false negative ratio thereby achieving high precision and recall rate.

1 Introduction

Identifying P2P traffic on today's Internet is challenging, since P2P based applications are growing rapidly [1]. P2P traffic classification schemes can be classified into broad two types namely, (i) port based analysis [1] and (ii) signature analysis of payloads [2]. As current P2P applications support dynamic port numbers, port based classification may not give correct results. Signature based analysis are not applicable for applications with encrypted payloads or padded payloads (as in case of Bit Torrent). To cater to these issues, statistical classification based schemes are recently being used for P2P traffic classification [3]. The basic idea proposed in [3] was to use hyperplanes to classify data points into multiple classes. The scheme [3] successfully classifies modern P2P traffic but also generates outliers due to the issue of inefficiency of classifying data as the number of SVMs grows superlinearly with the number of classes [4]. Using hyperspheres instead of hyperplanes can reduce the problem of outliers, because spheres create a tighter boundary along the data points it contains. Hypersphere based classifier [4] is a two-class classifier which use Support Vector description. However, P2P traffic separation is a multi class classification problem [3]. The present paper proposes *"nu- Maximal Margin Spherical Structured Multiclass Support Vector Machine (nu-MSMSVM)"* for P2P traffic classification which is basically a hypersphere based multi-class classifier. The volume of the hyperspheres created by *nu*-MSMSVM is as small as possible and at the same time the inter-sphere distance is as large as possible.

nu-MSMSVM needs to be first trained using labeled P2P traffic. Following that the trained model can be used to classify the unknown P2P traffic flows into different classes.

R. Kannan and F. Andres (Eds.): ICDEM 2010, LNCS 6411, pp. 80–84, 2012.
© Springer-Verlag Berlin Heidelberg 2012

1.1 Basic Architecture of nu-MSMSVM Based Classification

Our proposed P2P traffic classification method contains three steps as show in Fig.1. In the first step, network traffic data is collected from a switch (which has port mirroring enabled) and converted into trace files. In the next step, trace files are labeled according to the application type. The last step comprises constructing a classifier model which involves training with labeled application data and testing with unknown P2P network traffic using a decision rule. The third step is elaborated in the next section.

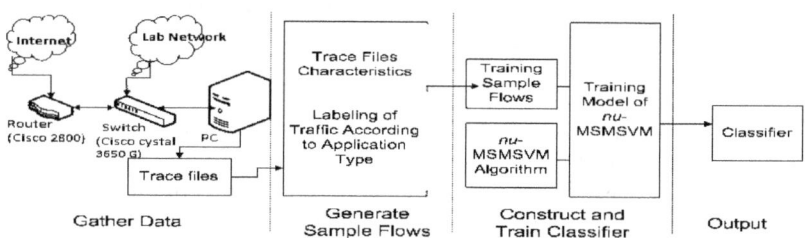

Fig. 1. Basic Architecture of the Proposed Classification Method

2 *nu*-MSMSVM Model Construction

Let data points to be classified be $\{(x_1),..(x_i),..,(x_m)\}$, $x_i \in D^n, 1 \le i \le m$, where D takes value from the input space. Hypersphere based multiclass classification problem is to find k hyperspheres with minimal radius in a higher dimensional feature space using a non-linear mapping $y_i = \emptyset(x_i)$ from input space D^n to a high-dimensional feature space D^F where $F > n$. Now the data points in the higher dimension are classified into K classes (where K is predefined), each enclosed by a hypersphere $S_k, 1 \le k \le K$. Mathematically, the hypersphere S_k is characterized by its center a_k and radius R_k, which can be found by solving the constrained quadratic equation given in eq. (1) [4], where ρ is the margin factor, $\vartheta, \vartheta_1 and \vartheta_2$ are user parameters (to control the degree of volume of sphere with respect to positive and negative data points), $m_k^+ and m_k^-$ are the number of points within the kth class., ξ_i, ξ_j are the slack variables.

$minimize:$ $R_k^2 - \vartheta\rho_k^2 + \left(\frac{1}{\vartheta_1 m_k^+} \Sigma_{l:y_i=k} \xi_l\right) + \left(\frac{1}{\vartheta_2 m_k^-}\Sigma_{j:y_j \neq k}\xi_j\right)$

$subjected\ to$ $\| \phi(x_i) - a_k \|^2 \le R_k^2 + \xi_i, \ \forall i : y_i = k,$ (1)

$\| \phi(x_j) - a_k \|^2 \ge R_k^2 + \rho_k^2 - \xi_j, \forall j : y_j \neq k, \xi_i \ge 0, \xi_j \ge 0 \ \forall i,j$

Converting equation (1) into primal problem with Lagrangian formulation we get equation (2).

$$L(R_k, \rho_k, a_k, \xi, \alpha, \beta) = R_k^2 - \vartheta\rho_k^2 + \frac{1}{\vartheta_1 m_k^+} \sum_{i:y_i=k} \xi_i + \frac{1}{\vartheta_2 m_k^-} \sum_{j:y_j \neq k} \xi_j - $$
$$\sum_i \alpha_i(R_k^2 + \xi_i - \| \phi(x_i) - a_k \|^2) - \sum_j \alpha_j(\| \phi(x_j) - a_k \|^2 - R_k^2 - \rho_k^2 + \xi_j) - \sum_i \beta_i \xi_i - \sum_j \beta_j \xi_j \tag{2}$$

where α_i, α_j, β_i and β_j $1 \leq i,j \leq k$ are nonnegative Lagrange multipliers. Equation (2) can be solved after converting it into its dual as given in equation (3)

$$maximize \sum_i \alpha_i K(x_i . x_i) - \sum_j \alpha_j K(x_j . x_j) - \sum_{i,l} \alpha_i \alpha_l K(x_i . x_l) + $$
$$2 \sum_{i,j} \alpha_i \alpha_j K(x_i . x_j) - \sum_{j,n} \alpha_j \alpha_n K(x_j . x_n) \tag{3}$$

$$s.t \sum_i \alpha_i = 1, \sum_i \alpha_i = 2\vartheta + 1, 0 \leq \alpha_i \leq \frac{1}{\vartheta_1 m_k^+}, 0 \leq \alpha_j \leq \frac{1}{v_2 m_k^-}$$

i,l correspond to positive class and j,n correspond to negative classes. $K(x,y) \equiv \langle \phi(x).\phi(y) \rangle$ is a kernel function used for mapping data from input space to feature space. Solving eq.(3), we obtain the Lagrange multipliers α_i and α_j, which gives the center of the hyperspher (a_k) as a linear combination of $\phi(x_i)$ and $\phi(x_j)$:

$$a_k = \sum_i \phi(x_i) - \sum_j \phi(x_j) \tag{4}$$

Now we can determine the distance of data point $\phi(x)$ to the center a_k of the kth hypersphere by the following equation

$$\| \phi(x) - a_k \|^2 = K(x.x) - 2\sum_i \alpha_i K(x.x_i) + 2\sum_j \alpha_j K(x.x_j) + \tag{5}$$
$$\sum_{i,l} \alpha_i \alpha_l K(x_i . x_l) - 2\sum_{i,j} \alpha_i \alpha_j K(x_i . x_j) + \sum_{j,n} \alpha_j \alpha_n K(x_j . x_n)$$

After a_k is determined, we can find the spherical radius R_k and the margin factor d_k of the kth hypersphere by exploiting the Karush-Kuhn-Tucker (KKT) conditions:

$$\alpha_i = \frac{1}{\vartheta_1 m_k^+} - \alpha_i (\xi_i - \| \phi(x_i) - a_k \|^2 \geq R_k^2) \text{ and } \xi_i \geq 0 \tag{6}$$

$$\alpha_j = \frac{1}{\vartheta_1 m_k^-} (\| \phi(x_l) - a_k \|^2 \leq R_k^2 + d_k^2 \text{ and } \xi_l \geq 0 \tag{7}$$

By applying above KKT conditions, we can determine the sphere radius and margin factor by setting

$$R_k^2 = \| \phi(x_i) - a_k \|^2 \; \forall i \text{ such that } 0 < \alpha_i < \frac{1}{\vartheta_1 m_k^+} \tag{8}$$

$$d_k^2 = \| \phi(x_j) - a_k \|^2 - R_k^2 \; \forall j \text{ such that } 0 < \alpha_j < \frac{1}{\vartheta_1 m_k^-} \tag{9}$$

2.1 nu-MSMSVM Model Testing

A data point x'_i from a new test data set $\{(x'_1),..,(x'_p)\}$ belongs to a hypersphere S_k if it satisfies equation (10).

$$R_k^2 \geq \| \phi(x'_i) - a_k \|^2 \qquad (10)$$

3 Experiments and Results

In the present experiment we have considered 4 classes namely, BitTorrent, PPLive, Skype and MSN thereby making $k = 4$. Experimental data (150 MB) was collected from one day's network traffic in an academic campus. The data comprised 19700 packets, where 9500 were from Bit Torrent, 6200 were from PPLive, 800 were from Skype and 3200 were from MSN. 35% of the packets were used for training and the rest were used for testing. The proposed *nu-MSMSVM* classifier was implemented using *nu*-Libsvm Library. The user defined values of the parameters of *nu*-MSM-SVM classifier parameters were: $\vartheta_1.\vartheta_2 = 0.001, \vartheta_2 = 0.01, \vartheta = 0.81, \rho = 1.09, \varepsilon = 0.5, \lambda = 9.46$ *and* fSVs = 0.811. Recall and precision rate obtained using the proposed *nu-MSMSVM*   for the data set and settings mentioned above is given in Table 1. The table also shows the results for the same dataset when classified using Multiclass-SVM [3] classifier.

Table 1. Results Based on nu-MSMSVM & Multiclass-SVM [4] Algorithm

Packets	Precision		Recall		F-Measure	
	*nu-*MSMSVM	Multiclass-SVM [3]	*nu-*MSMSVM	Multiclass-SVM [3]	*nu-*MSMSVM	Multiclass-SVM [3]
BitTorrent	0.991	0.908	0.983	0.976	0.986	0.941
PPLive	0.930	0.924	0.904	0.867	0.916	0.895
Skype	0.952	0.918	0.940	0.962	0.945	0.935
MSN	0.960	0.945	0.925	0.874	0.942	0.908

4 Conclusion

The concept of Hypersphere based classifiers being able to minimize the effect of outliers has been utilized in this paper to classify P2P traffic based on applications. However, traffic classification of P2P is a multi-class classification problem while the widely used Hypersphere based classifier performs two class classifications. In this paper we have developed a multi-class Hypersphere based classifier and shown that recall and precision rate of P2P traffic classification using this classifier is higher than that obtained using hyperplane based classifier.

References

1. Karagiannis, T., Faloutou, M.: Multilevel Traffic Classification in the Dark. In: SIGCOMM, pp. 468–474. ACM, USA (2005)
2. Yang, A.-M., Jiang, S.: A P2P Network Traffic Classification Method Using SVM. In: International Conference for Young Computer Scientist, China, pp. 398–403 (2009)
3. Hsu, C.W., Lin, C.J.: A comparison of methods for Multi-class support vector machines. IEEE Neural Networks 13, 415–425 (2002)
4. Wu, M., Ye, J.: A small sphere and large margin approach for Novelty detection using Training Data with outliers. IEEE 31, 2088–2092 (2009)

An Adaptive Image Retrieval System with Relevance Feedback and Clustering

K. Susheel Kumar, Pradeep Kumar Saroj, and R.C. Tripathi

Indian Institute of Information Technology Allahabad,
Department of Information Technology, Image Processing Lab.,
Allahabad, India
sus.iiita.932@gmail.com, pradeep_iet2007@yahoo.co.in,
rctripathi@iiita.ac.in

Abstract. The objective for this paper is to develop an adaptive image retrieval system with an innovative approach to use artificial neural networks and clustering techniques to retrieve images similar to the input image. This paper involves retrieving images from huge image databases which are visually similar to a query image. Due to the enormous increase in image database size, and its high usage in a variety of applications, need for the development of Content Based Image Retrieval arose. It summarizes the problem, the proposed solution, and the desired results. The system uses neural networks, relevance feedback and clustering. The system is made intelligent by making the system learn the user's preference as feedback. The relevance feedback is used to improve the precision of the system by analyzing user's relevance feedback for each retrieved image while neural network and clustering techniques are used to reduce the time complexity of the system. The system uses three-layered neural network to train the system using image clusters as training dataset by a supervised approach. Also after taking the feedback from the user, the image clusters are re-clustered by rearranging the images after a successful retrieval. Given a user query as an image, the neural system retrieves related images by computing similarities with images in the given image clusters. To provide preference, from all the retrieved images user selects an image as relevant one and all other are hence treated as irrelevant ones. So, the rank of the selected image is increased while the ranks of other images are decreased. With this feedback, the system refinement method estimates global approximations and adjusts the similarity probabilities.

Keywords: Artificial neural networks, clustering techniques, CBIR System, relevance feedback, GLCM Structure, Heuristic Algorithm.

1 Introduction

Image retrieval has been an active area of research since decades [1] but it was always restricted by the limited resources such as processing power and storage. Content Based Image Retrieval (CBIR) is a multidisciplinary domain closely related **to various computer science and research fields such as Databases, Artificial** Intelligence, Image Processing, Statistics, Pattern Recognition, Computer Vision, High Performance Computing and Human Computer Interaction.

R. Kannan and F. Andres (Eds.): ICDEM 2010, LNCS 6411, pp. 85–92, 2012.
© Springer-Verlag Berlin Heidelberg 2012

In the last few years, there has been a lot of effort made in the development of CBIR systems. The availability of large amount of visual data on the web underlines the need to create retrieval systems that offer precise and quick retrieval of desired images from the image database that meet the user requirements. Earlier due to technological limitations, the quick retrieval of desired images was not possible. The recent developments in processing capabilities, digital and networking have facilitated us to develop fast and efficient CBIR systems. Novel techniques have been proposed to retrieve images by their visual content [4]. Also efforts are going on to incorporate learning techniques in these systems. Many image retrieval systems (both commercial and research) have been developed using these novel techniques [2].

The existing methods of image indexing and text annotation are insufficient for retrieving images based on their visual contents. A lot of research is going on to develop CBIR systems that can retrieve visually similar images based on their visual features or the contents of the image. Hence, there is a lot of scope for the development of such CBIR systems using visual features.

This paper intends to provide a related work based on content-based image retrieval (CBIR) and architecture of CBIR system and next section implementation based on clustering and Heuristic Algorithm for similarity measurement and final section is implementing of result and conclusion.

2   Related Work

The aim of CBIR systems is to use the visual content of the image to search and retrieve visually similar images from an image database. These image features can be low-level information such as the color, texture and shape or it can be high-level information such as wavelets. It can be statistical values such as principle components etc.

2.1   Content-Based Image Retrieval

Various approaches and methodologies are proposed in research papers but there are mainly two basic steps in the CBIR systems. These are:

1. Feature Extraction. The first step is the extraction of image features
2. Matching. The second step involves matching those extracted features with features of existing images to retrieve visually similar images.

Step1: Extracting Image Features: Feature is the information in an image relevant for solving a task. More specifically Image features refer to characteristics of an image which describe its contents. These features can be low-level information such as the color, texture and shape or it can be high-level information such as wavelets [5]. It can be statistical values such as principle components etc. These features are extracted from the image using feature extraction algorithms.

Step2: Matching: A common measure for finding image similarity is color distance [3]. Two images can be compared by measuring the difference in the frequency of colors between them using some suitable color distance function. Several distance functions can be used for image comparison for example, Quadratic distance algorithm, Minkowski distance (Euclidean distance) algorithm etc.Approaches for texture features include the calculation of co-occurrence matrix of the image from which we can find texture features such as: correlation, energy, contrast, homogeneity, entropy etc.

2.2 CBIR Architecture

Fig. 2.1 shows the basic architecture of a CBIR system. In short, when a user inputs a query image, the features of that query image are extracted and are compared against the pre-calculated features of images in the image database. The similar images are retrieved and displayed on the user screen.

Query Methods: - Queries in the CBIR system are usually given by inputting a sample image or images. It is generally called Query-By-Example [9] approach. The image retrieval may also start with a browsing stage. The system first selects some random images from the database and displays it to the user then the user searches for suitable image as a query image to start with. The retrieved images are usually displayed to the user as thumbnails. And on user click or selection the full image can be displayed to the user.

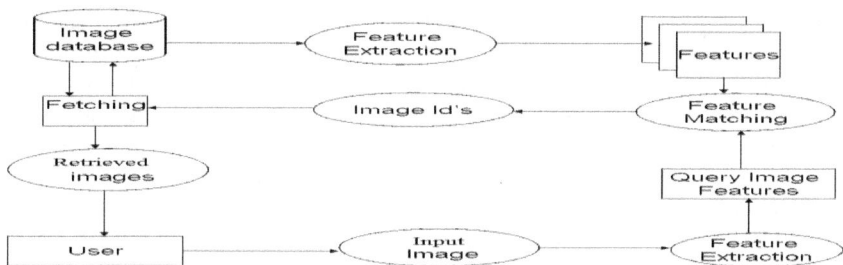

Fig. 2.1. Architecture of CBIR System [9]

3 Implementation

In this paper we proposed an Architecture which is divided in to two categories:

1. CBIR Engine (built using MatLab R2008a)
2. Web Server (built using ASP .NET with IIS Server)

3.1 CBIR Engine

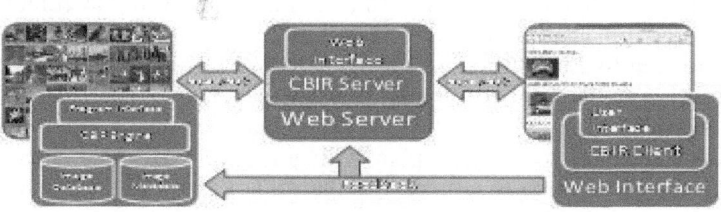

Fig. 3.1. Architecture of CBIR Engine

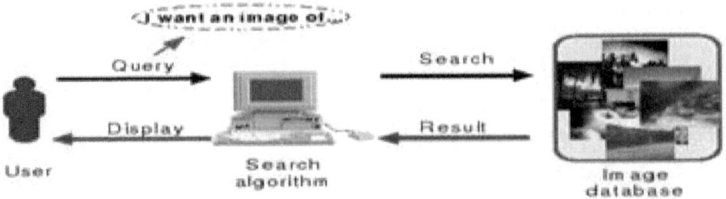

Fig. 3.2. Execution of CBIR System

3.1.1 Detailed Description of the CBIR System

The system takes an image as an input by the user, extracts features from the image, measures similarity of the image with existing clusters of images using neural networks and ranks the retrieved images using relevance feedback. The system works in two stages: training and testing. The training consists of features extraction of the all images in the training image dataset and then separate neural network is trained for each cluster of the image database. In this process features of all the images of each cluster are extracted and then input to train a separate neural network for each cluster. The image database consists of several clusters of images where each cluster contains images of a particular type. In our training dataset we have taken 10 different clusters of images e.g. 'Cars', 'Buildings', 'Flowers', 'Weapons' etc. Each cluster contains around 50 training images whose features are used to train a separate neural network for each cluster. Content of an image can be expressed in terms of different features such as color, texture, shape etc. Retrieval based on these features varies depends on how the features are extracted and used. Since features in color, texture, and shape are extracted using different computation methods, different features may give different similarity measurements. In our system we have used following texture features of an image: Entropy, Homogeneity, Energy, Correlation, and Contrast. These features are extracted from the image and then input to the neural network for training. In testing Process user is asked to input an image and then features are extracted from the image and input to all the trained neural network of each cluster and if output of one or more than one neural network is greater than a certain threshold then all the most relevant images of those image clusters are shown to the user as the most similar images to the input image

Stage One: Texture Features Extraction: - The first stage of the system is image processing and feature extraction. With initial clusters of images the feature extraction process is applied to each image, but before feature extraction all the images are resized to image of dimension 256 X 256 that is 256 rows and 256 columns. This is necessary as the dimensions of images in a cluster may vary. So, all the images of a cluster are resized to 256 X 256 and converted from RGB to Gray level image. Now the 'Correlation', 'Energy', 'Contrast', 'Homogeneity', 'Entropy' features are extracted from the image. First a gray-level co-occurrence matrix from image matrix is created by calculating how often a pixel with gray-level (grayscale intensity) value i occurs horizontally adjacent to a pixel with the value j. Now all the above mentioned features can be extracted from the co-occurrence matrix.

Correlation is a measure of how correlated a pixel is to its neighbor over the whole image and it is defined as:

$$\sum_{i,j} \frac{(i-\mu i)(j-\mu j)p(i,j)}{\sigma_i \sigma_j}$$

Energy is the sum of squared elements in the co-occurrence matrix and it is defined as:

$$\sum_{i,j} p(i,j)^2$$

Contrast is a measure of the intensity contrast between a pixel and its neighbor over the whole image and it is defined as:

$$\sum_{i,j} |i-j|^2 \, p(i,j)$$

Homogeneity is a measure the closeness of the distribution of elements in the co-occurrence matrix to the co-occurrence matrix diagonal and it is defined as:

$$\sum_{i,j} \frac{p(i,j)}{1+[i-j]}$$

Entropy is a statistical measure of randomness that can be used to characterize the texture of the input image and it is defined as:

$$-\sum_{i,j} p(i,j) \log\big(p(i,j)\big)$$

Stage Two: Testing using image as a query by User:-The testing starts when user inputs a test image to retrieve similar images or when user selects an image cluster from a given list of image category list. When user inputs an image, the image is input to all the neural networks representing different image cluster. If the probability of input image for one or more neural networks is more than a particular threshold which is 0.6, then the image belongs to those image clusters. It is possible for an image to be in more than one image cluster if the input image contains more than one object. For e.g. If an image contains 'Car', and 'Building' both then it belongs to both categories. So, images from both the clusters should be retrieved with rank according to the output of the heuristic algorithm which adds the neural network probability and the relevance value to determine the rank of the retrieved images. If the user clicks on one of the retrieved image then relevance measure of the retrieved image is increased by a value 0.1 while relevance measure of those images which are not clicked is decreased by 0.01. Also the input image by the user is stored in those relevant clusters whose probabilities are more than the threshold 0.6. The new image is stored in the training dataset. The image is indexed using heuristic algorithm, its features are extracted and the network is re-trained using the features of new image also. These steps are repeated at each query. If the user inputs an image:

Fig. 3.3. Test Image

Stage Third: Heuristic Algorithm for similarity measurement:-This is main underlying algorithm which decides the actual relevance of an image with all the clusters. It also manipulates the relevance measure of the image after each query. When an image's relevance drops to less than 0 then it also deletes that image file from the data-set. So, this algorithm also maintains the integrity of the dataset. When a new image is input to the system then first it creates the index of the input image in the form an array which contains the relevance of each cluster and the probability of each neural network.

An example index of a new image calculated by the algorithm is given below. Each column represents an image cluster while rows 1 and 2 represent the neural network probability and Relevance score respectively.

Cluster Name	Building	Car	Flower	Food	Space	Weapon
NN Probability	0.9	0.7	0.1	0.2	0.3	0.16
Relevance	0.1	0.1	0	0	0	0
Total	1	0.8	0.1	0.2	0.3	0.16

Fig. 3.4. Table used for Heuristic Algorithm

4   Results

Some of the training and testing images:

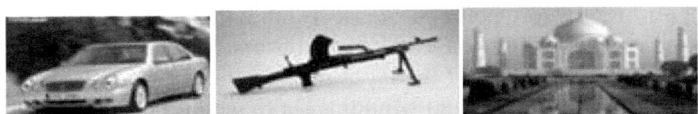

Fig. 4.1. Some Training and Test Images

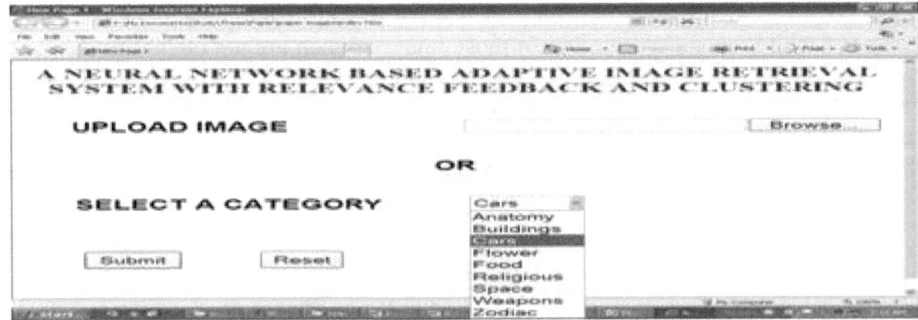

Fig. 4.2. Initial screen of the system

4.1 Graphical User Interface

In the web based GUI, user can access the system on LAN and can select the query image from his system and then submit for the retrieval of the similar images from the database or user can start by selecting a cluster.

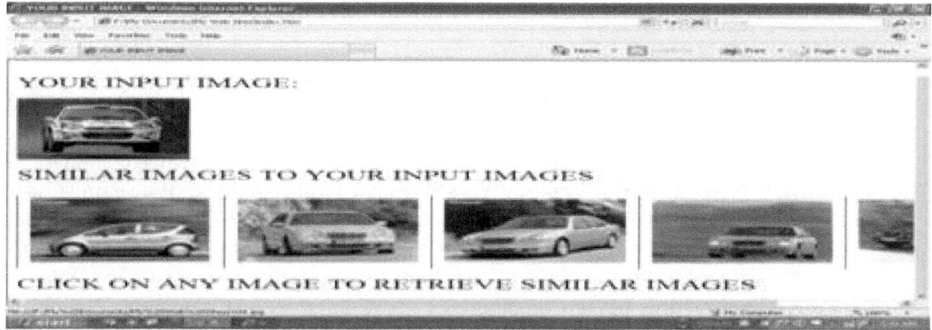

Fig. 4.3. Search results to the image query Car

Table 4.4. Accuracy of retrieved images

S.No.	Test Image	Correctly Matched	Incorrect	%Accuracy
1	Cars	9	1	90
2	Buildings	10	5	66.66
3	Flowers	18	2	90
4	Terrains	16	4	80
5	Food	7	3	70

5 Conclusion

The system has been tested on a wide variety of images, with many clusters and many images in a cluster giving very high accuracy. Still there are a number of directions for future work. The main suggestion is to use wavelets to extract high-level features. This may slow down the execution of the system but it will increase the accuracy of the system. The system is a bit slow because of training involved after each query. Other neural network architecture and different training algorithms can be also experimented with the system.

References

1. Gudivada, V., Raghavan, V.: Content-Based Image Retrieval Systems, vol. 28(9), pp. 18–22. IEEE Computer Society (1995)
2. Stanchev, P.L.: Content-Based Image Retrieval Systems. In: CompSysTech 2001, Bulgarian Computer Science Conference (June 21-22, 2001)

3. Zhang, L., Lin, F., Zhang, B.: A CBIR method based on color-spatial feature. Proceedings of the IEEE 1, 66–169 (1999)
4. Haralick, R.M.: Statistical and structural approaches to texture. Proceedings of the IEEE 67, 786–804 (1979)
5. Gonzalez-Garcia, A.C., Sossa-Azuela, J.H., Felipe-Riveron, E.M.: Image Retrieval based on Wavelet Computation and Neural Network Classification. In: Eight International Workshop on Image Analysis for Multimedia Interactive Services (WIAMIS 2007), p. 44 (2007)
6. Rui, Y., Huang, T.S., Ortega, M., Mehrotra: Relevance feedback: A power tool for interactive content-based image retrieval. IEEE Trans. Circuits Syst. Video Technol. 8(5), 644–655
7. Muneesawang, P., Guan, L.: A neural network approach for learning image similarity in adaptive CBIR. In: 2001 IEEE Fourth Workshop on Multimedia Signal Processing (2001)
8. Kuffner, A., Robles-Kelly, A.: Image Feature Evaluation for Contents-based Image Retrieval, Department of Theoretical Physics, Australian National University, Canberra
9. Nastar, C., Mitschke, M., Meilhac, C.: Efficient Query Refinement for Image Retrieval. In: Proceedings of the IEEE Computer Society Conference on Computer Vision and Pattern Recognition, June 23-25, p. 547 (1998)
10. Wojciechowski, K., Smolka, B., Palus, H., Kozera, R.S., Skarbek, W., Noakes, L.: Clustering method for fast content based image retrieval. In: Proceedings International Conference, ICCVG 2004, Warsaw, Poland (September 2004)
11. Manjunath, B.S., Ma, W.Y.: Texture Features for Browsing and Retrieval of Image Data. IEEE Transactions on Pattern Analysis and Machine Intelligence 18(8), 837–842 (1996)
12. Zhou, Z.-H., Chen, K.-J., Dai, H.-B.: Enhancing relevance feedback in image retrieval using unlabeled data. ACM Transactions on Information Systems 24(2), 219–244 (2006)
13. Hoi, Lyu, M.R.: A novel log-based relevance feedback technique in content-based image retrieval. In: Proc. of the 12th Annual ACM International Conference on Multimedia, pp. 24–31 (2004)

Using the Normalization for Typographic Errors in Numerals

Sachin N. Deshmukh[1], Suresh C. Mehrotra[1], and Hardeep Singh[2]

[1] Department of CS and IT, Dr B. A. M. University, Aurangabad. M.S. PIN 431003 India
[2] Department of CSE, Guru Nanak Dev University, Amritsar, Punjab India
sndeshmukh@hotmail.com, mehrotra_suresh@yahoo.com,
hardeep_gndu@rediffmail.com

Abstract. For numerical record fields such as date and age, many types of error are likely to yield small numerical differences between observed and true values. If, for example, two different sources provide separate case reports related to the same incident, the dates of onset may not match perfectly but are more likely to differ by a few days than by several years. In order to tackle the variations in numbers a few methods are available. The paper proposes a new normalization technique useful for the numerical record. A Comparison of Distance with the Smith Waterman Distance shows significant increase in the weight by the present technique.

Keywords: Record Linkage, Duplicate Record Detection, Deduplication, Numeric Data Comparison.

1 Introduction

Numbers play a central role in day to day work. Yet the current search engines and duplicate detection systems treat numbers as strings, ignoring their numeric values. For example, the search for 6798.32 on Google yielded two pages that correctly associate this number with the lunar nutation cycle [1]. For numerical record fields such as date and age, many types of error are likely to yield small numerical differences between observed and true values.

As on today, searching is widely used in search engines which search documents for the occurrences of a number. In the problem of deduplication of records, generally numbers are treated as a text and so the text matching algorithms are used. Available literature focuses on two categories of algorithms available for number search. They are number search in document and in record linkage.

2 Number Search Algorithms

The approach taken in the past to retrieve the numeric specification in documents has been to extract the attribute-value pairs contained in a document and store them in a database. Queries can now be answered using nearest neighbor techniques [3] [4]. There has been some research on automating the task of data extraction [5] [6].

R. Kannan and F. Andres (Eds.): ICDEM 2010, LNCS 6411, pp. 93–95, 2012.
© Springer-Verlag Berlin Heidelberg 2012

Agrawal and Srikant [2] proposed a new model in this regard. According to this model, it is not necessary to establish exact correspondences between attribute names and numeric values in the data. A user query can instead choose to provide only values, without specifying corresponding attribute names.

For numeric record fields such as salary, date and age, many types of error are likely to yield small numerical differences between observed and true values. At the same time, there are other types of errors (*e.g.* typing errors) for which large numerical differences are as likely as small ones. Both of these possibilities are handled in hit-miss mixture model [7] which include both 'misses' and 'deviations'.

Cosine similarity [8] is a measure of similarity between two vectors of n dimensions by finding the cosine of the angle between them, often used to compare documents in text mining. In addition, it is used to measure cohesion within clusters in the field of Data Mining [9].

3   Using the Normalization for Typographic Errors in Numerals

Chances of errors in the pure numeric fields are due to either typographic problems or unavailability of the data with the user. For example, at the time of entering the salary, typist may type 7000 instead of 70000 or user may not know the exact figure of the salary e.g. instead of exact salary of Rs. 12345/- the user may quote it Rs. 12000/-. Under these circumstances, it is difficult to find the similarity between these entity using string comparison algorithms. Here we proposed some steps for normalization of pure numeric data so that the errors listed above can be minimized.

Consider two records r_1 and r_2 with a numeric field 'salary'. Let $r_1(salary) = n$ and $r_2(salary) = m$. The normalization steps are as follows.

Let nl= Number of digits in n and ml= Number of digits in m

$$\text{Normalization}(n) = nn = \frac{n*10^{(ml-1)}}{10^{(nl-1)}*10^{(ml-1)}} = \frac{n*10^{(ml-1)}}{10^{(nl+ml-2)}} \tag{1}$$

$$\text{Normalization}(m) = nm = \frac{m*10^{(nl-1)}}{10^{(nl-1)}*10^{(ml-1)}} = \frac{m*10^{(nl-1)}}{10^{(nl+ml-2)}} \tag{2}$$

$$w_{salary}(r_1, r_2) = (1 - abs(nn\text{-}mm)) \tag{3}$$

where $w_{salary}(r_1, r_2)$ represents weight for 'salary' field in record r_1, r_2. $w_{salary}(r_1, r_2)$ Consider the example of two values representing the salaries of the person in the pair of record for which comparison is to be done *i.e.* n=12000 and m=1200.

$nn = (12000*1000)/(10000000) = 1.2$, $nm = (1200*10000)/(10000000) = 1.2$ and $w_{n,m} = 1 - abs(1.2 - 1.2) = 1$. Table 1 given below shows the comparison of distances calculated using Smith Waterman distance algorithm and the algorithm discussed above.

There is significant increase in the weights compared with Smith Waterman Distance. Weights for last two entries are 0.9655 which is false positive result. But it is to be noted that the weights of numeric values are not only going to decide the record linkage rather weights of other fields are also taken into considerations. The algorithm proposed above can be used for pure numeric data comparison.

Table 1. Comparison of Distance with Smith Waterman Distance

Value1	Value2	Smith Waterman Distance weight	Weight for our Method
12000	120000	0.8333	1.0000
12000	1200	0.8000	1.0000
120000	1200	0.6667	1.0000
12000	12345	0.4000	0.9655
120000	12345	0.3333	0.9655

4   Conclusions and Future Scope

Though there are large numbers of algorithm for comparison of   strings, still there is a need of efficient algorithm for comparison of numbers as currently many of the researchers are using string matching algorithms for numeric matches. Effect of change in the digit depends on the position of the digits. The errors in the number are either due to typographic errors or unavailability of exact data. The normalization technique can be used to tackle this problem to some extent. But still there is a vast scope of development in this direction as numeric data does not mean only numeric fields. Date fields and age fields are also prone to change in position of digits.

References

1. Kopal, Z.: Physics and Astronomy of the Moon. Academic Press (1962)
2. Agrawal, R., Srikant, R.: Searching with numbers. In: Proceedings of the 11th International World Wide Web Conference (WWW11), pp. 420–431 (2002)
3. Indyk, P., Motwani, R.: Approximate nearest neighbors: Towards removing the curse of dimensionality. In: ACM Symposium on Theory of Computing, pp. 604–613 (1998)
4. Roussopoulos, N., Kelley, S., Vincent, F.: Nearest neighbor queries. In: Proc. of the 1995 ACM SIGMOD Int'l Conf. on Management of Data, pp. 71–79 (1995)
5. Crespo, A., Jannink, J., Neuhold, E., Rys, M., Studer, R.: A survey of semi-automatic extraction and transformation,
   http://www-db.stanford.edu/crespo/publications/
6. Muslea, I.: Extraction patterns for information extraction tasks: A survey. In: The AAAI 1999 Workshop on Machine Learning for Information Extraction (1999)
7. Noren, G., Orre, R., Bate, A., Edword, I.: Duplicate detection in adverse drug reaction surveillance. Data Mining and Knowledge Discovery Journal, 306–328 (2007)
8. http://www.miislita.com/information-retrieval-tutorial/cosine-similarity-tutorial.htmlcosim
9. Tan, P.N., Steinbach, M., Kumar, V.: Introduction to Data Mining, ch. 8, p. 500. Addison-Wesley (2005) ISBN 0-321-32136-7

Performance Evaluation of Face Recognition
Based on PCA, LDA, ICA and Hidden Markov Model

N. Nallammal and V. Radha

Avinashilingam University, Coimbatore
msg2nalls@gmail.com
radharesearch@yahoo.com

Abstract. This paper describes a face recognition methods based on Principle Component Analysis (PCA), Linear Discriminant Analysis and Independent Component Analysis and Hidden Markov Model. Face recognition is an important research problem spanning numerous fields and disciplines. Face recognition draws a complex task and the changes in incident illumination ,head pose, facial expression, size and other external factors. HMM based framework for face recognition, face detection and it requires a one dimensional observation sequence and images are two dimensional, the images should be converted into either 1D temporal sequences or 1D spatial sequences. The paper presents with various face recognition techniques used for solving the problem. Traditional techniques such as holistic methods (PCA,LDA,ICA), feature based methods(Elastic Bunch Graph Matching, Dynamic Link Matching),model based methods(Active Appearance Model,3D Morphable Models) and hybrid method(Markov Random Field Method) are well known for face detection and recognition.

Keywords: Principle Component Analysis, Linear Discriminant Analysis, Independent Component Analysis, Hidden Markov Model, Hybrid methods.

1 Introduction

Face recognition employs automated methods to recognize a person. Face recognition techniques are strongly affected by variations in pose and illumination, accessories on face and aging effects.

2 Taxonomy of Face Recognition Methods

2.1 Holistic Methods

These methods are used the whole face region as the raw input and the face region is eigen picture based on PCA.

2.1.1 Principle Component Analysis
The objective of PCA is to reduce the dimensionality of the dataset but retain most of the original variability in the data and it is a way of identifying patterns in data and expressing the data to highlight their similarities and differences. It is discriminating

R. Kannan and F. Andres (Eds.): ICDEM 2010, LNCS 6411, pp. 96–100, 2012.
© Springer-Verlag Berlin Heidelberg 2012

input images into several classes.PCA transforms the image vectors into their subspaces (also called 'feature space").

PCA aims to maximize between-class data separation while LDA tries to maximize between-class data separation and minimize within class data separation.[1].

Basic steps of PCA algorithm
 Determine PCA subspace from training data. Store all p images in the matrix, Compute covariance matrix, eigenvalues and eigenvectors. Keep only the eigenvectors associated with non-zero eigenvalues. The matrix of eigenvectors forms the eigenspace. Visualized eigenvectors of the covariance matrix are called eigenfaces [4].The main advantage of PCA is to find the patterns to compress the data ie by reducing the number of dimensions without loss of information.

SMPCA: To solve the roots of the polynomial equation. Eigenvalues and eigen vectors will be used to generate all principle components simultaneously.

PGPCA: It does not solve the roots of the equation. The covariance matrices are reduced the subspace, so that principle components can be generated once at a time.

 SPCA: A Random initial vector is used to produce a projection vector to generate successive principle components.

PRPCA: It divides the image into equal size of sub images. The principle components are prioritized by the projection vectors.

2.1.2   Linear Discriminant Analysis
It finds to represent the face vector space by exploiting the class information. It differentiates individual faces but recognize the faces of same individual. The images in the training set are divided into the corresponding classes.

Basic steps of LDA algorithm[3]
LDA considers between a class correspondence of data. One class = one subject. 1.Determine LDA subspace from training data. Calculate the class scatter matrix. 2. All training images are projected to subspace 3.Test image is projected to same sub-space.

2.1.3   Independent Component Analysis
It minimizes second – order and higher – order dependencies in the input data and find the data are statistically independent. Two architecture of ICA. **I** – Statistically independent basis image. **II – Factorial code representation.**

Algorithm of ICA: Training Set :Step I: Learning **Centering:** Row subtracted from the second order statistics of the data. **Whitening**: Remove first and the second order statistics of the data **Step 2:** Calculate independent component and classify an input image. **Step 3:** Project test image into eigenfaces.**Step4:** Compute coefficient B_{test} ; $B_{test} = R_{test} * W_1^{-1}$ both B and Btest are used as feature vector .

3 Feature Based Methods

It is facilitating larger processing speed with good acting with face database in varied scales.

3.1 Elastic Bunch Graph Matching

Faces are represented as graphs with nodes positioned at fiducial points and edges are labeled with 2D distance vectors. Recognition is based on labeled graphs.

3.2 Dynamic Link Matching

Porbe images are distorted due to rotation in depth and changing facial expression. Probe images and gallery nodes are represented by layers of neurons interpreted as labeled graphs. Probe images are matched to the gallery of face models by DLM.

4 Model Based Methods

To create models of human faces using prior knowledge.

4.1 Active Appearance Model

A new image is interpreted a full appearance model and rough estimation of the position, orientation and scale.

4.2 3D Morphable Model

The model parameters of shape and texture recover from a single image of face. This model based on 3 training images of each person ie frontal, half-profile, profile view.

5 Hybrid Method

5.1 Markov Random Field

It is fully utilizing the noise immunity feature. The image is divided into smaller image patches and each having specific Id's. It includes two layers, i) Observable nodes ie., represented by squares (image patches) ii) Hidden nodes ie., represented by circle (Patch Id's).

6 Hidden Markov Model

HMM is defined as the triplet $\lambda = (A, B, \prod)$ .It is used to characterize the statistical properties of a signal and consist of two interrelated process:
a) Unobservable Markov chain with a finite number of states

b) A set of probability density functions associated with each state. HMM's have been successfully used for face recognition.   In[2], kuo and Agazzi have used a pseudo two dimensional HMM for character recognition to perform fast for binary image. Facial regions come in a natural order from top to bottom even if the images are taken under small rotations in the image plane. Pseudo two – dimension HMMs (P2D – HMM) for face recognition is developed by linking one dimensional left to right HMMs to form vertical super – HMM. Hybrid system comprising the neural networks and HMM shows the recognition rate equal to 100%.

Table 1. Comparative results on ORL Database

Methods	Recognition Rate
Eigenface	90.5%
Pseudo 2D HMM feature: grey values	94.5%
Convolutional Neural Network	96.2%
Pseudo 2D HMM feature: DCT coefficients	99.5%
Ergodic HMM + DCT	99.5%
Pseudo 2D HMM + Neural Network Coefficients	**100%**

Table 2. Recognition rate obtained from P2D-HMM's

Hidden Markov Models	The exact identification $100 - \frac{nerrors}{5.1}$
Pseudo 2D 3-3-3-3	99.80% (1 error on 510 photo)
Pseudo 2D 3-6-6-3	100%
Pseudo 2D 6-6-6-6	99.80% (1 error on 510 photo)
Pseudo 2D 6-6-6-6-6	99.80% (1 error on 510 photo)

6.1 Contour Matching Method

It is efficient technique that exact structure of the face can be extracted by 'contours' and the storage requirements are less because for matching purpose the whole face is not needed, only extracted contours are used.

The contours are compared using template matching for finding out maximum similarity between the input image and the registered image.[5]

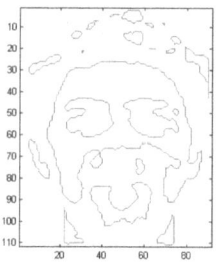

Fig. 1. Contour of given image

Table 3. Principal Component analysis System vs. contour Matching on Biold Face dataface

System	% Recognition Rate	Training Time Per Model	Test Time Per Image
Principal Component Analysis	95	6.52sec	2.73sec
Contour Matching	100	125.25 Sec	302.59 sec

7 Conclusion

Projection methods are (PCA,LDA ,ICA) efficient techniques for face recognition to solve a problem. The present study is hybrid system comprising the neural networks and HMM shows recognition rate equal to 100%.The challenge of the area faced by its ability to identify images which may be tampered or undectable due to various reasons. The poor performance of the system, the recognition rate reduces by varying lighting conditions and face expressions. To avoid these issues different image enhancement techniques can be employed. The report states a brief overview of some of the widely used methods.

References

1. Yambor, W.S.: Analysis of PCA – Based and Fisher Discriminant – Based Image Recognition Algorithms
2. Kuo, S., Agazzi, O.: Keyword spotting in poorly printed documents using Pseudo 2D HMMs. IEEE Transactions on Pattern Analysis and Machine Intelligence (1994)
3. Toygar, O., Acan, A.: Face recognition using PCA, LDA and ICA Approches on colored images. Journal of Electrical & Electronics Engineering 3 (2003)
4. Huang, R., Pavlovic, V., Metaxas, D.N.: A Hybrid Face Recognition Method using markov Random Fields. In: Proceedings of the 17th International Conference on Pattern Recognition (ICPR 2004), vol. 3 (2004) ISBN – ISSN: 1051 – 4651, 0 - 7695 - 2128-2
5. Gandhe, S.T., Talele, K.T., Keskar, A.G.: Face Recognition using contour Matching. IAENG International Journal of Computer Science 35(2) (2008); IJCS_35_2_06 (Advance online publication: May 20, 2008)

Comparative Study of Pattern Mining Techniques
for Network Management System Logs
for Convergent Network*

Bodhisattwa Gangopadhyay[1,2], Artur Arsenio[1,2], and Claudia Antunes[1]

[1] Instituto Superior Técnico,
Av. Rovisco Pais, 1, 1049-001 Lisboa
[2] Nokia Siemens Networks Portugal S.A.
Rua Irmãos Siemens 1-1A, 2720-093 Portugal
{Bodhisattwa.Gangopadhyay,Artur.Arsenio,
Claudia.Antunes}@ist.utl.pt
{Bodhisattwa.Gangopadhyay,Artur.Arsenio}@nsn.com

Abstract. The concept of Pattern Mining has obtained significant focus in Telecommunications Network Management Systems (NMS). A large volume of work has been dedicated to this field and valuable progress has been observed. Both sequential and structured pattern mining techniques were applied to NMS. In particular NMS logs (Performance and Alarm) pose several interesting issues for pattern mining, and it can help in various NMS activities such as alarm correlation, alarm associations, self-healing or pro-active fault management. In this paper, we present an overview of the different pattern mining techniques used in NMSs, compare them and present the most beneficial ones to NMS for Radio over Fiber (RoF) like convergent networks.

Keywords: Pattern Mining, Radio-over-Fiber, Network Management Systems.

1 Introduction

Communication networks with several radio access technologies, such as in the FUTON [1] infrastructure, have increasing complexity in terms of various network elements and also the network data generated, in a single infrastructure [1] [2]. This generated data in large quantity related to faults, warnings and Key Performance Indicators (KPIs) must be monitored for a rapid decision making process to enable a network management with self-healing and pro-active fault management capacities.

NMSs are aimed to possess the capability of pro-actively managing network configurations, traffic routing, fault and performance management in real time, thus

---

* This work is supported in part by the European Commission, in the context of the project FUTON "Fibre Optic Networks for Distributed, Extendible Heterogeneous Radio Architectures and Service Provisioning", grant agreement FP7 ICT-2007-215533.

   Bodhisattwa Gangopadhyay wishes to thank Fundação para a Ciência e a Tecnologia, Portugal, for support under grant SFRH/BDE/33799/2009.

R. Kannan and F. Andres (Eds.): ICDEM 2010, LNCS 6411, pp. 101–108, 2012.
© Springer-Verlag Berlin Heidelberg 2012

looking towards optimizing traffic throughput in the network [3]. Call detail data, network data and customer data are the types of telecommunication data. Our focus will be on network data (alarms, KPIs) where NMS acts on.

Data mining technology is imperative to the requirements mentioned here for extracting the hidden knowledge about the behavior of the network. The knowledge discovery in databases has different parts which involve data collection and cleaning, pattern discovery, post-processing of the discovered knowledge and finally using this discovered knowledge [4]. The authors in [5] argue that it is highly desirable that networks have the ability for detecting symptoms of the network exceptional conditions and enable proactive network management.

Pattern mining is a data mining technique employed to find the existing patterns in any available databases. The term "*pattern*" denotes a conjunction of propositions verified in a significant number of records in the database, and in its most basic form can be stated as an association rule. Though the original motivation behind this was related to analyze supermarket data, afterwards several works have been undertaken to employ pattern mining in telecommunication NMSs. History of pattern mining dates back to 1993 in the paper of Agarwal et.al. related to the market basket analysis in the form of association rule mining [6]. Work related to the application of pattern mining in telecommunications is found in [7] where the authors propose a solution procedure for identifying sequential alarms from the alarm data of a Global System for Mobile (GSM) system by employing constrained based sequential pattern mining. Observing the features of the alarm data, data is cleaned without compromising the quality of the obtained sequential alarm patterns. In telecommunication alarm correlation analysis for large alarm databases, mining of association rules is one of the primary methods while the efficiency of the algorithms is very important for these large datasets [8]. The work in [8] proposes an algorithm based on layered frequent pattern tree for mining frequent patterns and demonstrated a better time and space efficiency.

This paper concentrates on the study of the different pattern mining techniques aimed towards data originating from telecommunication NMSs. Specifically, the focus is on data related to the alarms and KPIs originating from the communication networks. The goal of this work is to study and find the best pattern mining technique for convergent networks (wireless and fixed) and the work falls in the scope of designing the pro-active NMS that can suit the best for heterogeneous network architectures such as FUTON. Selecting the wrong pattern mining technique can result in lower detection rates or an increased number of false alarms [9].

2   Pattern Mining and NMS

Knowledge Discovery in Databases (KDD) is used to find hidden knowledge from existing large databases and NMS alarm or performance data are perfect example of such databases. An example of an operation in network management is alarm correlation where the KDD method is often applied. The KDD method is comprised of various steps such as: knowledge requirement setting, data selection, data mining, result interpretation, and knowledge incorporation [10]. In the context of NMS, data mining techniques are restricted to pattern extraction or pattern mining in the available data [9].

A pioneer work in this field can be considered the Telecommunication Alarm Sequence Analyser (TASA) system [9], which exhibited the usage of knowledge discovery methods for almost the first time in the industry and was used for the knowledge extraction from the network alarm databases [9]. The pattern discovery used in TASA could be briefly mentioned as follows [4]: "Given a sequence S of alarms, a set E of alarm predicates, a class ε of episodes built from the predicates of E, a frequency threshold c, and window widths W and W´, find the confidences of all rules (α, e, W, W´) whose frequency is at least c.". TASA discovers episodic rules between alarms based on the temporal relationship existing between them [4]. An example of a rule can be cited as: "if alarms of type link alarm and link failure occur within five seconds, then an alarm of type high fault rate occurs within 60 seconds with probability 0.7"[11].

Also taking into account the fact that single fault conditions trigger multiple correlated alarms, fault management was proposed in [12] which took care of correlated alarms. In this scope they developed "Intelligent search of interesting patterns in sequences" to find correlated alarms. Alarm patterns on the basis of topology model were presented to the network operator for further decision related to matching the alarm pattern to a single triggering event.

The work done in [13] proposes a mining algorithm that used time constraints for restricting the time between the alarms. They also focused on a method for discovering sequential alarm patterns. But this work was limited to cleaning alarm events and finding sequential alarm patterns but did not provide correlated alarms for further processing.

3   Telecommunication Alarm Databases

It is well known that the first step in pattern mining lies in the understanding of the data. In case the generated data is not suitable for pattern mining, then possible steps are needed to change the raw data into a format which makes it suitable for pattern mining [10].

Before going to telecommunication alarm databases, it is worth mentioning the telecommunication network which is comprised of a network of links and nodes where messages are passed from one part of the network to another over multiple links and through various nodes. Switches, exchanges, transmission equipments are example of some of the components which form the network [4]. Whenever there is an abnormal condition in the network, alarms are generated by each of the components, sub-components and software modules. These alarms are usually generated in the form of messages and contain a time-stamp, the address of the node/component from where the alarm was generated, the severity of the alarm and the status of the alarm (whether cleared or not). The NMS at the operation and maintenance centre of the network receives these alarms and store them in the database. Also, the alarms are reported to the network operator for taking appropriate actions to eradicate the cause and bring the network back to normal.

4   Trends of Pattern Mining Usage in NMS

This section presents the comparative evaluation of state-of-the-art pattern mining techniques.

Table 1. Comparative evaluation

Techniques	Advantages	Disadvantages
Topographical proximity in Sequential Pattern Mining	Does not rely on predefined network configuration	Alarms conform to 3GPP FM standards while FUTON exhibits a heterogeneous environment
WINEPI algorithm	Efficiently identifies event sequences in sequential input data	Needs a-priori knowledge; Constraint on data processing in terms of both time and space
EW-WINEPI algorithm	Efficiently identifies event sequences in sequential input data; Reduces number of non-effective time window;	Still needs a-priori knowledge which might be a constraint for dynamic nature of FUTON network
Constrained based sequential pattern mining	Employs pre-cleaning Focuses on time sequence No compromise on data quality Important for pro-active fault management Increases performance of mining algorithm	Limited to GSM networks
Structural pattern mining	Mines structural pattern No focus on time sequence Supports scalability	Sample database was used to find results; not used on data originating from heterogeneous network architecture presented in FUTON
Mutually dependent pattern mining	Concept applicable towards an all IP-network Mutual dependency between faults, alarms and performance data can be used for proactive fault management	Might have limitations in a RoF infrastructure
Temporal data mining	Tested on telco networks Used as a pre-step to automation of fault detection in network equipments Applicable when datasets contains events Works in case of low predictive accuracy	Low availability of training data makes the system handicapped

A priori knowledge is required for the pattern mining algorithms applied to telecommunication data and it includes domain knowledge as well as detailed structural information [9]. With propagation of time, the nature of the system might change and this forces a change in the a priori knowledge. As studied in [9] and the functional part of TASA system, there are certain requirements needed by the data mining methods for the telecommunication data [7]: "*Application domain terminology and semantics used in user interface; Immediate, accurate and understandable results; Easy-to-use methods; Interfaces and integrability towards legacy tools; Adaptability to process information; Use of process information; Efficiency and appropriate execution time; Reduced iterations per task; Easy to learn; Increases efficiency of domain experts by reducing time spent per task*".

It is clear from the studies made that, pattern mining in transactional databases, mining classification rules for classifying data dependent on interesting features are some of the various pattern mining applications. Pattern mining in sequential patterns is the knowledge discovery being done on any ordered data. But it can inferred that, important information can be extracted from alarm data generated by telecommunication system by applying pattern mining techniques related to sequential data.

The algorithm described in [14] is based also on an a priori approach. They introduced new criteria for the selection of sequence where sequence plausibility and coherence is evaluated in network topology context. The algorithm is based on an assumption that depends on the closeness of the alarm-generating elements. They assume that closer the alarm generating elements a much greater relationship is plausible between the alarms. A priori knowledge related to the network configuration is not totally relied upon. The topographical information encoded within the alarms is used instead. Thus using the topographical information encoded within the alarms gives a much better performance of the pattern mining algorithms.

WINEPI algorithm described in [15, 16] uses a priori knowledge and aims toward mining temporal association rules in sequential data by employing sliding time window by employing a sliding time window. The maximum and minimum sequence duration constraint of the time window is specified by the user. This algorithm is capable of efficient identification of event sequences in sequential input data. But as the WINEPI algorithm have a constraint in terms of both time and space, formulation was done to reduce the number of non-effective windows, known as the EW-WINEPI algorithm. This work could bring a inference that, the number of episode rules which could be discovered depends on the time window, and with increase in the minimum Support and minimum confidence, the number of episode rules become smaller.

[7] observes that data cleaning is desirable before proceeding with pattern mining. As mentioned before, the work proposed in [7] also utilized the time constraints for restricting time difference between two alarm events. Also the quality of knowledge discovered was evaluated and the data cleaning was found to be an important measure for improving the functioning of the pattern mining algorithms. The quality of evaluation was determined by finding the ratio between difference in execution time before and after cleaning with execution time before cleaning. Thus differing from normal pattern mining algorithms, it becomes a fact that telecommunication alarm data contains not only valuable information but also lots of dummy information. Also for telecommunication alarm data, the reduction time in execution of pattern mining algorithm is an added value with pre-cleaning of the data.

The work in [17, 18], instead of acting on the time sequences as other works, concentrates on discovery of the structural data as the data collected from telecommunication NMSs is found to have explicit or implicit structural components. They used a computationally-constrained beam search.

Also, [19] looked into pattern mining of patterns which have mutual dependency. Telecommunication alarm data has exhibited a tendency to have mutual dependencies in alarm patterns. The mutual dependencies result from physical dependencies manifested as a set of events when an event is triggered. Thus mutual patterns can be used for constructing signatures for problematic situations. Also redundancy in alarm data generated by monitoring elements results in mutual alarm patterns, which makes it worth to inspect the mutual pattern mining.

[20] predicts telecommunication equipment failures from the network alarm sequences. This work is aligned with normal sequential pattern mining algorithms.

The work in [21, 22] looked into the distributed pattern mining where the alarm logs are divided into smaller logs according to topological location. This is for specific implication that pattern mining is done for alarms generated from the locally generated alarms. This marks a major difference from state-of-the-art sequential pattern mining algorithms resulting in scalability and also contributes to the resilience of the telecommunication system.

Overall, it can be concluded that pattern mining for telecommunication data follows sequential pattern mining techniques with slight variations, such as noticing the time stamps, the time difference between the data generated. In certain cases, distributed processing of the data from the telecommunication data are answers to scalability and resilience issues. It was also noticed that, directly running the pattern mining algorithms on telecommunication data is not the best method. A data pre-processing gives much better result in terms of time and accuracy when compared with the previous. Distributed processing does not fit for convergent radio-over-fiber infrastructures (such as case of FUTON) as a centralized processing is desired with all the computing facility stationed in the Central Unit overlooking the network and the alarm generating elements are very simple with least computational power.

5   Requirements for RoF Like Networks

Fault (FM) or Performance Management (PM) in convergent networks implies the management of all networks which forms portion of the integrated mobile and fixed wireless networks. This work makes us conclude that, almost no work was done related to the application of data/pattern mining in fault management or alarm handling specific to convergent networks. But it is also true that, the proposals and results obtained by the researchers in using data/pattern mining in FM replicates scenarios obtained in convergent networks. Our specific area of interest lies in RoF networks where alarms are generated both from fixed and wireless networks. The RoF part of the FUTON system is not prone to large number of alarms. For instance, a passive optical network (PON) is susceptible to fewer errors and alarms when compared to wide area network. This situation is similar to [20] where alarms are not generated in abundance and the training data is hard to be found. On the other hand there are new challenges: the correct identification of the faulty source, the impact on deployed services of such faults or performance impairments, and assurance of service levels over heterogeneous mobile networks are similar problems faced in all kinds of networks. The work proposed in [21] is a better solution for a high speed network, but the distributed processing of the faults oppose the idea of central processing of RoF Manager based on the fact that a centralized NMS is required to manage a highly distributed network for faults, congestion, and to assure adequate QoS across the whole network. The FM module of the RoF Manager requires functionalities such as fault localization, alarm correlation, and pro-active fault management. The referred literature in this survey has definitely shown that usage of pattern mining/ data mining is sure to add value to the system in terms of intelligence for achieving the required fault management functionalities. It is definite that frequent sequential pattern is the kind of patterns that will be found in the alarms generated from the RoF infrastructure. This is similar to alarms from other networks. Apriori algorithm can be a solution as the number of candidates is not very large. But it is certain that the algorithm needs to process numerical data rather than symbolic data.

Pattern mining for telecommunication alarm data stays limited to the steps such cleaning of alarm events and discovering sequential alarm patterns, and does thus not provide correlated alarms adopted for further processing. Further, data processing algorithms are thus a requirement for pro-active fault management.

6 Conclusions

This paper presents a survey on the usage of pattern mining in the area of NMSs. Specific interest is shown at fault management systems. Brief descriptions about pattern mining methodologies are stated at the beginning followed by the application of pattern mining techniques in Network Management Systems. The most famous and initial work in network management systems involving pattern mining techniques, TASA is also analyzed. We also briefly describe the kinds of data specific to telecommunication alarms on which pattern mining needs to be applied. We put forward state-of-the-art works from the field of pattern mining as applied on alarms originating from telco networks. At the end a critical analysis is done on the requirements of the pattern mining technique needed for convergent networks. This work highlighted some of the issues that affect the ability of pattern mining such as big volume of alarms generated from some part of the networks (e.g. wireless) or very rare events (such as alarms generated from PONs) or ability to work in real-time (using distributed data mining). Application of pattern mining techniques in NMSs is one of the oldest examples of usage of data mining because of the huge volume of data. Pattern mining usage is sure to accelerate for giving operators competitive advantage for performing alarm correlation or fault localization.

References

1. Pato, S., Pedro, J., Santos, J., Arsénio, A., Inácio, P., Monteiro, P.: On Building a Distributed Antenna System with Joint Signal Processing for Next Generation Wireless Access Networks: The FUTON Approach. In: 7th Conference on Telecommunications, Portugal (2008)
2. Santiago, C., Gangopadhyay, B., Arsenio, A., Ramkumar, M.V., Prasad, N.R.: Next Generation Radio over Fiber Network Management for a Distributed Antenna System. In: Wireless Vitae 2009, Aalborg, Denmark (2009)

3. Burn-Thornton, K.E., Garibaldi, J., Mahdi, A.E.: Pro-active Network Management Using Data Mining. In: Globecom 1998, vol. 2, pp. 1208–1211 (1998)
4. Toivonen, H., Ronkainen, P., Mannila, H., Klemettinen, M., Hätönen, K.: Knowledge Discovery from Telecommunication Network Alarm Databases
5. Kulkarni, P.G., McClean, S.I., Parr, G.P., Black, M.M.: Deploying MIB Data Mining for Proactive Network Management. In: 3rd International IEEE Conference on Intelligent Systems, pp. 506–511 (2006)
6. Agarwal, R., Imielinski, T., Swami, A.: Mining Association Rules Between Sets of Items in Large Databases. In: SIGMOD Conference 1993, pp. 207–216 (1993)
7. Ouh, J.-Z., Wu, P.-H., Chen, M.-S.: Experimental Results on a Constrained Based Sequential Pattern Mining for Telecommunication Alarm Data. In: 2nd International Conference on Web Information Systems Engineering, vol. 2 (2001)
8. Li, T.-Y., Li, X.-M.: A LFP-tree based method for association rules mining in telecommunication alarm correlation analysis. The Journal of China Universities of Posts and Telecommunications (2007)
9. Hätönen, K.: Data mining for telecommunication network log analysis. PhD Thesis, Series of Publications A, Report A-2009-1 (2009)
10. Vehviläinen, P., Hätönen, K., Kumpulainen, P.: Data mining in quality analysis of digital mobile telecommunications network. In: Proceedings of XVII IMEKO World Congress, Dubrovnik, Croatia, pp. 684–689 (2003)
11. Weiss, G.M.: Data Mining in Telecommunications. Dept. of Computer and Information Science. Fordham University
12. Tuchs, K.D., Jobmann, K.: Intelligent Search for Correlated Alarms Events in Databases. In: International Symposium on Integrated Network Management Proceedings, pp. 285–288 (2001)
13. Jain-Zhi, O., Pei-Hsin, W., Ming-Syan, C.: Experimental Results on a Constrained based Sequential Pattern Mining for telecommunication alarm data. In: Proccedings of the Web Information Systems (2001)
14. Devitt, A., Duffin, J., Moloney, R.: Topographical Proximity for Mining Network Alarm Data. In: SIGCOMM 2005 Workshops (2005)
15. Mannila, H., Toivonen, H., Verkamo, A.I.: Discovery of frequent episodes in event sequences. Data Mining and Knowledge Discovery, 259–289 (1997)
16. Hou, S., Zhang, X.: Alarms Association Rules Based on Sequential Pattern Mining Algorithm. In: International Conf. on Fuzzy Systems and Knowledge Discovery (2008)
17. Baritchi, A., Cook, D.J., Holder, L.B.: Discovering Structural Patterns in Telecommunication Data. In: Proceedings of FLAIRS 2000, American Association for Artificial Intelligence (2000)
18. Cook, D.J., Holder, L.B., Djoko, S.: Scalable discovery of informative structural concepts using domain knowledge. IEEE Expert 11(5) (1996)
19. Sheng, M., Hellerstein, J.L.: Mining Mutually Dependent Patterns for System Management. IEEE Journal on Selected Areas in Comm. 20, 726–736 (2002)
20. Weiss, G.M.: Predicting Telecommunication Equipment Failures from Sequences of Network Alarms. In: Handbook of Knowledge Discovery and Data Mining. Oxford University Press
21. Gardner, R.D., Harle, D.A.: Fault Resolution and Alarm Correlation in High Speed Networks using Database Mining Techniques. In: International Conf. on Information, Communications and Signal Processing, Singapore, pp. 1423–1428 (1997)
22. Manilla, H., Toivonen, H., Verkamo, A.I.: Discovery frequent episodes in sequences. In: 1st International Conference on Knowledge Discovery and Data Mining, Canada, pp. 210–215 (1995)

Analysis Patterns in Dimensional Data Modeling

Stephan Schneider and Dirk Frosch-Wilke

University of Applied Sciences Kiel, Institute of Business Information Systems,
Sokratesplatz. 2, 24149 Kiel, Germany
{stephan.schneider,dirk.frosch-wilke}@fh-kiel.de

Abstract. The construction of conceptual dimensional data models is one of the most important, fundamental and challenging tasks during the analysis phase in the systems development life cycle of a data warehouse system. Such data models are representing operational as well as strategic business requirements. Dimensional data models are used for implementing dimensional databases within the data warehouse system, which itself will be used for generating crucial information for decision-making. Although the enormous importance of conceptual dimensional data models is well known, the use of approved analysis patterns is not common practice. The non-consideration of analysis patterns can yield to poorly planned and therefore qualitative unproven dimensional data models respectively databases, which similarly yields to qualitative unproven generated decision-relevant information. Up to now the use of analysis patterns in dimensional data modeling is given no attention to in literature and in practice. This paper will overcome this gap in building data warehouse systems by introducing analysis patterns for dimensional data models which address well known and recurring problems in specific contexts.

Keywords: Analysis, Patterns, Dimensional Data Modeling, Data Warehousing.

1 Introduction

The methodical development of information systems is divided into the core phases analysis, design and implementation. The results of a preceding phase (e. g. analysis) in form of information models (e. g. conceptual data models) serve as inputs for the succeeding phase (e. g. design). The analysis phase is the first step in the development cycle of a system and therefore the fundamental and most important phase. All system requirements are defined in the analysis phase and documented in conceptual models.

A very effective and proven means for developing normalized conceptual data models is the use of analysis patterns like described in [8], [17], [18] and also in [5]. The use of analysis patterns leads to a time- and costsaving construction process and to qualitative proven data models.

Up to now the use of analysis patterns in dimensional data modeling for construction of information systems for business intelligence solutions is given no attention to in literature and in practice. Only in the books of [12], [13] and [14] some common exemplary problems and their solution approaches are described and modeled, but not in the form of patterns. Considering the enormous importance of the

R. Kannan and F. Andres (Eds.): ICDEM 2010, LNCS 6411, pp. 109–116, 2012.
© Springer-Verlag Berlin Heidelberg 2012

analysis phase, it must be noted that the non-consideration of analysis patterns in dimensional data modeling leads to poorly planned and qualitative unproven dimensional data models. In short, the non-consideration of analysis patterns is a research gap in dimensional data modeling and therefore as it is in data warehousing.

2 Dimensional Data Models

Since its introduction in 1990, data warehouse systems have been established as a solid and integrated part of the IT systems landscape of an enterprise [2], [6], [10], [12], [13], [14], [19]. A data warehouse system is used to improve and to optimize the data logistics within companies. A *data warehouse system* is an enterprise-wide information system, which consists of applications and databases harnessing the data warehouse [19]. A classic definition of a data warehouse was coined by William Inmon, who defines a data warehouse as a subject oriented, integrated, non-volatile and time variant collection of data in support of management's decisions [10]. Based upon this definition a *data warehouse* can be interpreted as an integrated pool of databases that is both target for integration activities on operational databases and source for generating crucial information within business intelligence applications [15], [16].

In the center of a data warehouse system is the data warehouse. A data warehouse is the hub within a data warehouse system and thus the basis for enterprise-wide data logistics. Depending on the architecture of the data warehouse system, a data warehouse is composed of different database types [16]. However dimensional structured databases are always part of a data warehouse. Such dimensional structured databases are used to generate crucial information for decision-making.

Dimensional structured databases based upon dimensional data models. A *dimensional data model* is a special data model representing the structure of multidimensional data on type-level, and therefor relies on the concepts "dimension" and "fact" [9], [13]. Multidimensional data can be seen as a n-dimensional data cube.

The cells of the n-dimensional data cube contain the facts. A *fact* is a quantitative measure, which describes an analyzable and a (business) relevant piece of information of a perceptible (economic) situation in a concentrated form [16].

The edges of the multidimensional cubes are representing the dimensions. A *dimension* is a unique, orthogonal structure element of multi-dimensional data [2].

Within the scope of an n-ary relationship all declared dimensions (classes) are combined to the fact table. A fact table is an association class whose primary key consists of the primary keys of all dimensions within the n-ary relationship. In addition, the fact table contains the facts as attributes.

3 Analysis Patterns

3.1 Problem-Solving Behavior of Experts

An *expert* is a person who is well grounded in a domain and has comprehensive domain knowledge, which is knowledge about one or more subject areas. According to [4], including the identification of relationships and watching out for repeatable structures as for superficialities are key properties of an expert's behavior. In addition, experts as distinguished from laity are normally characterized by a lot of successful solved problems and thereby solve upcoming problems not always from ground up, but draw on well-proven solution patterns for ancient problems [3], [7]. An expert draws on in using well known patterns for old problems to solve new problems. He doesn't reinvent the famous wheel anew, he adopts proven problem solving knowledge in new problem situations. Prerequisite for the usage of an already practiced solution is first, that the solution is principle applicable, and secondly, it exists in an appropriate level of abstraction. The elaborated and in an appropriate level of abstraction existing domain knowledge, which describes the solution for a recurring problem in a special context, is called a *pattern* [5], [16]. This easy-held definition also explains why it is spoken of a problem-solution-context triple in relation to a pattern.

The idea, to record and reuse knowledge in canonical form goes back to the architect Christopher Alexander. In his book "The Timeless Way of Building" he describes various patterns and their properties especially for usage in house building and urban planning [1].

In the year 1994 the published book "Elements of Reusable Object-Oriented Software" of [7] has exerts one of the greatest influences and an initiating effect for the pattern movement in software development history. Although the pattern movement records several roots [5], at least design patterns are an integral part of software development since the publication of this book. As the title of this book hinted, the presented patterns are design patterns for the design phase of the software development lifecycle.

The pattern concept as a successful artifact of reuse in the design phase has contributes to build and use patterns also in the analysis phase. In analogy to design patterns during the design phase patterns during the analysis phase are called analysis patterns. The term analysis pattern was introduced by Martin Fowler. In his book "Analysis Patterns: Reusable Object Models" [5] he defines a pattern as „an idea that has been useful in one practical context and will probably be useful in others." He deliberately leaves the definition open to indicate that a pattern could be anything in the end. The phrase "practical context" indicates that a pattern is the result of real and practical work and results from knowledge about a domain.

Every model construction process in software development can be seen as a problem, which must be solved from an expert's point of view with the help of patterns. Since the analysis phase is the most important phase in the whole systems development life cycle, therefore analysis patterns must be given a great importance.

3.2 Schema of the Description Form

For analysis patterns specification a minimalistically description form is chosen in this paper. This description form consists of the parts problem, context and solution. A more comprehensive pattern description structure offers [11]. In addition to problem, context and solution also methodological, organizational and economical aspects are used to describe patterns in a comprehensive way.

Unique Name. Each pattern is given a unique, precise and concise name.

Problem. For each pattern a description of the problem is made. The problem description outlines the problem, which can be defined as an unsatisfactory situation with negative impacts and recurs in a context. In addition, all the forces, which are necessary for the solution, are considered too.

Context. For each pattern a description of the context is made. A context identifies the real or intangible environment, where the perceived phenomena are located and a problem recurs. In addition, a context describes the conditions for the use of the pattern.

Solution. For each pattern a description of the solution is made. A solution can be defined as a satisfactory situation without negative impacts or in more general terms as the treatment of a recurring situation (problem). The pattern offers the solution for a specific problem in a graphical representation form. The graphical representation shows the pattern structure and its contribution to the problem solving.

4   Selected Analysis Patterns for Dimensional Data Models

Like mentioned in chapter 1 analysis patterns is given no attention to in literature and in practice. Only Kimball et al. [12], [13] and [14] describe some exemplary problems and their solution approaches in their graduate course on dimensional data modeling, but not in form of patterns.

The most practical experiences of the authors in data warehousing projects and the exemplary problem situations are suitable starting points for the construction and appropriate abstraction of analysis patterns. This chapter prepares some of these examples respectively experiences in a common way and presents the analysis patterns in the form of the triple problem-context-solution.

4.1   Different Change Intervals of Dimension Attribute Values

Name. Dimensions attribute values changing.

Problem. Normally a dimension has multiple attributes, which come from a normalized structured net of classes thru denormalizing processes. The conception of a dimension deliberately follows the principle of denormalization. On the principle of normalization built, and therefore divided among several classes, originally split attributes are brought together into one dimension. In the course of this reunion there is no distinction been made, what kind of change intervals the individually attribute values have.

The resulting dimensions are constituted of attributes, whose values have different change intervals.

The consequence of this inconsiderate attributes merge is a continuously increasing number of dimension objects that possesses a high degree of redundancy. The individual objects only differ in those attributes values that are often have been changed, while the rest of the attributes values have been retained unchanged.

For example, a normalized data model describes product data in a simple classification hierarchy as follows: product (n) → (1) product group (n) → (1) product family (n) → (1) product category. A product is classified into one product group, whereas one product group encompasses one or more products. A product group itself is classified into one product family, whereas one product family encompasses one or more product groups, and so on. The relationship-types between the different product classes are many-to-one relationship-types.

In the course of denormalization the attributes of the classes product, product group, product family and product category are brought together within the dimension product. It is common business practice that product category data are more often and faster be changed than product specific data.

Context. The context of this problem is all-encompassing. Any perceived problem domain is context of this problem.

Solution. The solution of this problem is shown in figure 1. As shown the origin dimension Dimension is split into two dimensions. The one dimension (Dimension A) contains those attributes that values are not often been changed, while the other dimension (Dimension B) contains those attributes that values are often been changed.

To prevent possible hierarchy information loss caused by splitting the attributes into two dimensions it's advisable to include hierarchy level attributes (static and dynamic attributes hierarchy level) in both dimensions. A hierarchy level attribute stands for the level of hierarchy of a specific attributes group within the dimension. For example, the hierarchy level of product specific attributes is 0. This hierarchy level represents the highest level of granularity (LoG). The hierarchy level of product group is 1, of product family 2 and of product category 3. Hierarchy level information is needed in drill-down and roll-up operations.

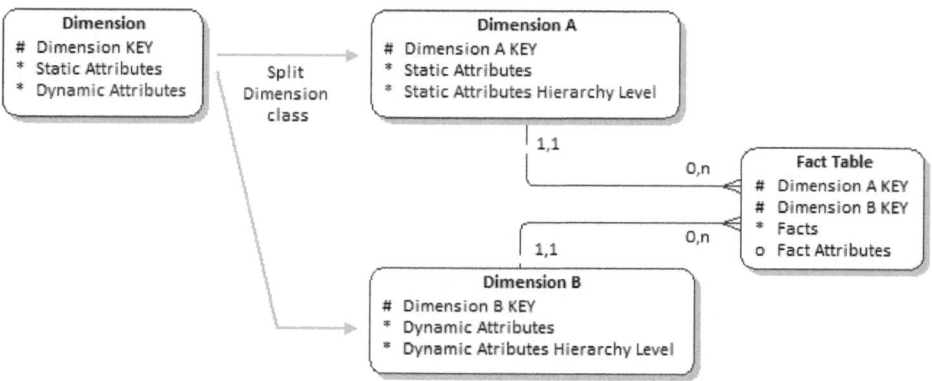

Fig. 1. Dimension attribute values changing Pattern

4.2 Multiple Occurrences of Dimension Objects per Fact(s) by Given Fact Table Grain

Name. Many-to-many Dimensions by given fact table grain.

Problem. The choice of the fact table grain (degree of detail) is a very important step during the construction process of a dimensional data model. The fact table grain determines what a fact table record represents. If the fact table grain is given because of impending analysis or reports, there may be dimensions, which objects (dimension records) occur several times per fact entry.

The non-consideration of this situation causes a violation of the fact table grain and a mutation of the fact values and thus to wrong results in the analysis of multidimensional data. The mutation of the fact values means that a priori additive facts become to semi-additive facts or non-additive facts, which will lead to significant conception losses.

As an example, an invoice in health care will be used. An invoice is basically composed of several invoice items (or invoice positions). Especially in health care an invoice item represents many diagnoses made by multiple practitioners and along with that many treatments. Practitioner, diagnosis and treatment as well as patient and time are dimensions of the dimensional data model. For reporting purpose in health care invoicing the fact table grain is to be fixated on an invoice item. That is, a record of the fact table represents an invoice item.

An immediate consequence of this fact table grain is a multiple occurrence of practitioners, diagnoses and treatments per fact entry. An opportunity to avoid the problem of multiple occurrences of dimension objects per fact entry is to fix the fact table grain on time × patient × practitioner × diagnosis × treatment. This solution, which implies a multiple insertion of the respective primary key of the corresponding dimension as foreign key in the fact table, is de facto a violation of the fact table grain. Therefore this solution will not been followed up.

Context. The choice of the fact table grain is one of the first steps in the conception process of a dimensional data model, and therefore essential in the whole conception of a dimensional data model [9], [13], [14]. The consequence of a fixation of the fact table grain can be a multiple occurrence of dimension objects per fact entry in any dimensional data model. Therefore the context of this problem is all-encompassing. Any environment that is perceived and leads to the construction of dimensions and facts is context of this problem.

Solution. The solution of this problem is shown in figure 2. Between Dimension and fact table there will be integrated a dimension bridge class (Dimension Bridge). The primary key of Dimension Bridge is a composite primary key that consists of Dimension Group Key and Dimension Key. Dimension Key is from Dimension and Dimension Group Key is a surrogate key that indicates a group. Under a Dimension Group Key the n-fold occurrences of dimension objects are subsumed. Instead of every single primary key (Dimension Key) of the dimensions the dimension bridge group key (Dimension Group Key) is set as a foreign key and part of the primary key in fact table.

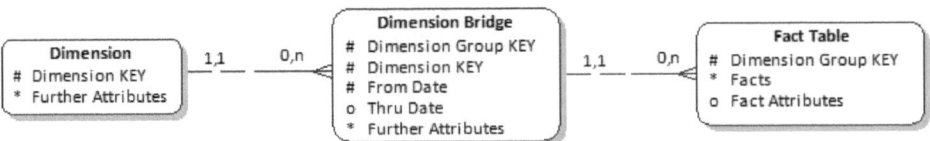

Fig. 2. Many-to-many Dimensions Pattern

5 Conclusion

The analysis patterns presented in this paper should be regarded as a first approach to address the pattern thought in dimensional data modeling. Research works, practical experiences as well as some exemplary problems treated in Kimball et al. in conjunction with the organization of data structures for decision-support tasks and their solutions in form of dimensional data models served as an introduction in this subject. The presented patterns help to solve problems recurring in certain contexts in a proven way. In addition, the used solutions promise an additional benefit effect with regard to the quality management for dimensional data models constructed with the help of analysis patterns.

In the course of further research and development work in the field of analysis patterns in dimensional data modeling the authors plan to build a wiki-based pattern repository for dimensional data models.

From the point of a strong scientific view it must be noted that this work is at the beginning of a research cycle. The explicated patterns are based on abstract units of knowledge. The knowledge base consists of own domain knowledge and own practical experiences as well as in parts foreign knowledge described in the literature. Moreover, this knowledge base is enhanced in an inductive and logical manner, transferred into abstract units of knowledge thru cognitive synthesis to build the basis for pattern construction. In the sense of the research objective of behavioral science, which seeks to develop and verify theories, the abstract units of knowledge have the state of hypotheses. Planned empirical studies must now provide evidence which leads to competent knowledge in the new research field of pattern driven dimensional data modeling development.

References

1. Alexander, C.: The Timeless Way of Building. Oxford University Press, New York (1979)
2. Bauer, A., Günzel, H. (eds.): Data-Warehouse-Systeme: Architektur, Entwicklung, Anwendung. Dpunkt, Heidelberg (2009)
3. Batra, D.: Conceptual Data Modeling Patterns: Representation and Validation. Journal of Database Management 16(2), 84–106 (2005)
4. Chi, M.T.H., Glaser, R., Farr, M.J. (eds.): The nature of expertise. Lawrence Erlbaum Associates, Hillsdale (1988)
5. Fowler, M.: Analysemuster: Wiederverwendbare Objektmodelle. Addison-Wesley, Bonn (1999)
6. Frosch-Wilke, D.: Data Warehouse, OLAP und Data Mining - State of the Art und zukünftige Entwicklungen. DuD - Datenschutz und Datensicherheit 10, 597–604 (2003)
7. Gamma, E., Helm, R., Johnson, R., Vlissides, J.: Design Patterns: Elements of Reusable Object-Oriented Software. Addison-Wesley, Reading (1994)
8. Hay, D.C.: Data Model Patterns: Conventions of Thought. Dorset House, New York (1996)
9. Imhoff, C., Galemo, N., Geiger, J.G.: Mastering Data Warehouse Design: Relational and Dimensional Techniques. Wiley, Indianapolis (2003)
10. Inmon, W.H.: Building the Data Warehouse. Wiley, Indianapolis (2005)

11. Jung, J., Sprenger, J.: Muster für Geschäftsprozessmodellierung. In: Schelp, J., Winter, R., Frank, U., Rieger, B., Turowski, K. (eds.) Integration, Informationslogistik und Architektur. LNI, vol. P-90, pp. 189–204. Köllen, Bonn (2006)
12. Kimball, R., Reeves, L., Ross, M., Thornthwaite, W.: The Data Warehouse Lifecycle Toolkit: Expert Methods for Designing, Developing, and Deploying Data Warehouses. Wiley, New York (1998)
13. Kimball, R., Ross, M.: The Data Warehouse Toolkit: The Complete Guide to Dimensional Modeling. Wiley, New York (2002)
14. Kimball, R., Ross, M., Thornthwaite, W., Mundy, J., Becker, B.: The Data Warehouse Lifecycle Toolkit: Practical Techniques for Building Data Warehouse and Business Intelligence Systems. Wiley, Indianapolis (2008)
15. Schneider, S.: Ein Ansatz zur Konstruktion generischer (Unternehmens-) Datenmodelle auf fachkonzeptioneller Ebene. In: Schelp, J., Winter, R., Frank, U., Rieger, B., Turowski, K. (eds.) Integration, Informationslogistik und Architektur. LNI, vol. P-90, Köllen, Bonn (2006)
16. Schneider, S.: Konstruktion generischer Datenmodelle auf fachkonzeptioneller Ebene im betrieblichen Anwendungskontext: Methode und Studie. Shaker, Aachen (2007)
17. Silverston, L.: The Data Model Resource Book. A Library of Universal Data Models for All Enterprises, vol. 1. Wiley, New York (2001)
18. Silverston, L.: The Data Model Resource Book. A Library of Universal Data Models By Industry Types, vol. 2. Wiley, New York (2001)
19. Winter, R.: Zur Positionierung und Weiterentwicklung des Data Warehousing in der betrieblichen Applikationsarchitektur. In: Jung, R., Winter, R. (eds.) Data Warehousing Strategie, pp. 127–139. Springer, Berlin (2000)

Mining Single Pass Weighted Pattern Tree

Olivia Castelino[1], Preetham Kumar[2], and Srivatsa Maddodi[2]

[1] Department of Computer Science and Engineering, Nitte Mahalinga Adyanthaya
Memorial Institute of Technology, An Autonomous Institution under Visveswaraiah
Technological University, Belgaum, India
[2] Department of Information and Communication Techonolgy,
Manipal Institute of Technology, Manipal University, India
oli.castelino@gmail.com, preetham.kumar@manipal.edu,
srivatsa.maddodi@gmail.com

Abstract. Weighted tree mining has become an important research
topic in Data mining. There are several algorithms for mining Frequent
Pattern trees. FP growth algorithm using FP tree has been considered
for frequent pattern mining because of its enormous performance and
development compared to the candidate generation model of Apriori.
The purpose of our work is to provide a tree structure for incremental
and interactive weighted pattern mining by only one database scan. It
is applied to existing Compact pattern (CP) tree. CP tree dynamically
achieves frequency-descending prefix tree structure with a single-pass
by applying tree restructuring technique and considerably reducing the
mining time. It is competent of using prior tree structures and acquires
mining outcomes to decrease the computation by incredible amount. Performance analysis show that our tree structure is very efficient for incremental and interactive weighted pattern mining.

Keywords: Compact Pattern Tree, Weighted, Association Rules.

1 Introduction

Data mining is the process of discovering interesting knowledge, such as patterns,
associations, changes, anomalies and significant structures, from large amounts
of data stored in databases, data warehouses, or other information repositories.
Data mining is the key step in the knowledge discovery process, and association
rule mining is a very important research topic in the data mining field (Agrawal,
Imielinski, Swami, 1993). The original problem addressed by association rule
mining was to find a correlation among sales of different products from the analysis of a large set of supermarket data for example market basket analysis. At
present, research work on association rules is motivated by an extensive range of
application areas, such as banking, manufacturing, health care etc. The discovery
of association rules is typically done in two steps: discovery of frequent itemsets
and the generation of association rules. In principle, data mining should be applicable to any kind of information repository. This includes relational databases,

R. Kannan and F. Andres (Eds.): ICDEM 2010, LNCS 6411, pp. 117–124, 2012.
© Springer-Verlag Berlin Heidelberg 2012

data warehouses etc. Based on the types of data, the challenges and techniques of mining may differ for each of the repository systems. Determining frequent itemsets, considered as one of the most significant responsibilities, has been the hub of many studies in the last few years. Many results have been proposed using sequential or parallel algorithms based on user defined minimum support [1].

Association rule mining algorithms currently proposed in the literature are not sufficient for large datasets [9][10]. Most of the existing algorithms discover all frequent itemsets based on user defined minimum support without considering the components of the transaction such as weight or quantity, cost and other relevant information of the customer which lead to profit. Moreover, the algorithms require at least two database scans to generate and test candidate patterns to obtain large item sets. Finding frequent patterns plays a crucial task in data mining. FP-tree based FP-growth mining technique proposed by Han et. al. [6][8] has been found one of the efficient algorithms using the prefix-tree data structure. The performance increase achieved by FP-growth is mainly based on the highly compact nature of FP-tree, where it stores only the frequent items in a frequency-descending order.

The prefix-tree based approach may suffer from the limitation of memory size when it tries to hold whole database information. But CP- tree [2] constructs a compact prefix-tree structure with one database scan and provides the same mining performance as the FP-growth technique by efficient tree restructuring process. Weighted pattern mining [3][4] can discover more important information evaluated to the conventional frequent pattern mining [6][8] by considering different weights of the items. Weights may correspond to special promotions on some products or profitability of different items. Let us consider an example, in a real world business database, frequency of diamond necklace is very low compared to the frequency of silver sold. Hence, knowledge about the patterns having low frequency but high weightage remains concealed by finding only frequent patterns. The main contribution of the weighted frequent pattern mining is to retrieve this concealed knowledge from database. Existing weighted frequent pattern mining algorithms [3][4] considered preset database and need multiple database scans to find the weighted frequent patterns. Our proposed tree structure is easy to construct and maintain for the incremental updating of the databases. It is highly suitable for interactive mining which is applied on CP tree. Our proposed tree structure needs only one database scan. Furthermore, it is competent of using prior tree structure and mining outcomes to decrease the computation by incredible amount. Performance study shows our tree structure is efficient in weighted frequent pattern mining. Furthermore, it generates fewer but more valuable patterns for users.

2   Related Work

Many weighted frequent itemset mining algorithms that have been proposed reflect the importance of items [5]. The main focus of weighted frequent itemset mining concerns satisfying the downward closure property. Most of the weighted association rule mining algorithms suggested so far have been Apriori based which use a candidate set generation and test mechanism. However, pattern growth algorithms are more efficient than Apriori based algorithms. WFIM [4] is the first FP-tree based weighted frequent pattern mining algorithm using two database scans over a fixed database. Seperate weight and support for each item were considered for pruning and the number of weighted frequent itemsets were reduced by using a minimum weight and a weight range.

3   Our Proposed Mining Single Pass Weighted Pattern Tree

3.1   Construction of Compact Pattern Tree

CP tree achieves a frequency-descending structure by capturing part-by-part data from the database and dynamically restructuring itself after each part by using efficient tree restructuring mechanism. Construction consists of two phases. In the first phase, insertion into CP-tree is done according to order of items and frequency count is updated. In the second phase, the items are arranged according to descending order of their frequency and the tree nodes are arranged.

Table 1. Transaction Table

TID	Transaction
10	c,a,e
20	b,d,f
30	a,b,d
40	b,d,e
50	f
60	g
70	f,e
80	c,f,e
90	f,e,d

The table shown above is a transaction database and then the step-by-step construction process of CP tree is shown. For the ease of explanation, it is assumed that the second phase is executed after inserting three transactions. Node traverse pointers in tree are maintained like FP-tree does.

Fig. 1. shows the tree structures and items list after inserting transactions 10, 20, and 30. In the second phase, rearrangement of the items I list in frequency descending order is done and then the tree is restructured according to that order. CP-tree at this stage is a frequency-descending tree.

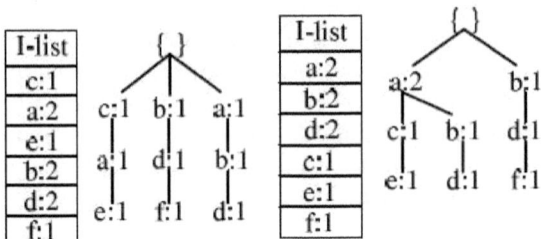

Fig. 1. After Insertion and restructuring TIDs 10-30

The next Insertion phase (for transactions 40, 50, 60) will follow the I-list order of a, b, d, c, e, f instead of previous order of c, a, e, b, d, f. Trees after second Insertion phase and Restructuring phase are shown in Fig. 2.

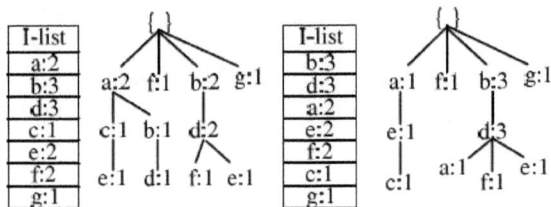

Fig. 2. After Insertion and restructuring TIDs 40-60

The final frequency-descending CP tree we get by performing the Insertion phase and Restructuring phase for last three transactions as shown in Fig. 3.

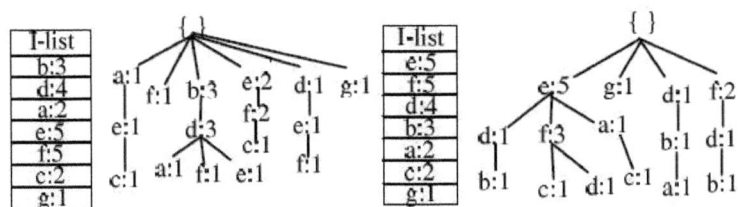

Fig. 3. After Insertion and restructuring TIDs 70-90

It is observed that items with higher frequency are arranged at the upper most portion of the tree. Mostly, databases share common prefix patterns among the transactions, so, the size of CP-tree tree is usually much smaller than its DB. One of the two primary factors to affect the performance of CP-tree is effectively switching to restructuring phase. Too much or too few restructuring operations both may lead to poor performance. Therefore, it can be initiated (i) after each user-given fixed sized slot, or (ii) when combined displacement of top-K items in I-list exceeds a given threshold.

The other performance factor is tree restructuring mechanism. Tree restructuring technique called Branch sorting method(BSM) is used that restructures by sorting unsorted paths in the tree one after another and the I-list in frequency-descending order. In the prefix-tree of Fig. 1. constructed based on first three transactions of transaction database, where I-list order c:1, a:2, e:1, b:2, d:2, f:1 is not in frequency-descendent order. To restructure the tree to such order, the I-list is sorted first to a:2, b:2, d:2, c:1, e:1, f:1 order. Secondly, tree restructuring starts with the first path in the first branch say,c:1→a:1→e:1. Since the path is not sorted according to new I-list order, it is removed from the tree, sorted (using merge sort technique) into a temporary array and then again inserted into tree in a:1→c:1→e:1 order. All unsorted paths in other remaining branches are processed using the same technique. If any path is found already sorted (e.g., the path of the last branch), it is not sorted, rather merged with previously processed common sorted path (if any). Thus, with the processing of the last path, the restructuring of the tree is completed and we get the frequency descending tree in second figure of Fig. 1. The performance of BSM depends on degree of displacement (DD) which uses merge sort approach with a complexity of $O(n\log_2 n)$, n being the number of items in path, therefore, the DD is immaterial on its performance. Sorted path handling feature of BSM reduces not only the number of sorting operations but also the size of data to be sorted.

3.2   Proposed Mining Single Pass Weighted Pattern Tree

All the items in transaction database contain the components such as item number, quantity, cost of the item bought and some other significant information of the customer. Most of the association rules mining algorithms do not consider quantity or weight or total profit. In large databases, it is possible that even if the items appear in very few transactions, they might lead to high profit. Therefore, weight is the most vital component that has to be considered and without which it may lead to drop of information [7]. Consider the transaction database, final frequency descending CP tree is obtained for that database in Fig. 3.

There is weight table below and the minimum threshold= 2. Here, the Maximum weight (MAXW) = 0.6 and after multiplying the frequency of each item with MAXW, the weighted frequency list is < g: 0.6, a: 1.2, c: 1.2, b: 1.8, d: 2.4, e: 3.0, f: 3.0 >. As a result, the candidate items (above minimum threshold) are "d: 2.4", "e: 3.0" and "f: 3.0".At first, the conditional tree of the item "d" in Fig. 4. is created by taking all the branches prefixing the item "d" and deleting the nodes containing an item which cannot be a candidate pattern with the item "d". For item "d", MAXW = 0.6 and we can get the weighted frequency list for item "d" by multiplying the other item's frequency with MAXW. Therefore, the weighted frequency list for the item "d" is < e : 3.0, f :3.0 >.

Table 2. Weight Table

Items	Weight
a	0.6
b	0.5
c	0.2
d	0.35
e	0.5
f	0.3
g	0.4

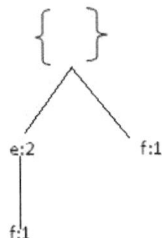

Fig. 4. Conditional Tree for Item d

Candidate patterns "df" and "de" are generated. Conditional trees for the patterns "df" and "de" are shown in Fig. 5.

Fig. 5. Conditional Tree for patterns df and de

Similarly, for item "e", item "f" and their candidate patterns are got and conditional trees are drawn. After testing all the candidate patterns with their actual weights and the weighted frequency, the resultant weighted frequent patterns are considered that are above the threshold.

4   Performance Analysis

Our experiments were performed on Netbeans IDE 6.7 installed on 2.1GHz Intel Core 2 Duo Processor with 2GB Memory and Windows Vista Operating Sys-

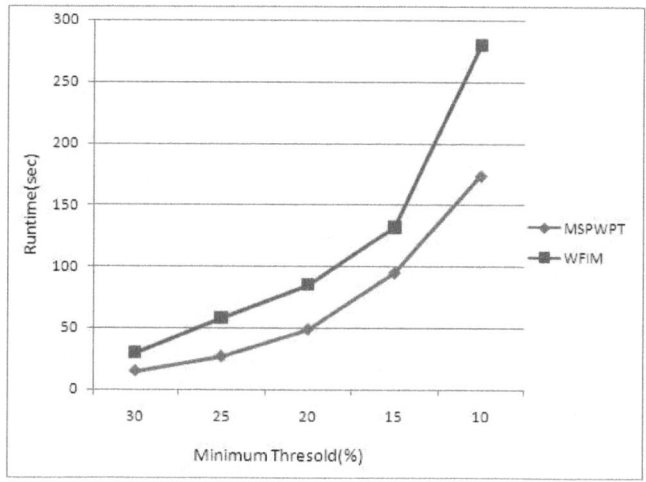

Fig. 6. Runtime Comparison

tem. To evaluate the performance of our proposed tree structure and algorithm, we have performed several experiments on the mushroom dataset. We have considered weight values of each item ranging from 0.1 to 0.9. Mushroom (0.56 MB, 8124 transactions, 119 distinct items) is a dense dataset having transaction length 23 for its every transaction. The running time comparison in mushroom dataset is shown in Fig. 6. Our algorithm gets benefit after the first mining threshold. After the first threshold our trees do not have to be constructed again. As the threshold decreases, new mining operation is needed. Fig. 6. demonstrates that MSPWPT outperforms WFIM by using a single database scan approach and interactive mining.

5   Conclusion

The purpose of our work is to provide a tree structure for incremental and interactive weighted pattern mining. Our proposed tree structure is easy to construct and maintain for the incremental updating of the databases. It is highly suitable for interactive mining which is applied on CP tree. CP-tree dynamically achieves frequency-descending prefix tree structure with a single-pass by applying tree restructuring technique and considerably reduces the mining time. Our proposed tree structure needs only one database scan. Furthermore, it is competent of using prior tree structure and acquires mining outcomes to decrease the computation by incredible amount. Extensive performance analyses show that our tree structure is very efficient for incremental and interactive weighted pattern mining.

References

1. Ananthanarayana, V.S., Subramanian, D.K., Murty, M.N.: Scalable, Distributed and Dynamic Mining of Association Rules. In: Valero, M., Prasanna, V.K., Vajapeyam, S. (eds.) HiPC 2000. LNCS, vol. 1970, pp. 559–566. Springer, Heidelberg (2000)
2. Tanbeer, S.K., Ahmed, C.F., Jeong, B.-S., Lee, Y.-K.: CP-tree: A Tree Structure for Single-Pass Frequent Pattern Mining. In: Washio, T., Suzuki, E., Ting, K.M., Inokuchi, A. (eds.) PAKDD 2008. LNCS (LNAI), vol. 5012, pp. 1022–1027. Springer, Heidelberg (2008)
3. Yun, U.: Efficient Mining of weighted interesting patterns with a strong weight and/or support affinity. Information Sciences 177, 3477–3499 (2007)
4. Yun, U., Leggett, J.J.: WFIM: weighted frequent itemset mining with a weight range and a minimum weight. In: Fourth SIAM Int. Conf. on Data Mining, USA, pp. 636–640 (2005)
5. Kim, Y., Kim, W., Kim, U.: Mining Frequent Itemsets with Normalized Weight in Continuous Data Streams. Journal of Information Processing Systems 6(1) (March 2010), doi:10.3745/JIPS.2010.6.1.079
6. Han, J., Pei, J., Yin, Y., Mao, R.: Mining frequent patterns without candidate generation: a frequent-pattern tree approach. Data Mining and Knowledge Discovery 8, 53–87 (2004)
7. Kumar, P., Ananthanarayana, V.S.: Discovery of frequent itemsets using weighted tree approach. IJCSNS International Journal of Computer Science and Network Security 8(8) (2008)
8. Han, J., Pei, J., Yin, Y.: Mining frequent patterns without candidate generation. ACM SIGMOD Record. In: Proceedings of the 2000 ACM SIGMOD International Conference on Management of Data, SIGMOD 22000, vol. 29(2) (May 2000)
9. Park, S., Chu, W.W., Yoon, J., Won, J.: Similarity search of time-warped subsequences Via a suffix tree (2002), doi: 10.1016/S0306-4379(02)00102-3
10. Geetha, M., D'Souza, R.J.: Discovery of Frequent Closed Itemsets using Reduced Pattern Count Tree. In: Proceedings of the World Congress on Engineering, WCE 2008, London, U.K, July 2-4, vol. I (2008)

Ontology Based Conceptual Framework of E-Learning System –The Future Perspective

N. Vanjulavalli

Department of Computer Science and Applications,
Periyar Maniammai University, Thanjavur
vanjulavallisn@gmail.com

Abstract. The e-learning community is aiming at having much more effective services than which is currently provided by any one of the available computer aided tutoring or learning management systems. Students and researchers need vast amount of material and spend considerable amount of time trying to learn about a particular subject or find relevant information. The success of the web information accessing has encouraged the researchers in the field of Intelligent Tutoring Systems (ITS) and LMS to focus on issues of interoperability and reuse. Ontologies are used and addressed by the community as an important requirement to define content semantics; assure the interoperability between educational systems. The use of ontologies and the advent of intelligent services for developing the web content, web filters, intelligent search engines and other applications are transforming the web of information into the semantic web. The aim of this paper describes the role of ontologies in the web learning management systems and the standards for describing, developing, exchanging, accessing, annotating, combining and qualifying educational resources. We conclude this paper by provoking the future ideas of research in the areas of ontologies and e-learning system.

Keywords: Ontology, Semantic web, Knowledge models.

1 Introduction

E-learning is just in time education integrated with high velocity chains. It aims at replacing old fashioned time/place/content predetermined learning with a just in time/customized/on-demand process of learning. It requires changes in the organizational behavior establishing a culture of "Learn in the morning, do in the afternoon". Thus an IT platform, which enables efficient implementation of such a learning infrastructure, is also needed. With wireless and mobile technologies, it is possible to realize anytime, anywhere, any way, any device for e-learning and educating.

The term ontology is originated from philosophy, where ontology is a semantic account of existence. Information on the web is commonly represented in natural language for human understanding. In order for the computer to understand its meaning it is necessary to represent the information in a form that can be semantically and syntactically. Such representations help in the processes of analyzing, extracting and integrating information on the web, making it easier the creation of solid knowledge

R. Kannan and F. Andres (Eds.): ICDEM 2010, LNCS 6411, pp. 125–130, 2012.
© Springer-Verlag Berlin Heidelberg 2012

bases that intelligent services can rely on to support users needs. The ontology is to formally describe shared meaning of the used vocabulary. In fact ontology constraints the set of possible mapping between the symbols and their meanings. But the shared understanding problem in e-learning occurs on several aspects of document usage. The shared understanding problem in e-learning occurs when one tries to define the content of a learning document in the process of providing learning materials as well as in the process of accessing to particular learning material.

Ontology as an informal conceptual system in the context of e-learning means the presence of an conceptual system to underlie a particular knowledge.

From an Artificial intelligence point of view, ontology can be seen as "The basic structure or armature around a knowledge base can be built". It means that ontologies try to explain how the world is configured by introducing a system of critical categories and their intrinsic relations which allows a shared understanding and semantic interoperability. It provides a set of fundamental concepts that includes the vocabulary, the semantic interconnections between concepts and simple rules of inference for some specific task or domain.

2 E-Learning and Semantic Web

The great success of the current www leads to a new challenge: a huge amount of data is interpretable by humans only, machine support is limited. Berner's lee suggests enhancing the web by machine processable information which supports the user in his tasks. For instance today's search engines are currently quite powerful but still return to offer too large or inadequate list of hits.

Semantic web technology can improve the effectiveness of the digital resource sharing. By using an ontology inference service, searching no longer need to be constrained to matching the content only, but also by inferring the true meaning of the concept it is possible to retrieve all knowledge equivalent resources.

The machine process able information can point the search engine to the relevant page that can improve the precision. To attain this goal the semantic web will be built up in different levels: Unicode/ Unified Resource Identifiers, XML, RDF ontologies, logical proof and so on. The important property of the semantic web architecture enabled by a set of suitable agents, establishes a powerful approach to satisfy the e-learning systems. Since it provides all means for e-learning ,ontology development, ontology based annotation of learning materials , the competition in learning courses and proactive of the learning materials through e-learning portals.

3 Metadata

Metadata means data about data to describe and how and when and by whom a particular set of data was collected, and how the data is formatted. Meta data is essential for understanding information stored in data warehouses and has become increasingly important in XML-based web applications. Metadata is structured information that describes, explains, locates, or makes it easier to retrieve, use, or manage an information resource.

Metadata contains object, person, time, subject, space and event. They make knowledge become static or dynamic and always include the following nine categories. General, lifecycle, meta-metadata, technological, educational, rights, relation, annotation and classification.

Learning object metadata describes learning resources using the following nine categories:

1. General: describe the general information of learning resource.
2. Lifecycle : describe the history and current state of learning resource and its evolution information
3. Metadata: describe the specific information about the metadata record itself, for example, this metadata record is created by whom, etc.
4. Technical: describe the technical requirements and characteristic of learning resource.
5. Educational: describe the key educational or pedagogical characteristics of the learning resource.
6. Rights: describe the intellectual property rights and conditions of use for the learning resources.
7. Relation: define the relationships among this resource and other targeted resource.
8. Annotation: provide comments on the educational use of learning resource, for example, this annotation is created by whom.
9. Classification; describe classification criteria and hierarchy of learning resource

4 Analysis of the Method for Building Ontology

There are various methodologies followed in the development of ontology. The skeletal methodology defines four main phases.

1. Identifying a purpose and scope
2. Building ontology capture(ontology coding, reusing existing ontology)
3. Evaluation(Verification and Validation)
4. Documentation

It provides with initial guidelines for ontology development; clarity for effective communication in future, coherence, extensibility, minimal ontological commitment.

According to Natalaya F.Roy it is a seven step method that describes the process of developing ontology in the following steps.

1. Determine the domain and scope of the ontology.
2. Consider reusing existing ontologies.
3. Enumerate important terms in the ontologies.
4. Define the classes and the class hierarchy.
5. Define the properties of classes-slots.
6. Define the facets of the slots.
7. Create instances.

In the process of developing ontology the first step is acquiring the domain knowledge (specification), the second step is designing the conceptual structure, the relationship between the concepts and the third step is ontology implementation and formation. Ontology evaluation and documentation also plays a major role in development process.

5 Knowledge Engineering and Ontology

Ontology Engineering is a subfield of Knowledge Engineering that studies the methods and methodologies for building ontologies. It researches the ontology development process, the ontology life cycle, the methods and methodologies for building ontologies and the tools suite and languages that support them. Ontology Engineering is still a relatively immature discipline so knowledge Engineering field uses the IEEE 1074-2006 standard for its use. It follows the software development lifecycle method. The ontology is developed mainly for knowledge acquisition. To implement it specification and conceptualization are needed. Evaluation works on Implementation and maintenance phase. Documentation works throughout the whole ontology development life cycle.

A brief description of Knowledge Engineering approach is presented below:

1. Identify the purpose and requirements specification: Concerns to clearly identify the ontology purpose, scope and its indented use, that is, the competence of the ontology.
2. Ontology acquisition: The goal is to capture the domain concepts based on the ontology competence. The relevant domain entities (e.g. concepts, relations, slots and role) should be identified and organized into hierarchy structure. The phase involves three steps as follows: i) Enumerate the important concepts and terms in the domain ii) Define concepts, properties and relations of concepts, and organize them into hierarchy structure iii) Consider reusing existing ontology.
3. Ontology Implementation: Aims to explicitly represent the conceptualization captured in a formal language.
4. Evaluation/Check: The Ontology must be evaluated to check whether it satisfies the specification requirements. It should be evaluated in relation to the ontology competence and ontology design criteria. The competency questions play an essential role in the evaluation of the completeness of the ontology, especially when considering the axioms.
5. Documentation: All the ontology development must be documented, including purposes, requirements, textual descriptions of the conceptualization and formal ontology. An approach to document on ontology is to use a hypertext, allowing browsing along term definitions, examples and its formalizations including the axioms.

The development and deployment of ontologies is not an easy task. It requires sophisticated methodology and still sometimes it is more an art rather than technology. In educational domain the problem of building ontologies has been tackled by different research groups providing many different approaches to deal with ontology development.

Ontology editors typically offer a graphical interface where it is possible to create / edit ontologies looking deeply on the fundamental concepts, their attributes. Properties and relationships, without making too much attention about how to represent them in a formal language such as OWL or RDF/RDFs. Free ontology editors currently available that can be used for educational purposes are TM4L, HOZO, Onto Edit and Protégé.

6 Case Study: Development of C Programming Ontology

In the process of development of C programming ontology we identify the purpose and requirements specification, ontology acquisition, implementation and evaluation.

The first phase is a step towards creation of sharable and reusable adaptive educational systems. The ontology as a conceptual courseware structure any greatly enrich the teaching process , also providing students an organizing axis to help them mentally mark their visions in the information hyperspace of the domain knowledge.

The second phase concentrates on working with the enumeration of important concepts and terms for teaching C programming course. It is followed by the definition of concepts, properties and relation of concepts. Taxonomic (is-a and part –of) relationship and non taxonomic relationship (participant –in).

Then at the next stage implementation of C programming ontology is done by organizing the concepts according to is-a, part-of and participant-in relations.

At the final stage of the development of c programming ontology evaluation is done from both perspectives as a knowledge base framework and as an interface framework. The structural consistency as a domain knowledge representation and the quality of ontology-based interface is to be evaluated on the subjective and objective levels.

7 Future Research Challenges and Directions

Semantic web has a big potential for improving technology enhanced learning in many respects. However the semantic web is still in its infancy we believe that one of the technologies that will help anytime, Anywhere, any body learning is ontology engineering which is a new knowledge generation technology to help people organize knowledge in a computer understandable manner.

Different research groups have been involved in ontology engineering research in recent years. Ontology engineering enables us to build the so called theory-aware systems, which can help learners to structure learning materials compliant with instructional learning theories and guide them to perform collaborative learning. The two other research questions are to develop an e- learning system where feedback is based on ontologies and these ontologies can be changed or reused, adopted and or extended. The focus in this research will be on the representation of ontologies using the language, grammar, grammar analysis techniques, algorithms and Artificial Intelligence testing to create feedback.

8 Conclusion

Semantic web technologies and applications are getting increasingly popular and adapted in different fields including education. Some of the distinctive features are:

1. More adaptive and personalized learning environments.
2. A better use of pedagogical to enhance instruction/learning.
3. Effective information sharing, storage and retrieval.
4. New form of collaboration with peers.

The ontology based search service enables customized search. The improved search performance using ontologies will extend reusability of learning contents and provide more systematic learning for learners. It is required to build domain ontologies for all subjects in future.

References

1. Boyce, S., Pahl, C.: Developing Domain Ontologies for Course Content. Educational Technology & Society 10(3), 275–288 (2007)
2. Dzemydiene, D., Lina Tankeleviciene, C.: On the development of domain ontology for distance learningcourse. In: 20th EURO Mini Conference Continuous Optimization and Knowledge-Based Technologies (EurOPT 2008) (2008)
3. Yas, A., Alsultanny, C.: e-learning system overview based on the semantic web. The Electronic Journal of e-learning (2006)
4. Garcia-Castro, R., Gomez-Perez, A., Munoz-Garcia, O.: The Semantic Web Framework: A Component-Based Framework for the Development of Semantic Web Applications. In: 19th International Conference on Database and Expert Systems Application, pp. 185–189 (2008) ISBN: 978-0-7695-3299-8
5. Luo Zhong, C.: Ontology and metadata for e-learning. In: International Conference on Computer Science and Engineering (2008)
6. Chang, B., Ham, D.-H., Moon, D.-S., Choi, Y.S., Jaehyuk Cha, C.: Educational Information Search Service Using Ontology. In: Seventh IEEE International Conference on Advanced Learning Technologies (ICALT 2007), pp. 414–415 (2007)
7. Raymond Sisun, R.: Using Domain ontologies for online learning, AAAI technical report (2006)

Developing Indian Medicinal Plant Ontology
Using OWL and SWRL

A. Raja Mohan and G. Arumugam

Department of Computer Science, Madurai Kamaraj University, Madurai, India
{prithivimohan,gurusamyarumugam}@gmail.com

Abstract. Semantic web, future web, will revolutionize the world with machine knowledge processing capabilities. Ontology is the building block of the semantic web. Earlier research on ontology design methodologies shows that manual construction of ontology is a complex process and it is very hard for a designer to develop a consistent ontology. In this paper, we present a methodology based on the usage of protégé 3.4.4 for developing and inferring the Indian medicinal plant ontology. Medicinal Plant Ontology is one of the useful ontology for people. Medicinal plants are belonging to the medicine category. The medicinal plants are very useful for curing diseases. The parts of the plants are also useful as a medicine for curing the diseases. The people should know all the properties of the plants such as height, color, taste. As per the design of Indian medicinal plant ontology, the Plant is implemented as a subclass of owl:Thing. Flowering plants, Non-Flowering plants, Parts of plants, Special names are implemented as a subclass of Plant. F_Plant_names is implemented as a subclass of Flowering plants. This paper describes the features of Protégé 3.4.4, the usage of inference rules framed by using SWRL, query by SQWRL and the inconsistency checking by Pellet reasoner.

Keywords: WWW Semantic Web Ontology Protégé Medicinal Plant.

1 Introduction

A new form of web content that is meaningful to computers will unleash a revolution of new abilities. The Semantic Web is an extension of the current web in which information is given well-defined meaning, better enabling computers and people to work in co-operation [1]. This is mainly accomplished by the use of ontologies which contain terms and relationships between terms that have been agreed upon by members of a certain domain. These agreed upon ontologies can then be published to be available for use by other members of the domain. Typical ontologies are: Dublin Core, http://dublincore.org/, UMLS, http://www.nlm.nih.gov/research/umls/, Open Biological Ontologies, http://obo.sourceforge.net/, The Upper Cyc Ontology, http://www.cyc.com/, Agrovoc, http://www.fao.org/agrovoc/. Indian Medicinal plants are highly useful in the Indian Siddha and Ayurvedic medicine. The medicinal plants and its parts are very useful as a medicine for curing diseases. All the properties of the plants such as height, color, taste might be known to the users and the practitioners.

R. Kannan and F. Andres (Eds.): ICDEM 2010, LNCS 6411, pp. 131–138, 2012.
© Springer-Verlag Berlin Heidelberg 2012

2   Knowledge Representation in Medicinal Plant Domain

Knowledge representation is the symbolization or formalization of the knowledge of the world. Various Knowledge representation methods are predicate logics, production rules, framework, ontology and so on. In this paper, we use the ontology and the rules to represent the medicinal plant knowledge. Ontology is an engineering artifact that is constituted by a specific vocabulary used to describe a certain reality (domain), plus a set of explicit assumptions regarding the intended meaning of the vocabulary. Insufficiency in expressivity and reasoning features are the problems affect the perfect-ness of ontologies. Rules can lay the foundation for expression and reasoning capabilities. Adding rules with the ontologies will solve the expressivity and reasoning problems.

2.1   Ontology and Its Need

Ontology defines the basic terms and relations comprising the vocabulary of a topic area as well as the rules for combining terms and relations to define extensions to the vocabulary [2]. It is necessary to define web resources more precisely and make them more amenable to machine processing. Ontology is classified as top level ontology, domain ontology, task or activity ontology and application ontology [3]. Top level ontology describes the very general concepts which are independent of a particular domain. Domain ontology describes the vocabulary related to a generic domain by specialize the concepts introduced in the top level ontology. Task ontology describes the vocabulary related to a generic task by specialize the concepts introduced in the top level ontology. Application ontology describes the concepts which correspond to roles played by domain entities while performing a certain tasks. The reasons for developing ontology are to analyze the domain knowledge, to enable the reuse of domain knowledge, to make the domain assumptions explicitly, to separate the domain knowledge from the operational knowledge and to share the common understanding of the structure of information among the people or the software agents.

2.1.1   Medicinal Plant Ontology
The medicinal plant ontology is defined as, MP = <MPC, MPP, MPI, MPR, MPA> where MP-ontology is the ontology which describes the concepts and their relations in the medicinal plant domain, MPC is a collection of concepts, MPP is a collection of attributes related to the concepts in MPC, MPI is a collection of individuals or instances of the concepts in MPC, MPR is a collection of relations between the concepts in MPC, MPA is the collection of axioms which are used to restrict the attributes and relations. Ontology can be constructed manually [4] or semi-automatically [5]. Manual extraction has been done for medicinal plant ontology.

2.1.2   Rules and Steps for Designing Ontology
The fundamental rules for designing the ontology are 1) There is no one correct way to model a domain, there are many alternatives. The best solution always depends on the application, 2) Ontology development is necessarily an iterative and a dynamic process [6] and 3) Concepts in the ontology should be close to objects in the domain of interest.

The steps to be followed for designing the ontology [7]

1. Determine the domain and scope of the ontology: Developers should determine the domain of interest and define the scope of the ontology.
2. Consider the reuse of existing ontology: Developers should reuse if ontology exist, otherwise develop it.
3. Enumerate important terms in the ontology: Developers should write down a list of all terms in the domain, either to make statements about or to explain to a user.
4. Define the classes and the class hierarchy: Classes has to be defined with appropriate names. The hierarchies have to be defined in three different ways, viz. top-down, bottom-up and hybrid. A top-down approach starts with the most general classes in the domain and subsequent specialization of the classes. A bottom-up approach starts with the most specific classes, the leaves of the hierarchy, with subsequent grouping of these classes into more general classes. A hybrid approach is a combination of the top-down and bottom-up approaches
5. Define the properties of classes: Properties describe the internal structure of classes. The object property relates one class to another class. The data type property assigns the value type to the class. The annotation property describes the generic comments of the class.
6. Define the facets of the properties: Properties can have different facets describing the value type, allowed values, the number of the values (cardinality), and other features of the values, the properties can have.
7. Create instances: At last create the individuals or instances of the classes.

2.1.3 Ontology Editors
Ontology editors are tools that enable the users for inspecting, browsing, codifying, and modifying ontology and support in this way the ontology development and maintenance task [8]. Existing editors vary in the complexity of the underlying knowledge model, usability, scalability, etc. Nevertheless, all of them provide enough support for the initial ontology development. Protégé [9], OntoEdit [10], OilEd [11], WebODE [12], and Ontolingua [13] are some examples of ontology editors.

2.2 Protégé

Protégé is a free, open-source platform that provides a growing user community with a suite of tools to construct domain models and knowledge-based applications with ontologies. Further, Protégé can be extended by way of a plug-in Architecture and a Java-based Application Programming Interface for building knowledge-based tools and applications.

2.2.1 Protégé OWL Editor
It enables the users to build ontology for the Semantic Web. OWL ontology may include descriptions of classes, properties and their instances. Protégé-OWL editor enables the users to Load and save OWL and RDF ontologies, Edit and visualize classes, properties, and SWRL rules, Define logical class characteristics as OWL expressions, Execute reasoners such as description logic classifiers and Edit OWL individuals for Semantic Web markup.

2.2.2 SWRL

Semantic Web Rule Language is a rule language. The SWRL-Tab is a development environment for working with SWRL rules in Protégé-OWL. It supports the editing and execution of SWRL rules. It provides a set of libraries that can be used in rules, including libraries to interoperate with XML documents, and spreadsheets, and libraries with mathematical, string, RDFS, and temporal operators. The SWRL-Tab has several software components, like, SWRL-Editor which supports editing and saving of SWRL rules in OWL ontology, SWRL Built-in Libraries which includes the core SWRL built-ins defined in the SWRL Submission and built-ins for querying OWL ontology.

2.2.3 SQWRL

Semantic Query enhanced Web Rule Language is built on SWRL rule language [14]. It takes rules' antecedent as a pattern specification for a query and takes rules' consequent as a retrieval specification. Any valid SWRL antecedent is a valid SQWRL pattern specification. That means SQWRL places no restriction on the left side of a query. It uses SWRL built-in libraries as an extension point [15]. SWRL-Editor can be used to generate and edit the queries. To execute the query SQ-Tab has to be added [16], by adding the jar file jess 7.1p2 in the protégé plug-in directory. The core operator is sqwrl:select. The select operator takes one or more arguments, which are variables in the pattern specification of the query, and builds a table using the arguments as the columns of the table. The built-ins like, sqwrl:count, sqwrl:orderBy, sqwrl:avg can be used as in SQL. SQWRL does not support sub-queries, but it is achieved by using the intermediate inferences made by SWRL rules. This mechanism is used to decompose the complex queries. The sqwrl:makeSet built-in is used to create a set. Using this set and sqwrl built-ins like, union, difference, isEmpty, size and intersection are used to do set operations. The SQWRL query tab provides a graphical interface to display the results of SQWRL queries.

3   Structure of MP-Ontology

In Indian medicinal plant ontology, Plant is a subclass of owl:Thing. Flowering plants, Non-Flowering plants, Partsofplants, Specialnames are subclasses of Plant. F_Plant_names is subclass of Flowering plants. The subclasses of F_Plant_names are Arattaip, Atutinappalaip, Betelnutp, Cabbagep, Garlicp, Groundnutp, Jackfruitp, Karumpanaip, Lady'sfingerp, Muntirip, Mustardp, Neemp, Nilavembup, Onionp, Papayap, Pineapplep, Pusanikkaip, Redgramp, Sugarapplep, Teaplantp. NF_Plant_names is a subclass of Non-flowering plants. The Subclasses of NF_Plant_names are Bamboop, Betelp, Chirpinep, Devilsugarcanep, Dhubgrassp, Horsetailp, Intappanaip, Mossesp, Myrrhp, Nutgrassp, Sacrificialgrassp, Sugarcanep, Wildsugarcanep. The subclasses of Partsofplants are Fruit uses, General uses, Oil uses, Seed uses, Stem uses, Leaf uses, Root uses, Null. The Subclasses of Specialnames are Botanicalname and Familyname.

The Object properties in MP-ontology are hasBotanicalname, hasFamilyname, hasFruituses, hasGeneraluses, hasLeafuses, hasoiluses, hasRootuses, hasSeeduses, hasstemuses,   is_a_Fruit_uses_of,   is_a_Leaf_uses_of,   is_a_Oil_uses_of, is_a_Root_uses_of, is_a_Seed_uses_of, is_a_Stem_uses_of, is_a_General_uses_of, whoseBotanicalname, whoseFamilyname. The Data type properties in MP-ontology are hasColour, hasHeight, hasTaste.

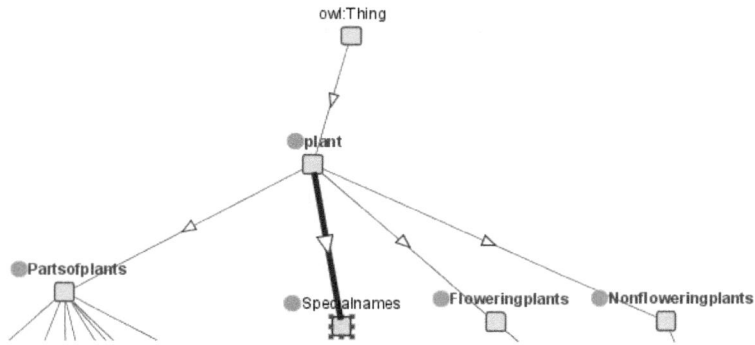

Fig. 1. Class tree of the MP-ONTOLOGY

3.1 MP-Ontology Based Reasoning

In our work, Pellet reasoner[17] is used to check the consistency of the ontology, classifying the classes and performing the individual detection etc. checking the consistency is used to identify the semantic contradiction which makes ambiguity in the description of the domain. Classifying the classes is used to test the subsumption relationship between classes and classes are classified into different level in the class hierarchy. Reclassification is necessary if inconsistency exists. Individual detection mechanism determines the appropriate concepts for certain individuals and classify the individuals according to the classes.

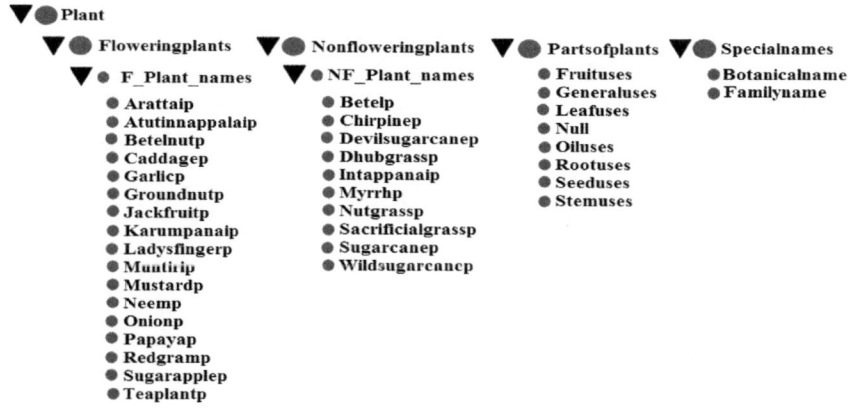

Fig. 2. Class Hierarchies in MP-ONTOLOGY

3.2 Rule Based Reasoning

In this work, SWRL is used for creating rules and SQWRL is used for supporting OWL queries.

Examples: The following SQWRL queries retrieve the information required by the users

To display the color of the plants

```
hasColour(?x,?y)→sqwrl:selectDistinct(?y)
```

To display the Non-flowering plant names whose family name is Poaceae, we can write

```
hasFamilyname(?x,Poaceae)→sqwrl:select(?x)
```

To display the general uses of the plant betel, we can write

```
Betelp(?x)∧hasGeneraluses(?x,?y)→sqwrl:count(?y)
```

To display the Botanical name and Family name of the plants with the column names, we can write

```
hasBotanicalname(?x,?y)∧hasFamilyname(?x,?z)→
sqwrl:select(?x,?y,?z)∧sqwrl:columnNames("Flowernames",
"Botanicalname","Familyname")
```

The following queries retrieve the botanical name for the individual cabbage and the Fruit uses for the individual cabbage respectively.

```
Cabbagep(?x)∧hasBotanicalname(?x,?y) → sqwrl:select(?y)
```

```
Cabbagep(Cabbage)∧hasFruituses(Cabbage,?x)→
sqwrl:select(?x)
```

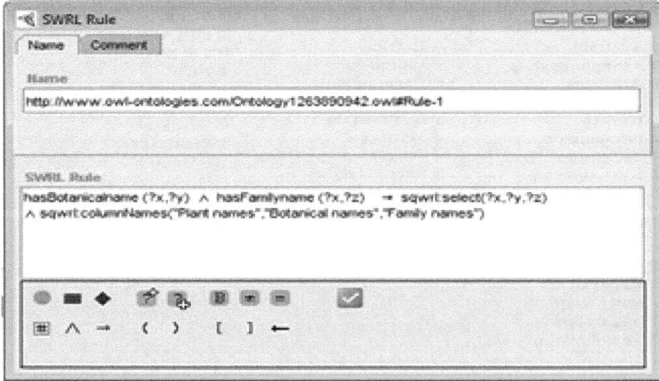

Fig. 3. SWRL Rule Editor

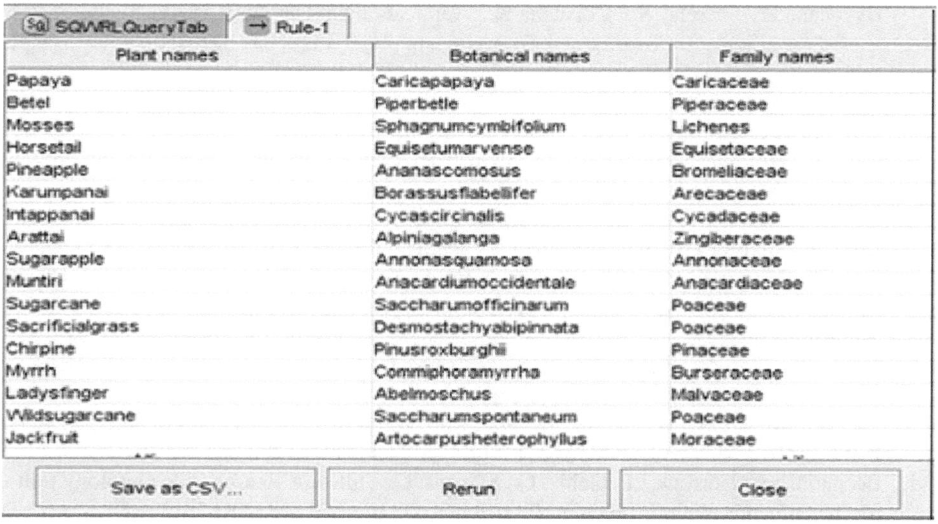

Plant names	Botanical names	Family names
Papaya	Caricapapaya	Caricaceae
Betel	Piperbetle	Piperaceae
Mosses	Sphagnumcymbifolium	Lichenes
Horsetail	Equisetumarvense	Equisetaceae
Pineapple	Ananascomosus	Bromeliaceae
Karumpanai	Borassusflabellifer	Arecaceae
Intappanai	Cycascircinalis	Cycadaceae
Arattai	Alpiniagalanga	Zingiberaceae
Sugarapple	Annonasquamosa	Annonaceae
Muntiri	Anacardiumoccidentale	Anacardiaceae
Sugarcane	Saccharumofficinarum	Poaceae
Sacrificialgrass	Desmostachyabipinnata	Poaceae
Chirpine	Pinusroxburghii	Pinaceae
Myrrh	Commiphoramyrrha	Burseraceae
Ladysfinger	Abelmoschus	Malvaceae
Wildsugarcane	Saccharumspontaneum	Poaceae
Jackfruit	Artocarpusheterophyllus	Moraceae

| Save as CSV... | Rerun | Close |

Fig. 4. SQWRL Tab and Query Result Interface

4 Conclusions

In this paper, we have attempted the semantic web approach for building the application for alternative medicine domain. The owl based ontology for Indian medicinal plants, MP-ONTOLOGY, was constructed with protégé 3.4.4, after following the listed steps for the ontology-development process. We have exploited the use of SWRL and SQWRL for inferring the constructed MP-ONTOLOGY. Consistencies checking of ontology and classification of classes have been done with the support of Pellet reasoner. Ontology design is a creative process and no two ontologies designed by different people would be the same. The potential applications of the ontology and the designer's understanding and view of the domain will undoubtedly affect ontology design choices. It is hoped that this ontology will be of immense use to the users and the practitioners of alternative medicine. In future, we will enhance the ontology with the local names of the plants with the natural language support. Also we will attempt to integrate this ontology with the other ontologies for alternative medicine and to evaluate the ontology.

References

1. Berners-Lee, T., Hendler, J., Lassila, O.: The Semantic Web. Scientific American, 28–37 (2001)
2. Neches, R., Fikes, R.E., Finin, T., Gruber, T.R., Swartout, W.R.: Enabling Technology for Knowledge Sharing. AI Magazine 12(3), 36–56 (1991)
3. Maedche, A.: Ontology Learning for the Semantic Web. Kluwer Academic Publishers, USA (2002)

4. Hyvonen, E., Saarela, S., Viljanen, K.: Application of Ontology Based Techniques to View-based Semantic Search and Browsing. In: First European Semantic Web Symposium on The Semantic Web and Applications, pp. 92–106. Springer, Berlin (2004)
5. Ohno, M.L., Gennari, J.H., Murphy, S.N., Jain, N.L.: The Guideline Interchange Format. American Medical Informatics Association 5, 357–372 (1998)
6. Das, A., Wu, W., McGuinness, D.: Industrial Strength Ontology Management. In: The Emerging Semantic Web. IOS Press (2002)
7. Noy, N., McGuinness, D.L.: Ontology Development 101: a Guide to Creating Your First Ontology. Stanford Medical Informatics Technical Report. SMI-2001-0880 (2001)
8. Sure, Y.: On-To-Knowledge – Ontology Based Knowledge Management Tools and their Application. German Journal Kuenstliche Intelligenz, Special Issue on Knowledge Management (2002)
9. The Protégé Project, http://protege.stanford.edu
10. Sure, Y., Erdmann, M., Angele, J., Staab, S., Studer, R., Wenke, D.: OntoEdit: Collaborative Ontology Engineering for the Semantic Web. In: Horrocks, I., Hendler, J. (eds.) ISWC 2002. LNCS, vol. 2342, p. 221. Springer, Heidelberg (2002)
11. Bechhofer, S., Horrocks, I., Goble, C., Stevens, C.: OilEd: A Reason-able Ontology Editor for the Semantic Web. In: Baader, F., Brewka, G., Eiter, T. (eds.) KI 2001. LNCS (LNAI), vol. 2174, pp. 396–408. Springer, Heidelberg (2001)
12. Arpírez, J.C., Corcho, O., Fernández-López, M., Gómez-Pérez, A.: WebODE: a Scalable Workbench for Ontological Engineering. In: KCAP 2001, Victoria, Canada (2001)
13. Farquhar, A., Fikes, R., Rice, J.: The Ontolingua Server: a Tool for Collaborative Ontology Construction. In: Tenth Knowledge Acquisition for Knowledge-Based Systems Workshop, Banff, Canada (1996)
14. SWRL Submission, http://www.w3.org/submission/SWRL
15. SWRL Bulit-ins, http://www.daml.org/2004/04/Swrl/builtins.html
16. SWRLTab Plug-ins, http://protege.cm3.net/cgi-bin/wiki.pl?SWRLTab
17. Pellet Reasoner, http://www.pellet.owldl.com

Detection of Web Users' Opinion from Normal and Short Opinionated Words

K.M. Anil Kumar and Suresha

Department of Studies in Computer Science
University of Mysore
Manasagangothri
Mysore, India
{anilkmsjce,sureshabm}@yahoo.co.in

Abstract. In this paper we present an approach to identify opinion of web users from an opinionated text and to classify web user's opinion into positive or negative. Web users document their opinion in opinionated sites, shopping sites, personal pages etc., to express and share their opinion with other web users. The opinion expressed by web users may be on diverse topics such as politics, sports, products, movies etc. These opinions will be very useful to others such as, leaders of political parties, selection committees of various sports, business analysts and other stake holders of products, directors and producers of movies as well as to the other concerned web users. Today web users express their opinion using normal words and short words. These short words, such as gud for good, grt8 for great etc., are very popular and are used by a large number of web users to document their opinion. We use semantic based approach to find users opinion from both normal and short words. Our approach first detects subjective phrases and uses these phrases along with intensifiers and diminishers to obtain semantic orientation scores. The semantic orientation score of these phrases is used to identify user's opinion from an opinionated text. Our approach provides better results than the other approaches on different data sets.

Keywords: Artificial Intelligence, Sentiment Analysis, Opinion Mining.

1 Introduction

The rapid development of web and its related technologies have fueled the popularity of the web with all sections of society. The web has been used by many such as governments, business houses, industries, educational institutions etc., to reach the masses. The individual user's are provided with an opportunity to obtain and share knowledge.

Today many web users document their opinion on different platforms like discussions forums, opinionated sites, e-commerce sites, blogs, personal web pages etc., the opinion expressed may be in a single line or multiple lines in an opinionated text. For last few years, web has seen new forms of written communications, which are quite popular with vast section of the web users. One such form of written communication popular with web users is using short words.

For example, word like excellent is written in short words as xllent, xlent etc., the use of short words are found to be very popular as it conveys message at less time.

R. Kannan and F. Andres (Eds.): ICDEM 2010, LNCS 6411, pp. 139–145, 2012.
© Springer-Verlag Berlin Heidelberg 2012

The limitation is that there are no standards for short words, making it very difficult for processing. A few web users use one or more short words in their communication and opinionated text are no exceptions. Following are the examples of opinionated text with normal and short opinionated words collected from opinionated site review centre and retained in same form.

Example 1. *Well it is one of the most **exciting** phones to ever come out. I do think it might be behind the times compared to older phones from Nokia like the N95 etc but it is still a **nice** phone.*

Example 2. *A **gr8** TV for the dollar. Samsung has designed and produced a **5n** TV. The picture quality is **excellent** with analog and high definition signal. Sound quality is **gud** to **excellent**. It has a wide angle of picture side vision. It is a very compact design for a TV of this size. Instructions are very **xllent** with simple set-up.*

Example 1 conveys opinion of a web user with normal opinionated words. Similarly, example 2 conveys opinion of a web user using normal and short opinionated words. The words in bold represent normal opinionated words, those that are bold and under-lined represents short opinionated words. The afore used short words like gr8, 5n, gud, xllent are commonly used to represent normal words great, fine, good and excellent.

In this paper we focus on detecting opinions expressed by web users using normal and short opinion words only on products. The remainder of this paper is organized as follows: In Section 2 we give a brief description of related work. Then, in Section 3, we discuss our methodology. In Section 4, the experimental results are discussed. Conclusion is discussed in Section 5.

2   Related Work

Opinion mining is a recent sub discipline of information retrieval which is not about the topic of a document, but with the opinion it expresses [1]. We have referred many literature on opinion mining, due to space constraint only a few are below mentioned.

Hatzivassiloglou and McKeown [11] have attempted to predict semantic orientation of adjectives by analyzing pairs of adjectives (i.e., adjective pair is adjectives conjoined by and, or, but, either-or, neither-nor) extracted from a large unlabelled document set.

Turney [9] has obtained remarkable results on the sentiment classification of terms by considering the algebraic sum of the orientations of terms as representative of the orientation of the document.

Wang and Araki [12] proposed a variation of the Semantic Orientation-PMI algo-rithm for Japanese for mining opinion in weblogs. They applied Turney method to Japanese webpage and found results slanting heavily towards positive opinion. They proposed balancing factor and neutral expression detection method and reported a well balanced result.

Kamps et al [7] have focused on the use of lexical relations defined in WordNet. They defined a graph on the adjectives contained in the intersection between the Turney's seed set and WordNet, adding a link between two adjectives whenever WordNet indicate the presence of a synonymy relation between them. The authors defined a distance measure d (t1, t2) between terms t1 and t2, which amounts to the length of the shortest path that connects t1 and t2. The orientation of a term is then determined by its relative distance from the seed terms good and bad.

Opinion observer [5] is the sentiment analysis system for analyzing and comparing opinions on the web. The product features are extracted from noun or noun phrases by the association miner. They use adjectives as opinion words and assign prior polarity of these by WordNet exploring method. The polarity of an opinion expression which is a sentence containing one or more feature terms and one or more opinion words is assigned a dominant orientation. The extracted features are stored in a database in the form of feature, number of positive expression and number of negative expression.

Our work differs from the afore mentioned studies, by finding opinion of a user not only from normal opinionated words, but also from short opinionated words in an opinionated text. Our work uses not only adjectives but other part-of-speech like verb, adverb etc., to capture opinionated words for efficient opinion detection.

3   Methodology

We collected four data sets for our work. The first data set consist of 250 opinionated texts collected from results of various search engines. The second data set is collection of 400 opinionated texts obtained from different opinionated sites like Amazon, CNet, review centre, bigadda, rediff etc. The third data set consisting of 140 opinionated texts is obtained from [2]. The fourth data set consisting of 100 opinionated texts is obtained from different opinionated sites.

The opinionated texts in these data sets are only on products and contained 50 % positive and 50 % negative opinionated texts. The first three data sets contain opinionated texts in which opinions are expressed using normal opinionated words, while the last data set contains opinonated text with normal and short opinionated words. In our approach opinionated texts from data sets 1, 2 and 3 are subjected to a part of speech tagger. The tagger used is Monty Tagger [6]. The tagged opinionated texts are then subjected to extraction patterns to obtain opinionated phrases that are likely to contain user's opinion. Table 1 shows a few extraction patterns used to find opinionated phrases, where JJ represent adjective and NN/NNS, VB/VBD/VBN/VBG, RB/RBR/RBS represent different forms of noun, verb and adverb.

An initial study undertaken by [4] showed that the extracted phrases also contain neutral phrases which can influence opinion of an opinionated text. In order to remove these neutral phrases we use Sentiment Product Lexicon (SPL) for capturing only subjective

Table 1. Extraction patterns

Slno.	First Word	Second Word	Third Word
1	JJ	NN or NNS	anything
2	RB,RBR or RBS	JJ	not NN nor NNS
3	JJ	JJ	not NN nor NNS
4	NN or NNS	JJ	not NN or NNS
5	RB,RBR or RBS	VB,VBD,VBN or VBG	anything

or opinionated phrases. Sentiment Product Lexicon is collection of General lexicon and Domain lexicon. General lexicon maintains a list of positive and negative words by collecting opinion words that are positive or negative from sources. Domain lexicon maintains a list of positive or negative words from the domain context. We found words like cool, revolutionary etc., appeared in negative list of General lexicon. These words were used to express positive opinion by web users. Hence we created a domain lexicon to have opinion words from the domain perspective. The details of construction of General lexicon and Domain lexicon are made available in [4].

Consider for example, an opinionated text **This is a bad phone.** When the tagger is applied to input text, we get the following tagged text **This/DT is/VBZ a/DT bad/JJ phone/NN ./.**. Application of extraction patterns from Table 1 will obtain **bad/JJ phone/NN** as opinionated phrase from the text. Sentiment Product Lexicon is used to detect neutral phrases. We consider the extracted phrases or words namely word1 and word2 from an opinionated text as neutral if none of the words extracted are found in Sentiment Product Lexicon.

From the above example word1 is bad and word2 is phone. We find whether word2 is in positive or negative list of Domain lexicon. If word2 is present in any one of the list in Domain lexicon, polarity of the word will be similar to polarity of list in which it is found. If it is not in positive or negative list of Domain lexicon, then positive and negative list of General lexicon is consulted to find the polarity of a word.

If word2 is neither present in Domain lexicon nor in General lexicon, we assume word2 to have neutral polarity, in such a case we use word1 instead of word2, and find polarity of word1 similar to polarity of word2 afore discussed. If polarity is found, then polarity is for the phrase consisting of both word1 and word2. If polarity is not found, we assume both word1 and word2 to be neutral. If a word, either word1 or word2, is present in both Domain lexicon and General lexicon, polarity of word will be similar to polarity of Domain lexicon. If word1 is a negator such as not, the polarity of word2 will be opposite to an earlier obtained polarity of word2.

For example the phrase "**not good**", here word1 is **not** and word2 is **good**. The polarity of word2 is positive, since word2 is prefixed by word1 i.e. **not**. The polarity of phrase is negative. We retain only those phrases that have a polarity and discard phrases that are neutral. We assign a score of +2 for positive phrases and -2 for negative phrases. we have used the values as discussed in [8].

The phrases obtained are subjected to a list of intensifiers and diminishers obtained from [10]. The objective is to assign a score to opinionated phrase based on occurrence of phrases that scales positive or negative opinion of the users. For example the opinionated text "**this phone is good**" is different from "**this phone is too good**". Here the phrase **too** is intensifying positive opinion of the user. Similarly, in the text "**This phone is barely good**" the phrase **barely** is dimishing the positive opinion of the user.

When the extraction patterns discussed in Table 1 are applied to the text "**this phone is too good**", the opinionated phrase **too good** is obtained. The SPL also outputs the phrase **too good** as positive opinion phrase with score +2. We pass the positive phrase to a list of intensifiers and diminishers.

Our intuition here is that, intensifiers or diminshers precede opinionated phrase. if the phrase is positive and preceded by an intensifier we add 1 to score of positive phrase(1+2). if the phrase is positive and preceded by an diminisher we subtract 1 to score of positive phrase(1-2). Similarly, if the phrase is negative and preceded by an intensifier we add -1 to score of negative phrase(-1-2). if the phrase is negative and preceded by an diminisher we add 1 to score of negative phrase(1-2). Therefore the score for the phrase **too good** is 3(1+2) and score for phrase **barely good** is 1(-1+2). We are unable to provide more examples because of the page limit guidelines of the conference.

We compute the average semantic orientation of the opinionated text by considering all scores of opinionated phrases as shown in Equation 1. We classify opinionated text as positive, if the average semantic orientation of opinionated text is greater than a threshold and negative when the average semantic orientation is less than a threshold. The threshold used here is 0.

$$SO(OpinionatedText) = \frac{1}{n}\sum_{i=1}^{n}(OpinionatedPhrase_i) \qquad (1)$$

For data set 4 which comprises of opinionated text with normal and short opinionated words. We built a lexicon of short words by collecting different words from different web sites. We collected around 220 short words and were analyzed by a group of 10 engineering students of different courses for identifying potential short words which conveys positive or negative opinion and its equivalent normal words. We add short words and its corresponding normal words into Short Word Lexicon (SWL), when there is 60% agreement by students on short words and its corresponding normal words.

We created a Short Word Lexicon of 170 short opinionated words with 92 positive and 78 negative short words along with normal words. The opinionated texts from data set 4 are subjected to SWL to identify the short words. The short words identified are translated to normal words in an opinionated text. Consider the text " **this is a gr8 phone**". Here gr8 is used to represent great. After part of speech tagging the text, we obtain **this/DT is/VBZ a/DT gr8/CD phone/NN**. Where DT,VBZ,CD and NN corresponds to determiner,verb,cardinal and noun. Application of extraction patterns from Table 1 does not obtain any opinionated phrases. Hence no opinion is obtained from the opinionated text. When we use SWL, the afore mentioned opinionated text is translated to **"this is a great phone"**. After the text is subjected to part speech tagging, we obtain **this/DT is/VBZ a/DT great/JJ phone/NN**. When the extraction patterns are applied, we obtain an opinionated phrase **great/JJ phone/NN**. The opinionated phrase is then subjected to SPL and a list of Intensifiers and diminishers to obtain a score used to find opinion of web users.

4   Experiments and Results

We used afore mentioned approach on different data sets namely data set 1, data set 2, data set 3 and data set 4. We compute the accuracy of our approach by considering true positives and true negatives divided by total number of opinionated texts. True positives represent number of opinionated texts classified correctly as positive, Similarly true negatives represent number of opinionated texts classified correctly as negatives. Table 2 shows accuracy of our approach on different data sets along with other results reported in literature. Table 3 shows accuracy of approach on data set 4 consisting of short words.

We obtained an positive accuracy of 90.85 % and negative accuracy of 88.88 % for Data set 1. An positive accuracy of 87% and negative accuracy of 72% is obatined for Data set 2. Similarly we obtained a positive accuracy of 92.85% and a negative accuracy of 60%for Data set 3. For Data set 4, we obtained a positive accuracy of 86% and a negative accuarcy of 80.28%. Fig. 1 shows positive and negative accuracy obtained by our approach on different data sets. We observe from Fig. 1, negative accuracy obtained is less than that of positive accuracy on all the data sets. This is due to presence of many positive pharses in negative opinionated texts. We found many web users expressed positive opinion on some features of the product, while summarizing the opinion of the product with few negative pharses such as "**i would not recommend this product to**

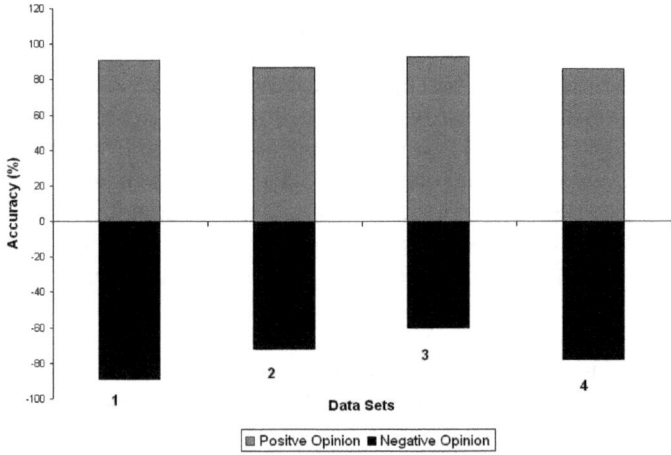

Fig. 1. Summary of Opinions on Different Data sets

Table 2. Results

Slno.	Approach	Number of opinionated text	Accuracy
1	Wang and Araki [12]	400	75%
2	Kennedy and Inkpen[2]	140	69.3%
3	Our approach	250	89.86%
4	Our approach	400	79.5%
5	Our approach	140	76.42
6	Our approach	100	83.14

Table 3. Results on Data set 4

Slno.	Approach	Number of opinionated text	Accuracy
1	Our approach(without consideration of short words)	100	64.40%
2	Our approach(with consideration of short words)	100	83.14%

anyone". The negative opinionated texts in Data set 3 also contained to many positive phrases leading to poor negative accuracy in that data set.

5 Conclusion

We have discussed an approach that detects opinion of a web user from an opinionated texts. The opinion expressed by the web users may be using normal words or short words. Our approach finds opinion of a web user from both normal and short word and classifies opinion as positive opinion or negative opinion. Our approach provides a better result than the other approaches discussed in literature and obtains better results on different data sets.

References

1. Esuli, A., Sebastiani, F.: Determining term subjectivity and term orientation for opinion mining. In: Proceedings of 11th Conference of the European Chapter of the Association for Computational Linguistics, Trento, Italy (2006)
2. Kennedy, A., Inkpen, D.: Sentiment Classification of Movie and Product Reviews Using Contextual Valence Shifters. In: Proceedings of FINEXIN 2005, Workshop on the Analysis of Informal and Formal Information Exchange during Negotiations, Canada (2005)
3. Anil Kumar, K.M., Suresha: Identifying Subjective Phrases From Opinionated Texts Using Sentiment Product Lexicon. International Journal of Advanced Engineering & Applications 2, 263–271 (2010)
4. Anil Kumar, K.M., Suresha: Detection of Neutral Phrases and Polarity Shifting of Few Phrases for Effective Classification of Opinionated Texts. International Journal of Computational Intelligence Research 6, 43–58 (2010)
5. Liu, B., Hu, M., Cheng, J.: Opinion Observer: Analyzing and Comparing Opinions on the Web, Chiba, Japan (2005)
6. Hugo: MontyLingua: An end-to-end natural language processor with common sense (2003)
7. Kamps, J., Marx, M., Mokken, R.J., De Rijke, M.: Using wordnet to measure semantic orientation of adjectives. In: Proceedings of 4th International Conference on Language Resources and Evaluation, Lisbon, Portugal, pp. 1115–1118 (2004)
8. Polanyi, L., Zaenen, A.: Contextual Valence Shifters. In: Computing Attitude and Affect in Text: Theory and Applications, pp. 1–10 (2006)
9. Turney, P.D.: Thumbs up or thumbs down? Semantic orientation applied to unsupervised classification of reviews. In: Proceedings of 40th Annual Meeting of the Association for Computational Linguistics, Philadelphia, US, pp. 417–424 (2002)
10. Stone, P.J.: Thematic text analysis: New agendas for analyzing text content. In: Roberts, C. (ed.) Text Analysis for the Social Sciences. Lawrence Erlbaum, Mahwah (1997)
11. Hatzivassiloglou, V., McKeown, K.R.: Predicting the semantic orientation of adjectives. In: Proceedings of 35th Annual Meeting of the Association for Computational Linguistics, Madrid, Spain, pp. 174–181 (1997)
12. Wang, Araki: Modifying SO-PMI for Japanese Weblog Opinion Mining by Using a Balancing Factor and Detecting Neutral Expressions. In: Proceedings of NAACL HLT 2007, New York, US, pp. 189–192 (2007)

Features for Art Painting Classification Based on Vector Quantization of MPEG-7 Descriptors

Krassimira Ivanova[1], Peter Stanchev[1,2], Evgeniya Velikova[3],
Koen Vanhoof[4], Benoit Depaire[4], Rajkumar Kannan[5],
Iliya Mitov[1], and Krassimir Markov[1]

[1] Institute of Mathematics and Informatics – Bulgarian Academy of Sciences, Sofia, Bulgaria
kivanova@math.bas.bg, mitov@mail.bg, kkmarkov@math.bas.bg
[2] Kettering University, Flint, MI, 48504, USA
pstanche@kettering.edu
[3] Faculty of Mathematics and Informatics, Sofia University, Sofia, Bulgaria
velikova@fmi.uni-sofia.bg
[4] IMOB, Hasselt University, Hasselt, Belgium
koen.vanhoof@uhasselt.be, benoit.depaire@uhasselt.be
[5] Bishop Heber College, India
rajkumarkannan@yahoo.co.in

Abstract. An approach for extracting higher-level visual features for art painting classification based on MPEG-7 descriptors is presented in this paper. The MPEG-7 descriptors give a good presentation of different types of visual features, but are complex structures. This prevents their direct use into standard classification algorithms and thus requires specific processing. Our approach consists of the following steps: (1) the images are tiled into non-overlapping rectangles to capture more detailed information; (2) the tiles of the images are clustered for each MPEG-7 descriptor; (3) vector quantization is used to assign a unique value to each tile, which corresponds to the number of the cluster where the tile belongs to, in order to reduce the dimensionality of the data. Finally, the significance of the attributes and the importance of the underlying MPEG-7 descriptors for class prediction in this domain are analyzed.

Keywords: Content-Based Image Retrieval (CBIR), Multimedia Semantics, MPEG-7 Descriptors, Clustering, Vector Quantization, Categorization.

1 Introduction

The digitalized art painting space gives us the opportunity to immerse in the ocean of accumulated culture. Earlier we could only dream to see some masterpieces. Now our computer moves us to every chosen place and time. These abilities increase the expectations for easy resource discovery by different criteria. While one user could be interested in art paintings from a specific movement or artist, others would search for images with particular theme or composition, and still others can be attracted by some pure aesthetic influence of the image. Many efforts are aimed at combining text-based and content-based search technologies in real-world image retrieval.

R. Kannan and F. Andres (Eds.): ICDEM 2010, LNCS 6411, pp. 146–153, 2012.
© Springer-Verlag Berlin Heidelberg 2012

MPEG-7 is an ISO/IEC standard developed by Moving Picture Experts Group. The formal name of MPEG-7 is "Multimedia Content Description Interface" (http://www.chiariglione.org/mpeg). The standard describes the multimedia content data that supports some degree of interpretation of the information meaning. The elements that MPEG-7 standardizes support a broad range of possible applications. The visual descriptors in the MPEG-7 standard describe different aspects of the image content such as dominant colors, edginess, texture, etc. The MPEG-7 descriptors are often used in the process of image-to-image matching, searching for similarities, sketch queries, etc. [1].

In this paper we apply a vector quantization method on the MPEG-7 descriptors as a possible approach for dimensionality reduction. For obtaining simple visual characteristics we use a clustering procedure over the tiles. The processes of obtaining these attributes are realized in our laboratory for art-painting semantic image retrieval APICAS. The significance analysis of received characteristics for class prediction of the artists' names or movements is conducted in the data mining analysis environment PaGaNe [2].

The rest of the paper is organized in the following way. Section 2 presents our methodology for extracting visual features from MPEG-7 descriptors based on vector quantization. Section 3 describes the software used for our research. Section 4 presents the received results. Finally, some conclusions and future work directions are highlighted.

2 Proposed Approach for Feature Extraction

MPEG-7 descriptors are complex descriptors, which provide a good presentation of different types of visual features. The description of the structure of MPEG-7 descriptors and algorithms is given in [3].

These complex structures need specific processing and cannot be put directly into generic classification algorithms.

In our work we are focused on following MPEG-7 descriptors:

- *Scalable Color (SC)* represents the color histogram in the HSV color space, encoded by a Haar transform. For presenting the image or a selected part, *Scalable Color* needs a vector with 64 attributes;
- *Color Layout (CL)* specifies the spatial distribution of colors using *YCbCr* color space. We use the first quantized *DCT* coefficient of the *Y*, *Cb* and *Cr* components, the next five successive quantized *DCT* coefficients of the *Y* component and the next two quantized *DCT* coefficients of the *Cb* and *Cr* component. Thus, the *Color Layout* vector has 12 attributes;
- *Color Structure (CS)*, which specifies both color content and the structure of the content. The descriptor expresses local color structure in an image by means of a structuring element that is composed of several image samples. We use a vector with 64 attributes for representing the *Color Structure*;
- *Dominant Color (DC)*. We reconfigured the presentation of this descriptor as three vectors, representing distribution of quantized hue, saturation and luminance. Such method is already precisely described and used by us in [4]. After this quantization we receive a vector with 23 attributes (13 for hue + 5 for saturation + 5 for luminance);

- *Edge Histogram (EH)* specifies the spatial distribution of five types of edges in local image regions. *Edge Histogram* descriptor produces a vector with 80 attributes;
- *Homogeneous Texture (HT)* characterizes the region texture using the energy and energy deviation in a set of frequency channels. A vector with 60 attributes is used, presenting *Energy* and *Energy Deviation*.

As a result we obtain a vector, which when taken together results more than 300 attributes. From other side each descriptor needs specific similarity measure.

Some of the MPEG-7 descriptors are alternative. For instance, Scalable Color, Color Layout, Color Structure and Dominant Color concern different aspects of the same phenomenon, i.e. distribution of the color within the image or region. It means that not all descriptors have to be given in the classification process. The first goal of this research is to examine which of them are more convenient to be used for extracting simple visual features for the purposes of class recognition.

Visual attributes can represent global characteristics, concerning whole images, or they can be extracted over the part of the images (specific region or tile of the image). Both approaches have their strengths: global attributes deliver integral temper of the image. Local attributes can capture more detailed information, which characterize the artists' styles or movements' specifics but introduce redundancy for the classifier. For reducing the computational weight and redundancy a possibility is to choose only part of the tiles – only chess ordered tiles, starting from the first tile $(1,1)$ or from the second one $(1,2)$ as well as taking into account only left sided or right sided tiles. In this paper we use all the tiles. The second goal of this research is to examine the trade of between the global and local approach.

In our approach we split the images into $m \times n$ non-overlapping rectangles (tiles). The tiles are marked as (i, j), where $i \in 1...m$ and $j \in 1...n$. Index i increases from the left tile to the right tile and index j increases from the top tile to the bottom tile of the image.

Let $I = \{I_p \mid p = 1...k\}$ be the observed set of k images. Each image is divided into non-overlapping $m \times n$ tiles and as a result a set of $k \times m \times n$ tiles $T = \{I_p^{ij} \mid p = 1...k, i = 1...m, j = 1...n\}$ is produced.

From the observed set, a subset $LI = \{I_q \mid q = 1...l, \ l < k, \ I_q \in I\}$ of representative images is extracted, which is used as learning set. The images of this subset produce a set of $l \times m \times n$ tiles $LT = \{I_q^{ij} \mid q = 1...l, i = 1...m, j = 1...n\}$.

For each MPEG-7 descriptor $X \in \{SC, CL, CS, DC, EH, HT\}$ the algorithm consists of following steps:

- for all tiles in LT, the MPEG-7 descriptor and the corresponding feature vector $X \in \{SC, CL, CS, DC, EH, HT\}$ is calculated;
- the tiles in LT are clustered. We used "repeated bisections". The number of the clusters can be different for different MPEG-7 descriptors, but in this realization for all descriptors an equal number α is used;
- the centroids of each cluster are calculated;

    -    for each tile a value, which corresponds to the number of the cluster where the tile belongs to, is assigned;

    -    for tiles which were not in the learning set $IT \setminus LT$, the membership of their centroids is calculated using L_1-metric, and the number of the corresponding cluster is assigned as a value of the tile.

As a result, each image of I is represented with a feature vector with $x \times m \times n$ numerical attributes, where x is the number of MPEG-7 descriptors. For instance in case of using all MPEG-7 descriptors for 3×3 tiling, the number of attributes in this vector is $6 \times 3 \times 3 = 36$. In case of selecting only a subset of the available tiles (chess order or left/right side), the number of features reduces.

A specific of this approach is that received attributes are nominal. The main purpose of the prepared datasets after implementing this approach is to examine the significance of the attributes and the local/global trade-off for class prediction.

3 Realization

In order to realize the proposed algorithm, our laboratory for art-painting semantic image retrieval "Art Painting Image Color Aesthetic and Semantic" (APICAS), firstly presented in [5], was extended with additional functions.

For obtaining the MPEG-7 descriptors our system refers to Multimedia Content Management System MILOS [6].

As clustering algorithm the program *vcluster*, which is part of the CLUTO open source software package [7], is implemented in the system. As clustering method we have used the default method "repeated bisections". The similarity between objects is computed using the correlation coefficient. As clustering criterion function, cluster maximization of sum of square root of sums of similarities of vectors, belonging to given cluster, is used. In this method, each cluster is represented by its centroid vector and the goal is to find the clustering solution that maximizes the similarity between each vector and the centroid of the cluster to which it is assigned.

As knowledge analysis and testing environment, we used the data mining analysis environment PaGaNe [2]. We have used PGN-1 classifier and implemented statistical analyzing tools for checking up our results and extracting regularities for artists' and movements' styles based on the extracted attributes.

4 Experiments

For our experiments we have used datasets that include 600 paintings of 18 artists from different movements of West-European fine arts and one group, which represent Orthodox Iconographic Style from Eastern Medieval Culture (Table 1). The pictures were obtained from different web-museum sources using ArtCyclopedia as a gate to the museum-quality fine art on the Internet as well as from different Eastern public virtual art galleries and museums for extracting Icons.

Table 1. List of the artists, which paintings were used in experiments, grouped by movements

Movement	Artist
Icons (60)	Icons (60)
Renaissance (90)	Botticelli (30); Michelangelo (30); Raphael (30)
Baroque (90)	Caravaggio (30); Rembrandt (30); Rubens (30)
Romanticism (90)	Friedrich (30); Goya (30); Turner (30)
Impressionism (90)	Monet (30); Pissarro (30); Sisley (30)
Cubism (90)	Braque (30); Gris (30); Leger (30)
Modern Art (90)	Klimt (30); Miro (30); Mucha (30)

We have made several experiments with different parameters for:

- the number of tiles – we have ran experiments with equal tiling over width and height from 1×1 (the whole images) up to 7×7 (i.e. $m = n \in \{1,...,7\}$);
- the number of clusters – the experiments were carried out with 20, 40 and 60 clusters;
- as class value, we have used "artists' names" and "movements".

As the set of attributes we have used $\{X(i,j)\}$, where $i = 1...m$, $j = 1...n$, X is SC, CL, CS, DC, EH, HT.

We have processed the datasets under the procedures of attribute selection in order to receive the order of significance of attributes for prediction. We have implemented several attribute evaluation methods – Chi square; Filter; Information Gain, and they give almost equal results for ordering the significance of the attributes, diverging the order for some attributes only in 2-3 positions. Later analyses are made using Chi square evaluation method.

We have summarized the obtained order of attributes by types of descriptors and positions of the tiles by width, respectively by height.

Fig. 1 shows the distribution of significance of MPEG-7 descriptors for class prediction. As it is shown, the *Color Structure (CS)* descriptor is the most informative for our datasets. The dominance of the features, based on the color descriptors (CS, SC, DC, CL) is obvious, which leads to these assumptions:

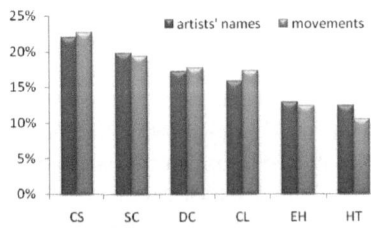

Fig. 1. Average distribution of significance by MPEG-7 descriptors over datasets, using different tiling and clustering, using Chi square evaluation method

- the artist's palettes, which are captured in color descriptors, are a powerful tool for creating the profiles of art painting images;
- using this approach, texture descriptors (EH, HT) can not produce sufficient quality attributes to present the specifics of the brushwork of the artists.

The analysis of the significance of the tile position for the horizontal splitting (Fig. 2) and vertical splitting (Fig. 3), shows that the increasing the number of tiles reduces the differences between the zones.

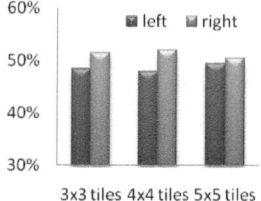

Fig. 2. Distribution of significance of left side and right side of the images for 3×3, 4×4 and 5×5 tiling

Fig. 3. Distribution of significance of upper and lower zone of the images for 3×3, 4×4 and 5×5 tiling

Furthermore, we can examine the significance of the tiles in respect to the position in the images. Fig. 4 shows the distribution of significance of the tiles in respect to the horizontal position. As we can see, the differences are not distinctive, which means that horizontally each zone of the image is relatively equal important.

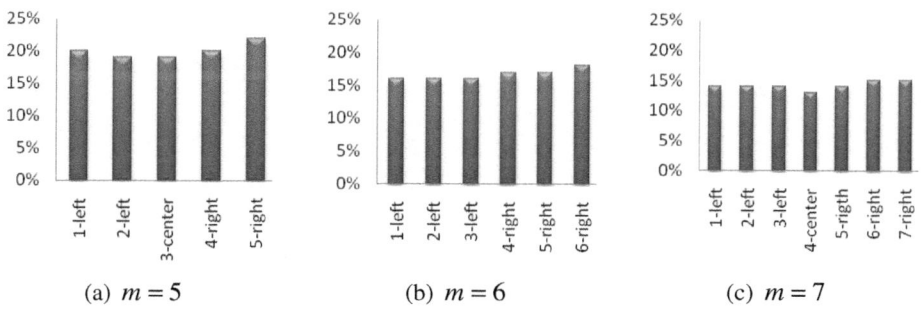

(a) $m = 5$ (b) $m = 6$ (c) $m = 7$

Fig. 4. Distribution of significance of the tiles by position of *width*, $i \in 1...m$ from left to right

The construction of many classical paintings is based on central symmetry. A little superiority of the right part of the image for a fewer number of tiling confirms the results from psychological theories for We attend to use this fact in further investigation with analyzing the tiles only of the right half of the image.

Similar analysis in respect to the vertical position of the tiles is shown on Fig. 5. Here, it becomes clear that outer tiles (and especially border tiles) are more informative (more distinctive for different classes) than inner tiles (and especially center tiles).

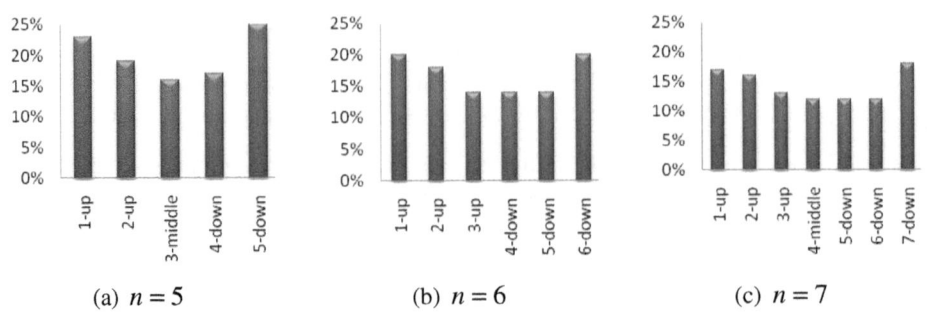

Fig. 5. Distribution of significance of the tiles by position of *height*, $j \in 1...n$ from up to down

This fact can also be explained with differences between constructions of composition in different styles [8]. While the central part of the image brings object or scene information, the borders are les burdened with this task. In order to supply the focus of the image, there are not usually specific objects found here, but only the ground patterns, which are specific for the artists or the school, in which the artists belongs. These patterns capture the ground of the artists' palette and brushwork.

Other experiments are focused on establishing the appropriate number of clusters in order to receive good classification results with lower computational cost. We have run ten-fold cross-validation over the datasets.

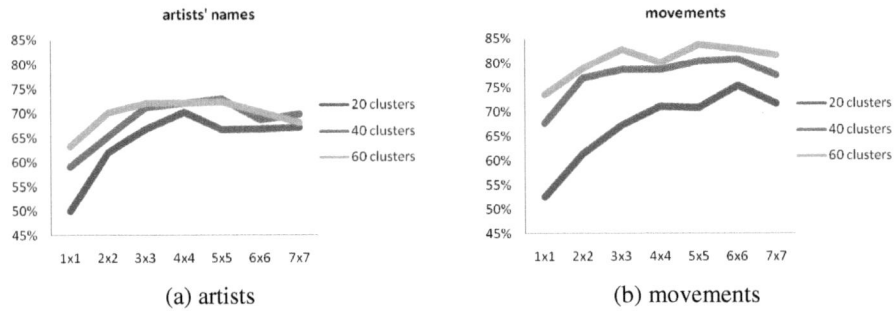

Fig. 6. Classification accuracy for datasets with classes artists/movementsusing 20, 40, 60 clusters and different numbers of tiling

The results displayed on Fig. 6, show that using vector quantization on MPEG-7 descriptors for the entire image (i.e. 1×1 tiling) is not so informative. Better but non-sufficient results are obtained for 2×2 tiling. Tiling 3×3 is the first with relatively good results. This result is also conceptually validated by the fact that 3×3 tiling corresponds to a rough approximation of the golden ratio, which usually lies in the compositions of the art paintings. The last observed tiling 7×7 shows a decreasing of accuracy, which can be explained by the fact that the pictures became too fragmented and the clusters fall not in the proper positions.

5   Conclusions

In this article we have presented an approach for analyzing visual characteristics, based on MPEG-7 descriptors. The method allows on one hand tiling and on the other hand a huge reduction of the dimensionality of the data. For the used data sets, 4×4 tiling and 40 clusters seemed optimal. From the analysis we learned that the artist's palettes, which are captured in color descriptors, are a powerful tool for creating the profiles of art painting images. The texture descriptors (*EH*, *HT*), in our particular presentation, can not produce sufficient quality attributes to present the specifics of the brushwork of the artists. Position analysis confirmed other research results.

In further research, we will look for combinations of characteristics in order to form profiles for artists or movements.

Acknowledgments. This work was supported in part by Hasselt University under the Project R-1875 "Search in Art Image Collections Based on Color Semantics" and by the Bulgarian National Science Fund under the Project D002-308/19.12.2008 "Automated Metadata Generating for e-Documents Specifications and Standards".

References

1. Stanchev, P., Green Jr., D., Dimitrov, B.: Some Issues in the Art Image Database Systems. Journal of Digital Information Management 4(4), 227–232 (2006)
2. Mitov, I., Ivanova, K., Markov, K., Velychko, V., Vanhoof, K., Stanchev, P.: PaGaNe – a Classification Machine Learning System Based on the Multidimensional Numbered Information Spaces. In: Fourth Int. Conf. Intelligent Systems and Knowledge Engineering (ISKE), Hasselt, Belgium, November 27-28. Printed in World Scientific Proceedings Series on Computer Engineering and Information Science, vol. (2), pp. 279–286 (2009)
3. International Standard ISO/IEC 15938-3 Multimedia Content Description Interface – Part 3: Visual,
   `http://www.iso.org/iso/iso_catalogue/catalogue_tc/catalogue_d`
   `etail.htm?csnumber=34230`
4. Ivanova, K., Stanchev, P.: Color Harmonies and Contrasts Search in Art Image Collections. In: First International Conference on Advances in Multimedia (MMEDIA), Colmar, France, July 20-25, pp. 80–187 (2009)
5. Ivanova, K., Stanchev, P., Dimitrov, B.: Analysis of the Distributions of Color Characteristics in Art Painting Images. Serdica Journal of Computing 2(2), 111–136 (2008)
6. Amato, G., Gennaro, C., Rabitti, F., Savino, P.: Milos: A Multimedia Content Management System for Digital Library Applications. In: Heery, R., Lyon, L. (eds.) ECDL 2004. LNCS, vol. 3232, pp. 14–25. Springer, Heidelberg (2004)
7. Karypis, G.: CLUTO: A Clustering Toolkit Release 2.1.1. University of Minnesota, Department of Computer Science, Minneapolis, MN 55455, Technical Report: #02-017 (2003)
8. Arnheim, R.: Art and Visual Perception: A Psychology of the Creative Eye. University of California Press, Berkeley (1974)

Content Based Image Retrieval Using Various Distance Metrics

Sanjay Patil[1] and Sanjay Talbar[2]

[1] Department of Electronics Engg.
Padmabhushan Vasantdada Patil Pratisthan's
College Of Engg., Sion-Chunabhatti, Mumbai. PIN 400 022, India
sanjayashri@rediffmail.com
[2] Shri Guru Gobind Singhji College of Engineering and Technology,
Vishnupuri, Nanded, PIN 431 606, India
sntalbar@yahoo.com

Abstract. Content based image retrieval (CBIR) provides an effective way to search the images from the databases. The feature extraction and similarity measures are the two key parameters for retrieval performance. A similarity measure plays an important role in image retrieval. This paper compares six different distance metrics such as Euclidean, Manhattan, Canberra, Bray-Curtis, Square chord, Square chi-squared distances to find the best similarity measure for image retrieval. Using pyramid structured wavelet decomposition, energy levels are calculated. These energy levels are compared by calculating distance between query image and database images using above mentioned seven different similarity metrics. A large image database from Brodatz album is used for retrieval purpose. Experimental results shows the superiority of Canberra, Bray-Curtis, Square chord, and Square Chi-squared distances over the conventional Euclidean and Manhattan distances.

Keywords: Content based image retrieval, Distance metrics, Similarity measures, Image features.

1 Introduction

Content based image retrieval has been an active and fast growing research area since 1990's. It is a technique which uses visual contents (color, texture, shape etc.) of the image to search images from large scale image database according to users applications. Before going in details of this system, we briefly discuss evolution of the content based image retrieval system. In the early 1990's due to advances in internet and new digital image technologies, number of digital images produced by scientific, educational, medical, industrial and other applications available to users increased rapidly [1].

In 1979, a conference on Database Techniques for Pictorial applications was held in Florence. This was the beginning of attraction and attention of researchers in the field of image database management technologies. But still research area in this era was not so active. In February 1992, United Nations National Science Foundation

R. Kannan and F. Andres (Eds.): ICDEM 2010, LNCS 6411, pp. 154–161, 2012.
© Springer-Verlag Berlin Heidelberg 2012

(USNSF) organized a workshop in Redwood, California to highlight research areas for visual information management systems and its applications in various fields [2]. Since then many researchers started work in this area. Development of methods which would increase retrieval accuracy and reduce retrieval time is the main challenges in CBIR.

Early techniques were not generally based on visual features but on the textual annotation of images. The images were first annotated by text and then searched using text based approach. However in many situations, text annotation scheme is inefficient. For the huge image data the vast amount of labor required in manual annotation. Also describing every visual feature within the images is very time consuming   and difficult. We know that, image speaks thousands of the words. So instead of manual annotations by text based keywords, images are indexed by their own visual features such as color, texture, shape the etc.

2   Architecture of Typical CBIR System

The general architecture of CBIR system is shown in fig.1. For the given image database, first extract features of individual one. The features can be visual features like color, texture, shape, region or spatial features or some compressed domain features. The extracted features are described by feature vectors. These feature vectors are then stored to form Image feature database.

For a given query image, we similarly extract its features and form a feature vector. This feature vector is matched with the already stored vectors in image feature database. The distance between the feature vector of the query image and those of the images in the database are then calculated. Obviously the distance of a query image with itself is zero if it is in database. The distances are then stored in increasing order and retrieval is performed with the help of indexing scheme.

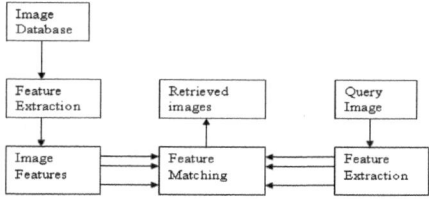

Fig. 1. Architecture of CBIR system

3   Image Features

A large amount of image database is added every moment of time, so the effective and efficient image retrieval system is needed. There are many features used in content based image retrieval but four of them are considered to be the main features. These features are color, texture, shape, and spatial properties. However, spatial properties are not generally taken into account, so main features to derive are color, texture, and shape [4].

3.1 Texture

There is one of the most important features of an image. It is characterized by the spatial distribution of gray levels in a neighborhood. In order to capture the spatial dependence of gray-level values, which contribute to the perception of texture, a two-dimensional dependence texture analysis matrix is taken into consideration. This two-dimensional matrix is obtained by decoding the image file; jpeg, bmp, etc.

3.2 Texture Representation and Features

The most popular statistical representations of texture are:

- Co-occurrence Matrix
- Tamura Texture
- Wavelet Transform

In the early 1970s, the co-occurrence matrix representation of texture features was proposed by Haralick *et al* [5]. In this approach, they highlighted the grey level spatial dependence of texture. Based on the orientation and the distance between image pixels, a co-occurrence matrix was first constructed and then meaningful statistics from the matrix are extracted. Many other researchers experimentally found out that contrast, inverse defence moment and entropy had the great discriminatory power.

Tamura *et al* [6] explored the texture representation which motivated by the psychological studies in human visual perception of texture. They found that in psychological studies computation approximation to the visual texture properties are important. The comparison between Tamura texture representation and co-occurrence matrix representation concluded that all the texture properties in Tamara texture representation are visually more meaningful. This characteristic gives tamura texture representation more importance in image retrieval.

In the early 1990s, many researchers began to use of the wavelet transform in texture representation. Smith and Chang [7] used the mean and variance extracted from the wavelet sub bands for texture representation. Chang and Kuo [8] was used tree structured wavelet transform to achieve better retrieval performance. Gross *et al* [9] used the wavelet transform combined with K-L transform and Kohenen maps to perform texture analysis. Kunda *et al* [10] proposed texture analysis using wavelet transform with a co-occurrence matrix to take advantage of both statistics based and transform based analysis.

4 Similarity Measures

Similarity measures also termed as distance metric plays important role in Content based image retrieval. Content-based image retrieval calculates visual similarities between a query image and images in a database. Therefore, the retrieval result is not a single image but a number of images ranked by their similarities with the query image. Different *similarity measures* will affect retrieval performances of an image retrieval system significantly so, it is important to find best distance metric for CBIR system. The query image will be more similar to the database images if the distance is smaller. If x and y are two d-dimensional feature vectors of database image and query image respectively, then the distance metrics are given by[11],

i. Euclidean distance,

$$d_E(x, y) = \sqrt{\sum_{i=1}^{d} (x_i - y_i)^2} \qquad (1)$$

ii .Manhattan distance,

$$d_{MAN}(x, y) = \sum_{i=1}^{d} |x_i - y_i| \qquad (2)$$

The Manhattan Distance was proposed in [13] for computing the dissimilarity scores between color images.

iii. Canberra Distance,

$$d_C(x, y) = \sum_{i=1}^{d} \frac{|x_i - y_i|}{|x_i| + |y_i|} \qquad (3)$$

iv. Bray –Curtis distance,

$$d_{BC}(x, y) = \sum_{i=1}^{d} \frac{|x_i - y_i|}{x_i + y_i} \qquad (4)$$

In the equation (3) and (4) the distance value will never be more than one, being equal to one when one of the attributes is zero. It avoids scaling effect and proved to be good metrics for retrieval performance.

v. Square chord distance,

$$d_{SC}(x, y) = \sum_{i=1}^{d} \left(\sqrt{x_i} - \sqrt{y_i} \right)^2 \qquad (5)$$

vi. Square Chi-Squared distance,

$$d_{CHI}(x, y) = \sum_{i=1}^{d} \frac{(x_i - y_i)^2}{x_i + y_i} \qquad (6)$$

The distance equations given in (5) and (6) respectively may also useful in image retrieval systems.

5   Retrieval Technique Used for Texture Images

In this section texture image database used for retrieval and image retrieval method are discussed.

5.1   Texture Image Database

We have used 108 textures from Brodatz texture album. Each texture pattern is containing set of nine images. So there are 972 different texture patterns [14]. The size of each texture is 643X 643. Each of 643X643 images is resized to 256X256 and saved in bitmap file format. The size conversion is done as in the databases generalised image size is 256X256 so we have developed software accordingly. Some of the specimen texture images in the database with set of their 9 different patterns are shown in figure 2.

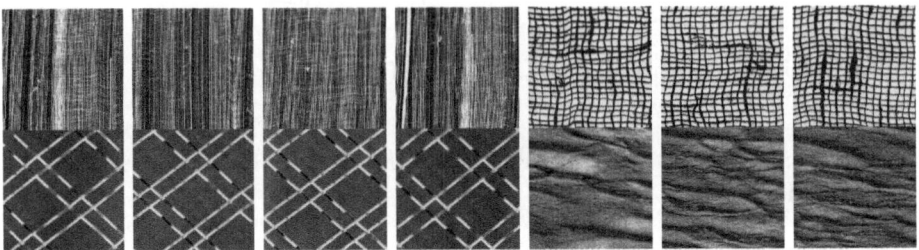

Fig. 2. Specimen texture images with 9 different patterns from Brodatz album

We used a method called the pyramid-structured wavelet transform for texture retrieval. It recursively decomposes sub signals in the low frequency bands. It is most significant for textures with dominant frequency bands. For this reason, it is mostly suitable for signals consisting of components with information concentrated in lower frequency bands [13]. As most of the image information exists in lower sub-bands, the pyramid-structured wavelet transform is highly efficient. The flow graph of pyramid structured wavelet transform is shown in figure 3.

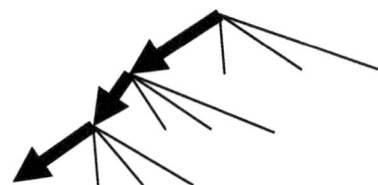

Fig. 3. Pyramid-structured wavelet transform

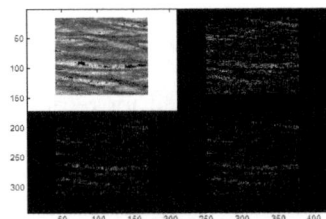

Fig. 4. First level wavelet decomposition of input image

Using the pyramid-structured wavelet transform, the texture image is decomposed into four sub images, in low-low, low-high, high-low and high-high sub-bands. The first level decomposition of input image is shown in figure 4. At this point, the energy level of each sub-band is calculated. This is first level decomposition. Using the low-low sub-band for further decomposition, we reached fifth level decomposition. The reason for this is the basic assumption that the energy of an image is concentrated in the low-low band. For this cause we used Daubechies wavelet as wavelet function.

5.2   Distance Algorithm

The query image is one of the 972 patterns from image database. The query image is decomposed and energies of the first dominant k-bands are determined. Similarly, all images in the database are decomposed and the first dominant k-band energies are calculated. Then distance between query image and database image is determined using different distance metrics [13]. This process is repeated until all the images in the database have been compared with the query image. It is obvious that the distance of an image from itself is zero. The distances are in the increasing order for the closest sets of pattern are then retrieved. Ideally, the nine topmost images are displayed as a result of the texture retrieval which is from same texture pattern.   Using the above algorithm, the query image is searched for in the image database. The distances are calculated between the query image and every image in the database.

6   Experimental Results

We have done the experiment with different distance metrics on the same set of images and compared the images with smaller distances. The image D371 is query image which is shown in figure 5. There are 9 similar images to the query image which retrieved sequently with the increasing distance which is depicted in the figure 7. The table 1 shows the retrieved images and their distances from query image for different distance metrics. It is observed from the table 1, the distance of query image from itself is zero. Also, it is clear that square chord and square chi-squared distances retrieve images with smallest distances as compared to traditional Euclidean or Manhattan distances.   The proposed retrieval system has been implemented in Matlab7.5 version on a Core2Duo, 2GHz processor. The figure 6 gives top 10 retrieved images from the database of 972 images for the given query image.

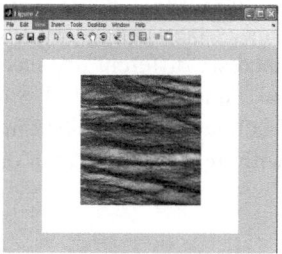

Fig. 5. The Query Image

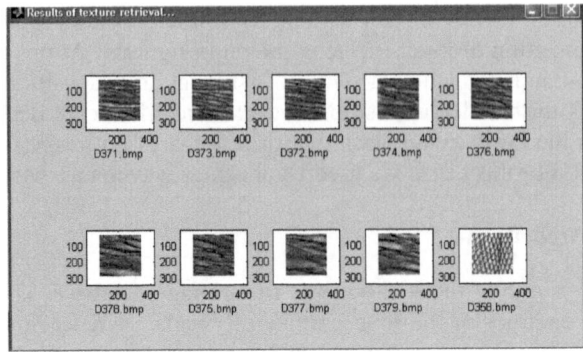

Fig. 6. Top 10 retrieved similar images from the database

Table 1. Retrieved images and their distances from query image

Retrieved Images	Distance between query image and database image for different Distance Metrics					
	Euclidean	Manhattan	Canberra	Bray-Curtis	Square Chord	Square Chi-squared
D371.bmp	0.0000	0.0000	0.0000	0.0000	0.0000	0.0000
D373.bmp	0.3480	0.7369	0.0317	0.0317	1.12×10^{-4}	0.0040
D372.bmp	0.3679	0.6275	0.0273	0.0273	1.30×10^{-4}	8.29×10^{-4}
D374.bmp	0.4403	0.7746	0.0334	0.0334	1.79×10^{-4}	0.0083
D376.bmp	0.4685	0.9669	0.0420	0.0420	2.07×10^{-4}	0.0076
D378.bmp	0.4707	0.8385	0.0360	0.0360	2.09×10^{-4}	0.0112
D375.bmp	0.4828	0.8350	0.0365	0.0365	2.24×10^{-4}	0.0067
D377.bmp	0.9706	1.6366	0.0707	0.0707	8.80×10^{-4}	0.0340
D379.bmp	1.0460	2.1135	0.0905	0.0905	0.0011	0.0504
D358.bmp	1.7690	3.0113	0.2341	0.2341	0.0017	0.0927

7   Conclusions

We have compared in detail six different distance metrics such as Euclidean, Manhattan, Canberra, Bray-Curtis, Square chord, Square chi-squared distances for texture image retrieval. A large database of 972 texture images is used. Using pyramid structured wavelet decomposition, energy levels are calculated. These energy levels are compared and distances between query image and database images are calculated using above mentioned six different distance metrics. From the results it is concluded that performance of Square chord and Square Chi-squared distances is better than the conventional Euclidean and Manhattan distances. Also Canberra and Bray-Curtis retrieves images with distances less than one, which avoids scaling effect as mentioned earlier.

References

1. Gudivada, V.N., Raghavan, V.V.: Content-based image retrieval systems. IEEE Computer 28(9), 18–22 (1995)
2. Kokare, M., Chatterji, B.N., Biswas, P.K.: A survey on current content based image retrieval methods. IETE Journal of Research 48(3&4), 261–271 (2002)
3. Long, F., Zhang, H., DagaFeng, D.: Fundamentals of content based image retrieval
4. Birgale, L., Kokare, M.: Color and texture features for CBIR. In: Proceedings of the International Conference on Computer Graphics, Imaging and Visualisation (2006)
5. Haralick, R.M., Shanmugam, K., Dinstein, I.: Texture features for image classification. IEEE Trans. on Sys. Man. and Cyb. SMC-3(6) (1973)
6. Tamura, H., Mori, S., Yamawaki, T.: Texture features corresponding to visual perception. IEEE Trans. on Systems, Man, and Cybernetics Smc-8(6) (June 1978)
7. Smith, J.R., Chang, S.F.: Transform features for texture classification and discrimination in large image databases. In: Proc. IEEE International Conference on Image Processing (1994)
8. Chang, T., Kuo, C.-C.J.: Texture analysis and classification with tree-structured wavelet transform. IEEE Transactions Image Processing 2(4), 429–441 (1993)
9. Gross, M.H., Koch, R., Lippert, L., Dreger, A.: Multiscale image texture analysis in wavelet spaces. In: Proc. IEEE Int. Conf. on Image Proc. (1994)
10. Kundu, A., Chen, J.-L.: Texture classification using qmf bank-based subband decomposition. CVGIP Graphical Models and Image Processing 54(5), 369–384 (1992)
11. Kokare, M., Chatterji, B.N., Biswas, P.K.: Comparison of Similarity Metrics for Texture Image Retrieval. In: TENCON (2003)
12. Swain, M., Ballard, D.: Color indexing. Internatiunal Journal of Compurer Vision 17(1), 11–32 (1991)
13. Siddique, S.: A Wavelet Based Technique for Analysis and Classification of Texture Images. Carleton University, Ottawa, Canada, Proj. Rep. 70.593 (2002)
14. Brodatz, P.: Textures: A photographic album for artists and designers. Dover, New York (1966)

An Efficient Content Based Image Retrieval Framework Using Machine Learning Techniques

B. Celia and I. Felci Rajam

St. Joseph's College of Engineering,
Chennai
{chirpiceli,felcirajam}@gmail.com

Abstract. A Content-based image retrieval (CBIR) framework is proposed for diverse collection of images with distinct semantic categories. For effective image categorization and retrieval, the semantic category of image is considered. The low-level features (color, texture, shape and edge) are extracted and its dimensions are reduced using Principal Component Analysis (PCA). To avoid misclassification in Support Vector Machine-"Pairwise Coupling Technique" (SVM-PWC), SVM-PWC with Fuzzy C-Mean (FCM) clustering techniques and entire DB search is used. To reduce image search space, the images are prefiltered using SVM-PWC and FCM techniques. Experiments are conducted over COREL dataset consisting of 1000 images with 10 distinct semantic categories. Analysis of precision-recall for SVM-PWC and SVM-PWC with FCM clustering techniques is reported. The accuracy and testing time for SVM-PWC, SVM-PWC with FCM and Prefiltered FCM is measured. The efficiency of proposed CBIR framework is measured in the reports.

Keywords: clustering, Fuzzy c-mean (FCM), Principal Component Analysis (PCA), statistical similarity matching, support vector machine (SVM).

1 Introduction

In the age of IT revolution, the applications of digital images in various domains are at rapid pace. As the images retrieved for the query should be in terms with the semantics perceived, the efficient semantic-based image retrieval technique has to be designed. CBIR has been active research area and it accommodates both the low level and high level features in its image retrieval technique.

1.1 Literature Review

The images retrieved based on image contents alone varies from its semantic perceived. The images with high feature similarities to the query image may be very different from the query image in terms of the semantics perceived by the user or semantics according to predefined categories is referred as *Semantic gap* problem.

In the CBIR system proposed by Mahmudur et al., [2], a machine learning approach with the statistical similarity matching technique and relevance feedback

R. Kannan and F. Andres (Eds.): ICDEM 2010, LNCS 6411, pp. 162–169, 2012.
© Springer-Verlag Berlin Heidelberg 2012

scheme have been used for efficient image retrieval. The probabilistic multiclass SVM and Fuzzy C-Mean clustering are used for image categorization and Prefiltering of images. To evaluate the performance of the proposed system, a medical database which contains the images of different modalities is used. Based on the precision-recall observation, the conclusion obtained is that the distance measures that utilize the category-specific feature distribution information perform better in a semantically organized database.

Support Vector Machine (SVM) is a supervised machine learning approach proposed primarily for binary classification and extended to multiclass classification. SVM-PWC is used for online prediction for query image. Hence, retrieved image considers the semantic property and semantic-based image retrieval is achieved [2].

1.2 Machine Learning Approach in CBIR

The dimensions of low-level features extracted are reduced using PCA technique. When images are retrieved based on the low-level features, the retrieved images aren't in terms with the semantics perceived by the user. Hence, to increase the accuracy of image retrieval, SVM-PWC technique is used. The main limitation of SVM-PWC is few misclassifications for the query image.

The main contributions of this paper are as follows: For efficient image classification, SVM-PWC has been used. When images are misclassified, the SVM-PWC with FCM and entire DB search is considered. The misclassified images in SVM-PWC and the SVM-PWC with FCM are removed and then entire DB search is performed to provide user with relevant images.

The remainder of this section is organized as follows: The section 2 describes image feature extraction and dimension reduction. In Section 3, Efficient image classification for CBIR Framework. In section 4, Experimental setup. In section 5, Result Analysis. Finally section 6, gives conclusion.

2 Feature Extraction and Dimension Reduction

The low-level features such as color, texture, edge and shape are to be obtained for query and DB images. The more distinct the low-level features, the more accurate the content based classification [2].

2.1 Feature Extraction

The first, second and third central moments of each color channel [6] are used to represent a color feature vector in the Hue, Saturation, Value in (HSV) color space. A gray level co-occurrence matrix with four different orientations (horizontal 0°, vertical 90° and two diagonals 45° and 135°) are constructed to obtain texture information. Higher order feature such as energy, contrast, homogeneity, correlation, entropy are measured on each gray level co-occurrence matrix [7]. The canny edge is used to detect the edges and corresponding edge directions are quantized into 72 bins of

5° each. Normalize the histograms with respect to the number of edge points in the image [2]. The shape feature vector is obtained by calculating seven invariant moments [5].

2.2 Dimension Reduction

Let $\Re^d$ be the feature dimension, where d= (9+20+72+7=108).To reduce the logical size and high computational complexity, the dimension reduction PCA technique is applied [1]. After applying PCA technique, the original feature vector in $\Re^d$ dimension for the query and database images are projected into $\Re^l$ dimension typically l<<min (d, M), where M corresponds to the feature vector of DB images. The statistical similarity measures such as Bhattacharyya and Mahalanobis distances are used for image retrieval [6]. The euclidean distance is outperformed by statistical similarity measures [8].

3   Efficient Image Classification for CBIR Framework

The SVM-PWC and FCM techniques are used for efficient image classification. Both SVM-PWC and FCM are discussed in sections 3.1 and 3.2 respectively. The entire DB search option is provided if images are misclassified while using both SVM-PWC and FCM.

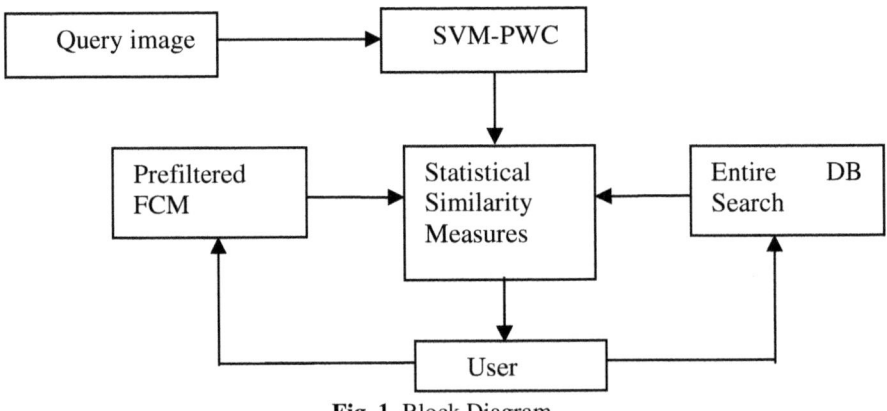

Fig. 1. Block Diagram

3.1 SVM-PWC

The one-against-one technique also known as "pairwise coupling" (PWC) technique is used to predict the class label for the query image [3]. This method trains $K\ (K-1)/2$ binary classifiers for k mutually exclusive classes, each of which provides a partial decision for classifying data point It then combines the output of all the binary classifiers to form a class prediction. For testing, each one of $K\ (K-1)/2$ classifiers vote for one class. The labels of K categories along with their probabilities, becomes annotation for testing images in the following format

<Image no><confidence class1>…<confidence class K>

When images are misclassified using SVM-PWC, the irrelevant images are displayed to the user [2]. To overcome the limitation, the FCM and entire DB search options are provided to the user is described in section 3.2 and 3.4.

3.2 FCM

The objective function [4] and steps involved can be defined as follows

$$J_k(U,V:X) = \sum_{i=1}^{M} \sum_{j=1}^{c} (u_{ji}^m) dist(X_i, v_j) \tag{1}$$

The $dist(X_i, v_j)$ can be calculated using Euclidean or Mahalanobis distance measures where cluster centers are v_j and X_i is reduced feature vectors. The fuzzy c-partition can be defined as c x M matrix and U corresponds to cluster membership.

The numbers of cluster centers, weighting components, termination criteria with iteration loops are initialized. The initial cluster centers are set to compute the initial cluster membership values. Update new cluster center and compute the cluster membership values till the termination criteria is met. The cluster center for the query image can be obtained using the feature vector of query image and the cluster center values of DB image.

The number of cluster centers is initialized to the number of semantic classes used in SVM-PWC. Each cluster center contains images from its corresponding semantic category is proposed. As the images retrieved based on FCM has less accuracy compared to SVM-PWC, the misclassified images of SVM-PWC alone can be overcome using FCM. The misclassified image becomes the input of FCM and its corresponding cluster centers are predicted for image retrieval.

3.3 FCM Prefiltering

The probability estimates of SVM-PWC and cluster membership values of FCM are effectively combined to reduce the image search space and time. The joint probability of SVM-PWC and FCM values are obtained for the predicted FCM label. The statistical similarity measures are applied to the prefiltered DB obtained and the topmost relevant images are displayed. Incase of refinements, the prefiltered DB reduces the search space time. The steps involved are:

Step1: Initialize the cluster number as c=K, where K is the number of semantic classes in SVM-PWC, M is the number of DB images and their semantic classes S=$\{S_1,...,S_K\}$ for FCM c cluster centers.

Step2: Project the original feature vector $f_q \in \Re^d$ of query image into $X_q \in \Re^l$ .For the query image q, find the cluster center using FCM.

Step3: Find the probability estimates (φ_s) and cluster membership values (ϑ_s) of DB image in the query image cluster center predicted using FCM.

Step4: Find the joint probability for probability estimates (φ_s) and cluster membership values (ϑ_s) of DB image in the query image semantic class such as $q_i = \varphi_s * \vartheta_s$.

Step5: Use the top d images obtained and measure the statistical similarity with respect to the query image and display the results.

3.4 Entire DB Search

When images are misclassified using SVM-PWC and FCM, the entire DB search option can provide user with few relevant images. Though only few relevant images are retrieved, it can provide user the option of selecting the most relevant images and further refinements are made based on the selected images.

The query image is first classified using SVM-PWC. When misclassified, FCM is used for classification. In case of misclassifications in both SVM-PWC and FCM, the entire DB search option is provided to the user. The misclassified label images are removed from the entire DB. Hence, K-2 or K-1 label images are used for image retrieval and the irrelevant images for query are removed.

The most relevant image for the query is selected and used for further image retrieval. The selected image for the query is classified again either using SVM-PWC or FCM if misclassified.

4 Experimental Setup

For SVM-based image classification, radial basis kernel function works well when the relation between attributes are non-linear. The two parameters to be considered while using RBF kernel are C and σ. To calculate C and σ, we perform 10-fold cross validation (CV) for the training set. For SVM-PWC method, *LIBSVM* software package is used.

For FCM, the cluster centers are set to the number of semantic classes. The cluster center values of DB images along with query image are used for label prediction. The statistical similarity measures are applied for image retrieval.

For evaluation and effectiveness of retrieval performance, the concepts of *Precision* and *Recall* are used. *Precision* is the ratio of the number of relevant images returned to the total number of images returned. *Recall* is the ratio of the number of relevant images returned to the total number of relevant images in DB.

A retrieved image is said to be a correct match if and only if it is in the same semantic category as the query image. Hence, Prefiltering DB based on the label prediction is justified. Performance of retrieval system, for SVM-PWC and SVM-PWC with FCM are analyzed using *Precision* and *Recall*.

5 Result Analysis

The reduced feature vectors with appropriate labels (1-10) are used for SVM training. Using LIBSVM, the best C and σ values are 150 and 0.023 with cross validation accuracy of 66.4 % and then the entire training set of 1000 images are tested again with this parameters to obtain final classifiers using SVM-PWC.

As the misclassified images of SVM-PWC are overcome in FCM, the SVM-PWC with FCM gives better results when compared to SVM-PWC. Precision and recall analysis in Fig.2 show SVM-PWC with FCM with better results.

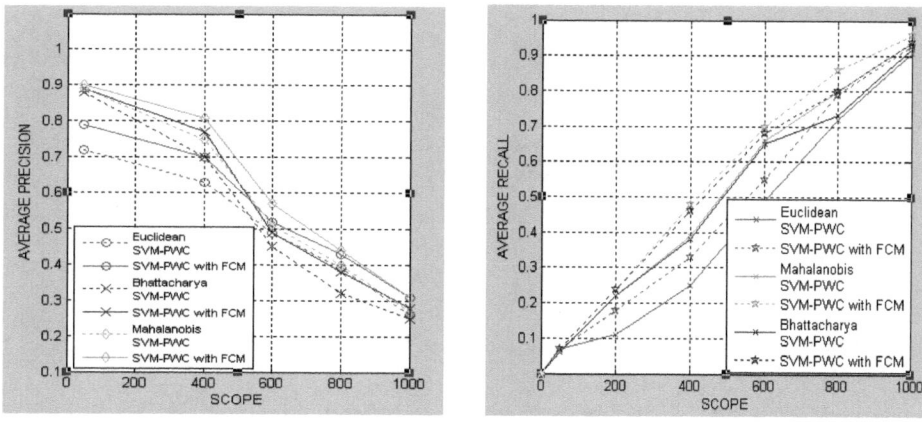

Fig. 2. Average Precision, Recall for SVM-PWC and SVM-PWC with FCM

In Fig 3, the misclassified images of SVM-PWC are classified correctly in FCM and the misclassified images of SVM-PWC and FCM are first given for entire DB search and refined using SVM-PWC.

Table 1. Accuracy and Time Analysis for Various Methods

Methods	SVM-PWC	FCM	FCM using Prefiltering
Accuracy	80	94.0	94.0
Testing time	1. 34	1.45	1.03

The Table 1 shows SVM-PWC with FCM with high accuracy (i.e.) 70%of misclassified images are classified accurately and the testing time is further reduced using the prefiltered DB search is measured. The remaining 30% of the images is classified using entire DB search. The time factor can be overlooked, when accuracy is considered.

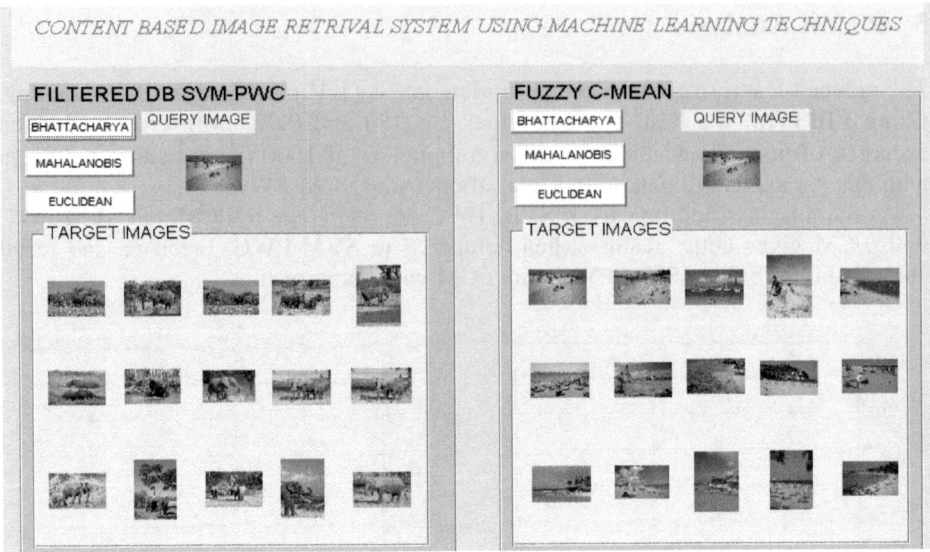

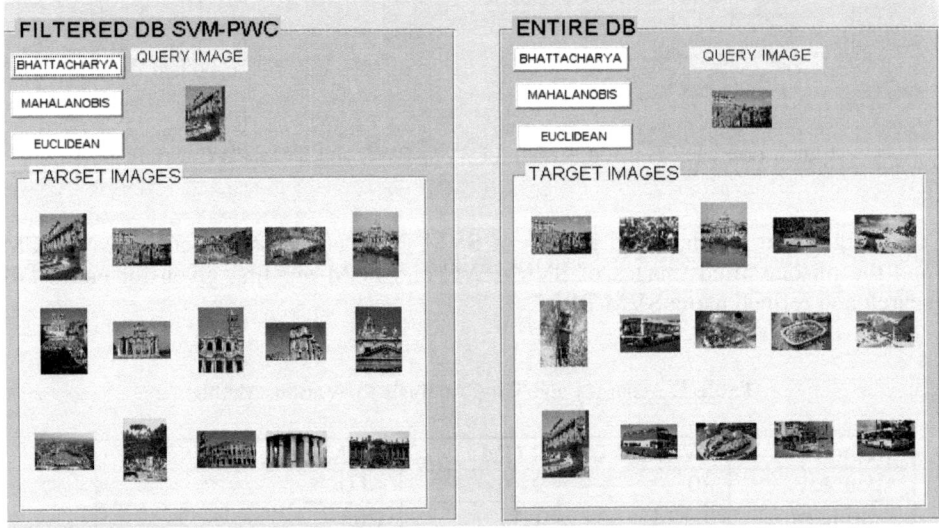

Fig. 3. Snapshot of SVM-PWC and FCM

6 Conclusion

In the proposed CBIR framework, SVM-PWC, FCM and entire DB search is used for increasing the accuracy of image classification. The misclassified images are classified using FCM and when it fails, entire DB search is provided. As the misclassified images are classified using FCM and entire DB again, the retrieval time is to be decreased using prefiltered DB. Hence, our proposed CBIR framework using SVM-PWC with FCM can be used as a front-end for image search which yields high accuracy and accessed within right time.

References

1. Jain, A.K., Chandrasekaran, B.: Dimensionality and sample size consideration in pattern recognition practice. In: Krishnaiah, P.R., Kanal, L.N. (eds.) Handbook of Statistics, Amsterdam, vol. 2, pp. 835–855. North Holland, The Netherlands (1987)
2. Rahman, M., Bhattacharya, P., Desai, B.C.: A framework for Medical Image Retrieval Using Machine Learning and statistical Similarity matching Techniques with Relevance Feedback. IEEE Transactions on Information Technology in Biomedicine 11(1) (2007)
3. Hsu, C.-W., Chang, C.-C., Lin, C.-J.: A Practical guide to Support Vector Classification, http://www.csie.ntu.edu.tw/~cjlin
4. Yang, J.F., Hao, S.S., Chung, P.C.: Color image segmentation using fuzzy c-means and eigenspace projections. Signal Process. 82, 461–472 (2003)
5. Dudani, S.A., Breeding, K.J., McGhee, R.B.: Aircraft identification by moment invariants. IEEE Trans. Computer C-26, 39–45 (1977)
6. Fukunaga, K.: Introduction to Statistical Pattern Recognition, 2nd edn. Academic Press (1990)
7. Haralick, R.M., Shanmugam, K., Dinstein, I.: Textural features for image classification. IEEE Trans.Syst., Man, Cybern. SMC-3(6), 610–621 (1973)
8. Aksoy, S., Haralick, R.M.: Probabilistic vs geometric similarity measures for image retrieval In: Proc. IEEE Conf. Computer Vis. Pattern Recognition, vol. 2 (2000)

Validating Data Warehouse Quality Metrics Using PCA

Rolly Gupta and Anjana Gosain

University School of Information Technology
Guru Gobind Singh Indraprastha University
Delhi, India
guptarolly02@yahoo.com, anajana_gosain@hotmail.com

Abstract. During the last decades researches, Data Warehouse is mainly concentrated on Quality. The best approach to quality evaluation goes through determining effective metrics on schemas. However, this set of metrics contains some redundant metrics. Generally, PCA (Principal Component Analysis) is used for defining principal metrics in the domain. In this study, we used PCA for dimensionality reduction on a set of 41 schemas, and we find out that instead of seven metrics [3], only 3 metrics were extracted as principal components. Our empirical validation experiment showed us that three principal components out of seven proposed metrics [3] seem to be practical indicators of the Quality Model for Data Warehouses.

Keywords: Data Warehouse Quality, Dimensional Modelling, Quality Metrics.

1 Introduction

Most of the organizations these days are deploying Data Warehouse for integrating data from various heterogeneous sources for management of information more efficiently and cost- effectively. Data Warehouse is treated as decision support systems for managing data. Since, Data Warehouse is crucial for the success of the organization, hence the information Quality of Data Warehouse should be assured. In data warehouse system quality [4][5], three different aspects are to be considered: DBMSs quality, data model quality and data quality. For such reasons, metrics have been used for the measurement of 'Quality' factors. Metrics helps to improve the process of software development (leading to better understanding), building predictive systems for database, maintaining projects and its quality, revealing problematic areas and detecting better ways to assist the researchers.

The objective of our work is to empirically validate the defined subset of metrics [3] using PCA (Principal Component Analysis), as PCA is a standard technique to identify the underlying, orthogonal dimensions that explain relations between the variables in a data set. Section 2 presents the data warehouse metrics used in our study. Section 3 is focused on the analysis methodologies used. Last section presents the experimental settings and results obtained by analysis.

R. Kannan and F. Andres (Eds.): ICDEM 2010, LNCS 6411, pp. 170–172, 2012.
© Springer-Verlag Berlin Heidelberg 2012

2 Metrics for Data Warehouse

Taking into account the characteristics expressed previously, we had empirically validated the following metrics [3] for data warehouses.

• NFT(Sc), NDT(Sc), NSDT(Sc), NAFT(Sc), NADT(Sc), NASDT(Sc), NFK(Sc).

3 Methodology

In this section we describe the methodology used, to analyze the metrics data computed from the 41 schemas. Principal Component Analysis (PCA) is a standard technique used to identify the underlying, orthogonal dimensions, explaining the relationships between the variables in a data set.

4 Experimental Setup

In this section, we present our empirical validation for the DW metrics defined in the previous section. In doing this, we firstly define the experimental settings and collected data. Finally, we analyze and interpret the results.

4.1 Experimental Settings and Collected Data

Information is "the" main organizational asset. We are analyzing a set of valid metrics [3] for measuring data warehouse model quality, which can help designers in choosing the best option among more than one alternative design. This experiment is carried out in order to empirically validate the metrics defined in Section2 using data collected from 41 schemas, as empirical validation plays a very important role in proving the practical utility of metrics.

Forty One Data Warehouse Schema are collected in order to perform this experiment. The domain of the schemas are different and we tried to select examples which represents the real world cases, through judging their utility in practical context. The values of Data Warehouse metrics for 41 schemas were calculated and analyzed.

4.2 Analysis Results

In this section, we present our empirical validation for the Data Warehouse metrics defined in the previous section. Figure shows the principal components that have been extracted. Three components were extracted (the three components that had an eigen value greater than 1).

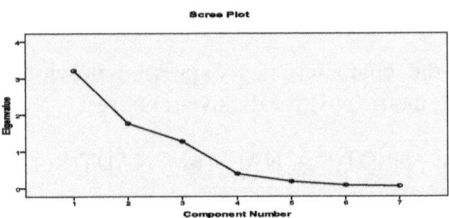

Fig.1. Screen Shot

4.3 Conclusion

We performed Principal Component Analysis which extracted three principal components. Principal Component1 consists of 3 metrics (NFT, NFK, NAFT). These measures are related to fact table, this component can be used as an abstract fact table metric. Principal Component2 consists of 2 metrics (NSDT, NASDT). These measures are related to count of shared dimensional table, this component can be used as shared dimensional table metric. Similarly, Principal Component3 consists of 2 metrics (NDT, NADT). Since, these measures are related to dimensional table, this component can be used as an abstract dimensional table metric.

Concluding this section, the presented principal Component Analysis technique (PCA) removes the interrelations constructed by independent components. This proves to be useful in dimension reduction by reducing the redundant metrics. This helped to reduce the effort required for further computation.

References

1. Calero, C., Piattini, M., Genero, M.: Developing quality complex database systems: practices, techniques & technologies. In: Metrics for Controlling Database Complexity, ch. III (2001)
2. Caro, A., Calero, C., Caballero, I., Piattini, M.: Defining a Data Quality Model for Web Portals. In: Aberer, K., Peng, Z., Rundensteiner, E.A., Zhang, Y., Li, X. (eds.) WISE 2006. LNCS, vol. 4255, pp. 363–374. Springer, Heidelberg (2006)
3. Calero, C., Piattini, M., Pascual, C., Serrano, M.A., Piattini, M., Genero, M., Calero, C., Polo, M., Ruiz, F.: Towards DW Quality metrics. In: Proceedings of the International Workshop on Design and Management of Data Warehouses (DMDW 2001) Interlaken, Switzerland (June 4, 2001); Foster, I., Kesselman, C.: The Grid: Blueprint for a New Computing Infrastructure. Morgan Kaufmann, San Francisco (1999)
4. Inmon, W.H.: Building the Data Warehouse, 3rd edn. John Wiley and Sons, USA (2003)
5. Serrano, M., Calero, C., Piattini, M.: An experimental replication with data warehouse metrics. International Journal of Data Warehousing & Mining 1(4), 1–21 (2005)
6. Sieniawski, P., Trawiński, B.: An Open Platform of Data Quality Monitoring for ERP Information Systems. In: IFIP Working Conference on Software Engineering Techniques - SET 2006, Warsaw, Poland (2006), http://www.ncbi.nlm.nih.gov
7. Signore, O.: Towards a Quality Model for Web Sites. In: CMG Conference, Warsaw, Poland (2005)

Utilization Analysis of Servers in a Data Centre

Girish Keshav Palshikar, Amrit Lal Ahuja, and Harrick M. Vin

Tata Research Development and Design Centre (TRDDC)
Tata Consultancy Services Limited,
54B, Hadapsar Industrial Estate, Pune 411013, India
{gk.palshikar,amrit.ahuja,harrick.vin}@tcs.com
http://www.tcs-trddc.com

Abstract. A *data centre* is a large centralized collection of IT infrastructure (servers, databases, application software etc.) for business functions. Analysis of the servers in a data centre with respect to their utilization characteristics is important for effective management the IT infrastructure - e.g., for reducing costs, improving reliability of business operations and capacity planning. Already saturated servers can crash with even a slight increase in workload and better usage of underutilized servers can save money and power. In this paper, we formalize several business questions related to utilization of servers in a data centre: already saturated, near saturation, under-utilized and interesting utilization patterns. We provide algorithms that use rigorous statistical techniques to automatically identify servers that satisfy such conditions. We present the results of utilization analysis of a real data centre.

Keywords: Data centre, Performance Monitoring, Server utilization, Capacity planning, Saturation, Wilcoxson signed rank sum test.

1 Introduction

Facilitated by fast and cheap computers and data storage devices, IT is now an integral part of the business functions in most large organizations. The bulk of the IT infrastructure for business functions is provided by the data centres. A *data centre* (or *server farm*) is a centralized collection of computing, data storage, communication and software infrastructure. A data centre runs a variety of software consisting of system software, operating systems, databases and business-specific applications. A data centre can be viewed as a loosely interconnected collection of communicating servers. Each *server* is a high-end computer equipped with data storage and appropriate software (applications, databases etc.). A data centre is often located in a single physical location such as a building. It is not uncommon for a data centre to include 10,000 or more servers. As an example, a data centre for a bank stores all the transactional data for all of its branches and works as the "back-end" of the application programs to provide the required services to its customers and employees. A large organization may also have multiple data centres, e.g., organized according to regions. Since a data

R. Kannan and F. Andres (Eds.): ICDEM 2010, LNCS 6411, pp. 173–180, 2012.
© Springer-Verlag Berlin Heidelberg 2012

centre is an expensive and critical resource, effective management and utilization of the IT infrastructure in it is important for smooth working of the business.

It is often the case that the IT infrastructure in a data centre grows in a rather *ad hoc* manner. Whenever a new business need arises (e.g., a new office is opened, a new business application system is added etc.), a number of servers are added to the data centre, without an adequate understanding of the current capacity and utilization of the already available servers. This is often done out of caution ("don't disturb what is working fine") and also for technical reasons such as compatibility of software versions. As a result, the workload is often non-uniformly distributed across the servers. Further, the utilization of a server may vary over time within a day, because of the complex and non-uniform temporal patterns of workload arrival. Also, some servers are often dedicated to handle a specific type of workload from a specific source. For example, a server dedicated to handle a cheque related service may remain heavily underutilized for most of the day, except for one hour in the evening when a burst of requests arrives, at which time it is saturated. Analysis of the servers in a data centre with respect to their utilization characteristics is important for effective management - e.g., for reducing costs, improving reliability of business operations and capacity planning. Following business questions need to be answered by analyzing the server performance data in a statistically rigorous manner:

1. Identify servers which are already saturated.
2. Identify servers which are near saturation.
3. Identify servers which exhibit *interesting* saturation patterns.
4. Identify servers which are very under-utilized.

Already saturated servers are prone to crash or can drastically reduce the response time of business functionality, even with a slight increase in workload, thereby adversely affecting the quality of service. Severely under-utilised servers can be used to host additional functionality (either new or transferred from already saturated servers) thereby improving utilization and reducing operational cots and capital investment costs for adding new infrastructure.

Answering these business questions rigorously is difficult, because the concepts (under-utilized, already saturated, near saturation, interesting saturation patterns), though intuitively clear, are not formally defined. Also, the very large number of servers in a data centre and complex temporal patterns in workload arrival and utilization prevent manual monitoring. An automated solution is required that can reliably detect when a server meets any of these conditions. The goal is not to monitor the servers for these conditions in real-time. Rather, we are interested in using long-term past data to produce historically justified answers to these business questions. For example, a server should be classified as already saturated only when it shows consistently at a high-level of utilization for long periods of time. A similar comment holds for detecting other conditions. In this paper, we formalize the concepts involved in answering the above business questions and provide statistically rigorous solutions for detecting servers which satisfy such utilization conditions. The paper is organized as follows. Section 2 formalizes the above business questions and discusses rigorous statistics-based approaches to solve them. Section 3 discusses the case study of a real-life data centre where these techniques were applied. Section 4 discusses related work. Section 5 provides conclusions and points out some further work.

2   Problem Formalization and Solution

Each server is monitored for parameters such as CPU and memory utilization, disk usage, data communication etc. For simplicity, we consider only one aspect of server utilization viz., CPU utilization. Thus there is a univariate time-series for each server, which measures CPU utilization (as a real number between 0% to 100%) at some regular time interval (say every 5 seconds). For servers having multiple CPUs, this number is the average of the utilizations of the individual CPUs in that period. We first formalize the notions of already saturated, near saturation and under-utilized servers, based on the CPU utilization time-series.

Throughout the paper, given time-series for a server S is denoted by $X_S = <(t_1, x_1), (t_2, x_2), \ldots, (t_N, x_N) >$ where x_i denotes the CPU utilization of S at the ith time instant t_i. For a uniformly sampled time-series, the difference $t_{i+1} - t_i$ is constant. But in practice this difference varies somewhat and for some time instants, the observations may be missing altogether. We pre-process the given time-series using techniques such as imputations and outlier detection and removal, so that the given time-series can be considered uniformly sampled.

Let $0 < M < 100$ be a user-specified *saturation level*. In general $x_i \geq M$ for say k among the N values in X_S and $x_i < M$ for the remaining $N - k$ values. Server S is said to be *near saturation* if k is "sufficiently large" i.e., if "sufficiently many" points in X_S out of N are above M. Next two subsection propose two solutions to formalize this concept.

2.1   Near Saturation: A Simple Approach

A simple approach would classify a server as near saturation if the fraction of the points above the given utilization threshold value M is above some user-specified threshold value $0 < h < 1$ i.e., if $k/N > h$, where k is the number of points above M. For example, if $h = 0.25$ then a server is near saturation if 25% points in the CPU utilization time-series are above the utilization level M. While it may be adequate for a high-level view, there are several difficulties with this simple approach. First, automatically determining the correct value for the threshold h is difficult. The approach totally ignores the temporal nature of the data. For example, a server heavily used for one particular hour every day and lightly loaded for the rest of the day is interesting because any workload increase will likely crash or severely slow down the server in that critical one hour period. Such scenarios are not detected by the simple approach.

2.2   Approach Using Wilcoxson Signed Rank Sum Test

To take time into account, we divide the given time-series into a sequence of consecutive non-overlapping windows e.g., each window may include one hour's data. We then apply the one-sample Wilcoxson signed rank sum test to the data points in a given window and classify whether the server is near saturation in that window or not. The idea is to examine how many of the points in the given window are above (and below) the given saturation level M. The one-sample Wilcoxson signed rank sum test is positive if the median of the data points in the window is $\geq M$ i.e., "close to" 50% points in the window are above M.

The one-sample Wilcoxson signed rank sum test is a non-parametric test to check the null hypothesis that the median of the data is equal to the given value M. The test is carried out as follows. Let n denote the number of data points in the given window. First remove all observations which are exactly equal to M and adjust n accordingly. Compute the signed difference $d_i = x_i - M$ for each data point in the window. Rank the d_is, ignoring the signs (i.e. assign rank 1 to the smallest $|d_i|$, rank 2 to the next etc.). For each group having an equal value for 2 or more observations/differences, average the rank between them. For example, suppose we have ranked first 4 data points and suppose the next two d_i values are equal; then assign the rank 5.5 to both the observations (average of ranks 5 and 6). Label each rank as $+$ or $-$, according to the sign of d_i. Compute W^+ and W^-, the sums of the ranks of the positive and negative d_is respectively. Check that $W^+ + W^- = \frac{n(n+1)}{2}$. Assuming $n \geq 20$, we use the normal approximation. Compute $\mu_W = \frac{n(n+1)}{4}$ and $\sigma_W = \sqrt{\frac{n(n+1)(2n+1)}{24}}$. Reduce the variance by $\frac{t^3-t}{48}$ for each group of t tied ranks. For example, if there was a group of 2 equal values, then $\frac{2^3-2}{48} = 0.125$ and the new value is $\sigma_W = \sqrt{\frac{n(n+1)(2n+1)}{24}} - 0.125$. Compute $z = \frac{W^+ - \mu_W}{\sigma_W}$. Under Normal approximation, z approximately follows the standard normal distribution. Probability (called p-value) of observing this particular value of z can be obtained from the standard table. If this p-value is less than the given *significance level* α (typically, $\alpha = 0.05$), then the null hypothesis is rejected and the server is not near saturation in this window.

The algorithm near_saturation accepts the utilization time-series X_S of a server S as input, divides it into a sequence of overlapping windows (each covering a period of b seconds) using subroutine divide_TS, performs the one-sample Wilcoxson signed rank sum test on each window using subroutine OSWSRS_test and returns sequence F_S of Boolean flags (near saturation or not) for each window. Later we analyze this sequence to detect *interesting* saturation patterns.

```
algorithm near_saturation
input X_S // CPU utilization time-series for server S
input b // window duration e.g., 60 minutes
input M // saturation limit
input α // significance level e.g., 0.05
output W_S, F_S; // sequence of windows over X_S, a Boolean flag for each window in W_S
W_S = divide_TS(X_S,b); // W_S contains m windows m ≈ N/b
for(i = 0; i < m; i + +) // do for each window
      F_S(i) = OSWSRS_test(W_S(i),M,α); // 1-sample Wilcoxson signed rank sum test
end for
return(W_S, F_S);
```

It is possible to use other tests instead of one-sample Wilcoxson signed rank sum test. For example, one could perform a hypothesis test that the fraction p of points above M is greater than some fixed constant p_0. Wilcoxson test implicitly uses $p_0 = 0.5$. The test statistic for the null hypothesis $H_0 : p = p_0$ is $\frac{(\hat{p} - p_0)}{\sqrt{\frac{p_0(1-p_0)}{n}}}$, where $\hat{p}$ is the observed fraction of points above M. This test statistic follows a standard Normal distribution and hence the p-value (probability) of observing that value of the test statistic can be computed using standard tables. The null hypothesis is rejected if this p-value is less than the required level of significance (e.g., $\alpha = 0.05$). This flexible approach allows testing whether the fraction of points above M is more than any given constant (p_0 need not be 0.5).

2.3   Identifying Already Saturated and Under-Utilized Servers

Let $0 < M_H, M_L < 100$ be a user-specified *high* and *low saturation levels*. Server S is *already saturated* (*under-utilized*) if "sufficiently many" points in X_S are above M_H (below M_L). Algorithm near_saturation can be re-used for identifying a server which is already saturated (under-utilized), by using M_H (M_L) instead of M. For example, $M_L = 20\%, M_H = 80\%$.

2.4   Identifying Servers with *Interesting* Utilization Patterns

Identification of temporal regularities and other interesting patterns in the CPU utilization of a server is useful from a practical perspective. In this paper, we consider only one such interesting pattern: is the server getting near saturation (or already saturated) at any particular hour of the day for many days? Algorithm int_pattern1 identifies the time periods which show near saturation on "significantly many" days. The idea is to create a time series which contains all the data points from the original time series which fall in the same period (e.g., 10:00 AM to 11:00 AM every day) but on different days. The algorithm examines this new time series as a whole (without dividing into windows) using the algorithm near_saturation. If the time series is declared as near saturation, then clearly, there are many data points above M during this particular time period across days. Hence the server is frequently getting near saturation during this particular time period across days.

We re-use algorithm near_saturation to divide the CPU utilization time-series X_S for a server into a sequence W_S of non-overlapping windows (each of duration b). Window w_d^i in W_S refers to the i-th time period in d-th day. We also get a corresponding sequence of Boolean flags F_S where flag f_d^i is 1 if the server is near saturation in window w_d^i and 0 otherwise. If there are "too many" 1's in this sequence of flags for a particular hour i, then the server is showing a *near saturation regularity* at the i-th hour on most days. To test this, we form a new time-series Y^i which is a concatenation of the windows in a fixed i-th time period on all days. Using one-sample Wilcoxson signed rank sum test on Y^i, we can test whether Y^i is near saturation or not. If yes, then we declare that the server S has near saturation regularity in the i-th time period of the day.

Table 1. Analysis of 7 Servers in a data centre

Server	#Windows	#Invalid Windows	#Near Saturation Windows	Summary Statistics		
				Mean	St. Dev.	Median
s1	506	2	343	56.08	30.16	73.06
s2	221	1	69	37.02	23.46	31.22
s3	60	0	23	63.11	18.64	52.71
s4	911	6	362	33.25	33.66	7.16
s5	1181	6	216	30.02	31.47	26.00
s6	305	5	13	25.38	18.08	19.69
s7	438	2	45	22.58	25.94	10.42

```
algorithm int_pattern1
input X_S // CPU utilization time-series for server S
input b // window duration e.g., 60 minutes
input M // saturation limit
input α // significance level e.g., 0.05
output W_S, F_S; // sequence of windows over X_S, a Boolean flag for each window in W_S
W_S, F_S = near_saturation(X_S, b, M, α);
for each time period i in a day do
      Y^i = w^i d_1 • w^i d_2 ... // • denotes concatenation
      if OSWSRS_test(Y^i, M, α) == 1 then
            print "Near saturation regularity in time period i"
      end if
end for
```

3   Experiments

We were given real-life performance monitoring data for 80 servers in a data centre. CPU utilization time-series for a period of about 21 days were collected for each of the servers. The CPU utilization was monitored at every 2 minutes. Some simple pre-processing and cleaning up steps were carried out on the time-series before using them for the experimental study. We use 1-hour windows ($b = 3600$ seconds) over each server's time-series. If a window contains less than 10 data points, then it is *invalid* and excluded from analysis. The saturation level is set at $M = 60\%$ and significance level at $\alpha = 0.05$. Table 1 shows the top 7 servers containing maximum number of windows detected as near saturation. For example, for server $s1$, 2 out of 506 windows were invalid and 343 among the remaining 504 windows were detected as near saturation. Fig. 1 shows the time-plot of the CPU utilization for server $s1$. In the beginning and towards the end of the monitoring period, the server has low utilization, but for the bulk of the period, the server is used quite heavily. The histogram in Fig. 1 shows a mixture distribution with peaks in the low and high utilization levels. The last part in Fig. 1 shows a matrix whose rows correspond to dates and columns to a specific window (time period). The ij-th entry shows a Boolean flag which is 1 if the server is near saturation in j-th window on i-th date. For example, column 1 corresponds to the window 00:00 AM to 01:00 AM; on 14 out of 21 dates, $s1$

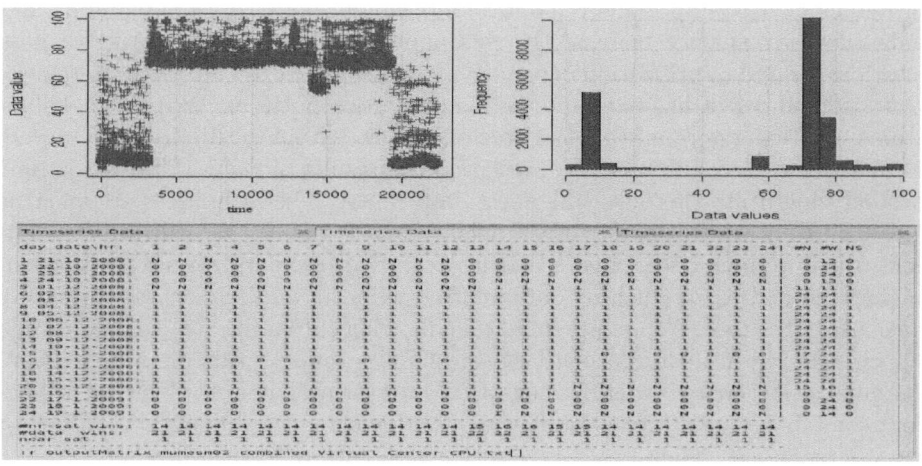

Fig. 1. Time-plot and histogram for CPU utilization of server $s1$

was near saturation in this period. Wilcoxson test is positive for the set of all data points in these 21 windows taken as a whole. Hence $s1$ is frequently near saturation from 00:00 AM to 01:00 AM on most days.

4 Related Work

Performance monitoring of servers and other resources is a well-developed area. Many tools are available to collect large amounts of performance data. We are focusing on *mining* this performance monitoring data to automatically identify opportunities for improving utilization and reducing operational costs of large data centres. A closely related area is that of constructing *models* of the server performance and use them for purposes such as explaining observed performance characteristics, performance forecasting, performance simulations under different workload conditions and identification of bottlenecks. The models are usually analytical [1], structural (e.g., Petri-net based [2]) or statistical (e.g., queuing theoretic [3], [4]; see also [5]). Related to our interesting utilization patterns, [6] proposes a Gini performance coefficient to measure regularity in the performance of a server. As in this paper, the profiling data has been used for various tasks such as capacity planning [7], server consolidation [8], server configuration [9] and performance improvement [10] etc. Unlike most such work, we have not attempted to relate CPU utilization to the workloads.

5 Conclusions and Further Work

Analysis of the servers in a data centre with respect to their utilization characteristics is important for effective management the IT infrastructure - e.g., for reducing costs, improving reliability of business operations and planning and budgeting for capacity increase. In this paper, we formalized several business questions related to utilization of servers in a data centre: already saturated, near saturation, under-utilized and interesting utilization patterns. We provided algorithms that use rigorous statistical techniques to automatically identify servers that satisfy such conditions. We presented the results of using these algorithms for analyzing utilization levels in a real data centre. The techniques are efficient and work well in identifying servers which satisfy any of the utilization conditions. Little domain knowledge, statistics expertise or experimentation is needed, so that the end-users (such as data centre engineers and managers) can easily make use of the tool. We are pursuing the following extensions: (a) using multiple aspects of server utilization together; e.g., CPU/memory utilization, disk usage, communication etc.; (b) discovering other interesting patterns of server utilization; e.g., spikes and their periodicities; (c) dependencies among utilizations of many servers; e.g., when two servers get nearly saturated together.

References

1. Kant, K., Won, Y.: Server Capacity Planning for Web Traffic Workload. IEEE Trans. Knowl. and Data Eng. 11(5), 731–747 (1999)
2. Praphamontripong, U., Gokhale, S., Gokhale, A., Gray, J.: An Analytical Approach to Performance Analysis of an Asynchronous Web Server. Simulation 83(8), 571–586 (2007)
3. Kant, K., Sundaram, C.R.M.: A Server Performance Model for Static Web Workloads. In: 2000 IEEE International Symposium on Performance Analysis of Systems and Software (ISPASS 2000), pp. 201–206. IEEE Press, New York (2000)
4. Cao, J., Andersson, M., Nyberg, C., Kihl, M.: Web Server Performance Modeling Using an M/G/1/K*PS Queue. In: 10th International Conference on Telecommunications (ICT 2003), pp. 1501–1506 (2003)
5. Hernández-Orallo, E., Vila-Carbó, J.: Web Server Performance Analysis Using Histogram Workload Models. Comput. Netw. 53(15), 2727–2739 (2009)
6. Ling, Y., Chen, S., Lin, X.: On the Performance Regularity of Web Servers. World Wide Web 7(3), 241–258 (2004)
7. Jiang, G., Chen, H., Yoshihira, K.: Profiling Services for Resource Optimization and Capacity Planning in Distributed systems. Cluster Computing 11(4), 313–329 (2008)
8. Spellmann, A., Erickson, K., Reynolds, J.: Server Consolidation Using Performance Modeling. IT Professional 5(5), 31–36 (2003)
9. Arlitt, M., Williamson, C.: Understanding Web Server Configuration Issues. Softw. Pract. Exper. 34(2), 163–186 (2004)
10. Hu, Y., Nanda, A., Yang, Q.: Measurement, Analysis and Performance Improvement of the Apache Web Server. In: IEEE International Performance, Computing and Communications Conference (IPCCC 1999), pp. 261–267. IEEE Press, New York (1999)

Subset Selection Approach for Watermarking Relational Databases

Burepalli V.S. Rao and Munaga V.N.K. Prasad

Institute for Development and Research in Banking Technology,
Hyderabad, India
burepallisri@gmail.com, mvnkprasad@idrbt.ac.in

Abstract. Information on the open medium like Internet is of great source of digital content. This can be copied easily, modified by the unauthorized users and shared among various unknown users of the Internet. This possesses threats in various forms to the owner of the digital information. In this paper we focus on copyright issue and propose a mechanism for proof of ownership based on the secure embedding of a robust imperceptible watermark in the relational database. It is achieved by formulating a watermarking method, which will watermark only the numeric attributes. This introduces a new way of dividing the database into different subsets and a meaningful watermark is embedded into database. Proposed watermarking technique avoids the synchronization problems and is resilient to subset selection attack, alteration attack, attribute cutting attack and subset addition attack.

Keywords: Digital watermarking, Information hiding, Digital rights, Security, Relational database.

1 Introduction

Recently, watermarking techniques have been extended from the multimedia context to relational databases. This is done to protect the ownership of data even after the data are published or distributed (i.e., piracy problem) [3]. To address this concern and to fight against data piracy, watermarking techniques have been introduced, first in the multimedia context [9-11] and now in relational database literature.

The extensive research has focused on various aspects of DBMS security, including access control techniques as well as data security issues [2, 4, 6, 8, 12, 13, 15, 16, 18, 19] little work has been done to secure proof of rights protection over relational databases. In recent years, researches have developed a variety of watermarking technique for protecting the ownership of relational databases [1, 5, 17, 22-24]. Most of the watermarking technique modifies numerical attributes [1, 5, 7, 22, 23, 14, 27, 28], while others swap categorical values [25, 26]. We analyze the current research on this issue and proposed a new watermarking technique.

The rest of paper is organized as follows. Section 2 presents Cryptographic algorithm - message authenticated code. Proposed watermark embedding and detection techniques are presented in Section 3. Experimental results are presented in section 4. Finally, conclusion is given in section 5.

R. Kannan and F. Andres (Eds.): ICDEM 2010, LNCS 6411, pp. 181–188, 2012.
© Springer-Verlag Berlin Heidelberg 2012

2   Cryptographic Algorithm – Message Authenticated Code

A message-authentication code (MAC) is a one-way hash function that depends on a key and our proposed technique depends on this algorithm. Let $H_2(K, r.P)$ be a MAC that randomizes the values of the primary key attribute r.P of tuple r and returns an integer value in wide range. $H_2(K, r.P)$ is selected with a private key K known only to the owner. The following secure Message Authentication Code (MAC) [20] is being used.

First Hash: $H_1(K, r.P) = H(K \circ r.P)$

MAC: $H_2(K, r.P) = H(K \circ H(K \circ r.P))$

Where o represents concatenation

Table 1. Parameters used in watermarking techniques

η	Number of tuples in the relational database
ν	Number of attributes available for marking
ξ	Number of least significant bits available for marking in an attribute
1/γ	Fraction of tuples marked
L	Number of bits in the watermark(WM)
K	Owner's secret key

3   Proposed Watermark Embedding and Detection Technique

The proposed watermarking algorithm in [1] that does not provide a mechanism for multi bit watermarks. They assume that the LSB bits in any tuple can be altered without checking data constraints. The watermark information is meaningless and which is not decided by the owner of the database. Sion, R., Atallah, M., Sunil Prabhakar [5] proposed a watermarking technique that embeds watermark bits in the data statistics. The data partitioning used is based on the usage of special marker tuples, which makes it vulnerable to watermark synchronization errors resulting from tuple deletion and tuple insertion. Min Huang, Jiaheng Cao, Zhiyong Peng and Ying Fang [14] proposed a watermark mechanism for numeric data. While detecting the watermark if the attacker modifies the database then it is very difficult to reconstruct the id value and subsets. Fei Guo, Jianmin Wang, Deyi Li [28] uses twice embedding insertion technique (i.e., for both fingerprint and owner's watermark) is used to embed the watermark bits. The fingerprint is meaningful but the owner's watermark information is meaningless. Moreover, it assumes that LSB bits in any tuple can be altered without checking data constraints. In order to avoid the above mentioned problems we proposed a watermark embedding and detection techniques which are shown in Fig 1 and Fig 2.

3.1 Proposed Watermark Embedding Technique

Watermarking for relational database introduces small changes in original database without affecting data usability. Thus, these small changes constitute the watermark. If we detect the watermark with high probability from a suspicious database, we can suspect piracy. The proposed watermark embedding technique divides the database into different subsets based on secret key K. The number of subsets is equal to the number of bits in the watermark. The data set R is a database relation with scheme $R(P, A_0, ..., A_{v-1})$, where P is the primary key attribute, $A_0, ..., A_{v-1}$ are v attributes which are candidates for watermarking and η is the number of tuples in R. The data set R is divided into L non-overlapping subsets (Subsets do not overlap, that is, for any two subsets s_i and s_j such that i ≠ j, we have $s_i \cap s_j = \{\}$) namely, $\{s_0, ..., s_{L-1}\}$, such that each subset s_i contains on the average η/L tuples from the data set R. For each tuple r∈ R, computes a MAC, which is considered to be secure [20] and is given by $H_2(K, r.P)$, where $r.P$ is the primary key of the tuple r, H() is a secure hash function. Using equation 1 the proposed watermarking technique calculates the subset number.

$$j \leftarrow H_2(K, r.P) \bmod L \tag{1}$$

For each tuple r the subset assignment is given by

$$Subset_j \leftarrow r \tag{2}$$

Furthermore, an attacker cannot predict the tuples to subset assignment without the knowledge of the secret key K and the number of subsets L, which are kept secret. Keeping L as a secret parameter is not a requirement but which introduces difficulty for an attacker in regenerating the subsets.

This approach equally divides the database into different subsets, which does not rely on special marker tuples for the selection of data subsets. This makes it resilient to watermark synchronization attacks caused by tuple deletion and tuple insertion. In the above way the proposed watermarking technique avoids the synchronization problems.Fig.1 shows the algorithmic steps for watermark embedding technique.

From Fig.1 before the changed data being stored into database, at line 7 we check for constraints whether it exceeds the data usability bounds or not. If it exceeds, we keep the primary key $r.P$ of tuple r in the false_array which is shown at line 8 and rollback the watermarking step. On the contrary, if the changed data is in the available changing range, we commit the change and store the new_data into the database which is shown at line 10. The constraint function includes basic data statistical measurement constraint, semantic constraints and structural constraints. Concretely mean and standard deviation of dataset are very common aspects in basic data statistical constraint. Semantic constraints and structural constraints are defined by user's input SQL statement according to relational table.

Watermark_Embedding (K , γ, ξ, v, WM, bounds)

    1)   L $\leftarrow$ Find number of bits in the watermark

    2)   foreach tuple r $\in$ R do

    3) $j \leftarrow H_2(K, r.P)$ mod L //finding subset number

    4) $Subset_j \leftarrow r$ //keeping the tuple r into the corresponding subset

    5)   for(j=0;j<L ; j++)

    6)   mark $Subset_j$

    7)   If(not Constraints. satisfied (new_data, bounds) then

    8)   { false_array[] $\leftarrow r.P$

    9)   Rollback}

    10)   else Commit

    11) Subroutine mark($Subset_j$)

    12)   foreach tuple t $\in$ $Subset_j$ do

    13)   if($H_1(K, t.P)$ mod γ equals zero)

    14)   attribute_index i= $H_1(K, t.P)$ mod v //mark attribute A_i

    15)   bit_index n = $H_1(K, t.P)$ mod ξ //mark n^{th} bit

    16) Set the nth bit of t.A_i to wm[j]

Fig. 1. Proposed watermark embedding technique

3.2 Proposed Watermark Detection Technique

Assume Alice suspects that the relation S published by Mallory has been pirated from her relation R. The set of tuples and attributes in S can be a subset of R. We assume that Mallory does not drop the primary key attribute or change the value of primary keys since the primary key contains valuable information and changing it will render the database less useful from user's point of view.Fig.2 shows the algorithmic steps for watermark detection technique.

    The proposed watermarking technique has the following advantages:

1. The MAC value ($H_2(K, r.P)$) controls the database dividing into different subsets and it is hard for an attacker to guess the subsets.
2. Meaningful watermark is embedded into the database.
3. This mechanism avoids the synchronization problems.
4. The constraints function will assure data's usability and retain properties of relational data.
5. The majority_voting method makes up for some small mistakes in the detection of watermark bit caused by subset selection, attribute cutting, alteration and subset addition attacks. So, that final detected watermark won't be affected badly.
6. This technique is very robust to subset selection, attribute cutting, alteration and subset addition attacks.

// K, γ, v, and ξ have the same values used for watermark insertion
  // L is the number of bits in the watermark (WM)
  //Watermak_Detection (k, γ, ξ, v, L, false_array [])

1)   foreach tuple s∈ S do
2) $j \leftarrow H_2(K, s.P)$ mod L // finding subset number
3) $Subset_j \leftarrow s$ // keeping the tuple in the corresponding subset
4)   for(i =0;i<L ; i ++)
5) $WM'[] \leftarrow$ detect($Subset_j$)
6)   subroutine detect($Subset_j$) return number
7)   foreach tuple m ∈ $Subset_j$ do
8)   If(($H_1(K, m.P)$ mod γ equals to zero) && ($m.P$ not in false_array))
      then
9)   attribute_index i= $H_1(K, m.P)$ mod v //get attribute A_i
10)   bit_index n = $H_1(K, m.P)$ mod ξ //get n^{th} bit
11)   ext [ ] $\leftarrow$ n^{th} bit of m.A_i
12) return majority_voting (ext [ ])

Fig. 2. Proposed Watermark detection technique

4   Experimental Results

The experiments conducted on Forest Cover Type dataset [21]. The dataset has 581012 rows. An extra attribute called id is added to serve as the primary key. The first ten integer-valued attributes were chosen as candidates for watermarking. The experiment has been done on a system of 2.40 GHz CPU and 256 MB of RAM. Proposed watermark embedding and detection techniques are coded in JAVA and executed on Windows 2000 platform. By using the proposed watermark embedding technique the watermark has been embedded into database with different values of γ and ξ and the mean and variance is observed. From those observation there is no change in the mean. But there is a slight variation in the variance which is shown in table 2. The subset selection attack, attribute cutting attack, subset addition attack and alteration attacks are performed to test the robustness of the proposed watermarking technique. The results of these attacks are shown in Fig 3 to 6.

4.1   Attribute Cutting Attack

Fig 4 shows the effect of omitting watermarked attributes from the database. The results for γ =9999, 999, 99 and 9 are plotted by varying the number of attributes dropped. Form this Fig as the number of dropped attributes is increases then the watermark detection ratio decreases. This proposed watermark mechanism is robust to attributes cutting attack.

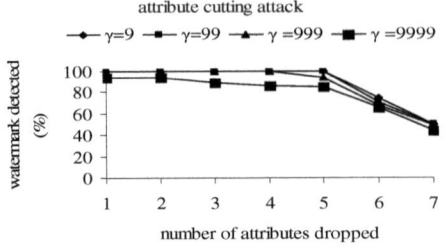

Fig. 3. Watermark detected in subset selection attack (ξ=1, ν=10)

Fig. 4. Watermark detected in attribute cutting attack (ξ=1, ν=10)

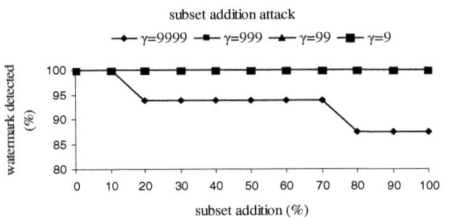

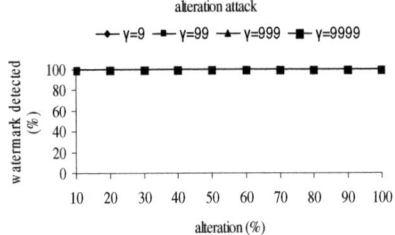

Fig. 5. Watermark detected in subset addition attack (ξ=1, ν=10)

Fig. 6. Watermark detected in alteration attack (ξ=1, ν=10)

Table 2. Change in variance introduced by watermarking

Attribute	Mean	Variance	γ=9999			999			99			9		
			ξ=1	4	8	ξ=1	4	8	ξ=1	4	8	ξ=1	4	8
Elevation	2959	78391								1	1			4
Aspect	155	12525									1			21
Slope	14	56									1			7
Horz-Dist-To-Hydrology	269	45177									2		+1	9
Vert-Dist-To-Hydrology	46	3398									-5			97
Horz-Dist-To-Roadways	235	2431276			-1							-1	-1	24
Hillshade-9am	212	717												3
Hillshade-Noon	223	391									2			27
Hillshade-3pm	142	1465									1			8
Horz-Dist-To-Fire-Points	1980	1753493				1						-1	+2	87

4.2 Subset Addition Attack

The attacker may add some tuples to the watermarked database. But this form of attack nearly has little impact to the watermark. The above experiment is conducted for different values of γ. Also, Fig 5 indicates that the watermark survives at least

87% when 100% of tuples were added to the watermarked database, but for the remaining values of γ =999, γ =99 and γ =9, 100% of the watermark were detected. From this, as the number of tuples added to the watermarked database increases then the detection ratio decreases. This shows that the algorithm is very robust to subset addition attacks.

4.3 Alteration Attack

In the alteration attack the attacker may randomly change some data in order to erase the watermark. In this experiment, if the attacker randomly changes 100% of tuples by resetting one bit of a value, we can detect 100% of watermark. The experiments were carried out with the values of γ=9, γ=99, γ=999 and γ=9999. For all the values of γ 100 % of the watermark is detected. In this way, the proposed watermark technique is very robust to attributes alteration attack which is shown in Fig 6.

5 Conclusion

In this paper, we study the numeric attributes digital watermark technology in relational database. Proposed watermark technique introduces the new way of dividing the database into different subsets, which embeds the meaningful watermark into the subsets. Our proposed watermark technique avoids the synchronization problems and is resilient to the subset selection attack, alteration attack, attribute cutting attack and subset addition attack. Further, the algorithm can be extended to mark non-numeric attributes and also to effectively protect the copyright of the relational database.

References

1. Agrawal, R., Kiernan, J.: Watermarking Relational Databases. In: Proceedings of the 28th VLDB Conference, Hong Kong, China, pp. 155–166 (2002)
2. Hale, J., Threet, J., Shenoi, S.: A Framework for High Assurance Security of Distributed Objects. In: IFIP TC11/WG11.3 International Conference on Database Security. Status and prospects: status and prospects, vol. X, pp. 100–199 (1997)
3. Vaas, L.: Putting a stop to database piracy. eWEEK, enterprise news and reviews (2003)
4. Bertino, E., Braun, M., Castano, S., Ferrari, E., Mesiti, M.: Author-x: A java based System for XML Data Protection. In: Proc. IFIP TC11/WG11.3 14th Annual Working Conference on Database Security: Data and Application Security Development Directions, pp. 15—26 (2000)
5. Sion, R., Atallah, M., Prabhakar, S.: Rights Protection for Relational Data. Transaction on Knowledge and Data Engineering 16(12), 1509–1525 (2004)
6. Shehab, M., Bertino, E., Ghafoor, A.: Watermarking Relational Databases Using Optimization-Based Techniques. IEEE Trancatiions on Knowledge and Data Engineering 20(1), 116–129 (2008)
7. Bertino, E., Jajodia, S., Samarati, P.: A Flexible Authorization Mechanism for Relational Data Management Systems. ACM Trans. Information Systems 17(2), 101–140 (1999)

8. Hildebrandt, E., Saake, G.: User Authentication in Multidatabase Systems. In: Proc.9th Int'l. Workshop Database and Expert Systems Applications, pp. 281–286 (1998)
9. Cox, I., Bloom, J., Miller, M.: Digital Watermarking. Morgan Kaufmann Publishers (2001)
10. Swanson, M., Kobayashi, M., Tewfik, A.: Multimedia Data Embedding and Watermarking Technologies. Proc. IEEE 86, 1064–1087 (1998)
11. Hartung, F., Kutter, M.: Multimedia Watermarking Techniques. Proc. IEEE 87(7), 1079–1107 (1999)
12. Jajodia, S., Samarati, P., Subrahmanian, V.S.: A Logical Language for Expressing Authorizations. In: Proc. IEEE Symp. Security and Privacy, pp. 31–42 (1997)
13. Jajodia, S., Samarati, P., Subrahmanian, V.S., Bertino, E.: A Unified Framework for Enforcing Multiple Access Control Policies. In: Proc. SIGMOD, pp. 474–485 (1997)
14. Huang, M., Cao, J., Peng, Z., Fang, Y.: A New watermark Mechanism for Relational Data. In: The Proceedings of the 4th International Conference on Computer and Information Technology, pp. 946–950 (2004)
15. Li, N., Feigenbaum, J., Grosof, B.N.: A Logic-Based Knowledge Representation for Authorization with Delegation. In: PCSFW: Proc. 12th Computer Security Foundations Workshop, pp. 162–174 (1999)
16. Nyanchama, M., Osborn, S.L.: Access Rights Administration in Role-Based Security Systems. In: Proc. IFIP Workshop Database Security, vol. 60, pp. 37–56 (1994)
17. Sion, R., Atallah, M., Prabhakar, S.: Resilient rights protection for sensor streams. In: Proc. of the very large Databases Conference, pp. 732–743 (2004)
18. Osborn, S.L.: Database Security Integration Using Role-Based Access Control. In: Proc. IFIP Workshop Database Security, vol. 201, pp. 245–258 (2000)
19. Rasikan, D., Son, S.H., Mukkamala, R.: Supporting Security Requirements in Multilevel Real-Time Databases, pp. 199–210 (1995)
20. Schneier, B.: Applied Cryptography, 2nd edn. John Wiley (1996)
21. http://kdd.ics.uci.edu/databases/covertype/covertype.html
22. Gross-Amblard, D.: Query-Preserving watermarking of Relational Databases and XML Documents. In: Proc. 22nd ACM SIGMOD-SIGACT Symp. Principles of Database Systems (PODS 2003), pp. 191–201 (2003)
23. Li, Y., Swarup, V., Jajodia, S.: Constructing a Virtual Primary Key for Fingerprinting Relational Data. In: Proc. ACM Workshop on Digital Rights Management, pp. 133–141 (2003)
24. Li, Y., Guo, H., Jajodia, S.: Tamper Detection and Localization for Categorical Data Using Fragile Watermarks. In: Proc. 4th ACM Workshop Digital Rights Management (DRM 2004), pp. 72–82 (2004)
25. Sion, R.: Proving ownership over categorical data. In: Proc. of IEEE International Conference on Data Engineering, pp. 584–596 (2004)
26. Bertino, E., Ooi, B.C., Yang, Y., Deng, R.: Privacy and ownership preserving of outsourced medical data. In: Proc. of IEEE International Conference on Data Engineering, pp. 521–532 (2005)
27. Sion, R., Atallah, M.J., Prabhakar, S.: On Watermarking Numeric Sets. In: Petitcolas, F.A.P., Kim, H.-J. (eds.) IWDW 2002. LNCS, vol. 2613, pp. 130–146. Springer, Heidelberg (2003)
28. Guo, F., Wang, J., Li, D.: Fingerprinting Relational Databases. In: Proceedings Symposium on Applied Computing, vol. 2(1), pp. 487–492 (2006)

Block Dependency Feature Based Classification Scheme for Uncalibrated Image Steganalysis

Deepa D. Shankar, T. Gireeshkumar, K. Praveen, R. Jithin, and Ashji S. Raj

TIFAC CORE in Cyber Security, Amrita Vishwa Vidyapeetham, Coimbatore, India
{sudee99,gireeshkumart,praveen.cys,
jithn_r550,ashjisraj}@gmail.com

Abstract. Steganalysis is a technique of detecting hidden information sent over a communication medium. In this paper, we present a powerful new blind steganalytic scheme that can reliably detect hidden data in JPEG images. This would increase the success rate of steganalysis by detecting data in transform domain. This scheme is feature based in the sense that features that are sensitive to embedding changes and being employed as means of steganalysis. The features are extracted in DCT domain. DCT domain features have extended DCT features and Markovian features merged together to eliminate the drawbacks of both. The blind steganalytic technique has a broad spectrum of analyzing different embedding techniques. The feature based steganalytic technique is used in the DCT domain to extract about 23 functionals and classify the dataset according to these functionals. The feature set can be increased to about 274 features by merging both DCT and Markovian features. The extracted features are being fed to a classifier which helps to distinguish between a cover and stego image. The classification is also done with inter block dependency features and intra block dependency features within the 274 features. Support Vector Machine is used as classifier here.

Keywords: Steganalysis, DCT, Extended DCT, Markov, Support Vector Machine.

1 Introduction

Steganography is a means of communication in a covert manner so that anyone who inspects the message being exchanged cannot collect enough evidence to prove that the message has data hidden in it. Steganography should thus make the communication invisible. In this paper we propose a new steganalytic technique which can be applied to different steganographic schemes and image format. However it can be ideally used in JPEG format.

Steganalysis can be broadly classified as Blind Steganalysis and Targeted Steganalysis. Targeted Steganalysis are designed for a particular steganographic algorithm. This technique is more robust since it has good detection accuracy for that specific technique when they used against the particular steganographic technique. Blind Steganalysis are schemes which are independent of any specific embedding technique are used to alleviate the deficiency of targeted analyzers by removing their dependency on the behavior of individual embedding techniques To achieve this, a set of distinguishing statistics that are sensitive to a wide variety of embedding operations

R. Kannan and F. Andres (Eds.): ICDEM 2010, LNCS 6411, pp. 189–195, 2012.
© Springer-Verlag Berlin Heidelberg 2012

are determined and collected. These statistics, taken from both cover and stego images are used to train a classifier, which is subsequently used to distinguish between cover and stego images.

Blind steganalysis is composed of two important components. These are feature extraction and feature classification. In feature extraction, a set of distinguishing statistics are obtained from a data set of images. There is no well defined approach to obtaining these statistics, but often they are proposed by observing general image features that exhibit strong variation under embedding. The second component, feature classification, operates in two modes. First, the obtained distinguishing statistics from both stego and cover images are used to train a classifier. Second, the trained classifier is used to classify an input image as either being a clean image or carrying a hidden message. Previous literature [1] state only the application of JPEG images in the either DCT domain or in the spatial domain [3] in terms of embedding and extraction. Feature based steganalysis [1] [4] is a technique wherein certain features that are sensitive to embedding changes but insensitive to image content is extracted. This paper intends to merge both DCT and Markovian features [2] with a possibility of eliminating the drawbacks of both with a feature selection. In order to reduce further computational complexity or costs, and to obtain reasonable success, SVM is used as a classifier for the DCT domain. Fridrich et al [2] used standard 274 features by merging DCT and Markov features for JPEG steganalysis.

In the next section, we will discuss about the general architecture of the system. Section 3 will deal with the implementation issues regarding the architecture. The experimental results are discussed in section 4. Section 5 will have a short note on the future work.

2   Implementation Details

The concept of feature extraction is combined with linear classification to devise an analytic system mainly for JPEG images. It has been understood in literature survey that calculating the features directly in JPEG domain is more sensitive to a wider type of embedding algorithms. The direct calculation also enables a more straight forward interpretation of the influence of individual features on detection as well as easier formulation of design principles leading to more secure steganography.

2.1   Feature Extraction

The goal of the paper is to merge new feature set which gives a better detection rate than any other steganalytic technique. The proposed feature set is used to construct a general linear classifier. The first step is to extract the features, and then Principal Component Analysis is used to find the optimal feature subset to improve the algorithm efficiency. Then the Support Vector Machine is designed with respect to accuracy, reliability and cost to give best results. The classification is then done on the same set of features, but differentiated as interblock dependency features and intra block dependency features [1, 2]. The SVM is trained by the obtained features and then it is subjected to testing on images which were used during training and also on images which are not trained. Fig. 1 shows the overall representation of the system.

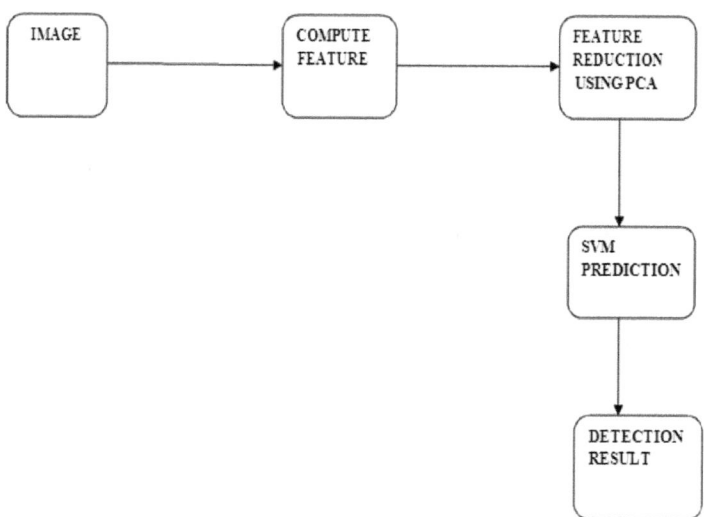

Fig. 1. System Architecture

Three types of features are extracted in DCT domain. They are First Order features, Extended DCT features and Markov features. The original DCT features [1] have 23 functional in them. The original DCT features can be extended to extended DCT features [2] which can extract about 193 functionals. The features of extended DCT are extracted within a range of -5 to +5 since DCT follows a Gaussian function and most of the important information is concentrated in values around zero. Another set of features is the Markov features [2] whose dimensionality can be reduced to 81.While the extended DCT features model inter-block dependencies between DCT coefficients, the Markov features capture intra-block dependency among DCT coefficients of similar spatial frequencies within the same 8X8 block. Hence they have been merged to eliminate the drawbacks of both. Markov features are also normalized to central values from -4 to +4. Another reason for merging the set is that the classifiers employing each feature set individually have complementary performance. Markov features are unable to detect short message lengths..All features in the merged feature set are uncalibrated. The same set of Extended DCT features are again distinguished as inter block dependency features and intra block dependency feature for low embedding rate. Here, the embedding is done by using two steganographic algorithms, F5 and PVD [9,10].

The Markov feature set as proposed in [2] models the difference between absolute values of neighboring DCT coefficients as a Markov process. The Markovian functionals taken together will comprise of 324 features. This has increased dimensionality, which can be reduced by taking the average of the four 81 dimensionality features. Thus we get a combined set of Extended DCT and Markov features as 274.

2.2 Feature Reduction

PCA or Principal Component Analysis is used to analyze the effective dimensionality of DCT and spatial based feature space. This is used to reduce the dimensionality of features and hence to retrieve optimal dataset. The extracted dataset is fed into a PCA. Relevant features were extracted from a total set of data. These data have the maximum amount of information which helps to classify the cover images and stego image from a dataset that is inputted [7].

2.3 Support Vector Machine Based Classification

Support Vector Machine is a supervised learning technique for classification. There are many techniques for classification like Neural Network, perceptron, Fisher Linear Discriminant and SVM. Out of this, SVM is widely popular in Machine Learning since it maps the data from the original space into a high dimensional feature space.

   When the kernel function is linear, the resulting SVM is a maximum margin hyperplane.Given a training sample, the hyper plane splits a given training sample in such a way that the distance from the closest cases to the hyper plane is maximized. The complexity of SVM depends on the training samples. Hence we can conclude that SVM guarantees generalization to a great extend [8].

3 Result and Discussion

3.1 Database of Images

One of the important aspects of any performance evaluation work is the dataset employed in the experiments. The dataset needs to include a variety of textures, qualities and image formats. A set of 420 images were taken both from JPEG format and compressed to a size of 256 X 256. We choose a large amount of JPEG format due to its wide popularity in transmission through the internet. A practical evaluation of project is presented by testing unconditional steganalysis for two different algorithms with diverse embedding mechanism: F5 and PVD. Unless stated otherwise, all results were derived on samples from the testing set that were not used in any form during training. 420 datasets of cover image and stego image is taken for analysis. Out of this, the images are used to extract different features like first order features, Extended features etc.Many features of these datasets maybe irrelevant. Hence these features maybe removed for better performance. This dimensionality reduction may be achieved by using Principal Component Analysis. The output of Principal Component Analysis is given to a linear SVM. Out of the 420 datasets used, 340 are used to train the SVM.80 datasets are used for testing.

3.2 Principal Component Analysis

A set of feature that have different statistics are extracted. The features are again reduced to obtain another set with lower feature dimensionality. This is only in terms of statistical outlook. The features can be further reduced by means of Principal Component Analysis. The first value found is called the Principal Component. The lower values are ignored after finding the Eigen values and Eigen vectors thus reducing the dimensionality. The Principal Component Analysis will reduce the dimensionality but may have a probability of eliminating the best features [7].

3.3 Linear SVM

The dimensionality reduction needs to be done because the classifier used here is linear SVM. There are many classifiers like Neural Network, perceptron, Fisher Linear Discriminant, SVM etc. Out of these, SVM is considered to be more powerful in terms of classification. The feature reduction is mainly due to the use of linear SVM to reduce the cost and computational complexity. Since the steganalysis system used was Blind, the SVM has to be trained before any testing occurs. Out of the 420 images, 340 images were used to train the data and the rest 80 were used to test the data [8].

A random set of 50 features were first extracted from an image. The extracted features were checked without inputting in the PCA. The classification results were only 50%. The feature set dimensionality was later reduced using PCA to a set of 20 features. The result was 90%.Thus the features have been reduced to give a more accurate classification. The reduced features are also proved to be a set of better features than before reduction. Two random steganographic algorithms, PVD and F5 are used for embedding into the images. The images are taken with various percentage embedding using F5 and PVD. All 274 features are taken into consideration here. The results are tabulated in Table 2.

Table 1. Classification using SVM

Data set	Percentage classification
Feature set without using PCA	50
Feature set using PCA	90

Table 2. Classification of uncalibrated images using SVM

Embedding Percentage	10	25	50	10-25-50-75
F5	59.5	46.6	60	50
PVD	52.7	54.5	83	50

When taken as a whole feature set of 274, the results shows results ranging from 50 to 60 %.Hence features are divided as interblock dependency features and intrablock dependency features [1,2]. Moment and Global Histogram is termed as intrablock dependency features since it depends only on values within a block. Variation, Blockiness, Co-occurance and Markovian features are termed as intra block features since it pertains to the values between two consecutive blocks. Global Histogram,Variation, Blockiness,Co-occurance are also said as Extended DCT Features. The separate feature gave a good classification rate than all features taken together. Moreover, the intra block dependency features gave a better classification result than inter block dependency features.

Table 3. Uncalibrated Image Classification with Separate Features

% Embedding	Moment	Global Histogram	Variation	Blockiness	Co-occurance	Markovian
10	66	60	80	100	83.4	80
25	75	40	75	83.33	66	71.4
50	50	57.14	80	60	69.23	85
75	57	57	75	100	83	88.7
10-25-50-75	55.2	50	80	69.2	71.42	75

4   Conclusion and Future Work

A set of features for steganalysis of JPEG images with a range of quality factors was developed. We considered features that take into account the numerical changes in DCT coefficient introduced by embedding. The feature set was obtained by merging and modifying two previously proposed feature sets with complementary performance (the DCT features that capture the inter-block dependencies among DCT coefficients and Markov features which capture intra-block dependencies). According to the experiments, the new merged feature set provides better results than previous results.

The present feature based system has PCA incorporated for reduced dimensionality thereby obtaining a better feature set. This feature set is being input into the linear SVM for classification between cover and stego image. Apart from the features mentioned, it has been decided to find a set of calibrated set of 274 features and uncalibrated set of 274 features [5]. Feature selection can be done using independent component analysis. These features can be later fed to a classifier, probably a soft margin classifier with Gaussian kernel [5]. The classification accuracy of the calibrated features as compared to uncalibrated features can be estimated.

Calibration can also used as a technique to analyze separate features with various steganographic algorithms. Separate feature extraction using inters block dependency features and intra block dependency features. Another enhancement of the paper can be an introduction to estimation of payload. This is called quantification, which can be achieved by means of Support Vector Regression [6]. The next enhancement is on the detection of message length. The method consists of a sequence of estimation procedures that use spatial domain representation of the cover and stego images to estimate the length of a message embedded.

References

1. Fridrich, J.: Feature-Based Steganalysis for JPEG Images and Its Implications for Future Design of Steganographic Schemes. In: Fridrich, J. (ed.) IH 2004. LNCS, vol. 3200, pp. 67–81. Springer, Heidelberg (2004)
2. Pevn'y, T., Fridrich, J.: Merging Markov and DCT Features for Multiclass JPEG Steganalysis. In: Proceedings SPIE, Electronic Imaging, Security, Steganography and Watermarking of Multimedia Contents IX, San Jose, CA, vol. 6505, pp. 301–314 (2007)

3. Yadollapour, A., Niami, H.M.: Attack on LSB Steganography in Color and Grayscale Images using Autocorrelation Coefficients. European Journal of Scientific Research 31(2), 172–183 (2009)

4. Kharrazi, M., Sencar, H.T., Memon, N.: Performance study of common image steganography and steganalysis techniques. Journal of Electronic Imaging 15(4), 041104 (2006)

5. Kodosky, J., Fridrich, J.: Calibration Revisited. In: ACM Multimedia and Security Workshop, Princeton, NJ, vol. 8, pp. 63–74 (September 2009)

6. Pevny, T., Fridrich, J., Ker, A.D.: From Blind to Quantitative Steganalysis. In: SPIE, Electronic Imaging, Media Forensics and Security XI, San Jose, CA, January 18-22, vol. 14, pp. 0C1– 0C14 (2009)

7. Miranda, A.A., Le Borgne, Y.A., Bontempi: New Routes from Minimal Approximation Error to Principal Components. Neural Processing Letters 27(3) (June 2008)

8. Cristianini, N., Shawe-Taylor, J.: An Introduction to Support Vector Machines and other kernel-based learning methods. Cambridge University Press (2000)

9. Wu, D.-C., Tsai, W.-H.: A steganographic method for images by pixel-value differencing. Pattern Recognition Letters 24, 1613–1624 (2003)

10. Fridrich, J., Goljan, M., Hogea, D.: Steganalysis of JPEG Images: Breaking the F5 Algorithm. In: Petitcolas, F.A.P. (ed.) IH 2002. LNCS, vol. 2578, pp. 310–323. Springer, Heidelberg (2003)

Indexing and Retrieval of Visually Similar Images in the Orthogonal Polynomials Transform Domain

R. Krishnamoorthy[1] and J. Kalpana[2]

[1] Anna University of Technology Tiruchirappalli, Tiruchirappalli
`rkrish26@hotmail.com`,
[2] Bharathidasan Institute of Technology
`kalpanalak@gmail.com`

Abstract. A Bayesian architecture for annotating, categorizing and retrieving 3D models of homogenous images given their 2D view is presented. Although the superiority of bayesian retrieval in a generic database has been studied, its ability to discriminate visually similar images, similarity being in colour, texture or shape has not been much reported. In the current work, we have established that continuous probabilistic image modeling based on mixture of Gaussians together with KL similarity measure, shows remarkable performance. For training, the characteristic view of the images is used. The features extracted are the polynomials transform coefficients. The algorithms used are simple, computationally efficient and do not require any prior segmentation. The dependence of the performance of the proposed architecture on the number of transform subspaces and the number of Gaussian mixtures has been studied. A comparative study with Daubechies wavelet shows that this architecture performs well with a small number of dimensions of transform subspaces and also with a small number of mixture of Gaussians, in addition to being fast.

Keywords: Bayesian retrieval, Expectation Maximization algorithm, Gaussian Mixture Model (GMM), Image Retrieval (IR), KL distance, Maximum Likelihood Estimate (MLE), Orthogonal Polynomials Transform (OPT),Visually similar images.

1 Introduction

The popularity and acceptance of compression techniques have led to the omnipresence of multimedia content in the compressed form. Since image processing in the transformed domain has a lower cost for computing and storing features, several applications in the spatial domain have been remodelled to work in the compressed domain. In the image retrieval (IR) front also, fortunately, as Khapli et al.in [1] review, these techniques are gaining importance in the recent past. In this context, there has been a great amount of research in assessing the suitability of different transforms to varied applications. Several works of the past decade have involved the use of floating point DCT coefficients as features [2]-[4] for the IR framework. With an aim of alleviating computation complexity, the conventional floating point transforms can be suitably replaced by integer based transforms and

R. Kannan and F. Andres (Eds.): ICDEM 2010, LNCS 6411, pp. 196–203, 2012.
© Springer-Verlag Berlin Heidelberg 2012

Orthogonal Polynomials Transform (OPT) is a promising one in this direction. As with any other transform, dimensionality reduction can be done because of the energy preserving property of the OPT.

The transform coefficients of Polynomials model are used as the feature set and the image is modeled as a mixture of Gaussians by grouping them into C segments, each assigned with a Gaussian distribution. Mixture of Gaussians are preferred because of their ability to model multimodal densities. To estimate the mixture parameters, the likelihood is maximized and the estimates are the Maximum Likelihood (ML) estimates for the parameters given the data. Indexing of query images is done by finding its KL distance with the training images. Although the superiority of such statistical methods for retrieval in a generic database have been studied, ts ability to accurately discriminate visually similar images has not been much reported and this work focusses on estimating the parameters that directly have an impact on accurate discrimination. For comparison w.r.t. the features extracted, we have taken the Daubechies 4 wavelet, (Daub4) as it is the most frequently used transform in IR.

This paper is organized as follows: In Section 2, the Orthogonal Polynomials Transform is briefly outlined. In Section 3, Gaussian Mixture model for an image is described followed by the bayesian retrieval crieterion in Section 4. The algorithm is summarized in Section 5. The experimental results and discussions are presented in Section 6 and conclusions are given in Section 7.

2 Orthogonal Polynomials Transform(OPT)

OPT employs polynomial basis functions and its energy compaction and image data decorrelation have been proved [5]. This transform is chosen because of the simplicity in computation owing to the integer arithmetic. For brevity, the details of the transform are omitted and complete details can be found in [6], [7]. For a two dimensional colour image $I(x, y, z)$ (x and y account for row and column and z for colour coordinate), the linear three dimensional image transformation can be defined by the point spread operator as follows:

$$\left.\left|\beta'_{ijk}\right|\right|^{n-1}_{i,j,k=0} = \left(|M| \otimes |M| \otimes |M|\right)^{t} I \tag{1}$$

Where $\otimes$ is the Kronecker product, $\left|\beta'_{ijk}\right|$ are the n^3 matrices arranged in the dictionary sequence and are the coefficients of transformation, $|I|$ is the image and the point spread operator is $|M|$. These transformed coefficients obtained with the Orthogonal Polynomials takes into account the effect of individual color planes as well as the interactions among the color planes.

Based on the energy grouping property of orthogonal polynomials transform, the energy vectors generated by point spread operator of the transform coding are rearranged so that the high energy transformed coefficients are grouped so that pruning low energy coefficients is made possible to reduce computational complexity.

For the convenience of point-spread operations, the elements of |M| are scaled to make them integers. Hence the transform model involves only integer arithmetic and as this facilitates a speedy retrieval, it has been adopted for feature transformation. The blocks of the image are taken with a sliding window of size $(n \times n)$, blocks being overlapped.

3 Gaussian Mixture Model

A representation of the image has been made with the transform coefficients as salient features. Keeping track of all the feature vectors extracted from an image will pose a major difficulty to any retrieval system and so there is a need for a feature representation to summarize the distribution of feature vectors. Ideally, the transform should provide dimensionality reduction necessary for density estimation to be feasible, and at the same time, be expressive enough to allow reasonably accurate estimates. The compressed domain transform coefficients capture the colour and the texture in the low frequency coefficients and hence can be used to model an image as a mixture of Gaussians.

As the Expectation-Maximisation (EM) algorithm is an efficient method for finding the mixture of Gaussians based on likelihood maximisation, it is used. The Minimum Description Length (MDL) principle serves to select among values of C. Using the center of each cluster, each block in the original image is affiliated with the most probable Gaussian, providing for probabilistic image segmentation. In this case, the function to be maximized is a mixture of multi dimensional Gaussian functions.

$$P(x) = \sum_{c \in C} w_c F(x | \mu_c, \sigma_c) \tag{2}$$

where x - input vectors, μ, σ - mean and variance vectors, C - number of Gaussians used, w weight of each Gaussian and F - probability of x given mixture components.

The success of the EM algorithm depends on the initial values and with a random initialization it may get trapped in local maxima. To avoid this, the component means was initialized with a variance-based technique. With proper initialization, the algorithm offers good performance in terms of convergence speed also. It was observed that stability was reached within the first few iterations.

4 Bayesian Evaluation

The image-matching problem is treated as a distribution-matching problem and the information-theoretic KL distance [8] is used as a distance measure between image mixtures. Probabilistic methods based on mixtures of Gaussians together with KL measure for image similarity, perform significantly better than geometric approaches like the nearest neighbor rule with city-block or Euclidean distances [9]. Greenspan et al. have proposed the closed form of the KL distance measure and have reported good results in the spatial domain[10]. Vasconcelos has proposed another closed form based on Mahalanobis distance [11] and accordingly, the matching function between the Gaussians $N_1(\mu_1, \Sigma_1)$ and $N_2(\mu_2, \Sigma_2)$ is given by

$$\pi(i) = \arg\min_j \left((\mu_{1,i} - \mu_{2,j})^T \Sigma_{2,j}^{-1} (\mu_{1,i} - \mu_{2,j}) \right) \tag{3}$$

As the KL-match variant of approximation via Mahalanobis match is an advantage with respect to computational complexity with compared to the one used in [10] and as we are interested in fast retrieval, this approximation was adopted.

5 Algorithmic Details

The algorithms used in the proposed architecture, OPTGMM, are given in this Section.

5.1 Algorithm for Feature Extraction and Feature Representation

Input: A database of ω_i classes each with images of characteristic views, M.

Output: Gaussian mixture parameters for each image of each class in the database
Begin

For every class, ω_i $(0 \le i < M)$

1:For every image $I_j \in \omega_i$ $(0 \le j < V_C)$

1.1:Divide I_j into B sub-blocks of size $(n \times n)$ with an overlap of p pixels between successive blocks

1.2:For $(\forall B)$

1.2.1:Extract the intensities at each location in RGB colour space and convert into YCbCr colour space

1.2.2:Interleave the pixel intensities of the 3channels

1.2.3:Apply OPT with pruning as outlined in Section 2. Let β denote the set of coefficients $[X_Y, X_B, X_R]_b$ for $\forall b \in \{1, 2...B\}$.This completes Feature extraction

2:With β as feature vectors extracted from blocks, find the Mixture of C Gaussians outlined in Section3.The conditional distribution is

$$P(\beta|I) = \sum_{c=1}^{C} w_I^c G\left(x, \mu_I^c, \Sigma_I^c\right)$$ where $\pi_I^c, \mu_I^c, \Sigma_I^c$ are the parameters for the

image I and mixture component C. This completes feature representation.

3:The conditional distribution of each class ω_i is the distribution of $\forall I \in \omega_i$.
End

The annotation algorithm processes the images in the validation set and then finds the largest posterior probability of the class that is the closest to the query.

5.2 Annotation Algorithm

Input: Query image database τ_Q, Class conditional distribution of every class ω_i

Output: A label for image $I_a \in \tau_Q$

Begin

1:For $\forall I_a \in \tau_Q$

 1.1:Process the image according to Step 1 and 2 of 5.1

 1.2:For every class ω_i compute the posterior probability

$$\log P(\omega_i|\beta) = \log P(\beta|\omega_i) + \log P(\omega_i) - \log P(\beta) \qquad (4)$$

where β is the set of features of I_a, $P(\omega_i)$ is the ratio of the number of images in ω_i to total images in τ_Q and $P(\beta)$ is a constant and $P(\beta|\omega_i)$ is calculated as outlined in Section 4

 2:Annotate I_a with the class $\hat{\omega}_i$, class with largest probability

End

5.3   Retrieval Algorithm

Input: Query by example I_r, τ_Q

Output: Top T Images from τ_Q ordered according to their posterior probability

Begin

1.For $\forall I_r$

 1.1:Process I_r according to Step 1 and 2 of Algorithm5.1

 1.2:Calculate its posterior probability with respect to $\forall I_q \in \tau_Q$ using equation (4)

 1.3:Rank images in τ_Q in order of decreasing probability,

 1.4.Retrieve the top T images.

End

6   Experimental Evaluation

The experiments in this section were conducted on a subset of the Columbia's COIL-100 database which consists of 2D views of 3D models of homogenous objects. A small subset of this database, the COIL-20 is available but it provides images that have striking colour or texture features. Since the ability to distinguish similar objects accurately was the intention of the work, a database with 10 classes of images that are homogenous either in colour, shape or texture was created. A sample of the database is shown in Figure 1. As can be seen, most of the objects are either wooden objects or share the same colour or shape in some views.

   Although the number of images for each class is 72, an image for every 5 degrees rotation a selection of the characterisitic views of the object.reduces the training images and also the training time Objects belonging to the same class present very

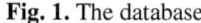

Fig. 1. The database   **Fig. 2.** Characteristic views of Roller

differently due to variations in scale as seen in Figure 2. Hence, we have chosen 9 images each spaced by 40 degrees to form the training set. A sample set of images for the 'roller class' has been shown in Figure 2. The training database thus consists of 90 images, 9 images for each class. The validation set consists of 100 images, 10 images from each class such that the images in the validation set are not there in the training set. The images are in JPEG format of the size 256 ×256. Annotation and Retrieval are performed on the validation set.

6.1 Results and Discussion

The metrics considered for the proposed retrieval system are precision and recall. In [12], Meng opines that what is more relevant to a user, is the number of irrelevant images he has to encounter, before getting a good number of relevant images and so this measure is also used for evaluating the performance.The intention was to study the interplay between accurate classification and the different parameters used in the feature extraction and feature representation phase.The transform features are obtained with a 8 ×8 window sliding by 4 pixels between consecutive samples. Diagonal covariances were used for the mixtures estimation. The iterations for the EM algorithm were fixed until changes less than a 0.1% occur.

For comparison in the feature extraction phase, features were extracted from the polynomials transform and with Daub4. The time needed for extracting the polynomials transform is 3.8 msec whereas that for Daub4 is 6.9 msec. It was inferred that since the computational complexity of the wavelet transform is more, more time is needed for feature extraction.

A comparison of the architecture has been made with respect to the total number of correct images retrieved when the features were extracted from the 2 different transforms. The results are summarised in Figure.3 for $C=16$ Gaussians. The OPT-GMM architecture outperforms Daub4GMM, the results being more pronounced for lower number of subspaces.

Daub4GMM gives an equivalent performance for a higher d. However, a good precision at lower d is an advantage as it implies more pruning and lesser computational complexity and this is attributed to the transform's good energy compaction property.

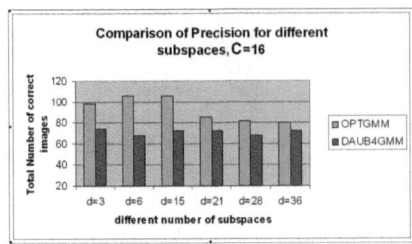
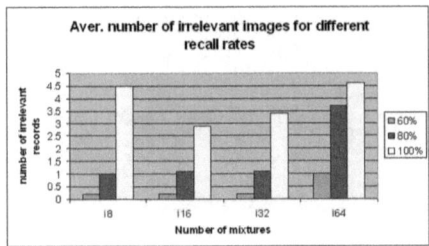

Fig. 3. Precision Coparison for 2 transforms   **Fig. 5.** No. of irrelevant images for various recall

For indexing, C was varied to study its impact on classification accuracy. The top 3 ranks have been considered. It was observed that $C=8$ was enough for rightly annotating most of the classes, with $d=21$. However, classes for which presentation of the object is very different because of rotation or scaling, such as that of the house block, $C=12$ were sufficient for correct annotation, with $d=6$. However, good annotation is obtained in the first rank, immaterial of the nature of the object, $C=16$ Gaussians.

Fig. 4.1. $C=16$ **Fig. 4.2.** $C=32$ **Fig. 4.3.** $C=64$

A sample of the study for a recall rate of 100% has been presented in Fig. 4. For a 100% recall, 16 mixture densities is sufficient, but gives unrelated results alongwith On analysing the retrieval performance for different C, it was evident that the results are perceptually more uniform for $C=16$, than those from $C=8$ for 15 subspaces. Perceptual uniformity in retrieval was further improved with 32 mixtures.

As the mixtures is increased beyond this, the performance falls sharply, i.e. the number of irrelevant results are more to achieve the desired recall rate, indicating inaccurate density estimates. It can thus be concluded that as many as 16 mixtures can provide acceptable results. All the results are presented for a subspace of 15.

Figure 5 shows the average number of irrelevant images the user has to encounter as a function of number of mixture of Gaussians for different recall rates. As evident, the number of irrelevant records is a constant for $C=16$ and 32 and increases rapidly after that indicating inaccurate density estimation. Although the performance for $C=8$ Gaussians is good for 60 and 80% recall, it worsens for 100% recall. So, the optimum parameters are 16 mixtures for a transform subspace of 15. Adding more than optimum subspaces leads to an inaccurate density estimation. Likewise,more the number of mixtures, more is the time needed to model the image.

7 Conclusion

The discriminating power of the Bayesian criterion when applied to homogenous images has been studied in this paper. The training database has been formed with a minimum set of characterisitic view of images. Images have been polynomial transformed. and modeled with a mixture of Gaussians. For a precise classification, it was found that 16 mixture densitites with 15 transform subspaces is sufficient. However, for a perceptually uniform retrieval, the number of Gaussians needed is 32. On comparison with Daub4 used for feature extraction, it is inferred that in addition to being fast, the proposed architecture distinguishes homogenous images accurately for a smaller number of mixtures and transform subspaces.

References

1. Khapli, V.R., Bhalchandra, A.S.: Compressed domain content based image retrieval: state of the Art, challenges and open issues. In: Proceedings of World Congress for Science, Engineering and Technology, Bangkok, vol. 36 (2008) ISSN 2070-3740
2. Bae, H.J., Jung, S.H.: Image retrieval using texture based on DCT. In: Proceedings of the International Conference on Info., Comm. and Signal Proc., Singapore, pp.1065–1068 (1997)
3. Qiu, K.J., Jiang, J., Xiao, G., Irianto, S.Y.: DCT-Domain Image Retrieval Via Block-Edge-Patterns. In: Campilho, A., Kamel, M.S. (eds.) ICIAR 2006. LNCS, vol. 4141, pp. 673–684. Springer, Heidelberg (2006)
4. Bajaj, M., Lay, J.: A Comparative Study of Performance Measures for Information Retrieval Systems. In: Proceedings of the IEEE Symposium on Computational Intelligence in Image and Signal Processing, pp. 271–274 (2007)
5. Krishnamoorthy, R., Bhattacharayya, P.: A new data compression Scheme using Orthogonal Polynomials. In: IEEE Proceedings of the International Conference on Info., Com. and Signal Proc., vol. I, pp. 490–494. Nanyang Technology Univ., Singapore (1997)
6. Krishnamoorthy, R.: Transform coding of monochrome images with a statistical design of experiments to separate noise. Pattern Recognition Letters 28, 771–777 (2007)
7. Krishnamoorthy, R.: A unified framework based on orthogonal polynomials for edge detection, and compression in colour images, Ph.D.thesis, IIT Kharaghpur (1997)
8. Kullback, S.: Information theory and statistics. Dover Publications, New York (1968)
9. Aksoy, S., Haralick, M.: Probabilistic vs. Geometric Similarity Measures for Image Retrieval. In: Proceedings of IEEE Conference on Computer Vision and Pattern Recognition, vol. 2, pp. 357–362 (2000)
10. Greenspan, H., Goldberger, J., Riddel, L.: A probabilistic framework for image matching. Journal of Computer Vision and Image Understanding 84, 384–406 (2001)
11. Vasconcelos, N.: On the complexity of probabilistic image retrieval. In: Proceedings of the International Conference. on Computer Vision, pp. 400–407 (2001)
12. Meng, X.: A Comparative Study of Performance Measures for Information Retrieval Systems. In: Proceedings of the 3rd International Conference on InfoTech., pp. 578–579 (2006)

Human Action Recognition and Localization in Video at Contextual Level

Mahendiran Arunothayam[1], Baskaran Ramachandran[1],
and Dhavachelvan Ponnurangam[2]

[1] Dept of Computer Science & Engg., CEGC, Anna University Chennai, India
[2] Dept of Computer Science, Pondicherry University, Pondicherry, India
{mahendirana,dhavachelvan}@gmail.com,baaski@cs.annauniv.edu

Abstract. This paper presents an investigation into the design of a computer based human action recognition system aimed at localizing and recognizing moving objects in a controlled environment. A system based on the object identifier and shape descriptor techniques is proposed. Automated visual perception of the real world by computers requires classification of observed physical objects into semantically meaningful categories (such as 'animal' or 'person' or 'objects').

This paper proposes a partially-supervised learning framework for classification of the moving objects especially vehicles and pedestrians that are detected and tracked in a variety of far-field video sequences, captured by a static camera. Introduction of scene-specific context features (such as image-position of objects using xml) is done to improve classification performance in any given scene. Along with this, a scene-invariant object annotation has been done to adapt this contextual model for new scenes.

Keywords: action recognition, context, video, xml, LabelMe.

1 Introduction

Computer vision is currently an active area of research, with the goal of developing visual sensing and processing algorithms and hardware that can see and understand the world around them. A central theme in computer vision is the description of a video (or image sequence) in terms of the meaningful objects that comprise it (such as persons, tables, chairs, books, cars, buildings and so on). While the concept of an `object' comes rather naturally to humans (perhaps because of our constant physical interaction with them), it is very difficult for a computer program to identify distinct objects in the image of a scene (that is, to tell which pixels in the image correspond to which object). As the main application of our research is to analyze activities in a scene, this paper restricts its attention to video sequences captured by static cameras and seeks to detect and classify objects that move in the scene.

2 Object Classification

2.1 Image Representation

Given a candidate image region in which an object might be present, the goal of object classification is to associate the correct object class label with the region of

R. Kannan and F. Andres (Eds.): ICDEM 2010, LNCS 6411, pp. 204–207, 2012.
© Springer-Verlag Berlin Heidelberg 2012

interest. Object class labels are typically chosen in a semantically meaningful manner, such as 'vehicle', 'pedestrian', 'bird' or 'airplane'. Humans can easily understand events happening around them in terms of interactions between objects. For a computer to reach a similar level of understanding about real-world events, object classification is an important step.

For our purposes, object classification is a process that takes a set of observations of objects (represented using suitable features) as input, and produces as output the probabilities of belonging to different object classes.

2.2 Recognition

There are several approaches can be used for determining the human action recognition and localization in the image. In most of the moving objects in videos separation work has been reported in [3, 4, 5] which is used performing an action video query on a test video sequence. In other cases the images are used for learning scene which comments on the objects in the frame are reported in [2]. In [1] provides an analysis of the Scene Based Context models and evaluates two of their representatives using the LabelMe dataset (open source library for web based image annotation tool).

2.3 Background Separation Algorithm

Thresholding will measure the foreground object's color or intensity value and compare it with the background. If the color intensity of the pixel is different from its neighboring pixels, the original pixel will be treated as the foreground. The one drawback to this approach is that it requires the foreground object to have a significant difference in the surface color than the background. This approach will not work because it relies heavily on the foreground and the background's difference in color.

2.4 Object Annotation

For this case, an annotation consists of a segmentation (represented by a polygon, and information about the object). The user begins the annotation process by clicking control points along the boundary of an object to form a polygon. When the polygon is closed, the user is prompted for the name of the object and information.

The entered information is recorded on the computer and the polygon is propagated across all frames in the video as if it were static and present at all times throughout the sequence. The user can further navigate across the video using the video controls to inspect and edit the polygons propagated across the different frames.

2.5 Object-Parts Hierarchies

When two polygons have a high degree of overlap, this provides evidence of either an object part hierarchy an occlusion. This paper can also take into account of viewpoint information and find parts, as demonstrated for the building object category. Notice that the object-parts are semantically meaningful.

Fig. 1. Objects and their parts. Using polygon information alone, automatically discover object-part relationships. The shown example parts for the building object classes, arranged as constellations, with the object appearing in the center of its parts.

Once the candidate parts have discovered for a set of objects, assign the specific part instances to their corresponding object. Using the intersection overlap heuristic, as above, and assign parts to objects where the intersection ratio exceeds the 0.5 threshold. For some robustness to occlusion, this paper compute a depth ordering of the polygons in the image and assign the part to the polygon with smallest depth that exceeds the intersection ratio threshold.

Fig. 2. Some examples of images and their annotations (From left to right) label, board, shelf, car, chair, lamp

2.6 Objects Relationship in Spatial Domain

The minimum distance between the two objects (polygons) were computed using the Euclidean distance method and/or that was used along with the overlap percentage which was computed from the two intersecting polygons.

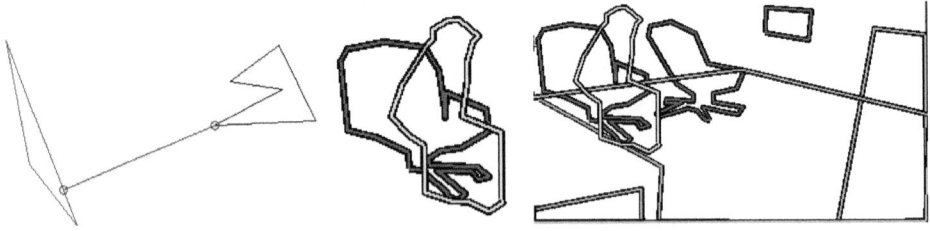

Fig. 3. (a) Shows the minimum distance measurement between the two polygons (b) shows two overlapping polygons, and (c) shows the entire environment of the office

First the all possible distance between the two polygons are computed. If the minimum distance is zero, then it computes another parameter called overlapping percentage of one polygon over other. From the percentage, program states a contextual description. And the object-part relationships were automatically discovered from the table. For example, the object- part relationship for the building were window, door, air conditioner, passage, entrance, pillar, marquee, text label, double door, balcony, chimney, shop window.

3 Conclusion

The concept of scene-specific features, as well as some new features (position using XML) are introduced and shown to benefit classification. Scene-independent and scene-dependent features are identified using mutual information estimate. At the same time, an algorithm has been proposed to adapt classifiers to scene-specific characteristics by carefully using unlabeled data.

It should be noted that selection of context features is task-dependent. For instance, if all the scenes considered have approximately the same scale, it makes sense to use object size as a scene-independent feature. Our intention here is to provide a principled mechanism to be able to decide on which features are scene-dependent. The key to correctly applying this mechanism to a specific problem lies in selecting a representative data set (that suitably models the variation across scenes) for mutual information calculation.

Acknowledgement. My sincere thanks to the [1] for suggestion in my project and paper.

References

1. Russell, B., Torralba, A., Murphy, K., Freeman, W.: Labelme: A database and web-based tool for image annotation. International Journal of Computer Vision 77(1), 157–173 (2008), http://labelme.csail.mit.edu/
2. Cour, T., Benezit, F., Shi, J.: Spectral segmentation with multiscale graph decomposition. In: IEEE Computer Society Conference on Computer Vision and Pattern Recognition, CVPR 2005, June 20-25, vol. 2, pp. 1124–1131 (2005)
3. Rabinovich, A., Belongie, S.: Scenes vs. objects: A comparative study of two approaches to context based recognition. In: IEEE Computer Society Conference on Computer Vision and Pattern Recognition Workshops, CVPR Workshops 2009, June 20-25, pp. 92–99 (2009)
4. Yeo, C., Ahammad, P., Ramchandran, K., Shankarsastry, S.: High-Speed Action Recognition and Localization in Compressed Domain Videos. IEEE Transaction on Circuits and Systems for Video Technology 18(8) (August 2008)
5. Zelnik-Manor, L., Irani, M.: Statistical analysis of dynamic actions. IEEE Transactions on Pattern Analysis and Machine Intelligence 28(9), 1530–1535 (2006)

Applications of Data Mining in e-Governance: A Case Study of Bhoomi Project

M. Hanumanthappa, B.R. Prakash, and Manish Kumar

Department of Computer Science & Applications, Bangalore University, Bangalore
hanu6572@hotmail.com, brp.tmk@gmail.com,
manishkumarjsr@yahoo.com

Abstract. E-government is a modern way that government department provides services for the public. The level of e government development is an important standard for a national information, e-government can improve government management efficiency, so it is very important that how to improve the public service by the public's need to e-government's development. This paper applies data mining technique in e-government construction by taking BHOOMI a project from government of Karnataka for helps to maintain and update the land records data systematically and securely. This can provide the better support for government decision, government department also provides the better services for public and achieves humanist truly.

1 Introduction

Data mining is a broad category of applications and technologies for gathering, storing, analyzing and providing access to data to help the decision makers in making decisions. Data Mining, also known as knowledge discovery in the database, refers to extract implicit potential useful information and knowledge from a large quantity of incomplete, noise, and blurring, random data which people do not know in advance [1]. Data mining method can usually be divided into two categories: first category is statistical, and its technology used probability analysis, relevance, cluster analysis and discriminated analysis; the other is machine learning in the artificial intelligence-based, through training and learning a large number of samples that need to set the mode or parameters.

ICTs (Information and Communication Technology) are effectively showing new dimensions to old institutional setups. There is a reinforced thrust for an informed and participatory citizenry for efficient e-governance. It goes without saying that impact of ICT on institutional changes is fast spreading across the boundaries of social and political arrangements of societies.

e-Governance is the application of Information and Communication Technology (ICT) for delivering Government Services, exchange of information, communication transactions, integration various stand-alone systems and services between Government and Citizens (G2C), Government and Business (G2B) as well as back office processes and interactions within the entire Government frame work. Through the e-Governance, the Government services will be made available to the citizens in a convenient, efficient and transparent manner. The Government being the service pro-

R. Kannan and F. Andres (Eds.): ICDEM 2010, LNCS 6411, pp. 208–218, 2012.
© Springer-Verlag Berlin Heidelberg 2012

vider, it is important to motivate the employees for delivering the services through ICT. To achieve this, the Government employees are being trained on technology and started realizing the advantage of ICT. The aim is to make them thorough with e-Governance applications and responsive to the technology driven administration.

What does E-Governance seek to achieve

- Efficiency
- Transparency
- Citizen's participation

Enabling e-governance through ICT contributes to

- Good governance
- Trust and Accountability
- Citizen's awareness and empowerment
- Citizen's welfare
- Democracy
- Nation's economic growth

ICT is the biggest enabler of change and process reforms with minimum resistance. Decades of attempts for government and process reforms fade in face of what ICT has achieved in few years. People would not so readily accept process change but in the name of ICT they do.

2 Recent Innovations

Indicative e-government innovations will now be examined to help understand why each was adopted, what's worked, and what hasn't. The services provided by the Government is not to allow the public to adapt to the settings and functions of the departments of the need, but government services should be the maximum from the needs of the public, based on "the interests of the public as the center" design services, and improve service efficiency, reduce service costs, improve service quality, providing the public with the largest service efficiency. Therefore, the Government's electronic public service is not just changes to the mode of service, but more important is government services awareness heightened and the concept of service innovation. Government public services need to attach importance to the principle of demand-oriented and then carry out all system construction and services work. To achieve this goal, government departments and the public must be interactive information on the public information needs, study the real need of public. With this caveat, the cases will be presented under five categories according to intended results: citizen participation, efficiency, effectiveness, service integration, and combating corruption.

3 Citizen Participation

There are many cases where ICT systems help enable the civic conversation necessary to political democracy. Before start the project establish the system of collection public opinion. Uses the computer technology fully, enables the different opinion of each aspect to reflect to the production public product department prompt and accurately. Secondly, public can be reflected in different categories for policy-makers with timely and accurate decision-making signal. Final collection public views should be finalized as a management system. One challenge facing many countries is that English is the lingua franca of ICT; there are an estimated 2200 languages used in Asia, and only 20% of Asians can use English. Making e-government widely accessible to citizens requires addressing this challenge.

3.1 Efficiency

E-government innovations often promise cost savings and/or increased tax revenue, and there is evidence in the region that this is being achieved in some cases. Efficiency gains can also accrue to citizens in terms of reduced waiting time and less money spent on bribes.

3.2 Effectiveness

In addition to efficiency gains, ICT-enabled reforms have yielded other benefits, including faster and more accurate response. For example, in India a national epidemiology service introduced ICT systems for gathering, processing, storing and reporting disease and public health data. System components used software packages for registration and analysis of diseases and public health risks. These created a single common system for information on specific diseases and public health risks, with local, regional and national databases searchable in various ways based on common data.

3.3 Combating Corruption

Many think that e-government can reduce opportunities for corruption. First, enhancing e-government can reduce opportunities for corruption by helping to measure performance better, facilitate outsourcing and contestability of public functions, reduce transaction costs, enforce rules more strongly, reduce discretion and increase transparency. Corruption is rooted in the cultural, political and economic circumstances of those involved. ICT does little to affect these root causes. It has a potential role, but a limited one that forms only part of a much larger picture. At the national level, one needs political will, public education, ethical watchdog agencies, and appropriate incentives for honest officials and effective punishment for the corrupt ones.

4   Data Warehouse and Data Mining Technology

Commonly used data mining technologies are based on analysis, study of the association rules and decision tree. Apply the Apriori Algorithm of association rules and Decision Tree algorithm to e- government data analysis and establish an E-government data analysis system based on data mining.

Data warehouse is a subject-oriented, integrated, time-variant, non-volatile collection of data, cutting across the enterprise. Until there is a repository of accurate data across the enterprise value chain, application of mining tools to analyze and aid in strategic government decisions is impossible. Currently, in most enterprises, the most difficult and resource consuming stage of development and deployment is data warehouse and mining application development.

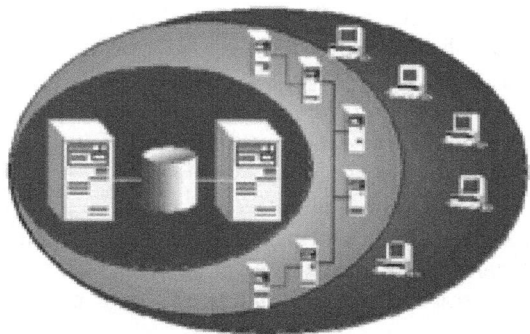

Fig. 1. Representation of data warehouse and data Mining

At times, government departments might come across shortages of resources in one department and excess of resources in the other. This could be due to non-availability of proper data and facilities to disseminate information. Even if government departments are computerized and networked more for the purpose of Internet usage and mail transfer, the information available in one department, which possess the data might not be utilized by other departments. This is because the information is stored in different formats, in different platforms and in heterogeneous data base systems. A look at the information requirements at each level and the information flow across levels shows a pattern. While information that flows from top (fund sanction, allocation and disbursement details) is split up to generate information for lower levels, information that flows from grass root level (such as expenditure details, benefits details, beneficiary details etc.) is consolidated to generate information for higher levels. This pattern makes the entire vertical domain of e-Governance framework, an ideal domain for development of data warehousing and use of data mining applications.

4.1 Data Mining on e-Governance Data Warehouse

Data mining is a broad category of applications and technologies for gathering, storing, analyzing and providing access to data to help the decision makers in making decisions. Typically, any Data Warehouse and Mining (DWM) application includes large data warehouse, decision support systems, query and reporting, On Line Analytical Process (OLAP), statistical analysis, forecasting and mining (a technology to extract unknown and hidden patterns and knowledge from within the data). DWM, therefore is well suited for e-Governance applications in the G2G (Government to Government) and G2C (Government to Citizen) environment. For effective implementation of a DWM solution, the de facto condition is a solid and reliable data warehouse on available e-Governance data from different sources.

4.2 DWM and e-Governance: The Need

- How to better understand our citizen's needs
- How to gain more operational effectiveness

- How to provide better, faster access to critical data about service status while increasing the value of information for those who make decisions on different levels of the government
- Develop project implementation plans on state and national level
- Propose extensive and effective databases for the e-Society
- Provide extensive data for support of e-Government
- Create effective data and system architectures for more goal oriented solutions to transitional problems Going by the e-Governance definition, with the use of DWM technologies, policy makers can get key conclusions from large amount of data that can be a critical component of any e-Governance initiative.

5   Different Data Mining Approach

Use of Historic Data: The availability of the basic data, right from the point of generation to meet the information needs at all level for all the time is still a problem in most of the government Departments. As current e-Governance framework is based on the use of computer technologies like Internet and Intranet that has further enhanced the utility of these databases as the main supportive system for planning and decision-making. There is still a vacuum in the analysis based decision systems. The growth of information technology and its adaptation over the years has been exponential, while at the same time the cost of both hardware and software are decreasing tremendously. New applications in all areas of planning and strategic operation are being developed and used at all levels.

  Generally on a day-to-day basis, a large volume of data is generated in order to fulfill various needs of the government. This data is generally associated with human resources, projects, plans, decisions, reports etc. As a matter of fact officials use to maintain at the most, one-year data or up to five years data in the system. As it occupies a lot of space and also tends to take lot of time for retrieval, with the kind of technology used at different levels, it was simply not possible to keep the historic data in the computer. But the historic data, which the officials could not use for various reasons, can play an important role for planning and analysis purpose and can lead to an important decision and/or can lead to lot of savings.

Knowledge Discovery Management

Knowledge Discovery Management (KDM) is the management of information, skill, experience, innovation, and discovering hidden aspects using machine intelligence. Gartner defines KDM as, "the creation, capture, organization, access and use of knowledge". It uses many technology categories, almost none of which are exclusive to KDM. KDM is a top down effort (practice) to try to understand and manage knowledge. KDM may use specific practices such as mining, collaboration, content management, e-mail, video conferencing, work place tools, portals and business applications. Knowledge management is the one, which ultimately is to be used for planning and implementation of various government schemes and projects. Managing knowledge involves managing domains of knowledge that are valued for achieving strategic objectives. The very nature of knowledge is that it changes fast and renders information

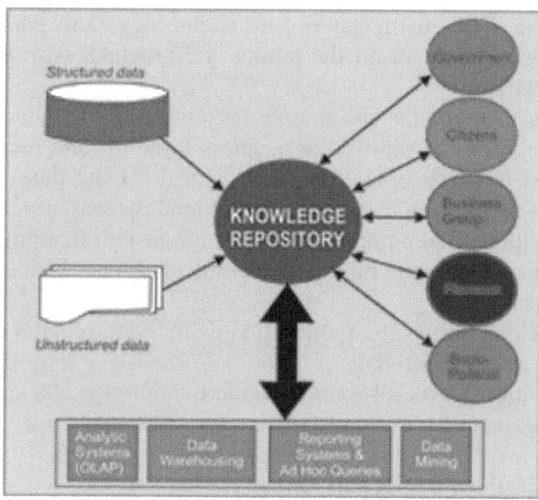

Fig. 2. Knowledge Discover Management

obsolete at a rapid pace. Building knowledge management requires identifying and storing the collected information in an enterprise knowledge repository known as a data warehouse.

5.1 Benefits of Data Warehouse and Mining for Better e-Governance

- Do not have to deal with heterogeneous and silo systems
- Dependence on IT staff minimized
- Can obtain easily decipherable and comprehensive information without the need to use sophisticated tools.
- Can perform extensive analysis of stored data to provide answers to exhaustive queries.
- Helps in formulating more effective strategies and policies for citizen facilitation

5.2 Beneficiaries of the System

From a layman's angle, the DWM technologies are more towards G2G than other forms. All the government plans and decisions can be arrived at, with the help of detailed multi-dimensional analyses of all the relevant data. In fact, it helps the citizens more than the government. The citizens can have a compact and compiled profile from the government as a web based report and the same can be used wherever the citizen wants.

6 Case Study

6.1 Introduction to Existing Bhoomi System

BHOOMI, online land records management system, has been designed and developed inhouse by National Informatics Centre, Karnataka State Unit, Bangalore for the

Revenue department, GoK, using state-of-art technology. This has been implemented by the Revenue Department in all the taluks of Karnataka with the implementation support from DIO/DIA.

BHOOMI helps to maintain and update the land records data systematically and securely. It has incorporated tightly the business logic of land records system. It has number of features for easy operations and security of the data. It has brought the transparency in the maintenance and updation of land records system.

It is also built with the three public interfaces for easier interaction with the public.

Manned LR Kiosk allows the public to take the land records documents on demand at fixed user charges.

Touch Screen Kiosk allows the public to view the land records documents without the intervention of revenue officials.

Manned Application Kiosk allows the public to apply for change of ownership and get the acknowledgement for the same.

6.2 Statistical Details of BHOOMI Data

Number of Districts: 27

Number of Taluks: 177

Number of Circles: 1000 (Approx.)

Number of Villages: 30000 (Approx.)

Number of Land Records Documents: 20000000 Number of Owners: 70 00 000 (Approx.)

6.3 Data in BHOOMI System

Land Records document of Karnataka contains the following information land parcel-wise Total extents of the land Unusable extents in that land Land Revenue to be collected Soil Type of the land Ownership details of that land - name of the owner, extents owned, khatha number, acquisition type with description, rights and liabilities of the owner Trees details with numbers of trees Irrigation details with extent irrigated Cultivator and tenancy details – year-wise, season-wise Year-wise, season-wise Land utilization and Year-wise and season-wise crop details with extents of the crops

6.4 Need for Business Intelligent System

Since BHOOMI system is operational since last 2000-2001. It has captured the change of ownership details , crops and season wise land utilization details". But to-day's requirement is not just the latest and updated information but the cross-functional information that can help decisions making activity as "on-line" process.

The Business Intelligence system will present to Government. decision-makers information based on data that is accurate and consistent. As the data elements of the warehouse will be captured at pre-determined strategic times, the information presented through the reporting function will remain consistent rather than changing on a continual basis as it now does when extracted from a transactional system.

Datawarehouse can collect information from a number of different disparate sources and it is the place where this disparity is reconciled, and it allows several different applications to make use of the same information.

Using OLAP tools, data can be accessed in the operational database across multiple-dimensions and statistical analysis tools (like cluster analysis, factor analysis etc.) can be applied on them.

6.4.1 Multi-dimensional Cross-Table Analysis

Multi-dimensional cross-table analysis showed that two or more variables joint frequency distribution table. It belongs to the scope of discrete multivariate analysis, cross-generation multi-dimensional or two-dimensional form, mainly used for the analysis of each things and phenomenon's differences, identify the inspection variables whether have relation. For example, to understand the different age levels and qualifications are concerned about the relationship between the content of the Government, the process can be used to form a two dimensional tables[1] [6]. To show that different age groups, all education levels are concerned about the number of different frequency content distribution, correlation, and to choose suitable way to carry out inspection. Multi-dimensional cross-table analysis of the selected output variables can choose between the correlation coefficient table below on the related analysis and correlation coefficients brief.

6.4.2 Correlation Analysis Method

Between the objective things are interrelated and mutual influence and mutual restraint. Reflect the interconnected between things to a quantity, that is correlation between variables. For instance height and body weight, income and expense [8]. The correlation analysis will find the latent rule that is valuable and description variable relates mutually from the data. Through several descriptions co-relational dependence statistics may determine between the variable's connection close degree and linear correlation direction.

Most commonly use is Pearson correlation coefficient, usually indicated with R. If variables X and Y carry on the observation, obtains a group of data: xi , yi (i = 1,2,..., n) , X and between Y the correlation coefficient formula is

$$R_{xy} = \frac{\Sigma (x_i - \bar{x})(y_i - \bar{y})}{\sqrt{\Sigma (x_i - \bar{x})^2 - \Sigma (y_i - \bar{y})^2}}$$

x, y respectively is the xi , yi (i = 1,2,..., n) Arithmetic average value. Where Rxy ≤ 1 . 0 < Rxy < 1 , x and y that is right relevant; if −1 < Rxy < 0 , that negative correlation between X and Y ; and I Rxy I closer to the 1, between the variables X and Y variables linear relationship is more remarkable. If Rxy closer to the 0, X and Y does not claimed related. When Rxy = 1, say X and Y completely related.

Since E-government affairs appear, it enhanced the government part work efficiency and transparency greatly, also accumulated massive data, but it is far from decision-making, and forecast, has not displayed effectiveness fully which its should have. For example each government website has similar nearly "public opinion investigation" column, it is a very good way of understanding the public's demand, but looked from the website announcement investigation result, the conclusion also pauses in calculation the total to the single question, and the proportion and so on in the simple isolation analysis.

---

[1] http://www.mapit.gov.in/compendium.pdf

6.5 Dimensions

Dimension Name	Dimension Description
Crop	Crop Details
Cultiv	Cultivator Details
Irrig	Irrigation Details
Mcrop	Mixed Crop Details
Owner	Owner Details
Util	Land Utilization Details
Tree	Tree Details
Mutation	Mutation Details
Land Class	Land Classification Details
Land Type	Land Type Details
Location	Location Details
Patta	Patta Inam Details
Time	Normal Time Dimension
Cropping Pattern Time	Cropping Pattern Time Dimension
Soil	Soil Description

Attributes

Cultiv_no	Cultivator Number
Owner_no	Owner Number
Owner	Owner Name
Acqui_type	Acquition Type
Acqui_code	Acquition Code
Login_tah	Tahsildar Name
Login_sir_up	Approved Sirstaedaar
Login_deo	Data Entry Operator
Login_ri	Revenue Inspector

Facts

Fact Name	Fact Description
Scrop_Acre	Single Crop Extent in Acres
Scrop_Gunta	Single Crop Extent in Guntas
Scrop_Fgunta	Single Crop Extent in Fraction of Gunta
Larea_acre	Extent in Acre w.r t to Cultiv Type
Larea_gunta	Extent in Gunta w.r t to Cultiv Type
Crop_acre	Mixed Crop Extent in Acre
Crop_gunta	Mixed Crop Extent in Gunta
Kharif_acre	Extent in acre of crop grown in Kharif season
Kharif_gunta	Extent in Gunta of crop grown in Kharif season
Rabi-acre	Extent in acre of crop grown in Rabi season
Rabi_gunta	Extent in gunta of crop grown in Rabi season
Garden_acre	Extent in acre of crop grown in Garden season
Garden_gunta	Extent in gunta of crop grown in Garden season
Amount	Amount received for Mutation
Tree_no	No of Trees
Total_Mut_Time	Total time for Mutation
Tah_Delay	Tahsildar Delay
RI_Delay	Revenue Inspector Delay
Notice_Delay	Delay In Notice Issue
SirNotice_Delay	Sirastaedar Notice Delay
Sir_Delay	Sirastaedar Delay
New_acre	Extent Acre Modified
New_gunta	Extent Gunta Modified
Sold_acre	Extent in Acre Sold
Sold_gunta	Extent in Gunta Sold
NoofMut	No of Mutations
Ext_acre_own	Extent in Acre Land Owned
Ext_gunta_own	Extent in Gunta Land Owned
Ka_acre_own	Extent in acre of Kharab a
Ka_gunta_own	Extent in gunta of Kharab a
Kb_Acre_Own	Extent in acre of Kharab b
Kb_Gunta_Own	Extent in gunta of Kharab a
Ext_acre_util	Extent in Acre Utilized w.r.t to Land Class
Ext_gunta_util	Extent in Gunta Utilized w.r.t to Land Class
Ext_fgunta_util	Extent in Fraction of Gunta Utilized w.r.t to Land Class

Table 1. Governance Projects and Service Delivery (efficiency, accountability and equity) in India

Nature of e-governance project	Type of government application	Efficiency (time/effort/money for getting the job)		Accountability(transparency/ speed money/ wastage/harassment)		Empowerment (participation/ accessibility/equity)	
		Before	After	Before	After	Before	After
CARD, AP/Kaveri in Karnataka	Valuation of property	Few days	Few minutes	Middlemen, harassment Rs.50 to 500	Reduced	Secrecy/ discretion	Information access
CARD, AP/ Kaveri in Karnataka	Land registration	7-15 days	2-3 hours	2-5% of the value	Minimised	Ambiguity	Display
Bhoomi, Karnataka	Obtaining land title certificates	3-30 days	5-30 minutes	Rs.50-500	Rs.15	Secrecy	Transparency
Inter-state check posts, Gujarat	Collect fines for over loading	30 minutes	2 minutes	Harassment, corruption	Minimised	Discretion	Penalties are displayed
Mandal computers, AP	Issue of caste certificates	20-30 days	15 minutes	Rs.50-100	Rs.10	Discretion	Transparency/ Citizen Charter
FAST in AP	Issue of licences/ vehicle registration	delays	Stipulated time	Rs.50-300	Reduction of speed money	Discretion	Transparency/ Citizen Charter
SKIMS in AP	Net working of Secretariat, departments	Red tapism/ delays/ tedious procedures	Speedy communication/ reduction of cost, staff/time/paper	Absence of accountability/	Transparency accountability/ accessibility of information for quick monitoring & actions	Complexity/ secrecy	Transparency/ access to information for quick action

7 Conclusion

At present, the application of data mining in the e-government public services is relatively small, this paper through data mining in government e-government public services application, the question of independence be linked together, demonstrate the nature and potential link of the problem, provide better decision-making information and support to the Government for the actual work, we can understand the actual needs of the public by these knowledge, enhance the accuracy and scientific decision-making of departments, better service to the people. A framework for 'Data Warehousing and Mining' in e-Governance is presented in this paper. A large number of e-Governance applications are already in operation in most of the states and at the centre. The necessary DWM infrastructure has been created at the headquarter and sufficient number of officials have been trained on DWM. This is the right time for introducing DWM in the e-Governance arena and to further strengthen the e-Governance system. In order to incorporate the DWM system and implement it, initially one or two sectors may be identified and the DWM system built over it as a proof of concept. Once the desired results are achieved, the same can be replicated in other sectors of the government. Once the complete system is in place at the national level for use, a knowledge bank can be created for the entire e-Governance environment.

References

1. Hart, J., Kamber, M.: Concept and Technique of Data Mining. Machine Industry Press, Beijing (2001)
2. Ester, M., Wittmann, R.: Incremental Generalization for Mining in a Data Warehousing Environment. In: Schek, H.-J., Saltor, F., Ramos, I., Alonso, G. (eds.) EDBT 1998. LNCS, vol. 1377, pp. 135–152. Springer, Heidelberg (1998)

3. Fayyad, U., Piatetsky-Shapiro, G., Smyth, P.: Knowledge Discovery and Data Mining: Towards a Unifying Framework. In: Proc. 2nd Int. Conf. on Knowledge Discovery and Data Mining, Portland, OR, pp. 82–88 (1996)
4. Gueting, R.H.: An Introduction to Spatial Database Systems. The VLDB Journal 3(4), 357–399 (1994)
5. Han, J., Cai, Y., Cercone, N.: Data-driven Discovery of Quantitative Rules in Relational Databases. IEEE Transactions on Knowledge and Data Engineering 5(1), 29–40 (1993)
6. "Business Intelligence And E-Governance" Analytics & Modeling Division National Informatics Centre Department Of Information Technology Ministry of Communication & IT New Delhi - 110003
7. http://www.mapit.gov.in/compendium.pdf

Tracking of Nose Tip: An Alternative for Mouse

T. Gireeshkumar[1], K.J. Poornaselvan[2], Sattviksharma[1], Gulshankumar[1],
and R. Sreevathsan[1]

[1] Amrita Vishwa Vidyapeetham, Coimbatore, Tamilnadu, India
[2] Govt. College of Technology, Coimbatore, Tamilnadu, India
{gireeshkumart,sattviksharma,gulshan92,
sreevathsan.ravi}@gmail.com,
poornakj@yahoo.co.in

Abstract. Gesture recognition is mainly apprehensive on analyzing the functionality of human wits. The primary goal of gesture recognition research is to create a system which can recognize specific human gestures and use them to convey information or for device control. The purpose of this paper is to interface machines directly to human wits without any corporeal media in an ambient environment. This work pertains to reckoning on tracking of nose tip. In the pragmatic phenomenon the nose tip is tracked and mouse positioning event is generated on how the nose tip moves on the real world domain. In effectuation phase a single camera based computational paradigm is used for tracking nose tip, and recognizing gestures. Reference point location tracking method is used to spot nose tip in successive frames.

Keywords: Gesture recognition, Human wits, Nose tip detection, Reference point location tracking.

1 Introduction

Gesture recognition tends its way to pattern recognition problem when it comes to bottom stage analysis. In the pragmatic world any vision or image processing problem breaks down to pattern recognition way of solving. More in a transpired way gesture motions are time-varying motion patterns which constitutes towards using statistical pattern recognition as a tool in solving this type of problems. Pattern Recognition concomitants itself after feature extraction has been done [8][9][10].

Modeling of human behavior is becoming an increasingly important and active area of research in computer vision. In many earlier gesture recognition systems, hand tracking and gesture recognition were achieved with the assistance of specialized devices (e.g., data glove, markers, etc.), but this paper focalizes on interacting with the system without any of the special devices [1][2].

The ultimate purpose of this paper is to automate a real time system using a nose in a relatively normal environment. The rest of this paper is organized as follows: Section 2 describes the system Architecture. Section 3 derives the components of gesture recognition systems and implementation of the above system. Section 4 describes the performance analysis and test report. Section 5 describes the conclusion and future enhancements.

R. Kannan and F. Andres (Eds.): ICDEM 2010, LNCS 6411, pp. 219–225, 2012.
© Springer-Verlag Berlin Heidelberg 2012

2 System Architecture

Fig.1 depicts the general flow of the process. It starts with the initialisation phase where the perceptual user interface (PUI).Frames are cleaved from the video sequence which are passed to object detection phase. Firstly the nose tip is detected and located based on the luminance pattern extracted from the initialisation phase. The returned cartesian co-ordinates are used to position mouse onscreen. Further if the frames return the same co-ordinates successively accounting for static head posture then gesture recognition phase that does blink detection is initialised.. Later eye region is extracted and the RGB image is converted to YCbCr space. The luminance map is generated for this region, on which we perform adaptive thresholding. The thresholded image is post-processed with connected component analysis, which includes a set of geometric tests.

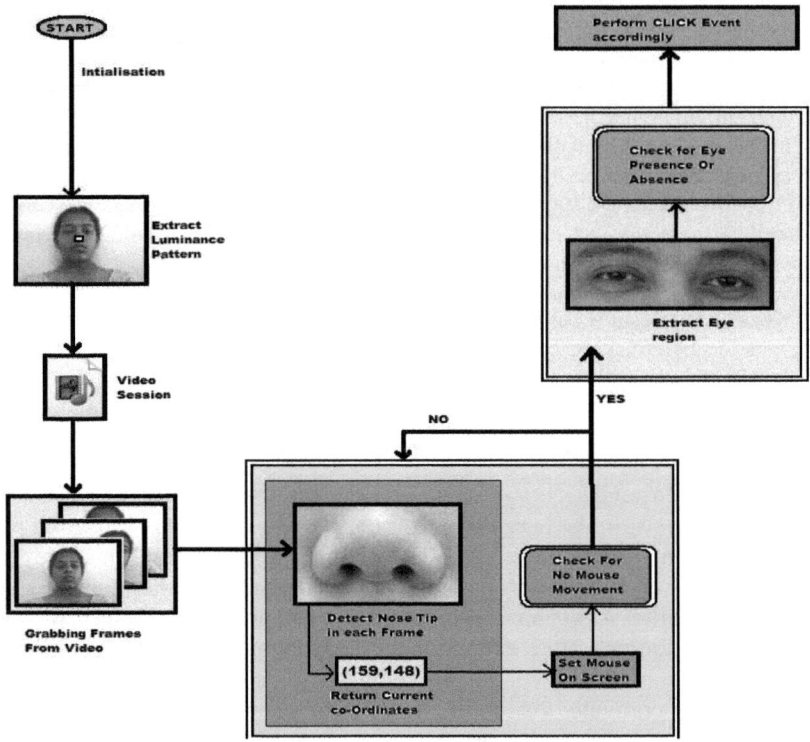

Fig. 1. General flow of system architecture

3 Components of Gesture Recognition System

The conceptual view of the work consists of an image acquisition system, pre-processing system, object tracking system and finally an event handling system. Specifically the process consists of the following modules:

1. Device Integration
2. Video Footage and Grabbing Frames
3. Image Enhancement
4. Nose Detection and Tracking
5. Event Handling

3.1 Image Acquisition

This bundles the operations of device integration, initiating the video footage and grabbing frames from the recorded session [3].

1. Process includes Installing and configuring the image acquisition device. The following are the steps that are to be followed in general to install and configure the device.

   - Installing the frame grabber board in your computer.
   - Installing any software drivers required by the device.
   - Connecting a camera to a connector on the frame grabber board.
   - Verifying that the camera is working properly by running the application software that came with the camera and viewing a live video stream [4].

2. Retrieve information that uniquely identifies the image acquisition device to the Image Acquisition Toolbox.
3. Next a Video Input Object is created which is used by the toolbox to represent the connection between MATLAB and the acquisition device.
4. When both the device and MATLAB are ready to acquire image, a preview of the same is shown to ensure the image acquisition is going to be satisfactory.
5. The object properties which triggers, interval between grabbing of frames etc. are configured according to the requirements of the developing system. On a maximum MATLAB can cleave one second video stream to 30 frames.
6. Once the frame are cleaved the image data thus obtained from webcam is brought to MATLAB workspace which are used in the following modules. The data is acquired on a frame to frame basis.

3.2 Image Enhancement

The principal objective of image enhancement is to process an image so that the resultant image is more suitable to operate on for the specific application. Image enhancement in most of the applications becomes a pre-processing step [2].

3.3 Nose Detection and Tracking

In this section the nose feature is detected in initial frames and tracked in successive ones. According to this method a convex shape such as the shape of the tip of the nose, is a robust object for precise, smooth location and tracking with the webcam as its luminance pattern undergoes very small or almost no change during the video session. The location of the nose can be tracked with pixel and subpixel accuracy [3].

Intially the tri channel RGB video image is converted to YCbCr space and the flow relates to first defining an X-spot in the Ycomponent(luminance component) of the converted image, which is generally either a point on the tip of the nose closest to the webcam or slightly off from it,thus defined X-spot moves therefore on the tip of the nose as the user changes his head pose. A video image of the X-spot and its immediate vicinity is stored as an X-luminance pattern [3].

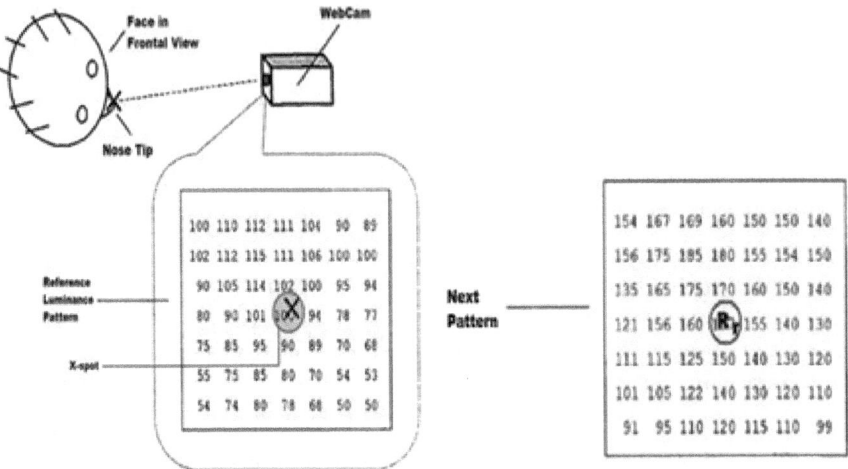

Fig. 2. Initial and successive patterns with located reference point

Generally, the size of this pattern is one sixteenth of the size of image. In subsequent video frames, a best match for the stored X-luminance pattern is found by comparing luminance pattern on a pixel-by-pixel basis, thereby determining the two-dimensional location of the reference point in each video frame with pixel accuracy. [7].

Implementation of the reference point location tracking method depends on corresponding video-based X-spot defining, X-luminance pattern storing, reference point defining, video image registering, video image comparing and average weighting means(Fig. 2).In the successive frame the best match is searched only in the area inside the defined search window. The area of the search window depends on the size of the X-luminance pattern and hence on the size of the image. This area remains constant for a specific video session(Fig. 3).

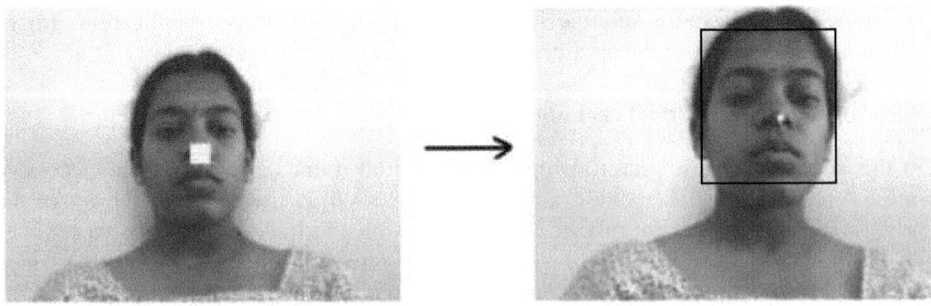

Fig. 3. Initial frame and nose tip in the next with template

3.4 Event Handling

The module takes as an input either the nose tip co-ordinate or the flag which recognises the blink gesture. Normalisation of the nose tip position is done in order to match the system screen size with the size of the image [5][6]. The change in the nose position is shown using a graphical object, similar to that of mouse.

3.5 Nose Tracking Algorithm

Real-time online recognition is done by acquiring the data at that moment of time since the motion patterns in the gesture vocabulary are more complex. So at each instance of time a gesture model is defined and manipulated. Basically, a gesture is defined as an ordered sequence of states in the spatial-temporal space. Some basic protocols are followed which are domain specific are listed here. Embedding intelligence makes the system more perspicacious and thus making the system more resourceful. Any kind of noises has to be dislodged using image processing techniques because noises affect the recognition process drastically. The algorithm is given below

1. Procure the continuous stream of video from   the perceptual user interface.
2. Cleave the input video into sequence of frames.
   {The obtained image (frame) is a RGB tri- channel image}
   Convert the frame into YCbCr tri channel image.
3. Image enhancement {Remove noise from the image by unsharp masking and morphological Erosion operation}
4. Calculate the nose template size as one sixteenth of image size
5. Extract the X- luminance pattern from the centre of the initial frame which is of size calculated in step4 {User must place the nose tip at centre initially.} Centre of the pattern defines the X-spot which gives initial nose tip location
6. Grab next frame
7. Define search window in the current frame using previous nose tip location such that it encloses the facial region
8. Search for best matching pattern in the search area by performing overlapping sliding of X- luminance pattern {this locates nose tip to pixel accuracy}
9. To detect the next reference point, perform weighted averaging and identify the location with maximum correlation. This will give results to sub-pixel accuracy.
10. Location of reference point gives the nose tip position and hence the current mouse position.
11. Place mouse onscreen in the specified location

4   Testing and Performance Analysis

The experiment was conducted for 25 persons with 453 different poses in nose tips for the size of 320X240 samples of 235 numbers and for the size of 160X120 samples of 200 numbers, the test result as shown in Table1.

4.1   Test Result for 25 Persons

Illumination: Average   Image Size   : 320X240

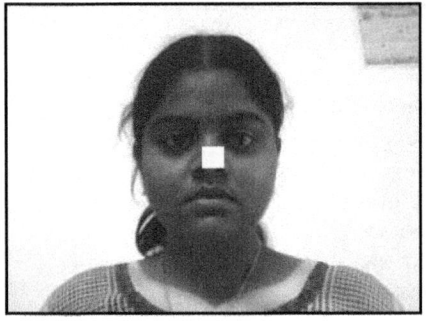   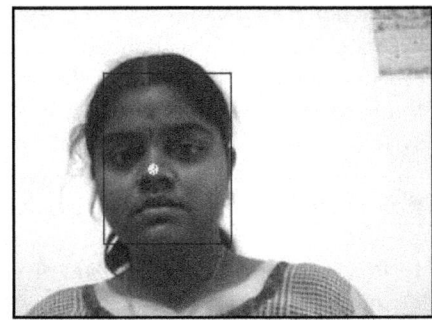

Initial X: 120   Initial Y: 160   Displaced X: 123   Displaced Y: 110

Fig. 4. Showing the nose and nose template

Table 1. Performance of Nose Tip Detection System

Total number of persons whoses faces were analysed	25nos
Total number of samples tested	435 nos
Number of 320 X 240 samples	235 nos
Number of 160 X 120 samples	200 nos
Number of samples in which Nosetip was correctly detected	420 nos
Execution Time - 320 X 240 samples	2.33–5.5 sec
Execution Time - 160 X 120 samples	0.8 – 1.1 sec
Efficiency	96.55%

5   Conclusion and Future Augmentation

This paper proposed and demonstrated a gesture recognition system and its cogency and robustness is checked through a slew number of experiments (Fig.4). Experimental results describe the effectiveness of the approach and the efficiency of the system. It is shown theoretically and by extensive experiments that this technology can be used to operate computer hands-free. It exhibits robustness and precision which are sufficient for many applications and which allow a user the flexibility and convenience of motions. An idea for extending this paper in the future includes introducing the detection of eyebrow raises to do some extended operations as users need.

References

1. Kubota, N.: Human Detection and Gesture Recognition Based on Ambient Intelligence. In: Face Recognition, p. 558. i-Tech, Vienna (2007)
2. Jackway, P.T., Deriche, M.: Scale-Space Properties of the Multiscale Morphological Dilation-Erosion. Proceedings of IEEE Transactions on Pattern Analysis and Machine Intelligence 18(1) (1996)
3. Gorodnichy, D.O.: Method for Video Based Nose Location Tracking and Hands Free Computer Input Devices Based Thereon. Patent Application Publication, United States (2005)
4. Mohamed Berbar, A., Hamdy Kelash, M., Amany Kandeel, A.: Faces and Facial Features Detection in Color Images. In: Proceedings of the Geometric Modelling and Imaging, New Trends (GMAI 2006) (2006)
5. Gorodnichy, D.O., Malik, S., Roth, G.: Nouse Use Your Nose as a Mouse a New Technology for Hands-free Games and Interfaces. In: VI 2002, Calgary, pp. 354–361 (2002)
6. Kumar, R., Kumar, A.: Black Pearl: An Alternative for Mouse and Keyboard. Proceedings of ICGST- GVIP 8(III) (2008)
7. Gorodnichy, D.O., Gerhard, R.: Affordable yet robust and precise face tracking using USB cameras with application to designing hands-free user interfaces. In: Proceedings of the ACM Conference on Software and Technology of Human-Computer Interfaces (2002)
8. Chau, M., Betke, M.: Real Time Eye Tracking and Blink Detection with USB Cameras, Boston University Computer Science Technical Report No. 2005-12 (2005)
9. Zhang, L., Lenders, P.: Knowledge-Based Eye Detection for Human Face Recognition. In: Proceedings of Fourth International Conference on Knowledge-Based Intelligent Engineering Systems & Allied Technologies, Brighton, UK (2000)
10. Peng, K., Chen, L., Ruan, S., Kukharev, G.: A Robust Algorithm for Eye Detection on Gray Intensity Face without Spectacles. Proceedings of JCS&T 5(3) (2005)

A Wireless Sensors Based Feedback System for Human Body Movement Practices

Alex Aravind and Viswanathan Manickam

Computer Science Program
University of Northern British Columbia
Prince George, BC, Canada - V2N 4Z9
{csalex,manickam}@unbc.ca

Abstract. Tracking human body movements is a fundamental and complex problem. Recent times, body worn wireless sensors based systems are becoming effective tools to solve such complex problems. In this paper, we present a wireless sensor network based feedback system to assist training human body movements. We have designed an experimental system using Sun SPOT sensors to capture the movement and then analyze them to offer meaningful feedback to both the trainer and trainees. We conducted a limited number of experiments for some basic movements and the preliminary results are encouraging. The proposed wireless sensors based feedback system is simple, generic, efficient, cost effective, and user friendly. Therefore, it has the practical appeal.

Keywords: Movement tracking, wireless sensor networks, body worn sensors, inertial sensors, feedback assisted training.

1 Introduction

Tracking human body movement is a complex and challenging problem. The difficulty arises due to a number of biochemical and environmental factors that influence human movement. Human movement tracking involves high computation and generally data intensive. The problem has been the subject of extensive studies since the 1980s[6,13,14]. There are several types of movements based on the body parts involved and the applications intended. In that, whole body movement, facial expression, gestures - which commonly originate from facial and hand movements, and movements involving specific body parts such as hand and leg have attracted strong interest due to various applications. Some of the potential applications include visual surveillance, advanced user interface, virtual reality, diagnosis and identification, dance choreography, personalized training, physiotherapy, and rehabilitation.

Computing and communication revolutions, constantly feeding each other, have transformed the world into new levels in recent decades. We are approaching another technological revolution and this time sensors and actuators join with computing and communication to feed each other to create synergy. Wireless sensor network is a such system and it is becoming a powerful infrastructure for numerous applications.

R. Kannan and F. Andres (Eds.): ICDEM 2010, LNCS 6411, pp. 226–233, 2012.
© Springer-Verlag Berlin Heidelberg 2012

The motivation of this project arises from both ends - technological push and application pull. On the technological side, we are entering into a new era of miniature devices (e.g. smart dusts) capable of sensing, computing, and communicating and exchanging data with one another using radio or optical communications. They can self organize into ad hoc network capable of solving variety of problems[12]. Recent breakthroughs in DNA computing indicates that such miniature devices will be available in a cost effective manner sooner than expected[1]. On the application side, mainly due to economic and social changes, the demand for personalized physical training in sports, entertainment, fitness, physiotherapy, and rehabilitation increase steadily. Human body movement practice is common to a range of applications including the above mentioned.

There are four key factors influence the increasing demand for activities involving human body movement. First, automation has been infiltrating every aspect of human life and hence more and more professions are becoming to involve a little or no physical work of the employees. Second, thanks to the computing, communication, and entertainment technology revolutions, every day people spend considerable amount of their time on phone, TV, and Internet which again involve little or no physical movement. Third, availability of rich and unhealthy food is becoming increasingly common and the number of people who can offered such food is steadily increasing. Fourth, as awareness increases through media, more and more people want to involve or trained in several activities. In a nutshell, less physical activity and less time to travel and get training from traditional training centers. Therefore, personal training involving body movements - whether it is sports, entertainment, fitness, physiotherapy, or rehabilitation - at home in convenient times is an attractive option. However, hiring such a personal expert is not affordable to most people for several reasons (e.g. time, money, security). Despite its accuracy, capturing motion using video camera has several limitations. First, most people may not want their image to be captured on video camera. Second, video camera requires line of sight. Third, due to the volume of data, it requires high storage and complex processing. The above analysis motivates us to investigate and develop a simple, non-intrusive, cost effective, and user friendly feedback system for training practices.

This paper describes a wireless sensors based feedback system for human body movement practices. It presents the architecture, prototype hardware setup using Sun SPOT sensors, introduces concepts and ideas for movement pattern mapping and feedback system, discusses the implementation and early experiments. The preliminary results indicate that the proposed system is capable of performing meaningful movement pattern mapping and offer useful feedback.

2 Human Body Movement Tracking – A Brief Survey

Numerous approaches have been proposed in the literature to track various types of human body movements. Based on the types of equipments used, human motion tracking is broadly classified, in [6], into three categories: visual tracking, non-visual tracking, and robot-aided tracking. Visual based tracking uses optical sensors (e.g. cameras) to collect data (e.g. videos, photos, etc.) and track the movement. Again, visual based tracking is classified as visual marker based and visual marker-free. In visual marker based techniques, visual markers (identifiers) are attached to human body and the optical sensor tracks the movement of these markers. Visual marker-free approach uses only optical sensors to track the movement. A combined approaches use both body movement and marker movement. Non-visual based tracking uses other types of sensors such as inertial sensors (e.g. accelerometer and gyroscope), magnetic sensors, and acoustic sensors.

Based on the methods used, tracking is classified as model based tracking, region-based tracking, active contour based tracking, and feature based tracking[13]. Model based tracking uses simplified representation of body segments. Popular representations are lines (stick figure), two dimensional contour (2-D ribbons), and three dimensional volume (elliptical cylinder, cone, sphere, etc.). Region based tracking uses the idea of identifying a connected region associated with each moving object in an image and then track it over time. Active contour based tracking, also known as snakes, uses bounding contour of the object and updated dynamically over time. It aims at extracting the shape directly from the subject. The above three methods track the objects as a whole. Instead, feature based tracking uses some distinguishable points or lines on the objects to achieve the task. This approach has the advantage of tracking efficiency. The accuracy depends on choosing suitable feature, and its extraction and matching. The study described in this paper involves a particular case of human body tracking problem based on inertial sensors. Inertial sensors typically has two components, accelerometer to produce linear acceleration and gyroscopes to produce the rate of turn or tilt.

Applications to dance have been actively studied since early 70s[2,5,7,9,11]. In these studies modeling, annotation, and animation aspects are focused in [7,11]. Dynamic programming has been used to check the similarity between observed dance movements in [2,5]. Aylward and Paradiso used inertial sensors to record and transmit the expressive motion of a group of dancers[9]. They study the correlation between the movement of a group. Inertial sensors have also been used to study walking motion[4], gait training[10], motion detection of human upper limbs[8], and motion recognition for equipment operation[3].

3 Feedback Assisted Movement Training System

The proposed system is sensors based human interactive software system. In a higher level, it consists of the following four main components: (i) *Trainer* - who creates a sequence of movement patterns; (ii) *Trainees* - who try to imitate or reproduce the chosen pattern created by the trainer. The process of creating movements by a trainee is referred to as *practice*; (iii) *Sensors* - attached to the human subject (trainer or trainee) during the creation of a movement pattern in order to collect the movement data and feed into a software system; and (iv) *Software System* - to provide feedback to the trainees during a practice and to the trainer after practices.

We refer the movement patterns created by the trainer as *templates* and the movement patterns produced by the trainees as *practice patterns*. We make the following assumptions: (A1) Movement data of templates and practice patterns are obtained from the same equipment based on same technique; and (A2) A set M of basic movements are known and a template is a finite sequence of elements from M.

The movement tracking problem in the above setup is simpler compared to traditional human body movement problem studied in the literature. The templates and association of a movement pattern to be tracked to its corresponding template are supplied by the user. Also, the system has the knowledge of the basic movement patterns. For many practical applications, these assumptions are reasonable. These are unknown in the traditional body movement tracking and without this knowledge the problem is hard to solve.

The system starts with an initial set of well defined basic movements, and the set can be updated when new basic movements are identified. Each of these basic movements is attached with associated information that can be used for educated feedback and performance calculations. From these basic movements, the trainer can create templates for practices. A trainee can choose a template from the template database to practice that movement. The system can then match the created practice pattern with its template. The result of the assessment is stored in the feedback database, and a suitable feedback is generated and communicated to the trainee when requested. The feedback database can be used to analyze more than one practice.

Pattern assessment involves matching two movement patterns - specifically a practice pattern and its template. Let us denote the movement patterns (a practice pattern and its template) as P and T, which are graphs in the three dimensional inertial space.

3.1   Movement Pattern Matching

Accurate matching of movement patterns is crucial for the usefulness of the system. In our case, the movement patterns P and T are basically time series. Several ways P and T may be aligned or mapped end to end and produce an alignment score. Such a numerical score for the entire alignment may not be very helpful to offer any useful feedback, particularly the movement pattern is sufficiently long. However, such a global alignment may be used as a reference to see the accuracy of the other improved techniques. Useful feedbacks must be specific enough to indicate which parts of the movement are accurate or acceptable and which parts are incorrectly practiced. This requires the identification of smaller meaningful segments in P and T. For that, we need to identify meaningful points in the pattern that we refer to as **markers**. Using the alignment of the identified smaller segments, the system can offer more specific and useful feedback.

There are several ways markers can be produced. We introduce three ways of producing the markers: (i) *Random* - choose time points randomly; (ii) *Periodic* - divide the time interval into n equal parts; and (iii) *Feature based* - extract distinguishable points from the movement patterns. Random and periodic markers are simple, but do not dependent on the content of the data. These type of markers may be useful for theoretical analysis and we do not see much use in the real applications. Markers derived based on some key features from the data can be more useful in practice, but the challenge is choosing meaningful features and their identification. We again classify the feature based markers as *system derived* and *trainer specified*. System derived markers are logical points in the data, based on some interesting features such as sharp turn and sudden change. Trainer can specify the markers based on higher level logical steps or movements, either during the data generation (by explicit signal) or after the data generation based on data analysis, visualization, and personal expertise.

We compute the alignment score between the segments using two simple methods: (i) Average distance method; and (ii) Dynamic programming. The average distance method computes the distances between every two points (one from first the segment and the other from the second segment in the same index) and then the average of these distances is considered as the alignment distance.

Optimal alignment between P and T can be obtained by suitably warping (stretching) the time axis of one series to align with the other (referred to as *dynamic time warping*). Dynamic programming is a powerful optimization technique to create such a time warping. Conceptually, dynamic programming recursively builds the solution in a bottom up fashion - from simpler case to more complex case. Computationally, it first constructs a matrix (using P as columns and T as rows), and then computes and fills the matrix using the specified recurrence equation starting from the upper left corner to the lower right corner. The value of the cell (i, j) is computed based on the values of the cells $(i-1, j), (i-1, j-1)$, and $(i, j-1)$. Then, from the lower right corner cell, the optimal path can be retraced. Construction of a suitable recurrence equation and its initialization are the keys to the accuracy of the alignment.

4   System Architecture and Experimental Setup

We use inertial sensors for our experiments. Initial experiment uses a single Sun SPOT sensor attached to the wrist, as shown in Fig.2., for simple hand movements. Later experiments are expected to use multiple sensors. The software captures the movement information using Sun SPOT sensors in a regular interval. The system differs between the trainer and the trainees. When the trainer uses the software, she can feed the new templates and assess all the practices done by the trainees. When a trainee uses the software, she can do practices on the given templates. The software architecture of the system is shown in Fig.1.

The software has the following logical modules.

◇ *Movement databases*: There are three movement databases in the software. First one represents the basic movement knowledge base which comprises of the information about the basic movements. Second, the template pattern database contains patterns created by the trainer. Finally, the practice pattern database contains the practice pattern produced by the trainees. By

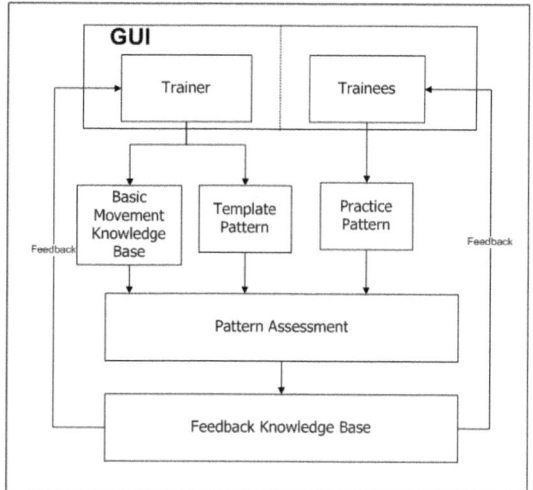

Fig. 1. Architecture   **Fig. 2.** Experimental Setup

developing knowledge base on the possible movements, the system can offer more informed and intelligent feedback. Based on the mapping score of the practice movement, necessary information about the movement can be extracted from the database to prepare and offer suitable feedback.

◇ *Pattern Assessment*: Pattern Assessment is responsible for analyzing the practice pattern against its template pattern. It compares the movement based on the reading tilt and acceleration across 3 dimensional axis and assign a comparison value. The trainers can assess the trainee performance by checking the scores which is calculated based on the pattern matching or she can check the movements using graphical display.

◇ *Feedback Knowledge Base*: Feedback knowledge base is an interesting module in the software as it provides the feedback about the movement. Also, the module provides information about which part of the movement needs more importance and attention. Based upon the user login to the system, this module suggests techniques to improve the movement. If a trainer login, the feedback mostly concentrates on the movements that most of the trainees find it difficult or performed well. If a trainee login, the trainee will be provided with information about the missed moves or least matched moves.

We have conducted a limited number of experiments. Initially we tried with templates using hand movement for basic regular geometric shapes such as triangle, rectangle, and circle. We used sharp turn as the markers and implemented the marker based discrete segments approach. We captured a set of practices against the templates and divided the practice pattern by identified marker and analyzed the pattern matching. The obtained results is in the range of scores between 50 - 80%. We represented the comparison pattern in a graphical way as shown in Fig.3.

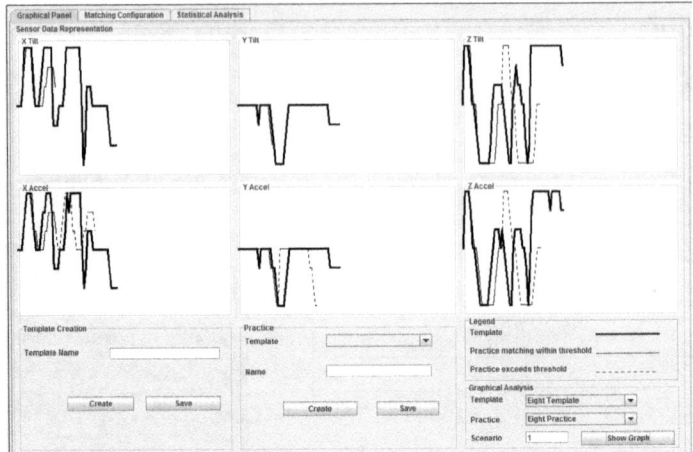

Fig. 3. An Experimental Result

The graph is drawn with the tilt and acceleration values of the three axes against the time line. The thick line represents the template and thin line (continuous and dashed) represents practice pattern. The thin continuous line indicates that the practice is close to the template and therefore acceptable. The thin dashed line indicates that the score is not satisfactory and needs more attention.

During our experiment, we observed that dynamic programming gives more accurate alignment score than average distance method. The crucial component is marker identification. In a simple experiment, our system identified 7 markers from the template pattern, 7 markers from the practice 1, and 6 markers from the practice 2. The alignment scores are given in the table below.

Scores	S1	S2	S3	S4	S5	S6	S7	Total
Practice 1	90	75	65	100	100	90	35	79.28571
Practice 2	75	55	60	90	90	40	-	58.57143
Practice 2	75	55	60	90	90	-	55	60.71429

If you look at the scores for the practice 1, the segments S1, S4, S5, and S6 were performed well, and the segments S2 and S3 were performed above average, and the segment S7 was performed very poorly. Clearly this table offers more useful information in the segment level. The problem arises when some markers are missed or some unintended markers are fetched. In the former case, the alignment of some segments may be adjusted to see a better overall score (as shown in the table) and in the latter case unintended markers must be filtered.

5   Conclusion and Future Directions

In this paper we discussed a template based movement tracking system for personalized training purposes using wireless sensor networks. We discussed some preliminary approaches and algorithms that can be used to implement and conducted a limited number of experiments. The work can be expanded in several directions including implementing tuned dynamic programming based alignment, more customized feedback system, and new creative display options. We leave these for our future work.

References

1. Pistol, C., Mao, V., Thusu, V., Lebeck, A.R., Dwyer, C.: Moleucular Logic Gates: Encoded Multichromophore Response for Simultaneous Label-Free Detection. Small 6(7), 843–850 (2010)
2. Fujimoto, M., Fujita, N., Takegawa, Y., Terada, T., Tsukamoto, M.: A Motion Recognition Method for a Wearable Dancing Musical Instrument. In: Proc. of the International Symposium on Wearable Computers, pp. 11–18 (2009)
3. Tanaka, H., Kimura, R., Ioroi, S.: Equipment Operation by Motion Recognition with Wearable Wireless Acceleration Sensor. In: Proc. of the International Conference on Next Generation Mobile Applications, Services and Technologies, pp. 114–118 (2009)
4. Ito, T.: Walking Motion Analysis using 3D Acceleration Sensors. In: Proc. of the Second UKSIM European Symposium on Computer Modeling and Simulation, pp. 123–128 (2008)
5. Sadeghi, H., Moallem, P., Monadjemi, S.A.: Feature Based Dense Stereo Matching Using Dynamic Programming and Color. International Journal of Computational Intelligence 4, 179–186 (2008)
6. Zhou, H., Hu, H.: Human Motion Tracking for Rehabilitation - A Survey. Biomedical Signal Processing and Control 3, 1–18 (2008)
7. Ramadoss, B., Rajkumar, K.: Modeling and Annotating the Expressive Semantics of Dance Videos. International Journal of Information Technologies and Knowledge 1, 137–146 (2007)
8. Zhou, H., Hu, H.: Intertial Sensors for Motion Detection of Human Upper Limbs. Sensor Review 27(2), 151–158 (2007)
9. Aylward, R., Paradiso, J.A.: Sensemble: A Wireless, Compact, Multi-user Sensor System for Interactive Dance. In: Proc. of the International Conference on New Interfaces for Musical Expression, pp. 134–139 (2006)
10. Negard, N.-O., Schauer, T., Raisch, J., Shumacher, S., Homberg, V.: Control of FES-assisted Gait Training after Stroke using Inertial Sensors. In: Proc. of the 11th Annual Conference of the International FES Society, pp. 74–76 (2006)
11. Calvert, T., Wilke, L., Ryman, R., Fox, L.: Applications of Computers to Dance. IEEE Computer Graphics and Applications, 6–12 (2005)
12. Darrin, M.A., Carkhuff, B.G., Mehoke, T.S.: Future Trends in Miniaturization for Wireless Applications. John Hopkins APL Technical Digest 25(4), 343–347 (2004)
13. Wang, L., Hu, W., Tan, T.: Recent Developments in Human Motion Analysis. Pattern Recognition 36, 585–601 (2003)
14. Gavrila, D.M.: The Visual Analysis of Human Movement: A Survey. Computer Vision and Image Understanding 73(1), 82–98 (1999)

Performance Analysis of Classification Techniques Using Different Parameters

Gaurang Panchal, Amit Ganatra, Y.P. Kosta,
and Devyani Panchal

Department of Computer Engineering, Charotar Institute of Technology
(Faculty of Technology and Engineering),
Charotar University of Science and Technology, Changa, Anand-388 421, India
{gaurangpanchal.ce,amitganatra.ce,ypkosta.adm,
devyanipanchal.it}@ecchanga.ac.in

Abstract. Data mining technique is the process of analyzing data from different perspectives and summarizing it into useful information. Classification refers to the data mining problem of attempting to predict the category of categorical data by building a model based on some predictor variables. The goal of data classification is to organize and categorize data in distinct classes. It does not require any priori knowledge of the class statistical distribution in data sources. ANN can be trained to distinguish the criteria used to classify and it can do so in a generalized manner allowing successful classification of new inputs not used during training. Back propagation as a training algorithm for ANN works well for classification. This Paper shows the issue of improving the fitness of BPN algorithm and the performance analysis of various classification techniques like Naïve Bayes, Bayesian network, Support Vector Machine and GABPN discussed.

Keywords: Classification, Neural Network, Naïve Bayes, Bayesian Networks, SVM.

1 Introduction to Classification Techniques

An information extraction activity whose goal is to discover hidden facts contained in databases. Using a combination of machine learning, statistical analysis, modeling techniques and database technology, data mining finds patterns and subtle relationships in data and infers rules that allow the prediction of future results.

Typical applications include market segmentation, customer profiling, and fraud detection, evaluation of retail promotions, medical diagnosis, and credit risk analysis.

Classification refers to the data mining problem of attempting to predict the category of categorical data by building a model based on some predictor variables. Neural networks are most effective and appropriate artificial intelligence technology for pattern recognition. Superior results in pattern recognition can be directly applied for business purposes in forecasting, classification and data analysis [1]. This new approach gives an extra advantage in solving "real-world" problems in business and engineering. However, to bring proper results, neural networks require correct data pre-processing, architecture selection and network training. In general terms, an

R. Kannan and F. Andres (Eds.): ICDEM 2010, LNCS 6411, pp. 234–241, 2012.
© Springer-Verlag Berlin Heidelberg 2012

artificial neural network consists of a large number of simple processing units, linked by weighted connections.

The Naive Bayes (NB) algorithm makes predictions using Bayes Theorem, which derives the probability of a prediction from the underlying evidence. NB affords fast model build. NB assumes that each attribute, or piece of evidence, is independent from the others. In practice, this assumption usually does not degrade the model's predictive accuracy significantly.

Bayesian Network: It is a probabilistic graphical model that represents a set of variables and their probabilistic independencies.

Support Vector Machine Algorithm (SVM): Support Vector Machine (SVM) is a classification and regression prediction tool that uses machine learning theory to maximize predictive accuracy while automatically avoiding over fit of the data. Neural networks and radial basis functions, both popular data mining techniques, can be viewed as special cases of SVMs. SVMs perform well with real-world applications such as classifying text, recognizing hand-written characters, classifying images. There is no upper limit on the number of attributes and target cardinality for SVMs. The SVM kernel functions currently supported are linear and Gaussian.

2 Problem Definition

Classification is a data mining (machine learning) technique used to predict group membership for data instances. Classification means evaluating a function, which assigns a class label to a data item. Classification is a supervised learning process, uses training set which has correct answers (class label attribute). The problem is to develop the classification model using the available training set which needs to be normalized. Large scale data mining applications involving complex decision making can access billions of bytes of data.. Hence, the efficiency of such applications is paramount.

3 Data Analysis

We need to analyze your dataset to define column parameters and detect data anomalies. Data analysis information needed for correct data pre-processing. By default, data analysis options will be applied to all columns in the input data set. But they can be different for every column.

Missing values: It is necessary to remove the missing values. We can remove the missing value by mean, median, minimum or by maximum value.

Outliers: Outliers is column values that are far away from the majority of the column data. Outliers mean values that are "far" from the majority of others. Outliers can be just extreme cases or measurement errors. Outliers can significantly degrade the performance of the neural network. It is necessary to remove the outliers.

Wrong type values: It is necessary to remove the wrong type value. Wrong type values usually resulted from a data entry error (e.g. a column with values "102, 43, 15, 8, abc, 89, 1" having abc as a wrong type value). These values prevent correct column type identification and should be removed.

4 Data Pre Processing

The Value with min and max for all accepted numeric columns from your input data file. You can change the minimum and maximum values if you know that future data for forecasting will be lower than the minimum and higher than the maximum presented in your input data file.

Scaling Numeric Columns: Numeric columns are automatically scaled during data pre-processing [2]. By default, numeric values are scaled using the following formula.

$$SF = (SR_{max} - SR_{min}) / (X_{max} - X_{min}) \tag{1}$$

$$X_p = SR_{min} + (X - X_{min}) * SF \tag{2}$$

Where X is actual value of a numeric column, X_{min} is minimum actual value of the column, X_{max} is maximum actual value of the column, SR_{min} is lower scaling range limit, SR_{max} is upper scaling range limit, and SF is scaling factor and X_p - pre-processed value. We have scale inputs with scaling range[-1...1] and output column with scaling range [0...1], all the Categorical column like Sex , Marital Status with two state, Children with 3 State, Education with two state and Retention Probability with two state. We scale the data for better performance of Neural Network

5 Architecture Selection

The Number of retrains parameter specifies how many runs (network retrains) with different weight initialization will be made for each architecture configuration. For example, if you set 3 retrains per configuration, each architecture will be retrained 3 times and the best result from these 3 retrains will be selected to compare with results of others topologies.

For employee retention probability we have total 11 inputs. We have started searching best architecture with minimum hidden nodes. Using Akakies Information Criterion (AIC) we can find the best architecture.

$$AIC = n * \ln(RSS / n) + 2 * K \tag{3}$$

Using the Akaiks Information Criterion we can build best neural network Architecture. The Lowest AIC is best for any Neural Network Architecture. Though there are many more techniques but the AIC is the best method for Model Selections

6 Dataset for Analysis

Nursery Database was derived from a hierarchical decision model originally developed to rank applications for nursery schools. The data set taken for classification is as below, all attributes here are nominal. Here Number of Instances in Training set is 7494, Number of Instances in Testing set is 3498, Number of Attributes: 16 input+1 class attribute All input attributes are integers in the range 0...100.The output attribute is the class code 0..9.The Data sets are taken from ftp://ftp.ics.uci.edu/pub. Performance analysis of the system is considered based on below data sets. Weka[16] is a collection of machine learning algorithms for data mining tasks. The algorithms can either be applied directly to a dataset or called from your own Java code. Weka contains tools for data pre-processing, classification, regression, clustering, association rules, and visualization. It is also well-suited for developing new machine learning schemes.[16]

Table 1. Attribute Name and Attribute values taken in Analysis

Attribute Name	Attribute values
Parents	Usual, pretentious, great_prêt.
has_nurs	proper, less_proper, improper, critical, very_crit.
Form	Complete, completed, incomplete, foster.
Children	1, 2, 3, more.
Housing	Convenient, less_conv, critical.
Finance	Convenient, inconv.
Social	Nonprob, slightly_prob, problematic.
Health	Recommended, priority, not_recom.
Classes	Not_recom, recommend, very_recom, priority, spec_prior

7 Performance Analysis

Here we have taken No of Iterations is 600,No of Hidden Layers is 1,No of Hidden Nodes is 10,Error Tolerance is 90%,Mutation Rate is 0.2,Cross Over Rate is 0.3,Generations is 25,Population is 300.

Table 2. Performance Analysis based on various ways

based on Iterations			Based on number of Hidden nodes.			based on number of Hidden layers			
Iterations	Accuracy %	Time (Sec)	Hidden Nodes	Accuracy %	Time (sec)	Hidden Nodes in layer1	Hidden Nodes in layer 2	Accuracy %	Time in sec
100	80	17	8	73	40	6	3	82	26
200	81	34	9	84	45	7	2	74	29
300	83	53	10	80	46	8	1	39	27
500	83	1.23	11	81	50	6	4	83	28
1000	84	2.37	-	-	-	5	5	81	27

Table 3. Performance Analysis based on Learning Rate

Base on Learning Rate		
Learning Rate	Accuracy %	**Time (Sec)**
0.3	80	1.2
0.4	77	1.16
0.5	79	1.17
0.6	78	1.22

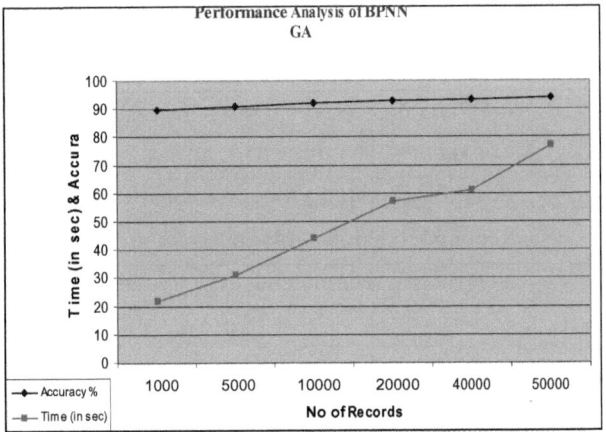

Fig. 1. Performance Analysis of GA Based BPN

Table 3 and Figure 1 shows the Performance analysis based on learning rate and Chart shows the Performance analysis based on GA base Back Propagation.

8 Comparison Performance with Different Classification Techniques

Comparing the proposed system with MLP training, Naïve Bayes and some other were done using a tool WEKA. Data set taken for testing is Nursery Data set, having # variants 12120 and training set is having no of variants 12960.[16]

1. Naïve Bayes
2. Bayesian network
3. Support Vector Machine

Naive Bayes Algorithm: The Naive Bayes (NB) algorithm makes predictions using Bayes Theorem, which derives the probability of a prediction from the underlying evidence. NB affords fast model build and applies. NB assumes that each attribute, or piece of evidence, is independent from the others. In practice, this assumption usually does not degrade the model's predictive accuracy significantly [7].

Bayesian Network: It is a probabilistic graphical model that represents a set of variables and their probabilistic independencies. It is a framework for representing uncertainty in our knowledge, a Graphical modeling framework of causality and influence, a Representation of the dependencies among random variables. It is a compact representation of a joint probability of variables on the basis of the concept of conditional independence [7].

Support Vector Machine Algorithm (SVM): Support Vector Machine (SVM) is a classification and regression prediction tool that uses machine learning theory to maximize predictive accuracy while automatically avoiding over fit of the data. Neural networks and radial basis functions, both popular data mining techniques, can be viewed as special cases of SVMs. SVMs perform well with real-world applications such as classifying text, recognizing hand-written characters, classifying images. There is no upper limit on the number of attributes and target cardinality for SVMs. The SVM kernel functions currently supported are linear and Gaussian [7].

Performance Study with Other Methods

Table 4. Performance Analysis of Various Classification Techniques

Algorithm Name	Accuracy
Bayesian network	0.803047372
Naive Bayes	0.80386569
Support Vector Machine	0.815737546
BPNN GA	0.9222595

After the Performance analysis, the Support Vector Machine and Back Propagation Neural Network with Genetic Algorithm give better result in terms of accuracy. [15]

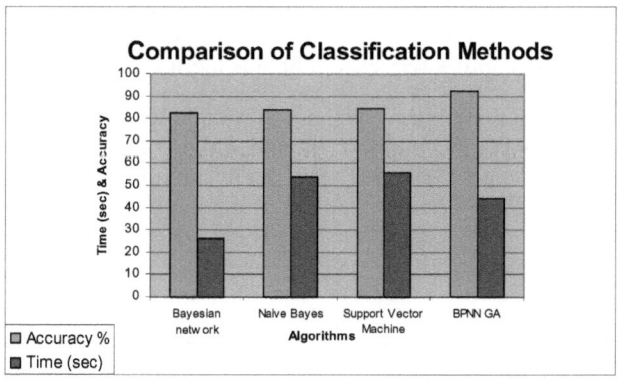

Fig. 2. Comparision of Various Classification Techniques

Also Genetic Algorithm based Back Propagation Neural Network give better performance as show in table.

The result is generated using WEKA.

Table 5. Performance of various classifiers

Classifier	CCR(%)	Incorrect CCR (%)	RMS Error (%)	Time (Sec.)
Multilayer Perceptrons	85.71	14.28	0.2543	0.08
SMO	64.28	35.71	0.4303	0.53
bayes.net	50	50	0.4385	0.02
NBTree	50	50	0.4418	0.03
ZeroR	35.71	64.28	0.4702	0.0
Filtered Classifier	64.28	35.7143	0.3883	0.02
Multi Class Classifier	57.14	42.8571	0.4173	0.01
Bagging	71.42	28.5714	0.3958	0.02

By observing result analysis of various Classification techniques, Genetic Algorithm
Based Back Propagation Network and SVM give better result.

9   Conclusion

Both Genetic Algorithm and back propagation are search and optimization techniques. The goal of this hybrid algorithm is to perform weight adjustment in order to minimize the Mean Square Error between obtained output and desired output. It is better to apply back propagation algorithm first, so that the search space of Genetic algorithm will be reduced. Hence one can overcome the problem of local minima. The proposed algorithm exploits the optimization advantages of GA for the purpose of accelerating neural network training. BP algorithm is sensitive to initial parameters and GA is not. BP algorithm has high convergence speed and while GA is having slow convergence. So the proposed system blends merits of both BP and GA.

Acknowledgement. The authors' wishes to thank all the colleagues for their guidance, encouragement and support in undertaking the research work. Special thanks to the Dean and Principal for their moral support and continuous encouragement.

References

1. Goldberg, D.E.: Genetic algorithms in search, optimization, and machine learning. Pearson Education (2001)
2. Gupta, R.K., Bhunia, A.K.: An Application of real-coded Genetic Algorithm for integer linear programming. AMO-Advanced Modeling and Optimization 8(1) (2006)

3. Srinivas, V., Thompson, G.L.: Benefit-cost Analysis of coding techniques for the Primal Transportation Algorithm. Journal of the Association for Computing Machinery 20, 194–213 (1973)
4. Mohan, M., Gupta, P.K.: Operations research, Methods and Solutions. Sultan Chand and Sons, Reading (1992)
5. Mak, B.L., Sockel, H.: Info. & Mgmt, A confirmatory factor analysis of IS employee motivation and retention (2001)
6. Hornik, K., Stnchcombe, M., White, H.: Multilayer Feedforward Networks are Universal Approximators. Neural Network 2, 359–366 (1989)
7. Garg, P.: Advanced in Computer Science & Engineering. MacMillan Publication (2009)
8. Vijyalakshmi Pai, G.A., Rajasekaran, S.: Neural networks, fuzzy logic and genetic algorithms. In: Synthesis and applications. Prentice-Hall of India, Reading (2004)
9. Kullback, S., Leibler, R.A.: On Information and Sufficiency. The Annals of Mathematical Statistics 22(1), 79–86 (1951)
10. Akaike, H.: A new look at the statistical model identification. IEEE Transactions on Automatic Control 19(6), 716–723 (1974)
11. Linhart, H., Zucchini, W.: Model Selection. John Wiley and Sons (1986)
12. Hurvich, C.M., Tsai, C.: Regression and Time Series Model Selection in Small Samples. Biometrika 76, 297–307 (1989)
13. Cavanaugh, J.E.: Unifying the Deriviations for the Akaike and Corrected Akaike Information Criteria. Statistics & Probability Letters 33, 201–208 (1997)
14. Zhang, M.: Artificial Neural Networks. Victoria University of Wellington
15. Plagianakos, V.P., Magoulas, G.D., Vrahatis, M.N.: Learning rate adaptation in stochastic gradient descent, Department of Mathematics, University of Patras
16. http://www.cs.waikato.ac.nz/ml/weka/

Revenue Estimation and Quantification in Sponsored Search Auctions: An Inductive Learning Approach

Madhu Kumari and Kamal K. Bharadwaj

School of Computer and System Sciences,
Jawaharlal Nehru University, New Delhi, India
madhu.jaglan@gmail.com, kbharadwaj@gmail.co.in

Abstract. Sponsored Search Auctions (SSA) are major contributors to the search engine's revenue because of their highly targeted customers and all time available on-line arenas. The Involvement of search users induces a fairly complex dynamics in SSA. It encompasses a gamut of multi-disciplinary research problems starting from modeling users' clicking behavior to mechanism design. In the proposed work we focus on the users' response towards advertisements based on the time of query, keywords used in query and position of advertisements. This paper is an effort to estimate and quantify search engine's pay off using inductive learning which in turn implicitly models users' clicking behavior and as a byproduct it can help search engine to induce optimality in the auction without sacrificing much of the efficiency of the ranking. Experimental results are presented to demonstrate effectiveness of the proposed scheme.

Keywords: Sponsored Search Auctions, Search Engine, Auctions Contexts, Inductive Learning, Users' Search Behavior.

1 Introduction

In comparison to the traditional auctions these auctions have three players, advertiser, search engine and user therefore it becomes quite arduous to understand the nature of interaction and responses of each player towards others. It is natural for bidder to bid upon the keywords but what is the right commodity to be sold user will decide and its value as well. Although there are many users preference models in SSA [1],[2],[4] but literature pertaining to the revenue prediction of auctioneer based on users' behavior modeling is sparse. This paper addresses natural questions like: How to estimate auctioneer's pay-off under a certain mechanism and what are the important factors which influence revenue?

This paper focuses on the following aspects: effect of number of clicks on auctioneer's revenue, the right commodity to bid upon (to be clicked) and to develop a technique that increases optimality of the auction without losing much in terms of efficiency of ranking.

R. Kannan and F. Andres (Eds.): ICDEM 2010, LNCS 6411, pp. 242–244, 2012.
© Springer-Verlag Berlin Heidelberg 2012

2   Proposed Scheme

2.1   Applying Inductive Learning to Classify the Situation in Sponsored Search Auctions

2.1.1   Choosing Attributes for Classification

Although there are several attributes which constitute a SSA conditions, but in this paper we are considering only seven of these, based on their generality to capture the real situations and informational aspects in clicking decisions. Selected attributes are Domain Search Frequency(DSF), Type of keywords in query(Keyword), Type of the match of advertisement to query(Match) ,Time of query (Time), Relevance of advertisement(Relevance) and Position of the advertisement(Position). Based on the above parameters inductive learning based on information gain heuristics is used (C5 method) [5].

2.2   Estimation of Revenue Based on the Extracted Rules

2.2.1   Revenue Estimation

In the proposed framework we have considered that any SSA can be described by a vector C, $C = \{ q, L, CPC, time \}$ representing its context as: $C = \{ q, L, CPC, time \}$ where q is query on which SSA is called , L is an ordered list of candidate advertisements for this query, CPC is an ordered list of cost per click of an ad on particular position and $time$ is a timestamp. Revenue of search engine or auction provider in a particular auction A_C is computed as:

$$R(A_C) = \sum_{i=1}^{n} C(p_i) * CPC(ad_j, p_i) \tag{1}$$

where $C(p_i)$ is clicking decision of user at position p_i and $CPC(ad_j, p_i)$ is cost per click of advertisement ad_j at position p_i . In real situations, C can easily be mapped to the classifying attributes and based on the values of these attributes (using the rules extracted from logs) it is possible to estimate that how many clicks a particular context C can lead to. Hence auctioneer can estimate revenue with almost the same accuracy as that of inductive rules.

2.2.2   Revenue Quantification

Search engine's revenue of SSA is a collective price combination of commodities position, time and keywords which are sold to advertisers. Analysis of discovered rules which are obtained from the data logs based on the contexts of auctions can be used to quantify auctioneer's revenue. Hence auction provider's revenue $R(A_C)$ can be expressed as a weighted sum of $R_T(A_C)$, $R_K(A_C)$ and $R_P(A_C)$ (time, keyword and position dependent fraction of revenue respectively):

$$R(A_C) = w_1 R_K(A_C) + w_2 R_T(A_C) + w_3 R_P(A_C) \tag{2}$$

where weights can be obtained from coverage of the rules related to the considered attributes and $w_1 + w_2 + w_3 = 1$.

244   M. Kumari and K.K. Bharadwaj

3   Experiments

For carrying the experiments in this work we have considered five query domains: Automobiles, Holidays, Drinks, Airways and Laptops, and considered 40 to 50 queries for each domain and analyzed data for the features explained above.

Table 1. Sample data

S.N	DSF %	in Keyword	Match	Time	Relevance (0 - 10)	Position (1 - 4)	Clicking decision
1	5	Specific	Exact	AH	3.2	2	Yes
2	8	General	Exact	PH	4.1	2	Yes
3	7	General	Broad	AH	2.0	3	No
4	7	Specific	Broad	PH	5	1	Yes
5	10	General	Exact	AH	3.5	1	Yes
6	3	Specific	Exact	PH	2.5	2	No
7	10	Specific	Broad	OH	4.0	1	No
8	8	General	Exact	OH	4.7	1	No
9	10	Specific	Broad	PH	1.2	4	No
10	5	General	Broad	PH	4.5	3	Yes

4   Conclusions and Future Work

This work is to leverage the informational model of users clicking behavior, to motivate auctioneers to disintegrate revenue in to different ingredients for effective pay off prediction and thereby to facilitate advertisers to bid on the appurtenant commodity. Major contributions of this paper are to estimate and quantify auctioneer's revenue by using inductive learning techniques which synthesizes a tacit users clicking model. Future work includes capitalizing revenue quantification for setting up optimal auctions without forfeiting efficiency of ranking schemes and ingraining proposed scheme with fuzzy logic based effective bidding range computation [3].

References

1. Aggarwal, G., Feldman, J., Muthukrishnan, S., Pál, M.: Sponsored Search Auctions with Markovian Users. In: Papadimitriou, C., Zhang, S. (eds.) WINE 2008. LNCS, vol. 5385, pp. 621–628. Springer, Heidelberg (2008)
2. Feldman, J., Muthukrishnan, S.: Algorithmic Methods for Sponsored Search Advertising Tutorial. In: SIGMETRICS (2008)
3. Kumari, M., Bharadwaj, K.K.: Fuzzy Logic Based Effective Range Computation and Bidder's Behavior Estimation in Keyword Auctions. In: IEEE 2nd International Advance Computing Conference, pp. 299–303 (2010)
4. Ostrovsky, M., Edelman, B., Schwarz, M.: Internet Advertising and the Generalized Second Price Auction: Selling Billions of Dollars Worth of Keywords. American Economic Reviews 97(1), 242–249 (2006)
5. Quinlan, J.R.: C4.5: Programs for Machine Learning. Morgan Kaufmann Publishers (1993)

Using MySQL and JDBC in New Teaching Methods for Undergraduate Database Systems Courses

Anil L. Pereira, Mehdi Raoufi, and Jerrod C. Frost

Department of Accounting, Computer Science and Entrepreneurship
Southwestern Oklahoma State University
Weatherford, Oklahoma 73096, U.S.A.
{Anil.Pereira,Mehdi.Raoufi,FrostJ}@SWOSU.edu

Abstract. This paper describes how the open source database software MySQL and Java Database Connectivity (JDBC) are used in new teaching methods for undergraduate Database Systems courses. Traditionally, the content of these courses include database design and an implementation using SQL. The wide spread use of database in ecommerce demands a different approach for teaching students, who, are not only interested in database, but also in programming database in Web application development. We have complementarily blended SQL and Java to enhance students' learning and understanding of Database Systems and its programming. The lab component uses MySQL which can be installed on different operating systems. Java is used for building GUIs and transaction processing in the term project. Database connectivity and transaction processing via embedding SQL statements in Java are achieved using JDBC and MySQL Connector/J driver. Course components are evaluated based on feedback from students who completed the course.

Keywords: Undergraduate Database Systems Course, MySQL, Java Database Connectivity, Query Tree, and Relational Algebra.

1 Introduction

The use of relational databases is pervasive in many ecommerce applications today. More and more people are committing to trade and transactions via the World Wide Web, popularly known as the Internet [1]. Diverse applications such as online banking, airline ticketing and reservation, payment of utility bills, etc. are available on the Internet. Technical knowledge of ecommerce application development, Database transaction processing, Structured Query Language (SQL) [2], and Relational Database Management Systems (RDBMSs) is critical to the Web application developer.

The proposed approach was adopted in a Database Systems course. The course blends Database design, SQL and the Java programming language [3]. Java Database Connectivity (JDBC) [3] and MySQL [4] are used to help students to better understand SQL and programming database transactions. Relational algebra [5] and query trees [5] are used to help students better understand the development of database queries in SQL and the optimization of those queries. The term project [6, 7]

R. Kannan and F. Andres (Eds.): ICDEM 2010, LNCS 6411 , pp. 245–248, 2012.
© Springer-Verlag Berlin Heidelberg 2012

involves the design and implementation of a real world application such as a car rental system, hotel reservation system, and pharmacy database system.

2   The Deficiencies of the Traditional Approach

Most introductory undergraduate Database Systems courses do not cater to the needs of acquiring skills in Web and ecommerce application development. The development of many ecommerce applications demands knowledge of the client-server paradigm, Graphical User Interface (GUI) programming, server-side transaction management, and the Structured Query Language (SQL). Students are usually not exposed to the mathematical fundamentals and visual tools for query processing and optimization.

Relational algebra must be covered in introductory undergraduate Database Systems courses. We have observed that knowledge and experience of query development in relational algebra allows a student to better visualize 1) operations such as multiple Joins in complex SQL queries and 2) reordering of operations in query optimization.

3   Our Approach to Teaching Database Systems

Topics covered in the course include relational algebra, SQL, Entity Relationship (ER) modeling [5], Mapping ER to the relational model [5], and database normalization [5, 8] up to the 3rd normal form. Students in our computer science and information systems programs learn Java programming during the introductory courses Computer Science I and Computer Science II. Our Database Systems course includes a review of Java and the object oriented process. Java Database Connectivity (JDBC) and examples of embedded SQL statements for querying and updates are covered. Students use multiple embedded statements to create database transactions.

3.1   Relational Algebra and SQL

We first cover concepts in relational algebra and SQL keeping in mind the pre-requisite for the course which is Computers and Information Access (CIA), a general education requirement. In CIA, students learn basic concepts in relational databases and SQL using Microsoft Access. SQL is an industry wide standard used to create databases and specify database queries and updates. In our course, examples of SQL statements for querying and updating databases are implemented in MySQL.

Relational algebra provides mathematical foundation for SQL operations such as SELECT and UPDATE. It allows students to understand complex operations like Multiple Joins. In our approach to teaching SQL and query optimization we adopt the use of query trees. The query tree is a data structure representing the sequence of operations in a query. It is used by a Relational Database Management System (RDBMS) for query optimization. Query optimization is realized by reordering the sequence of operations in a query. This reduces the cost in terms of space and time for execution of centralized and distributed queries. This also reduces the cost in terms of data communication between sites for distributed queries. We have found that query

Trees help students to visualize the effect of reordering operations in a query. Query optimization in both centralized and distributed Databases is taught.

3.2 Java and MySQL

The software used in the course includes MySQL and Java. They are interfaced via JDBC as shown in Fig. 1. MySQL is an open source RDBMS. MySQL is platform independent, and supports command line and Graphical User Interfaces. It can be installed and configured on Windows and Linux operating systems. Students use MySQL script files to create databases and implement SQL queries and updates on those databases. Java is an object-oriented computer programming language that is platform independent. The Java Virtual Machine (JVM) can be installed on multiple different platforms such as UNIX, Linux, Windows and Mac OS. Java is widely used to program Web and ecommerce applications. Java due to its intensive computer networking packages lends itself well to programming applications based on Sockets (software ports for applications to communicate), Transmission Control Protocol/Internet Protocol (TCP/IP) and User Datagram Protocol (UDP). Java supports both client-side and server-side programming.

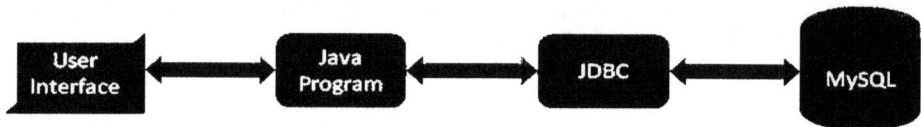

Fig. 1. Interfacing Java to MySQL

The JDBC Application Programming Interface (API) allows for connectivity to several RDBMSs via corresponding JDBC drivers. JDBC allows for database transaction processing via embedded SQL statements. It also allows for embedded SQL queries and retrieval of query results. In the course, we begin with a review of Java topics that include types, variables, control structures, arrays, classes and objects. Students learn to implement different database queries and transactions by embedding SQL statements in JDBC. Database implementation is done in MySQL.

4 Evaluation of the Approach Taken in the Course

Students who completed the course were asked to rank the following statements as: "1" if you strongly agree, "2" if you somewhat agree, "3" if you are neutral, "4" if you somewhat disagree, "5" if you strongly disagree.

A. Relational algebra helped in my understanding of SQL and distributed query processing.
B. Query trees helped in my understanding of query optimization.
C. Java and JDBC helped in my understanding of database transactions.

D. MySQL helped in my understanding of database creation, updates and views.
E. The term project helped in my understanding of the database design process.

Out of seven students who completed the course six students responded to the survey. Feedback from the students was positive regarding the approach and open source software tools adopted in the course. 67% of the students strongly agree with statement A and 33% somewhat agree. For statement B, 17% strongly agree and 83% somewhat agree. For statement C, 33% strongly agree and 67% somewhat agree. For statement D, 100% strongly agree. For statement E, 67% strongly agree, 17% somewhat agree and 17% are neutral.

5 Conclusion

Relational algebra, query trees, MySQL, JDBC and the term project helped students learn important concepts in Database Systems. Large number of different examples including creation of database views on MySQL helped in student's learning of SQL. A possible improvement to the course as suggested by the students is: Covering more examples on Java GUI programming. Other possible improvements include covering Java Servlets for Server-side programming. This will provide students with additional skills to develop Web-based applications.

References

1. Raoufi, M., Maniotes, J., Patel, H.: A course in E-commerce Web Development for the Undergraduate Curriculum in Information Technology/Information Systems/Computer Science. In: Proc. of Society for Information Technology & Teacher Education International Conference, Chesapeake, Virginia, 3595–3597 (2006)
2. Melton, J., Simon, A.: SQL:1999: Understanding Relational Language Components, 1st edn. Morgan Kaufmann Publishers Inc., San Francisco (2001)
3. The Java Programming Language, http://java.sun.com/
4. MySQL, http://www.mysql.com/
5. Elmasri, R., Navathe, S.: Fundamentals of Database Systems, 6th edn. Addison-Wesley (2011)
6. Van Der Vyver, G., Lane, M.: Using a Team-Based Approach in an IS Course: An Empirical Study. J. Info. Tech. Edu. 2, 393–406 (2003)
7. Swanson, D.K., Lynch, C.S.: WebLab: A New Approach to Undergraduate ME Laboratory Training at Georgia Tech. In: Proc. of American Society for Engineering Education Annual Conference and Exposition, Nashville, Tennessee, pp. 2149–2156 (2003)
8. Kung, H., Tung, H.: An Alternative Approach to Teaching Database Normalization: A Simple Algorithm and an Interactive e-Learning Tool. J. Info. Sys. Edu. 17(3), 315–324 (2006)

A Novel Approach to Morphological Generator for Tamil

R.U. Rekha[1], M. Anand Kumar[1], V. Dhanalakshmi[1], K.P. Soman[1], and S. Rajendran[2]

[1] Computational Engineering and Networking,
Amrita Vishwa Vidyapeetham, Coimbatore - India
[2] Department of Linguistics, Tamil University,
Thanjavur, India
{m_anandkumar,v_dhanalakshmi,kp_soman}@cb.amrita.edu,
raj_ushush@yahoo.com

Abstract. Tamil is a morphologically rich language. Being agglutinative language most of the categories expressed are suffixes. Tamil is a post positional inflectional language. The Morphological Generator takes lemma and a Morpho-lexical description as input and gives a word-form as output. It is a reverse process of Morphological Analyzer. Morphological generator system implemented here is a new data driven approach which is simple, efficient and it does not require any rules and morpheme dictionary. We have developed an individual system to handle nouns and verbs. Any automated machine translation system requires morphological analyzer of source language and morphological generator of the target language. Using this morphological generator we have also developed a verb conjugator and noun declension. Here.

Keywords: Morpho-lexical inflection, Paradigm, Inflection table, Sentence generation.

1 Introduction

Natural Language Processing (NLP) has been developed in 1960. The aim of NLP is studying the problems in the automatic generation and understanding of natural languages. Tamil verbs are inflected into several grammatical features. In Tamil language the verb specifies almost everything like gender, number, and person markings and also with auxiliaries it represents mood and aspect [1]. These are the morphological information of the root words. This makes the work challenging in Tamil. Morphological generator generates a word form from a lemma, word class, and the type of *Morpho-lexical inflection* required. In Tamil language some time the root word undergoes morphological change when it attaches to the inflection. Morphological generator can be an individual module or integrated with several NLP applications like machine translation, Automatic sentence generation. In this paper we describe a fast and simple morphological generator for Tamil. This novel approach can be applied to any morphologically rich languages.

2 Morphological Generator for Tamil

Generally, morphological generator tool is developed using rule based approach. Where the rule based approach requires a set of morphosyntactic rules, spelling rules

R. Kannan and F. Andres (Eds.): ICDEM 2010, LNCS 6411 , pp. 249–251, 2012.
© Springer-Verlag Berlin Heidelberg 2012

and morpheme dictionary. In this novel approach rules and dictionaries are not required it only requires the inflection table and paradigm classifier program. Here, the morphological generator receives an input in the form of *lemma+word_class+ Morpho-lexical Information*. The *Morpho-lexical Information* has been extracted from our Morphological Analyzer tool [2].

2.1 Inflection Table Formation

Number of paradigms for each word class (noun/verb) is defined. In Tamil there are 32 paradigms for verb and 25 for noun [1]. For every paradigm a word is selected this is termed as head word. For this head word all Morpho-lexical forms are created. There are more than thousand word forms are possible for a head word. Here we have selected 1500 most frequently used Morpho-lexical forms for verb including auxiliary and clitics and for noun it is 325 including postpositions. This verb/noun Morpho-lexical forms creation uses an order which is followed for all the paradigms. A *Morpho-lexical Information list* is also created for the above Morpho-lexical forms. Using all the word forms a table is created each column of the table corresponds to its paradigm. For each column remove the stem. This table is represented as an *inflection table*. In this table row indicates the Morpho-lexical inflection .

3 Methodology

The morphological generator system needs to handle three major things first One is the lemma part, then the word class and another is the Morpho-lexical information.

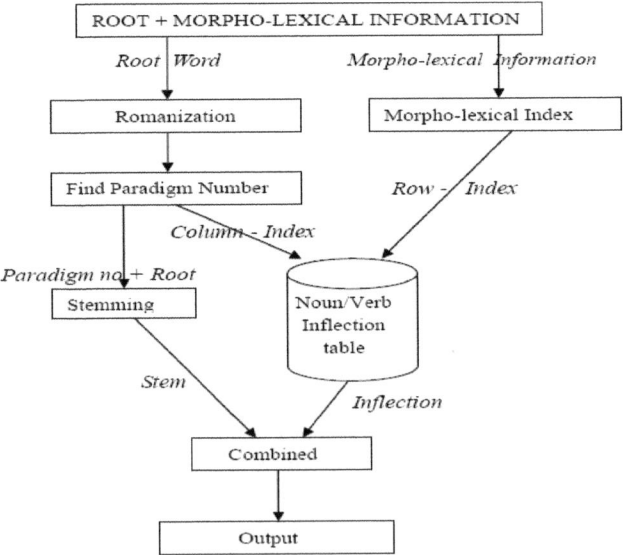

Fig. 1. Morphological Generator System

By the way the generator is implemented makes it distinct from other morphological generator. The input which is in Unicode format is first Romanized and then the paradigm number is identified by end characters. For this process a Perl program has been written this paradigm number is referred as column index. The Morpho-lexical information of the required word class is given by the user as input. From the Morpho-lexicon information list the index number of the corresponding input is identified this corresponds to the row index. A verb and noun inflection tables are used in this system. Using the word class specified by the user it uses the corresponding inflection table. In this Two-Dimensional inflection table rows are Morpho-lexical information index and columns are paradigm numbers. For each paradigm we have created a complete set of morphological inflections corresponding to the Morpho-lexical information list. Finally using the *column index* and *row index* morphological inflection is retrieved from the inflection table. This inflected form is affixed with the stem. In this work a morphological generator is designed for each of the syntactic categories and then combined to generate a complete sentence. Figure 1 shows the implementation of this methodology.

4   Conclusion and Future Work

Morphological generator which is explained here is a novel approach .It is developed using a very simple and efficient method. This is not a language specific method .So this can be applicable for all the morphologically rich languages. Using this approach currently we are developing morphological generator for Malayalam and Telugu. This system is unique that handles auxiliaries and clitics. It does not require any spelling rules and dictionary. This methodology can be implemented for any language. This work can be further used for implementing morphology based translation system between any languages to Tamil.

References

1. Rajendran, S., Arulmozi, S., Ramesh Kumar, Viswanathan, S.: Computational morphology of verbal complex (2001); Language in India, vol. 3 (April 4, 2003)
2. Anand Kumar, M., Dhanalakshmi, V., Soman, K.P., Rajendran, S.: A Novel Apporach For Tamil Morphological Analyzer. In: Proceedings of Tamil Internet Conference 2009, Cologne, Germany, pp. 23–35 (October 2009)
3. Lehmann, T.: A Grammar of Modern Tamil, 2nd edn. Pondicherry Institute of Linguistics and Culture, Pondicherry (1992)

Morphological Analyzer for Malayalam
Using Machine Learning

V.P. Abeera[1], S. Aparna[1], R.U. Rekha[1], M. Anand Kumar[1], V. Dhanalakshmi[1],
K.P. Soman[1], and S. Rajendran[2]

[1] Amrita Vishwa Vidyapeetham, Ettimadai, Coimbatore-641105
[2] Tamil University, Thanjavur
abeeravp@gmail.com, m_anandkumar@cb.amrita.edu,
kp_soman@amrita.edu

Abstract. An efficient and reliable method for implementing Morphological Analyzer for Malayalam using Machine Learning approach has been presented here. A Morphological Analyzer segments words into morphemes and analyze word formation. Morphemes are smallest meaning bearing units in a language. Morphological Analysis is one of the techniques used in formal reading and writing. Rule based approaches are generally used for building Morphological Analyzer. The disadvantage of using rule based approaches are that if one rule fails it will affect the entire rule that follows, that is each rule works on the output of previous rule. The significance of using machine learning approach arises from the fact that rules are learned automatically from data, uses learning and classification algorithms to learn models and make predictions. The result shows that the system is very effective and after learning it predicts correct grammatical features even for words which are not in the training set.

Keywords: Natural Language Processing, Machine Learning, Morphemes, Morphology.

1 Introduction

Morphological analysis is the process of segmenting words into morphemes and analyzing the word formation. Morphological Analyzers are used in search engines, speech synthesizer, speech recognizer, lemmatization, noun decompounding, spell and grammar checker and machine translation. Malayalam is a morphologically rich language and belongs to Dravidian Language family. It is an agglutinative language. Generally rule based approaches are used for building Morphological Analyzer [1]. A novel approach using machine learning technique is implemented for Tamil Morphological Analysis [2]. Here the same technique is used for Malayalam with the help of SVMTool which explores a new methodology for Morphological Analyzer. This paper briefly describes about data creation, supervised learning technique and various stages in building the Morphological Analyzer.

R. Kannan and F. Andres (Eds.): ICDEM 2010, LNCS 6411 , pp. 252–254, 2012.
© Springer-Verlag Berlin Heidelberg 2012

2 Morphological Data Creation for Malayalam Language

For any machine learning approaches data creation plays the key role. It needs only corpora with linguistical information. The morphological or linguistical rules are automatically extracted from the annotated corpora. the nouns and verbs were classified into paradigms. Each paradigm root word will be inflected with similar set of inflections. In the case of Malayalam Morph Analyzer being discussed here, 26 noun paradigms were identified, each of which contained 453 inflections, and 28 verb paradigms with 458 inflections were identified, which constitutes the first stage. The second stage is to collect the noun and verb list and categorize them based on the paradigms. Fig.1 explains the preprocessing steps involved in the development of morphological corpus. Developed corpus undergoes following modifications to create the training data used for machine learning.

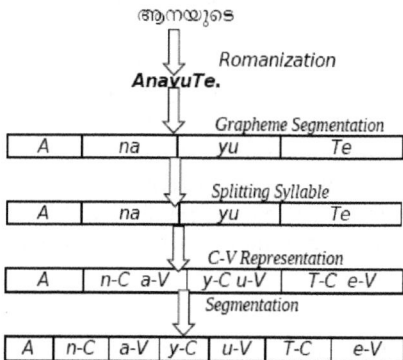

Fig. 1. Preprocessing steps

3 Implementation of Morphological Analyzer

Using Machine Learning Approach the Morphological Analyzer for Malayalam is developed. We have developed separate engines for noun and verb. Fig. 2 gives an outlook of the Morphological Analyzer system [2]. Three phases are involved in our Morphological Analyzer.

Preprocessing: The surface form is converted into sequence of units which is given as the input for the Morphological Analyzer tool.

Segmentation of Morphemes: Preprocessed words are segmented into morpheme according to the morpheme boundary. The input sequence is given to the trained model 1. The trained model predicts each label to the input segments.

Identifying Morpheme: The Segmented morphemes are given to the trained model 2. It predicts grammatical categories to the segmented morphemes. We have trained the system to give multiple outputs to handle the compound words.

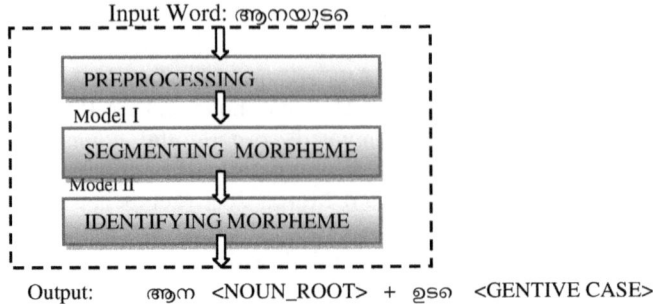

Fig. 2. Schematic Representation

4 Morphological Analyzer Using Machine Learning

Recently Machine Learning Approaches are dominating the computational linguistics field. Machine learning approaches don't require any hand coded morphological rules .It needs only corpora with linguistical information. These morphological or linguistical rules are automatically extracted from the annotated corpora. The SVMTool [3] is a simple and effective generator of sequential tagger based on Support Vector Machines. We has applied the SVMTool to the problem of Morphological Analysis. During training SVM models (weight vectors and biases) are learned from the training corpus.

5 Result and Conclusion

In this paper we have presented an effective and interesting methodology of performing Morphological Analyzer for Malayalam implemented using SVMTool. The result shows that the system is very effective and after learning it predicts correct grammatical features even for words which are not in the training set.

References

1. Rajendran, S., Arulmozi, S., Ramesh Kumar, Viswanathan, S.: Computational morphology of verbal complex. Paper read in Conference at Dravidan University, Kuppam (December 26-29, 2001)
2. Anand Kumar, M., Dhanalakshmi, V., Soman, K.P., Rajendran, S.: A Novel Apporach For Tamil Morphological Analyzer. In: Proceedings of Tamil Internet Conference 2009, Cologne, Germany, pp. 23–35 (October 2009)
3. Gimenez, J., Marquez, L.: SVMTool Technical Manual v1.3., TALP Research Center, LSI Department, Salgado, Barcelona (2006)

Improved Algorithm for Automatic Word Alignment for Hindi-Punjabi Parallel Corpus

Karuna Jindal and Vishal Goyal

Department of Computer Science
Punjabi University, Patiala
jindal.karuna@yahoo.com
vishal.pup@gmail.com

Abstract. This paper describes an alignment system that aligns texts at the word level in Hindi-Punjabi parallel corpus. The previous aligner was based on length based estimation approach. In the previous version, multi-word unit & sometime one-to-one produces alignment errors. In this improved version, different techniques like Boundary Detection, Dictionary-Lookup (DL), Nearest-align-Neighbor (NAN) and Scoring based Minimum distance function to improve the accuracy has been used. Alignment of words means to identify correspondences between words in source language and target language sentences. This automatic word alignment of Hindi-Punjabi corpus is very useful in automatically developing Hindi-Punjabi dictionary. In the previous version, the system accuracy was claimed to be 89.5 % approximately but after rigorous testing, it is found to be 65%. After implementing above techniques in the improved system explained here, system accuracy was found to be 99.09% for one-to-one word alignment and 80% accuracy for multi-word alignment.

Keywords: Automatic word alignment, Automatic Hindi-Punjabi Dictionary generation, scoring, boundary-detect, nearest-align-neighbours, dictionary lookup.

1 Introduction

A parallel corpus is a text in one language together with its translation in another language. Parallel Corpus is usually defined as a collection of original texts translated to another language where the texts, paragraphs, sentences, and words are typically linked to each other. Alignment of corpus is basically of three types: Paragraph-wise, Sentence-wise and Word-wise. Paragraph alignment of parallel corpus is the identification of the corresponding paragraph in both of parallel texts in terms of number of sentences in it. Sentence alignment of parallel corpus is the identification of the corresponding sentences in both halves of the parallel text. Basically the shorter sentences are aligned with shorter sentences and longer sentences are aligned with longer sentences. Word alignment of parallel corpus is the identification of the corresponding words in both halves of the parallel text. Automatic word alignment means without the human interaction the parallel corpus should be aligned with the

R. Kannan and F. Andres (Eds.): ICDEM 2010, LNCS 6411 , pp. 255–263, 2012.
© Springer-Verlag Berlin Heidelberg 2012

machine accurately. Alignment in Hindi-Punjabi corpora has been an active research topic.

2 Related Work

Researchers have worked for non-Indian languages but very little work has been done for Indian languages & that is the focus of our project. Word alignment is a crucial part because it is the process of determining which words in a given source & target language sentences pair are translations of each other. This is a token level task, meaning that each word in the source text is aligned with its corresponding translation in the target text. A parallel text consists of a source language text & its translation into some target language. If we have determined which words are translations of each other then the text is said to be word aligned & these types of words that are translations of each other are known as word pair.

Mukda Suktarachan et al. (1997) developed a method for unknown word alignment based on English-Thai language. They used two techniques for word alignment. First technique is that matches two words together. Second one is to count number of characters. For sentence alignment, statistical alignment is used. There is a drawback in Thai language that there is no sentence delimiter & no blank space in between the words [1].

Aswani et al. (2005) They used a simple sentence length approach to sentence alignment & local word grouping, dictionary lookup & a nearest aligned neighbours approach to deal with many-to-many word alignment for Hindi-English parallel data [2].

Gale & Church (1993) estimate translation probabilities & use these probabilities to search for most probable word alignment. The translation probabilities are estimated using a method based on Brown et. al's Model [3].

Lakhbir et al. (2009) developed length based estimation approach to perform word alignment. They used dictionary lookup method when number of words in source language & target language are not same. Multi-words units & sometime 1:1 produces alignment error [4].

Somboonphol et al.(2002) used statistical technique for estimating word correspondences using the estimation functions. They used Gale's method, threshold function & new condition for estimating the word correspondence. They used simple method based on the number of word correspondence by co-occurrence-frequency [5].

D.Wu, (1994) applied two methods for the word alignment. Firstly, the gale's method is used to Chinese & English which applies the length-based method. Next to adding lexical cues to a length–based method. The accuracy is increased from 86% to 92% by adding the lexical cues.[6]

Robert et al. (2005) used hybrid, multi-feature approach to perform word alignment. They used Transliteration Similarity, Local word grouping, Dictionary lookup, Expected English Words & Nearest aligned neighbours approach to deal with many-to-many word alignment [7].

In the previous algorithm, minimum distance function & DL is used for alignment. But after testing, we found that minimum distance function doesn't work. Only 1-1 mapping & DL is used for word alignment.

3 Overview of Alignment Algorithm

In order to keep high precision in words alignment, several steps are used with the human & computer cooperation.

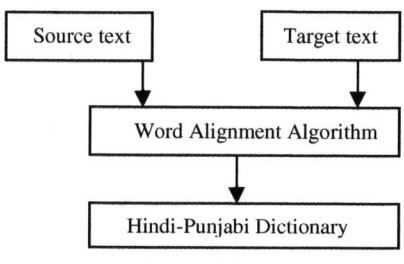

Fig. 3.1.

3.1 Basic Concepts

3.1.1 Source Text is the Hindi text. This is sentence aligned text. The format of these text files is in Unicode Standard. The Font used in these files is Arial MS Unicode.

3.1.2 Target Text is the Punjabi text here which is the exact translation of the source text. This is sentence aligned text.

3.1.3 Word alignment means deciding which pairs of words can be the translation of each other in source & target language.

3.1.4 Hindi-Punjabi Dictionary means after deciding which pairs of words can be matched are taken & stored in the database.

3.1.5 Parallel Text

A parallel corpus is a collection of texts, each of which is translated into one or more other languages than the original. The simplest case is where two languages only are involved: one of the corpora is an exact translation of the other. Example of parallel text is as below:

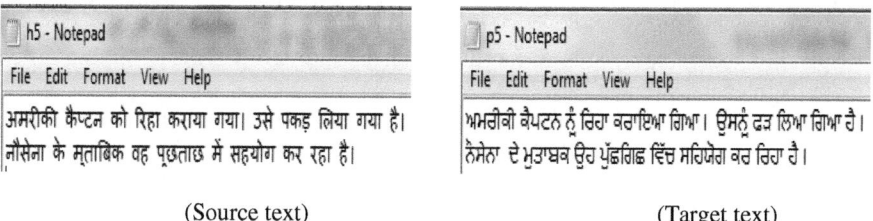

(Source text)   (Target text)

The above example represents the parallel corpus in which on the left hand side, there is a source text & on the right hand side, there is exact translation of source text that is target text.

The parallel text is sentence aligned and the user can optionally give the location to the source and target files. A text in a source language and the corresponding text in a target language are given to the alignment system. Our aim is to identify an appropriate translation for a particular word in the source language text among the words in the target language text. The Automatic alignment is done which gives the percentage of words aligned. The parallel corpus has been collected from resources like EMILLE corpus and others for the word alignment. Parallel Corpus was also developed using the existing Hindi to Punjabi Machine Translation System available online at website http://h2p.learnpunjabi.org. The Hindi text was downloaded from number of online hindi newspaper websites like BBC Hindi, Dianik Jagram, Bhaskar etc. Hindi-Punjabi parallel corpus used comprised of 50K sentences of variable lengths.

3.2 Improved Word Alignment Algorithm

The algorithm works on the principle that a shorter sentence tends to translate in shorter sentence and a longer sentence tends to translate in a longer sentence. An algorithm uses the fact that the length of a text is highly correlated with the length of its translation. Here we used the Boundary-Detection, Dictionary Lookup, Nearest-align-Neighbours & the scoring given by the minimum distance function. This distance function is actually used to find the best alignment of the words from the various possible cases. After mapping the sentences, the words are aligned according to minimum distance function called scoring technique. We calculate a score between all combinations of words pairs. The Hindi & Punjabi words are simply marked by spacing as in ordinary written text. It considers only 1:1, 1:2, 2:1, 1:3 & 3:1 type of words alignments. Links between parallel texts are showed by attributes of Alignment. All words units without 1:1 are known as multi-words. For the implementation, we used .net tool. The computer language which we used that is ASP.net with VB.net. [8][9]

3.2.1 Algorithm
1. Load bilingual sentence aligned text file.
2. Input these two files into the align function that do the whole processing of the two files.
3. Statistical Analysis of two files are done i.e the number of sentences & words are counted.
4. Split the source sentences & target sentences into word order & create arrays of words in each sentence.
5. Then one by one each sentence of source & target files is taken & words of these sentences are matched. The matching is based on Boundary-Detection, Dictionary Lookup, Nearest-align-Neighbours & the scoring given by the minimum distance function. It considers only 1:1, 1:2, 2:1, 1:3 & 3:1 type of words alignments.
6. The words are aligned and started into the database.

3.2.2 Boundary Detection with Dictionary Lookup

In Boundary-Detection functions both Hindi & Punjabi sentences are divided in two halves than from each part corresponding first & last Hindi & Punjabi words are matched with Hindi-Punjabi dictionary of most common words, if words are found in dictionary than according to the Nearest-align-Neignbours alignment is performed. If any one of these words are not found in dictionary than the minimum distance with scoring technique are used for alignment. If the last word of first half & first word of last half are not found in dictionary then these words will be match with the previous & the next word corresponding to Punjabi text. If any one of these word is found, then alignment is performed according to the Nearest-align-Neignbours approach. If not, than the minimum distance with scoring technique are used for alignment.

3.2.3 Nearest-Align-Neighbors

At the end of the Boundary-Detection & Dictionary Lookup stage of the word alignment process, many words remain unaligned. Here we introduce a new approach, called the "Nearest-aligned-Neighbours approach". As we know Hindi-Punjabi language are very closely related & follow a similar order. The Nearest Aligned Neighbours approach works on this principle & aligns one or more Hindi words with one of the Punjabi words. We find the nearest Hindi word that is already aligned with one or more Punjabi words. We assume that the words in Hindi-Punjabi sentence follow a similar order & align the rest words in that group accordingly. An example of alignment using the Nearest Aligned Neighbours approach is given in Figure 3.2.

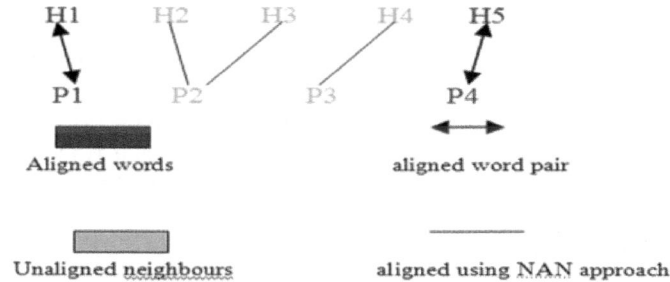

Fig. 3.2. Nearest Aligned Neighbours Approach

In the above figure, Word H1 & H5 are already aligned with P1 & P4. Now H2, H3 & H4 are yet to be aligned. Then according to the minimum distance, the unaligned words will be aligned. In the above example, the case which takes P2= H2, H3 having the minimum score. So H4 is align with P3, H2 & H3 are align with P2. It means, by using the minimum distance, we will find the nearest neighbour.

3.2.4 Scoring Technique

While calculating the scores of words pairs with in sentence pairs, the length of word is measured in terms of number of characters in it. These measurements on the basis of number of words give the precise results especially between Hindi-Punjabi texts. There are number of possible cases for the alignment of the words in sentence pairs.

So finding the distance for all the possible cases, the case having minimum score is taken into consideration that it is best aligned case of all the possible cases of words pairs with in sentence pairs. Accordingly aligning will be done. After aligning one sentence, the next mapped sentence is taken & again found the case having the minimum score .The same procedure mentioned above will be executed for all the mapped sentences.

3.2.5 Minimum Distance Function

In this function, sentence having greater number of words is assumed as target sentence & other one is assumed as source sentence. Suppose the source text i.e. Hindi Text contains sentence consisting of 4 words & target text i.e. Punjabi text contains sentence consisting of 5 words. There are four possible cases how these words are corresponding to each other.

Case 1: When first word in Source text is mapped to two words of target Text
S1=T1, T2; S2=T3; S3=T4; S4=T5
Distance1 = ABS (S1-(T1+T2)) + ABS (S2-T3) + ABS (S3-T4) + ABS (S4-T5)
Case2:
S1= T1; S2= T2, T3; S3= T4; S4=T5
Distance2= ABS (S1-T1) + ABS (S2-(T2+T3)) + ABS (S3-T4) + ABS (S4-T5)
Case3:
 S1= T1; S2= T2; S3= T3, T4; S4=T5
Distance3 = ABS (S1-T1) + ABS (S2-T2) + ABS (S3-(T3 + T4)) + ABS (S4-T5)
Case4:
S1= T1; S2= T2; S3= T3; S4= T4, T5;
Distance4 = ABS (S1-T1) + ABS (S2-T2) + ABS (S3-T3) + ABS (S4-(T4 + T5))

Min (Distance1, Distance2, Distance3 & Distance4) will be taken as final result. If the difference of words in between both the sentence is more than 1, then we will use the same formula as we have already defined but the mapping will be different.

3.3 Evaluation Method

The accuracy of the system is calculated by the following formula:
    Accuracy percentage = (Number of correctly aligned words/Total number of words)*100

4 Limitations of the Previous System and Comparison with Improved Algorithm

There are various limitations which lie with the previous system. We will define these limitations & comparison with the improved algorithm below one by one:

1) If any of these categories 2:1 & 1:2 occur simultaneously in a one sentence then it will be difficult for the previous program to align those words.

For example

जब माता पिता और स्कूल साथ मिलकर काम करते है (10)
(Jab mata pita aur school saath milkar kaam karte hai)
ਜਦੋਂ ਮਾਪੇ ਅਤੇ ਸਕੂਲ ਨਾਲ ਮਿਲ ਕੇ ਕੰਮ ਕਰਦੇ ਹਨ (9)
(Jadon mape ate school naal mil ke kamm karde han)

Hindi_Words	Punjabi_Words
और	ਅਤੇ
जब	ਜਦ
साथ	ਨਾਲ

hindi_words	punjabi_words
जब	ਜਦੋਂ
है	ਹਨ
स्कूल	ਸਕੂਲ
और	ਅਤੇ
माता पिता	ਮਾਪੇ
साथ	ਨਾਲ
करते	ਕਰਦੇ
काम	ਕੰਮ
मिलकर	ਮਿਲ ਕੇ

Previous algorithm   Improved algorithm

2) If the sentence contain 3:1 word then it will be difficult for the previous program to align that word.

For example

सदस्यों की ओर से की जा रही आलोचनाओं से खिन्न चल रहे थे। (13)
(Sdasyo ki aur se ki ja rahi aalochnaoo se khinn chal rahe the)
ਮੈਬਰਾਂ ਵਲੋਂ ਕੀਤੀ ਜਾ ਰਹੀ ਆਲੋਚਨਾਵਾਂ ਤੋਂ ਉਦਾਸ ਚੱਲ ਰਹੇ ਸਨ । (11)
(Mebran vlao ki ja rahi aalochnavan ton udaas chall rahe san)

Hindi_Words	Punjabi_Words
की	ਵੀ
जा	ਜਾ
से	ਤੂੰ

hindi_words	punjabi_words
सदस्यों	ਮੈਬਰਾਂ
थे	ਸਨ
जा	ਜਾ
की ओर से	ਵਲੇ
की	ਵੀ
रही	ਰਹੀ
आलोचनाओं	ਆਲੋਚਨਾਵਾਂ
से	ਤੋ
खिन्न	ਉਦਾਸ
चल	ਚੱਲ
रहे	ਰਹੇ

Previous algorithm   Improved algorithm

3) Previous program can't solve the problem which totally languages related & make alignment error.

For example

जब माता पिता और स्कूल साथ मिलकर काम करते है तो सब ठीक होता है।
(Jab mata pita aur school saath milkar kaam karte hai to sab theek hota hai)
ਜਦੋਂ ਮਾਪੇ ਅਤੇ ਸਕੂਲ ਨਾਲ ਮਿਲ ਕੇ ਕੰਮ ਕਰਦੇ ਹਨ ਤਾਂ ਸਭ ਠੀਕ ਹੁੰਦਾ ਹੈ ।
(Jadon mape ate school naal mil ke kamm karde han tan sabh theek hunda hai)

Hindi_Words	Punjabi_Words
है	ਹੈ
साथ	ਨਾਲ
तो	ਤਾਂ
ठीक	ਠੀਕ
जब	ਜਦ
और	ਅਤੇ

hindi_words	punjabi_words
जब	ਜਦੋਂ
है	ਹੈ, ਹਨ
काम	ਕੰਮ
करते	ਕਰਦੇ
तो	ਤਾਂ
ठीक	ਠੀਕ
होता	ਹੁੰਦਾ
माता पिता	ਮਾਪੇ
और	ਅਤੇ
स्कूल	ਸਕੂਲ
साथ	ਨਾਲ
मिलकर	ਮਿਲ ਕੇ
सब	ਸਭ

Previous algorithm   Improved algorithm

4) If the input text is 1:1 then in some cases, the alignment is not done completely.

For example

मैडोना के वकील ने इस सिलसिले में फिर से अर्ज़ी दाख़िल की है। (13)

(Medona ke vakeel ne is silsile mein phir se arjhi daakhil ki hai)

ਮੇਡੋਨਾ ਦੇ ਵਕੀਲ ਨੇ ਇਸ ਸਿਲਸਿਲੇ ਵਿੱਚ ਫਿਰ ਤੋਂ ਬੇਨਤੀ-ਪੱਤਰ ਦਾਖ਼ੀਲ ਕੀਤੀ ਹੈ । (13)

(Medona de vakeel ne is silsile vich phir ton benti-pattar daakhil kiti hai)

Hindi_Words		Punjabi_Words	
है		ਹੈ	
सिलसिले		ਸਿਲਸਿਲੇ	
में		ਵਿੱਚ	
ने		ਨੇ	
के		ਦੇ	
से		ਤੋਂ	
की		ਜੀ	
इस		ਇਸ	

hindi_words	punjabi_words
मैडोना	ਮੇਡੋਨਾ
है	ਹੈ
सिलसिले	ਸਿਲਸਿਲੇ
के	ਦੇ
वकील	ਵਕੀਲ
ने	ਨੇ
इस	ਇਸ
में	ਵਿੱਚ
फिर	ਫਿਰ
से	ਤੋਂ
अर्ज़ी	ਬੇਨਤੀ-ਪੱਤਰ
दाख़िल	ਦਾਖ਼ੀਲ
की	ਕੀਤੀ

Previous algorithm   Improved algorithm

5 Results

The previous version of the word aligner is based on length based Estimation Approach, which contains multi-words unit problem & sometime 1:1 makes alignment error. The method is based on a simple statistic model. In this version, boundary detection with dictionary lookup, nearest-align-neighbours and scoring based minimum distance function has been used for present version. For the automatic word alignment, Hindi-Punjabi parallel corpus is needed the parallel corpus has been collected from resources like EMILLE corpus and others for the word alignment. Parallel Corpus was also developed using the existing Hindi to Punjabi Machine Translation System available online at website http://h2p.learnpunjabi.org. The Hindi text was downloaded from number of online hindi newspaper websites like BBC Hindi, Dianik Jagram, Bhaskar etc. Hindi-Punjabi parallel corpus used comprised of 50K sentences of variable lengths. After implementing above techniques in the improved system explained here, we have removed the limitations of the previous system & accuracy was found to be 99.09% for one-to-one word alignment and 80% accuracy for multi word alignment. The model was motivated by the observation that the longer regions of text tend to have longer translations, and that the shorter regions of text tend to have shorter translations.

References

1. Kawtrakul, A., Thumkanon, C., Oovorawan, Y., Varasrai, P., Suktarachan, M.: Automatic Thaiunknown word recognition. In: Proceedings of the Pacific Rim Symposium on Natural Language Processing, Thail, pp. 341–348 (1997)
2. Aswani, N., Gaizauskas, R.: Aligning words in English-Hindi parallel corpora. In: Proceeding of the ACL Workshop on Bilingual & Using Parallel Texts, Ann Arbor, pp. 115–118 (June 2005)

3. Dagan, I., Church, K., Gale, W.: Robust Bilingual Word Alignment for Machine Translation. In: Proceedings of the Workshop on Very Large Corpora (1993)
4. Goyal, V., Garcha, L.: Automatic Word Alignment Algorithm for Bilingual Hindi-Punjabi Parallel Text. In: Proceeding of the IACC, Patiala (2009)
5. Somboonphol, N., Sornlertlamvanich, V.: Statistical Technique for Estimating Word correspondence for Bilingual Dictionary Development. In: Proceedings of SNLP-Oriental COCOSDA (2002)
6. Wu, D.: Aligning a Parallel English-Chinese Corpus Statistically with Lexical Criteria. In: Proc. of the 32nd Annual Conference of the ACL, Las Cruces, NM, pp. 80–87 (1994)
7. Gaizauskas, R., Aswani, N.: A hybrid approach to align sentences & words. In: Proceeding of the ACL Workshop on Bilingual & Using Parallel texts, Ann Arbor, pp. 57–64 (June 2005)
8. Moore, K.: The Ultimate VB .NET and ASP.NET Code Book
9. Macdonald, M.: Beginning ASP.NET in VB .NET: From Novice to Professional

A Fast and Effective Partitioning Algorithm
for Document Clustering

Rajeev Kumar[1], Alok Ranjan[1], and Joydip Dhar[2]

[1] Department of Information Technology
[2] Department of Applied Sciences
ABV - Indian Institute of Information Technology and Management, Gwalior, India
{rajeevkumariiitm,iiitm.alok}@gmail.com,
jdhar@iiitm.ac.in

Abstract. Fast and high quality document clustering is one of the most important tasks in the modern era of information. With the huge amount of available data and with an aim to creating better quality clusters, scores of algorithms having quality-complexity trade-offs have been proposed. Some of the proposed algorithms attempt to minimize the computational overload in terms of certain criterion functions defined for the whole set of clustering solution. In this paper, we have proposed a novel algorithm for document clustering using a graph based criterion function. Our algorithm is partitioning in nature. Most of the commonly used partitioning clustering algorithms are inflicted with the drawback of trapping into local optimum solutions. However, the algorithm proposed in this paper usually leads to the global optimum solution. Its performance enhances with the increment in the number of clusters. We have carried out sophisticated experiments wherein we have compared our algorithm with two well known document clustering algorithms viz. k-means and k-means++ algorithm. The results so obtained confirm the superiority of our algorithm.

Keywords: Document clustering, partitioning clustering algorithm, Graph based criterion function, k-means, Optimization.

1 Introduction

Document clustering is the task of segregation of documents into groups of similar or nearly similar documents. The documents within each group should exhibit a relatively higher degree of similarity while the similarity among documents belonging to different clusters should be as small as possible [1].

Developing an efficient and accurate document clustering algorithm has been one of the most favorite areas of research in various scientific fields including statistics, machine learning and pattern recognition. A number of algorithms aimed at document clustering have been proposed over the years [2, 3, 4, 5, 6]. According to Jain et.al [7], these algorithms can be broadly categorized into two types viz. hierarchical [8, 9, 10] and partitioning [11, 12, 13, 14].

As far as partitioning algorithms such as k-means [15], k-medoids [15] or graph partitioning-based [15] are concerned, they consider the whole data as one single

R. Kannan and F. Andres (Eds.): ICDEM 2010, LNCS 6411, pp. 264–271, 2012.
© Springer-Verlag Berlin Heidelberg 2012

cluster and then seek the clustering solution by partitioning it into predetermined classes. They aim to optimize i.e. either minimize or maximize a certain criterion function. The value of the criterion function used determines the quality of clustering solution involved. In [16, 17], seven criterion functions are described.

In this paper, we have proposed a novel clustering algorithm which is partitioning in nature. This algorithm works in two stages viz. initial clustering stage and refinement stage. We have devised the initial clustering stage in such a way that the algorithm has a minimal chance to trap in any local optimum. Moreover, we have used the graph based criterion function [18, 19] as the objective function to optimize. We have compared our approach with two well known algorithms viz. the k-means algorithm [2] and the k-means++ algorithm [3].

2 Graph Based Criterion Function

The documents available with any dataset can be easily modeled with the help of graphs. In [18, 19], the authors have proposed two types of graphs to model the document in the context of clustering. The first graph is the graph obtained by computing the similarities between the documents taken two at a time, and the second graph can be obtained by visualizing the documents and the terms as a bipartite graph.

The graph model we are following visualizes the various documents and their terms as a bipartite graph $G_b = (V, E)$, where V is composed of two sets V_d and V_t. The vertex set V_d denotes the documents whereas the vertex set Vt denotes the terms. In this model, if the jth term is contained by the ith document, we can say that an edge connects the corresponding i^{th} vertex of V_d to the jth vertex of V_t. The weights of these edges are determined utilized the concept of the *tf-idf* model elaborated in [20].

In terms of such a bipartite graph, the problem of clustering converges into the computation of a simultaneous partitioning of the documents and the terms thereby optimizing the criterion function defined on the edge-cut. In our paper, we have used an edge-cut based criterion function known as the normalized cut. This criterion function is defined as

$$minimize \ G_2 = \sum_{r=1}^{k} \frac{cut(V_r, V - V_r)}{W(V_r)}. \tag{1}$$

Here Vr corresponds to the set of vertices belonging to the rth cluster, and $W(Vr)$ corresponds to the sum of the weights of the adjacency lists of the vertices belonging to the rth cluster. The rth cluster will consists of the vertices from both documents as well as terms i.e. V_d and V_t. This criterion function has the unique characteristic of computing a clustering solution which is composed of the documents along with the terms associated with these documents.

3 Cluster Validity Measures

A cluster validity measure maps a clustering on a real number [22]. The number indicates to what degree certain structural properties are developed in the clustering. In our experiments, we have used two measures viz. Entropy and F-measure.

3.1 Entropy

Entropy measure utilizes the class label of a document of any cluster in order to evaluate the quality of the clustering solution [21]. The smaller the value of entropy, the better the clustering solution is. In an ideal clustering solution, the entropy would become zero.

In a particular cluster S_r having size N_r, the entropy of this cluster is defined to be

$$E(S_r) = -\frac{1}{\log q} \sum_{i=1}^{q} \frac{N_r^i}{N_r} \log\left(\frac{N_r^i}{N_r}\right). \tag{2}$$

Where q denotes the number of classes in the dataset, and N_r^i denotes the number of documents available to the i_{th} class which were assigned to the r_{th} cluster. The overall entropy of the cluster will be given by the following equation

$$\text{Entropy} = \sum_{r=1}^{k} \frac{N_r}{N} E(S_r). \tag{3}$$

3.2 F- Measure

The F-Measure [22] is one of most widely used cluster validity measure in the research arena. Let D denotes the set of documents and let $C = \{C_1, \ldots, C_k\}$ be a clustering solution of D. Let $C^* = \{C_1^*, \ldots, C_l^*\}$ denotes the human reference classification. Then the recall of cluster j with respect to class i, $rec(i, j)$, is defined to be $|C_j \cap C_i^*|/|C_i^*|$. The precision of cluster j with respect to class i, $prec(i, j)$, is defined to be $|C_j \cap C_i^*|/|C_j|$. The F-Measure combines both values as follows:

$$F_{i,j} = \frac{2}{\frac{1}{prec(i,j)} + \frac{1}{rec(i,j)}}. \tag{4}$$

Based on this formula, the overall F-Measure of a clustering is given by:

$$F = \sum_{i=1}^{l} \frac{|c_i^*|}{|D|} \cdot \max_{j=1,\ldots,k} \{F_{i,j}\}. \tag{5}$$

It is noteworthy that a perfect clustering solution leads to an F-Measure score of 1, which is the greatest possible value of the measure.

4 Algorithm Description

Unlike the other partitioning clustering algorithm such as k-means, our algorithm uses a greedy approach. We have divided our algorithm into two phases viz. initial clustering and refinement.

4.1 Initial Clustering

In this phase, we, first of all, determine initial clustering solution. I.e. we segregate the given documents into the desired number of clusters, although this configuration is expected to change in the refinement phase.

K documents are chosen in the beginning of the algorithm. We henceforth refer to these documents as seeds. We utilize these seeds as the first centroids of k clusters required. Now, we choose the document having the minimum sum of squared distances from the already chosen documents. This process results in the document possessing the largest minimum distance from the already chosen documents.

Suppose at some point of time, we are having m documents in the chosen list, we, now, evaluate the sum $s = \sum_{l=1}^{k}(Dist(d_l, a))^2$ for all documents a in set A, where set A consists of the documents possessing the greatest sum of distances from already chosen m documents. We choose the document having the least value of S as the next entrant in the list i.e. the $(m+1)^{th}$ document. We continue with this process unless we do not have k documents in the chosen list.

4.1.1 Pseudocode of the Algorithm Proposed for Initial Clustering

> D → Determining variable
> N → number of document vectors
> K → number of clusters required
> SEEDS_VECTOR →list of seeds initially empty

Step1: Put a randomly chosen document into SEEDS_VECTOR.

Step2: Choose a new document residing at the maximum distance from the current documents in SEEDS_VECTOR and put it into SEEDS_VECTOR.

Step3: Loop through steps 4 to 6 until the number of documents in SEEDS_VECTOR is less than K.

Step4: Initialize a variable STORE and put into it the pairs of sum of distances of all current seeds from each document and ID of the document.

Step5: Loop through Step 6 D times.

Step6: Add the document with the least sum of squared distances from the un-chosen seeds to SEEDS_VECTOR.

Step7: Loop through steps 8 and 9 for the remaining documents.

Step8: Choose any document.

Step9: Put the chosen document into the cluster possessing its closest seed.

4.1.2 Description of the Algorithm Proposed for Initial Clustering

First of all, we insert a randomly chosen document into SEEDS_VECTOR which is initially empty. SEEDS_VECTOR is a set used to hold seeds. Seeds are the documents representing clusters. This phase is basically aimed at choosing k seeds each representing a single cluster. Now, the most distant document from the already chosen seed is inserted into SEEDS_VECTOR. Once the two initial seeds are chosen, an iterative process, in order to select other documents, is started comprising of multiple iterations. During each iteration, first of all, we order the documents in the decreasing order of their sum of distance from the current seeds residing in SEEDS_VECTOR Next, we pick the first D (the Determining variable which is decided keeping in view of the total number of documents, desired number of clusters K and the distribution of clusters in K- dimensional space) documents. Now we use these documents to find the document having least sum of squared distances from the current seeds in the list. The document found is added into SEEDS_VECTOR. We continue this process until we have K seeds in SEEDS_VECTOR.

Once, we get K seeds in SEEDS_VECTOR, we assume these seeds as the centroids of the initial clusters. The remaining N-K documents are assigned to the cluster according to its nearest seed.

4.2 Refinement

The refinement phase involves the repeated change in the cluster configuration. We consider each document and each term as vertices. We term them as document-vertices and term-vertices. This phase involves multiple iterations. Each iteration is carried out in two stages. In the first stage, the documents are visited in a randomly manner. Each document is visited exactly once. The visited document is now put in every other k-1 cluster except to its original cluster. If a movement results in an improvement i.e. decrease in the value of the criterion function, the document is shifted to that cluster. Now, the second stage of the refinement phase begins. This stage involves the same procedure as adopted in the first stage with documents replaced with terms. Thus, in this stage terms instead of the documents are visited. Each term is visited exactly once. The visited term is now put in every other k-1 cluster except to its original cluster. If a movement results in an improvement i.e. decrease in the value of the criterion function, the term is shifted to that cluster.

Once all the documents and terms are visited, the iteration is finished. However if in an iteration, no migration of any document or term occurs, the second stage hence the refinement phase ends.

4.2.1 Pseudocode of the Algorithm Proposed for Refinement

IN_CLS← Set of clusters obtained from initial clustering.

G← criterion function of IN_CLS

Step1: Loop through steps 2 to 14 while at least a single document or term or both moved from one cluster to another.

Step2: Empty the array A.

Step3: Loop through steps 4 to 8 while each document is not included in A.

Step4: Choose a random document X from IN_CLS.

Step5: If X is not included in A, perform Steps 6 and 7.

Step6: Include X in A.

Step7: Move X to a cluster different from original cluster of Y which leads to decline in the value of G. In case no such cluster is found, let X be in its cluster.

Step8: Loop through steps 9 to 13 until even a single term moved between clusters.

Step9: Loop through steps 10 to 13 while each term is not included in A.

Step10: Choose a random term Y from IN_CLS.

Step11: If Y is not included in A, perform Steps 12 and 13.

Step12: Include Y in A.

Step13: Move Y to a cluster different from the original cluster of Y which leads to decline in the value of G. In case no such cluster is found, let Y be in its cluster.

5   Implementation Details

We have carried out sophisticated experiments wherein we have compared the working of our algorithm against the k-means algorithm [2] and the k-means++ algorithm [3]. We have used real dataset downloaded from [23]. They comprise of two datasets viz. re0 and re1. We have also synthesized our own dataset which we henceforth call synthetic dataset.

Table 1. Synthetic Dataset

Class label	Number of documents	Class label	Number of documents
Architecture	100	Maths	100
Art	100	Medical	100
Business	100	Mythology	100
Crime	100	Politics	100
Economics	100	Space	100
Engineering	100	Sports	100
Geography	100	Terrorism	100
History	100		

Table 2. Real Dataset

Data	Source	Number of documents	Number of classes
re0	Reuters-21578	1504	13
re1	Reuters-21578	1657	25

6 Results and Analysis

In this paper, we have evaluated the quality of the clustering solution using two well known cluster validity measures viz. entropy and F-measure. We have calculated entropy values of ten executions and taken their average. The same is done in case of F-measure. Now, we plot these values against four different values of number of clusters i.e. k. We have shown the experimental results as graphs [see Fig.1-6]. The results clearly indicate that the entropy values of the clustering solutions generating out of our approach is always smaller while F-measure is greater than those of k-means [2] and k-means++ [3]. Hence our algorithm is found to be outperforming the two algorithms (i.e. k-means and k-means++). Also it can be easily concluded with the help of the graphs that entropy decreases while F-measure increases with the increment in the number of clusters.

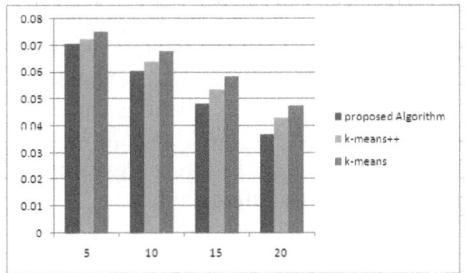

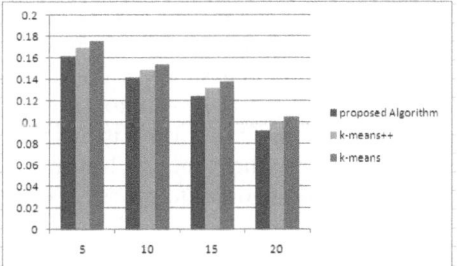

Fig. 1. Variation of entropy Vs number of clusters for synthetic dataset (# of classes 15)

Fig. 2. Variation of entropy Vs number of clusters for dataset re0 (# of classes 13)

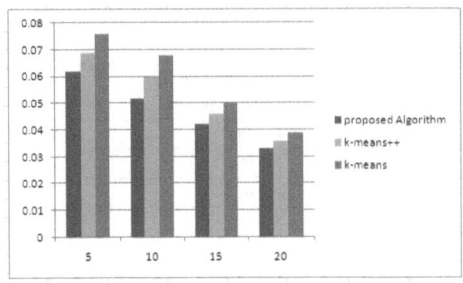
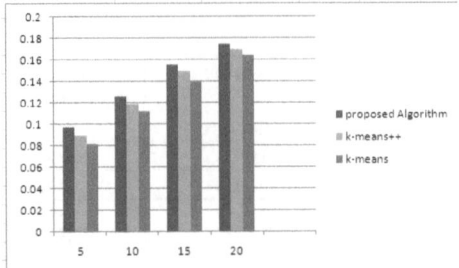

Fig. 3. Variation of entropy Vs number of clusters for dataset re1 (# of classes 25)

Fig. 4. Variation of F-Measure Vs number of clusters for synthetic dataset (# of classes 15)

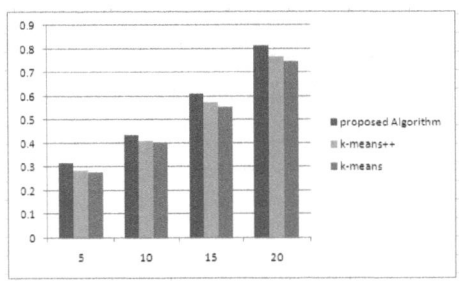
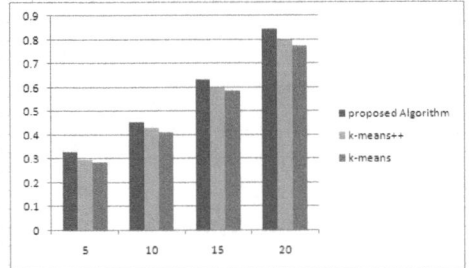

Fig. 5. Variation of F-Measure Vs number of clusters for dataset re0 (# of classes 13)

Fig. 6. Variation of F-Measure Vs number of clusters for dataset re1 (# of classes 25)

7   Conclusions and Future Work

This paper introduces a new algorithm for document clustering. This algorithm attempts to minimize a graph based criterion function in order to get an accurate clustering solution. From the literature, it is apparent that most of the earlier suggested algorithms have a relatively greater chance to get stuck in a local optimal solution. However, unlike them our algorithm is so astutely devised that it minimizes the fear of getting stuck in any local solution. In most of the cases, it successfully reaches the desired global solution. It is also evident from the results obtained that the performance of our algorithm keeps on enhancing with increase in the number of clusters required.

Our algorithm is basically a greedy one. It, in some way or the other, exhaustively checks all the possible solutions, with some pruning, before reaching the global optimal solution. This is why, its execution time is relatively more in comparison to some other algorithms such as k-means [2] and k-mean++[3]. In future, research may be concentrated in order to get rid of this shortcoming of our algorithm.

References

1. Berkhin, P.: Survey of clustering data mining techniques, Accrue Software Paper (2002)
2. Hartigan, J., Wong, M.: Algorithm AS136: A k-means clustering algorithm. Applied Statistics, 100–108 (1979)

3. Arthur, D., Vassilvitskii, S.: K-means++: the advantages of careful seeding. In: ACM-SIAM Symposium on Discrete Algorithms (2007)
4. Mahdavi, M., Abolhassani, H.: Harmony k -means algorithm for document clustering. Data Mining and Knowledge Discovery (2009)
5. Cui, X., Potok, T.E., Palathingal, P.: Document clustering using particle swarm optimization. In: Proceedings IEEE Swarm Intelligence Symposium, pp. 185–191 (2005)
6. Kanungo, T., Mount, D.M., Netanyahu, N.S., Piatko, C.D., Silverman, R., Wu, A.Y.: An efficient k-means clustering algorithm: Analysis and implementation. IEEE Trans. Pattern Anal. Mach. Intell. 24(7), 881–892 (2002)
7. Jain, A.K., Murty, M.N., Flynn, P.J.: Data Clustering: A Review. ACM Computing Survey 31(3), 264–323 (1999)
8. Guha, S., Rastogi, R., Shim, K.: Rock: A robust clustering algorithm for categorical attributes. Information Systems 25(5), 345–366 (2000)
9. Guha, S., Rastogi, R., Shim, K.: Cure: an efficient clustering algorithm for large databases. SIGMOD Rec. 27(2), 73–84 (1998)
10. Karypis, G., News, V.K.: Chameleon: Hierarchical clustering using dynamic modeling. Computer 32(8), 68–75 (1999)
11. Han, E.H., Karypis, G., Kumar, V., Mobasher, B.: Hypergraph based clustering in high-dimensional data sets: A summary of results. Data Engineering Bulletin, 15–22 (1998)
12. Ng, R., Han, J.: Efficient and effective clustering method for spatial data mining. In: Proceedings of the 20th VLDB Conference, Santiago, Chile, pp. 144–155 (1994)
13. Zahn, K.: Graph-theoretical methods for detecting and describing gestalt clusters. IEEE Transactions on Computers, 68–86 (1971)
14. Chandrasekharan, M., Rajagopalan, R.: An ideal seed non-hierarchical clustering algorithm for cellular manufacturing. International Journal of Production Research, 451–464 (1986)
15. Jain, A.K., Dubes, R.C.: Algorithms for Clustering Data. Prentice Hall (1988)
16. Zhao, Y., Karypis, G.: Empirical and theoretical comparisons of selected criterion functions for document clustering. Machine Learning 55(3), 311–331 (2004)
17. Zhao, Y., Karypis, G.: Evaluation of hierarchical clustering algorithms for document datasets. In: CIKM Proceedings of the Eleventh International Conference on Information and Knowledge Management, pp. 515–524. ACM Press (2002)
18. Zha, H., He, X., Ding, C., Simon, H., Gu, M.: Bipartite graph partitioning and data clustering. In: CIKM (2001)
19. Dhillon, I.S.: Co-clustering documents and words using bipartite spectral graph partitioning, Technical Report, Department of Computer Science, University of Texas, Austin (2001)
20. Salton, G.: Automatic Text Processing: The Transformation, Analysis, and Retrieval of Information by Computer. Addison-Wesley (1989)
21. Zhao, Y., Karypis, G.: Criterion functions for document clustering: Experiments and analysis, Technical Report, University of Minnesota, pp. 01–40 (2001)
22. Stein, B., Eissen, S.M.Z., Wißbrock, F.: On cluster validity and the information need of users. In: Proceedings Artificial Intelligence and Applications, pp. 373, 522, 531, 533 (2003)
23. Dataset from Karypis Lab, http://glaros.dtc.umn.edu/gkhome/fetch/sw/cluto/datasets.tar.gz

Low-Rank Matrix Factorization and Co-clustering Algorithms for Analyzing Large Data Sets

Archana Donavalli[1], Manjeet Rege[1], Xumin Liu[1],
and Kourosh Jafari-Khouzani[2]

[1] Department of Computer Science, Rochester Institute of Technology,
Rochester, NY, USA
{axd2687,mr,xl}@cs.rit.edu
[2] Department of Radiology Research, Henry Ford Hospital, Detroit, Michigan, USA
kjafari@rad.hfh.edu

Abstract. With the ever increasing data, there is a greater need for analyzing and extracting useful and meaningful information out of it. The amount of research being conducted in extracting this information is commendable. From clustering to bi and multi clustering, there are a lot of different algorithms proposed to analyze and discover the hidden patterns in data, in every which way possible. On the other hand, the size of the data sets is increasing with each passing day and hence it is becoming increasingly difficult to try and analyze all this data and find clusters in them without the algorithms being computationally prohibitive. In this study, we have tried to study both the domains and understand the development of the algorithms and how they are being used. We have compared the different algorithms to try and get a better idea of which algorithm is more suited for a particular situation.

Keywords: Co-clustering, Matrix factorization, Isoperimetric Co-clustering.

1 Introduction

Today with the ubiquitous presence of data, it is becoming increasingly important to extract meaningful information out of very large data sets and to use it effectively. There are several data mining techniques like classification, clustering, associations, visualization, summarization, deviation detection etc. that are currently being used for this purpose. Clustering is one of the most popular techniques, which is used to find groups or clusters based on similar patterns in data. Traditional clustering is also known as one-way clustering. One of the newer techniques in data mining is co-clustering of data, which is becoming increasingly important for applications such as web mining, market-basket analysis, bioinformatics etc. While clustering concerns with one type of data such as clustering documents, images or words, co-clustering extends clustering to include n-type of data while forming clusters. For example, consider a scenario where we want to know which documents contain what kind of words and are

R. Kannan and F. Andres (Eds.): ICDEM 2010, LNCS 6411, pp. 272–279, 2012.
© Springer-Verlag Berlin Heidelberg 2012

published in which conferences. Such information is generated from three kinds of data in text mining - documents, words and categories (i.e. conferences, in this case).

One of the early research endeavors on co-clustering was Bipartite Spectral Graph Partitioning by, [2]. There have been several other papers which have proposed many interesting algorithms for co-clustering of data. Some of them are graph partitioning based co-clustering methods like Isoperimetric Co-clustering algorithm by Rege, et al.[7], matrix-factorization based co-clustering methods like Block Value Decomposition by, Long, et al. [5] etc.

With the size of data sets increasing with each passing day, it has become more and more difficult to practically use the co-clustering algorithms on such data sets without being prohibitively expensive computationally. One area of research that targets this very problem is the low-rank matrix factorization which basically aims to convert the high dimensional sparse matrix into a representative small matrix and find clusters based on that. This field has been of interest to both the data mining as well as the mathematical community. Many algorithms have been developed over the years for solving this very problem. We have tried to select a few interesting ones from both the communities- CUR-type decomposition by Petros, et al.[3] and Compact Matrix Decomposition (CMD) by Sun, et al. [8].

In the following sections we have tried to explain the algorithms and the motivation for developing them. We have also tried to compare and contrast the algorithms based on the experimental results provided in the papers.

2   Co-clustering Algorithms

2.1   Bipartite Spectral Graph Partitioning

This approach to co-clustering of data sets was proposed by Dhillon [2], in the KDD, 2001 conference. The author first presents a general idea for applying clustering algorithms to document collections. The first step to achieve this objective is to create a vector-space model. This is done by first extracting unique content-bearing words from the set of documents and to treat them as features. Then each document is represented as a vector in this feature space. Hence, the entire document collection can now be represented by a word-by-document matrix A such that the rows refer to words and the columns refer to documents. if an entry in A say, $A_{i,j}$ is zero then it indicates that the ith word is not present in the jth document and similarly, if $A_{i,j}$ is non-zero then it indicates the number of times the ith word occurs in the jth document. The motivation for this work came from the fact that existing document clustering methods like agglomerative clustering, partial k-means algorithm, projection-based methods, self-organizing maps, multidimensional scaling etc. are computationally expensive for large collections. This is because the computation required to form the graph is quadratic in the number of documents.

Word clustering has found use in applications such as in the automatic construction of a statistical thesaurus, automatic classification of documents, in the enhancement of queries etc. The underlying idea in such applications is to group or cluster words based on the documents in which they appear. The assumption being that words occurring together must belong to the same context or domain. The author proposes to consider co-clustering both words and documents simultaneously. To do so he plans to consider this problem as that of finding the minimum cut vertex partitions in a bipartite graph between documents and words.

To explain his model, the author introduces a bipartite graph model for representing a document collection. Two sets of nodes are considered: documents and words. An edge between a document and a word exists if the word is present in that document, else the edge is absent. Another way to do this is to have edge weights representing the frequency or the number of times a given word occurs in a given document. The author considers traditional graph partitioning techniques but renders them as inefficient because they have a tendency to get stuck in local minima. So, he decides to consider spectral partitioning instead. Spectral partitioning in comparison gives a better global solution. Along with the spectral graph partitioning the author uses eigenvectors as optimal partition vectors and ratio-cut and normalized-cut objectives to arrive at the algorithm. Thereafter, Singular Value Decomposition (SVD) is used to find the clusters.

Not only has the author successfully developed his bipartition algorithm but he has also extended it to a multi-partitioning algorithm to solve the problem of finding k word and clusters. Instead of just using the bipartition algorithm recursively the author decides to use the k-means algorithm to obtain the desired k-way multi-partitioning. He considers this to be a more efficient way than recursively calling the bi-partitioning algorithm. The author has used three popular publicly available data sets for his experiments. He also created his own data set by mixing all three data sets. Confusion matrix is used to capture the goodness of the document since, the actual class labels are known. And the measures of purity and entropy are derived based on that. The author also shows in his experimental results that his algorithm is more robust to the presence of noise words because of the fact that it uses a global spectral heuristic of using singular vectors.

2.2   Isoperimetric Co-clustering Algorithm (ICA)

This approach to co-clustering of data sets was proposed by Rege, et al. [7], in the sixth International Conference on Data Mining (ICDM'06). In this paper, they propose a new graph-partitioning based approach to solve the problem of document-to-word clustering, which is basically a two-way clustering. The problem of document-to-word clustering has found considerable interest because of the problems in text, Web and multimedia documents. In this work the basic idea is to model the words and documents as the two vertices of a bipartite graph and then use their Isoperimetric Co-clustering Algorithm to partition the bi-partite graph to get the relevant clusters. Thus, they transform the document-word co-clustering problem to a bi-partite graph partitioning problem. The idea here is to cluster documents based on commonly occurring words in them and to cluster words based on the common documents in which they appear. To implement their algorithm they model the entire data set as word-document matrix and name it as B. This matrix consists of words as the rows and documents as the columns. So, the relevance of the ith word in the jth document is represented by the value of $B_{i,j}$. Thereafter, by simultaneously clustering rows and columns of B, the co-clustering of documents and words was achieved. This is done by representing the data set as an undirected bipartite graph and then applying isoperimetric co-clustering algorithm to partition it.

They represent the set of words say W and the set of documents say D by the two vertices of the weighted bipartite graph. Co-clustering is then achieved by partitioning this bipartite graph. A graph partitioning algorithm basically assigns a set of values to each vertex in the graph and a vector consisting of the values for each of the vertices is called the indicator vector of the graph. The partitioning algorithm proposed in this paper is motivated by the classic isoperimetric problem which aims to determine a plane figure of the largest possible area whose boundary has a specified length. In other words it seeks to find the shape with minimum perimeter for a fixed area. They assume that since the number of documents and words are finite, the bipartite graph too has finite number of vertices. Using the definitions of the isoperimetric constant of a continuous manifold and the isoperimetric number for a bipartite graph, they derive a system of linear equations for the combinatorial volume. They then derive the isoperimetric ratio as the ratio of the boundary area to the volume of the region of the manifold.

A partition is considered to be more optimal if the isoperimetric ratio for it is low. The goal of their algorithm is to derive partitions with low isoperimetric ratio. They have also used a vertex removal strategy to solve the system of linear equations. They used a dumbbell shaped graph consisting of 21 document and word vertices with uniform weights to analyze whether to remove a document vertex or a word vertex or both together. From this analysis they conclude that although it doesn't matter which vertex is removed as long as it is densely connected in the graph. But, if a sparsely connected vertex is removed then it causes imbalanced partitions. Thus, they decide to remove the vertex with the maximum degree in their algorithm.

They claim that their algorithm is an improvement over the popular spectral partitioning methods which have some drawbacks like- they fail to produce the best partition for certain families of graphs like the roach graphs, which gets its name from the fact that it is shaped like a cockroach and consists of two path graphs, each on $2k$ vertices. The ICA has the inherent advantage of solving linear equations instead of solving eigenvalue problem or solving Singular Value Decomposition (SVD) in case of the spectral approach, which makes it computationally more efficient. Moreover, in case the desired eigenvector is very close to the other eigenvalues of the matrix, the solution to the eigenvector problem and SVD has been found to be less stable to minor perturbation of the matrix in comparison to the solution to a system of linear equations.

To validate their theory, the authors perform a series of extensive experiments to compare their algorithm with other Spectral-SVD bipartite graph partitioning approaches. They decide to use the isoperimetric ratio to evaluate their algorithm. They decide not to use traditional clustering reporting techniques such as confusion matrix because the goal of co-clustering is not to achieve perfect clustering of one data type but to achieve the optimal co-clustering of the two data types together. Using the isoperimetric ratio for evaluation is also justified by the fact that both ICA and Spectral-SVD algorithms aim to minimize the isoperimetric ratio. While the former achieves this by solving a system of linear equations the later achieves this by solving the eigenvalue or the SVD problem.

3   Low Rank Matrix Factorization Techniques

3.1   CUR-Type Decomposition

In many applications, the data consists of an $m \times n$ matrix A which may be stored on disk but is too large to be read into random access memory (RAM) or to perform superlinear polynomial time computations on it. This paper by Petros, et al. [3], aims to address this problem by developing fast Monte Carlo algorithms for performing useful computations on large matrices. Such computations generally require time which is superlinear in the number of nonzero elements of the matrix, the authors expect their algorithms to be useful in many applications where the data sets are modeled by matrices and are extremely large. The algorithms basically decompose the large matrix into three smaller matrices.

In the first algorithm, the LINEARTIMECUR algorithm, c columns of A and r rows of A are randomly sampled. Then $m \times c$ matrix C consisting of m rows and c columns of A is formed along with $r \times n$ matrix R consisting of r rows and n columns of A. Then using C and R, the $c \times r$ matrix U is computed. The advantage of this algorithm is that it can be implemented without having to store the matrix A in RAM, provided it can make two passes over the matrix stored in the external memory and use $O(m+n)$ additional RAM. In the second algorithm, the CONSTANTTIMECUR algorithm is different from the first algorithm in the approach that it randomly samples a constant number w of rows of C. This has the advantage over the previous algorithm that, it now requires only constant additional RAM but has the disadvantage that it requires a third pass over the data and has additional error.

The authors state that their CUR approximations have been used both practically and theoretically. Practically, they have been used in applications such as the reconstruction of a matrix given a sample of the matrix in a recommendation system context and for similarity query problems which are widely used in areas such as information retrieval. In theoretical context, the CUR approximations have been used in applications such as designing and analyzing approximation algorithms for the max-cut problem. Thus, CUR approximations are useful in applications where the use of constant additional space and time framework is essential. Thus, to solve the problem of not being able to perform useful computations because of not being able to store the whole of the large matrices in the main memory, the authors present two successful algorithms. One which computes an approximate CUR decomposition of a matrix A using linear (in m and n) additional space and time and another which computes a description of an approximate CUR decomposition of a matrix A using only constant additional space and time.

3.2   Compact Matrix Decomposition (CMD)

Large, real graphs are often very sparse. For example, the web graph, the Internet topology graph, who-trusts-whom social network graph etc. This paper proposed by Sun, et al. [8], aims to address the problem of finding patterns and anomalies in the large sparse graphs. This is particularly useful for applications such as network traffic monitoring, research citation network analysis, social network analysis, regulatory networks in genes etc. Although some of the existing methods like SVD and CUR are very useful for identifying hidden and associated structures in high dimensional data, these methods often ignore the sparseness of the graph. As a result of this, they incur a high memory and computational cost because of which they are not practically used.

In the proposed algorithm the authors plan to address this problem by computing sparse low rank matrix approximations. Because of this CMD reduces the computation cost and space requirements and hence performs better than the existing algorithms. The authors list the desirable properties of their algorithms as: fast, space efficient and use in anomaly detection. They define the problem by using an adjacency matrix for representing a directed graph with weights such that every row or column in A corresponds to a node in the graph. They have kept their definition of the adjacency matrix is more general because of the fact that they omit rows and columns that have no entries. This makes it feasible to include special cases like bi-partite graphs, in which the rows and columns refer to different sets of nodes or the traditional graphs, in which the rows and columns refer to the same set of nodes.

The reasoning behind their approach is that since most graphs from real applications are large but sparse, i.e. the number of edges |E| is roughly linear in the number of nodes |V|, they can be stored very efficiently by using sparse matrix representation by only keeping the nonzero entries. This reduces the space overhead from $O(|V|^2)$ to $O(|V|)$. To efficiently identify a low dimensional summary while preserving the sparsity of the graph, the authors consider the patterns of the graph as a low dimensional summary of the adjacency matrix. Thus, they formulate the problem as a matrix decomposition problem. They consider two general classes of graph mining problems: the static graph mining and the dynamic graph mining. In case of the static graph mining, the input data is a given static graph represented as its adjacency matrix. So, the objective is to find patterns, outliers and summarize the given sparse matrix. In case of the dynamic graph mining, the input data are raw event records that need to be pre-processed. So, the objective in this case is to find patterns, outliers and summaries from the given timstamped pairs such as the source-destination pairs from network traffic or email messages and IM chats.

The CMD algorithm consists of two parts: the first part involves the construction of a subspace for a given input matrix and the second part involves computing its low rank approximation. For the subspace construction, the authors choose to use the sampled columns to represent the subspace as the subspace is spanned by the columns of the matrix. To achieve this objective they use biased sampling followed by duplicate column removal. In biased sampling, the columns are picked with replacement biased towards the ones with higher norms. So, the columns with higher entry values will have the higher chance of being selected multiple times. This method of sampling is good and yield an optimal approximation but at the expense of a lot of duplicated samples. As a result they have to then carry out duplicate column removal. Doing this reduces both the storage space required and the computational effort. Thus, a very important step in the subspace creation is to scale up the columns that are sampled multiple times while removing the duplicates. The scaling up is done based on the square root of the number of times it is being selected. For the second part of low rank approximation, the main objective is to form an approximation of the original matrix by using the sampled columns. This is done by projecting the original matrix onto the span of the sampled columns and then reducing the cost by removing the duplicate rows.

The authors also provide a practical technique for mining dynamic graphs using CMD in case of applications which continuously generate data for graph construction and analysis. They claim that the results got can be directly fed into applications such as anomaly detection and historical analysis. In this scenario, the data source is assumed to generate a large volume of real time event records for constructing large graphs and since it is hard to buffer and process all data that are streamed, the authors propose an intermediate step of sparsification, to reduce the incoming data volume by sampling and scaling data to approximate the original full data. After the input data has been summarized as a current matrix A, the next step is matrix decomposition which is the core component for computing low-rank matrix approximation. In the end, an error measure is used to quantify the quality of the mining result. They use sum-square-error (SSE) and relative SSE for measuring the error.

Their sparsification algorithm is based on the idea that for each time window, they can incrementally build an adjacency matrix A, by updating its entries as data records are coming in. Each new record triggers an update on an entry (i, j) with a value increase of v, i.e. $A(i, j) = A(i, j) + v$. This is done by sampling updates with a certain probability p, and then scale the sampled matrix by a factor of $1/p$ to approximate the true matrix. After having constructed the adjacency matrix, it has to be compactly summarized. In this step the authors consider three different kinds of low-rank approximation techniques. They consider SVD, because it is traditional and optimal. They consider CUR, because it preserves the sparsity property and they consider CMD because it achieves significant performance gains over both SVD and CUR. Using their experimental results the authors conclude that CMD is ten times faster than SVD and CUR and requires 1/10 of the space for the same reconstruction accuracy

4 Conclusion

We presented some of the representative works on co-clustering and low rank matrix factorization. Of the many existing co-clustering algorithms, not all have been used effectively because of the practical limitations. We have also tried to compare and contrast the algorithms based on the experimental results provided in the papers. Our future work and goal is to study some of the other works in both these domains such as the Co-clustering on Manifolds by Quanquan, et al. [4], Algorithm 844 by Berry, et al. [1], CRD framework by Pan, et al. [6] etc.

References

1. Berry, M.W., Stewart, G.W., Pulatova, S.A.: Algorithm 844: Computing sparse reduced-rank approximations to sparse matrices. ACM Transactions on Mathermatical Software 31 (2005)
2. Dhillon, I.S.: Co-clustering documents and words using bipartite spectral graph partitioning. In: 7th ACM SIGKDD International Conference on Knowledge Discovery and Data Mining (KDD), San Francisco (2001)
3. Drineas, P., Kannan, R., Mahoney, M.W.: Fast monte carlo algorithms for matrices iii: Computing a compressed approximate matrix decomposition. Society for Industrial and Applied Mathematics (SIAM) 36, 184–206 (2006)
4. Gu, Q., Zhou, J.: Co-clustering of manifolds. In: 15th ACM SIGKDD International Conference on Knowledge Discovery and Data Mining (ICDM), Paris (2009)
5. Long, B., Zhang, Z., Yu, P.S.: Co-clustering by block value decomposition. In: 11th ACM SIGKDD International Conference on Knowledge Discovery and Data Mining (KDD), Chicago (2005)
6. Pan, F., Zhang, X., Wang, W.: Crd: Fast co-clustering of large datasets utilizing sampling-based matrix decomposition. In: ACM SIGMOD/PODS Conference, Vancouver (2008)
7. Rege, M., Dong, M., Fotouhi, F.: Co-clustering documents and words using bipartite isoperimetric graph partitioning. In: 6th IEEE International Conference on Data Mining (ICDM), Hong Kong (2006)
8. Sun, J., Xie, Y., Zhang, H., Faloutsos, C.: Less is more: Complex matrix decomposition for large sparse graphs. In: 7th SIAM International Conference on Data Mining (ICDM), Minneapolis (2007)

Biclustering and Feature Selection Techniques in Bioinformatics

Bhavik Desai[1], Pankaj Andhale[1], Manjeet Rege[1], and Qi Yu[2]

[1] Department of Computer Science, Rochester Institute of Technology,
Rochester, NY, USA
{bxd9449,pma7893,mr}@cs.rit.edu
[2] Department of Information Sciences and Technology,
Rochester Institute of Technology, Rochester, NY, USA
qi.yu@rit.edu

Abstract. The paper describes several data mining techniques, developed to solve problems which are faced by biologists in Bioinformatics.Several biclustering algorithms which perform clustering on the two dimensions simultaneously are described. Other techniques described in this paper include feature selection methods which help in reducing noise and improving the performance of the classification model.

Keywords: biclustering, data transform, feature selection, filter methods.

1 Introduction

Biology is the most important science because understanding various biological processes in living organisms provide reasoning for several or possibly all diseases. Tremendous amount of data is being constantly generated from several biological experiments which are part of genomics research. The biologists needed techniques to interpret this data, which led to the introduction of Bioinformatics.

2 Biclustering Algorithms

Clustering algorithms can either cluster genes or conditions with respect to set of conditions or genes respectively, but it cannot cluster genes and condition simultaneously.In general, Biclustering algorithms can cluster along two dimensions, row and column simultaneously. The important points that one should know about biology while applying biclustering to gene expression data are: a cellular process consists of small numbers of active genes (participating genes) and this process becomes active in only set of conditions, and a gene can participate in several cellular process simultaneously. To meet these criteria while biclustering, a cluster of genes/conditions should be defined with respect to set of conditions/genes respectively, the clusters formed should not be exhaustive or/and exclusive and gene/condition should be able to belong to several or no clusters. The problem of biclustering becomes complex due to presence of noise in gene expression data generated from various experiments.

R. Kannan and F. Andres (Eds.): ICDEM 2010, LNCS 6411, pp. 280–287, 2012.
© Springer-Verlag Berlin Heidelberg 2012

2.1   Biclustering Algorithm

Problem Defination

While explaining several biclustering algorithms, we would be using definition described in this section. The gene expression data is represented as $m \times n$ matrix, where m is the number of genes and n is the number of conditions and $a_{i,j}$ is a real value representing the expression level of gene i in condition j.

	Condition 1 .... Condition j .... Condition n			
gene 1	a_{11}	....	a_{1j}	.... a_{1n}
gene i	a_{i1}	....	a_{ij}	.... a_{in}
gene m	a_{m1}	....	a_{mj}	.... a_{mn}

Fig. 1. Gene expression data matrix

In the given matrix, row cluster is defined as subset of rows (I) that show similar behavior across all the columns (n) whereas column cluster (J) is defined as subset of columns that show similar behavior across all rows (m). A bicluster (I, J) can be defined as subset of genes (I) that exhibit similar behavior across subset of conditions (J) or vice-versa where $I = \{i_1, ..., i_k$ such that $k \leqq m\}$ and $J = \{j_1, ..., j_s$ such that $s \leqq n\}$. Thus a bicluster (I, J) is $(k \times s)$ sub-matrix of the original $(m \times n)$ matrix.

2.2   Weighted Bipartite Graph Representation of Data Matrix

A weighted bipartite graph is defined as $G(V, E)$, where E is the set of edges in the graph and V is the vertices divided into two sets: L and R such that $V = L \cup R$ and all the edges in E have one end in R and the other end in L. The gene expression data matrix defined in the previous section can be viewed as weighted bipartite graph where in $'m'$ genes would be nodes belonging to L and $'n'$ conditions would be nodes belonging to R and the matrix element $a_{i,j}$ would be the weight of the edge from node $i \in L$ to node $j \in R$. The weighted bipartite graph for the gene expression data matrix is show in the Fig.2.

The complexity of determining bicluster in matrix depends upon the score function used to determine the quality of bicluster. In Fig.3, even if we consider the weights $a_{i,j}$ to be 0 or 1 then still finding a bicluster is equivalent to finding biclique in the bipartite graph, which is a NP-complete problem. The case becomes more complex when weights $a_{i,j}$ are real values rather than 0 or 1. Using the graph theory, it is proved that all the variants for determining biclusters are NP-complete problem. Thus, most biclustering algorithm use heuristic approach, some of them apply data preprocessing techniques before actually applying the algorithm in order to better find the pattern of interest.

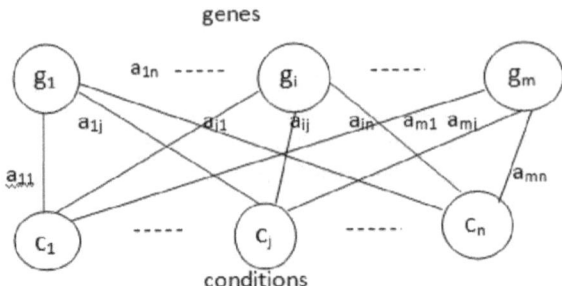

Fig. 2. Weighted Bipartite graph for gene expression data matrix

2.3 Types of Bicluster

There are four major types of biclusters: (1) bicluster with constant values, (2) bicluster with constant values on rows or columns, (3) bicluster with coherent values and (4) bicluster with coherent evolution. The first 3 types of biclusters analyze the data matrix and try to discover subset of rows or columns that shows similar behavior. While in coherent evolution type of bicluster, the elements of matrices are considered as symbols and the behavior is examined, to find if they follow certain order, or shows coherent positive or negative changes with respect to normal values. Thus in this type of bicluster the coherent behavior is found without taking into account its exact numeric value.

2.4 Weighted Bipartite Graph for Gene Expression Data Matrix

In Fig.3, the $table(a)$ shows the ideal bicluster with constant values whereas $table(b)$ and (c) shows constant rows bicluster and constant columns bicluster respectively. The $table(d)$ shows additive model of coherent value type of bicluster whereas $table(e)$ shows multiplicative model of coherent values $table(f)$ shows the actual constant value bicluster which is contaminated with noise. The $table(g), (h), (i), (j)$ are examples of coherent evolution where in $table(g)$ and (h) the state changes along rows and columns respectively.

In $table(i)$ the value increases from 1st column to second then decreases and then again increases in column four $table(j)$ shows negative or positive changes with respect to normal value, irrespective of their numeric value.

Notations
Consider a data matrix $A = (X, Y)$ where X is the set of rows and Y is the set of columns. Let (I, J) be the bicluster consisting of I rows which are subset of X and J columns which are subset of Y. $a_{i,j}$ is an element at i^{th} row and j^{th} column of the matrix. We will use the following notations:

Mean of ith row of bicluster

$$a_{i,J} = (1/|J|) * \sum j \epsilon J a_{i,j} \qquad (1)$$

Mean of jth row of bicluster

$$a_{I,j} = (1/|I|) * \sum i\epsilon I a_{i,j} \tag{2}$$

Mean of the bicluster

$$a_{I,J} = (1/|I||J|) * \sum j\epsilon J, i\epsilon I a_{i,j} \tag{3}$$

For finding a constant bicluster, the approach involves arranging rows and columns in such a order that similar values cluster together but this can be done with noiseless ideal data matrix. Ideally, in a constant value bicluster (I, J), were all values are same, for all $i\epsilon I$ and $j\epsilon J$, $a_{i,j} = \mu$, where μ is the mean of all the values in the cluster.But for real data with noise $a_{i,j} = \mu + \eta_{i,j}$ where $\eta_{i,j}$ is the noise associated with the data. In Fig.3.a shows the ideal bicluster with constant values whereas (f) shows constant bicluster in noisy data.The most common merit score function used to determine the quality of constant bicluster is the variance. Variance

$$(I, J) = \sum i\epsilon I, j\epsilon J (a_{i,j} - a_{I,J})^2 \tag{4}$$

Cheng and Church [3] used mean square residue as the merit function to evaluate the quality of the bicluster. The residue $r(a_{i,j})$ of an element $a_{i,j}$ in a bicluster with coherent values is defined as

$$r(a_{i,j}) = a_{i,j} - a_{i,J} - a_{I,j} + a_{I,J} \tag{5}$$

The mean square residue is defined as

$$H(I, J) = (1/|I||J|) * \sum i\epsilon I, j\epsilon J r(a_{i,j})^2 \tag{6}$$

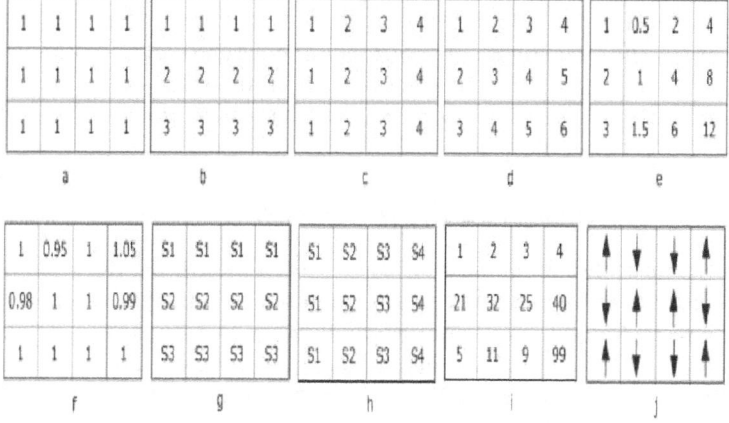

Fig. 3. Types of bicluster

This merit function needs to be minimized to determine better bicluster with coherent values. In Fig.3, d and e shows bicluster with coherent values.[1] describes bicluster as Order preserving sub-matrix (OPSM) wherein a bicluster is set of rows whose values are in linear order across set of columns. In Fig.3.i, the coherent evolution bicluster has the order $a_{i,4} > a_{i,2} > a_{i,3} > a_{i,1}$. In such bicluster with coherent evolution the emphasis is on order of values across columns rather the exact numeric values. In Fig.3.g and h the state changes across rows and columns respectively thus it is an example of coherent evolution. Whereas j portrays sign change across rows and columns irrespective of their numeric values. There can be an overlapping bicluster that consist of two different type of bicluster . Types of bicluster are shown in Fig.3.

3   Biclustering Methods

3.1   Iterative Row and Column Clustering

For biclustering, the first method that comes in mind is using the existing clustering algorithms on rows and columns of data matrix separately then combining the result to get the bicluster. Coupled two-way clustering (CTWC) [4]uses iterative row and column clustering approach. CTWC starts with one pair of columns and rows wherein each pair consists of set of all columns and set of all rows. To find stable row and column clusters, hierarchal clustering algorithm is applied on each set of rows and columns, thus finding a set of bicluster at a time. A tunable parameter T is used for controlling the decision of biclustering. At the beginning $T = 0$, when there exist a single bicluster with all rows and columns. With the increase in the value of T the current bicluster gets divided at each step, until at certain high value of T which consist of bicluster with single row and column. The stability of a bicluster is measured by the control parameter T by fixing the range of value $\triangle T$ at which the cluster remained unchanged. $\triangle T$ generally constitutes the range of values required to break the data into single row and column. CTWC maintains two lists for stable clusters (rows and columns clusters) and a list for pair of rows and columns subset. At each step one subset of rows and one subset of columns are clustered and combined. The new formed bicluster is added to the rows and columns list. The iteration continues until cluster of predefined size is formed and no new cluster that satisfies the stability criteria is found.

4   Recent Biclustering Approaches

Important approaches in computer science such as greedy iterative search, exhaustive and divide and conquer is implemented by Block Clustering for biclustering. These technique are computationally very fast but one may miss a good bicluster as it can be divided before being determined. Distribution parameter identification approach assumes certain statistical model and determines the parameter used to generate the data by minimizing certain score functions in various iterations. Kluger et al.[7]. Techniques [8] used to improve Minimum Sum Squared Residue Coclustering are as follows

4.1 Data Transformation

Data transformation is performed as a preprocessing step and is important in various data mining tasks as variance of the variable will decide its relevance in the model.

4.2 Incremental Local Search(LS)

The local search strategy basically searches for the move of some row/column that maximizes the change in the score function. This strategy overcomes the problem described above. The detailed description about how the local search is performed can be found in [3].[8] described improved Minimum Sum Squared Residue Coclustering algorithm that uses local search to escape the local minima. The algorithm is described wherein the updating the cluster and local searching is performed alternately. In first step the row and column clusters are updated then in the second step, the local search is performed to check for row/column that can be moved in order to improve the score value. Each iterations performs this two steps.

A very different approach of biclustering is presented in [6] which explain diametrical clustering of anti-correlated genes. It is observed that genes which are functionally related exhibit strong anti-correlation in their expression levels. This can be the case because a gene may be strongly suppressed in order to allow some other to be fully expressed. Such genes which are functionally related still get clustered into different groups. The algorithm described in [6]clusters highly correlated and anti-correlated genes into a diametric cluster. The positively and negatively correlated genes can be separated using a simple post processing step.

5 Feature Selection Techniques

One of the important steps in discriminant analysis is feature selection wherein a subset of features are selected for the discriminant system instead of using all the attributes or features within the data. The computational cost reduces with reduction in the features or dimensions. The classification accuracy is improved with reduction in noise. More interpretable features are available which can help in identifying and monitoring the function type or target diseases. For example, Golub et al [5] showed that 50 informative genes are usually sufficient for a two class cancer subtype classification. Feature selection is usually performed under two approaches: filters and wrappers. The features are selected on the basis of their intrinsic characteristics which basically determine the discriminative power with respect to the target class. In wrapper type method the feature selection process is wrapped around the learning algorithm *i.e.* the feature is selected by determining its usefulness by estimating the accuracy of the learning method.There are two approaches for starting the search of best features. *Forward selection* and *Backward elimination*.

Filter methods are much faster than Wrapper methods but classification accuracy is better delivered by wrapper than that delivered by filters. The disadvantage of wrapper method is that it requires classifier to be called repeatedly during the feature selection process.

Some of the above described methods are: (a) Filter methods: Filter methods filters for selecting genes from among all the genes. Some of the filters are: Information gain(I): This parameter measures the significance of the feature with respect to the class.

$$Information\ gain = H(class) - H(class/feature) \tag{7}$$

$$H(class) = -\sum class_i \epsilon class^{P(class_i)}.log_2(P(class_i)) \tag{8}$$

$$H(class) = -\sum class_i \epsilon class^{P(class_i)}.log_2(P(class_i)) \tag{9}$$

$$H(class/feature) =$$
$$-\sum feature_i \epsilon feature^{P(feature_i)} \times$$
$$\sum class_i \epsilon class^{P(class_i/feature_i)} \times \tag{10}$$
$$log_2(P(class_i/feature_i))$$

But information gain is biased for feature with high variance. This biasness was removed in symmetric uncertainty [9] as

$$SU = 2 \times information\ gain/(H_{(class)} + H_{(feature)}) \tag{11}$$

The filter methods can be applied in two steps as follows: 1. Rank all the features using certain filters similar one described above. 2. Choose the higher ranked n-1 features as the best feature subset. (b) Wrapper method: The feature selection can be performed using wrapper methods in following steps: 1. Select a machine learning algorithm like Naïve Bayes to evaluate the score of the feature subset. 2. Select a searching algorithm like forward selection explained above. 3. Search the feature space for subset of features by keeping track of the best subset of features. 4. The best subset is considered as output of feature selection. The feature selection for unsupervised clustering is like chicken and egg problem as the feature selection needs to be performed depending upon the prior knowledge of cluster structure which in turn needs to be determined. Approach described in [2] identifies irrelevant genes rather than relevant genes and improves clustering by discarding them and using the remaining relevant genes. In this technique the non-discriminant genes are ordered in middle thus can be discarded.

6   Conclusion

Data mining techniques such as clustering, biclustering, feature selection, discriminant methods and graph models have been explained throughout the paper.

One can combine two or more approaches or methods explained above to derive a method that performs better than the existing algorithm to solve a particular problem. Apart from the application of these techniques to the field of bioinformatics, the algorithms presented in this paper are domain independent.

References

1. Ben-Dor, A., Chor, B., Karp, R., Yakhini, Z.: Discovering local structure in gene expression data: The order-preserving submatrix problem. In: 6th Computational Biology International Conference (2002)
2. Ding, C.H.Q.: Unsupervised feature selection via two-way ordering in gene expression analysis. NERSC Division, Lawrence Berkeley National Laboratory, University of California, Berkeley, CA, USA
3. Dhillon, I.S., Guan, Y., Kogan, J.: Iterative clustering of high dimensional text data augmented by local search. In: 2nd IEEE International Conference Data Mining, ICDM (2002)
4. Getz, G., Levine, E., Domany, E.: Coupled two-way clustering analysis of gene microarray data. Proc. Natural Academy of Sciences US (2000)
5. Golub, T., Slonim, D.K., et al.: Molecular classification of cancer: class discovery and class prediction by gene expression monitoring
6. Dhillon, I.S., Marcotte, E.M., Roshan, U.: Diametrical clustering for identifying anti-correlated gene clusters. Bioinformatics, 1612–1619 (2003)
7. Klugar, Y., Basri, R., Chang, J.T., Gerstein, M.: Spectral biclustering of microarray data: Coclustering genes and conditions. Genome Research, 703–716 (2003)
8. Livne, O.E., Golub, G.H.: Scaling by binormalization. Numerical Algorithms, 97–120 (2004)
9. Press, W.H., Flannery, B.P., Teukolsky, S.A., Vetterling W.T.: Numerical recipes in c (1988)

A Comparative Study between Dynamic Web Scripting Languages

Alok Ranjan[1], Rajeev Kumar[1], and Joydip Dhar[2]

[1] Department of Information Technology
[2] Department of Applied Sciences
ABV - Indian Institute of Information Technology and Management, Gwalior, India
{iiitm.alok,rajeevkumariiitm}@gmail.com,
jdhar@iiitm.ac.in

Abstract. Nowadays websites generate dynamic responses to the user requests. This leads them to dynamic web scripting languages. PHP, JSP and ASP.NET are the three most popular web scripting languages in the world. PHP is particularly useful for lightweight web applications. JSP which employs Java in its implementation is useful for the systems which require extra security. ASP.NET which is a Microsoft product combines some of the fine features of both PHP and JSP. All the three languages have pros and cons associated with them. In this paper, we have compared the impacts of these three languages on the performance of a web server. We have described and analyzed the results of conducting experiments on four benchmarks: calculating the factorial of 100, determining whether a random word having 1 million characters is a palindrome or not, sorting a list of 1 million random integers using merge sort, running Dijkstra's algorithm on a graph with 1000 nodes and 5000 edges. We employed famous web servers viz. Apache 2.2.6, Apache Tomcat 6.0.26 and IIS 7.5. We have shown the results using both built-in modules and self-written codes. Moreover, we have used C# with ASP.NET which being an object oriented language provides built-in modules.

Keywords: ASP.NET, Dijkstra's Algorithm, JSP, Merge Sort, PHP.

1   Introduction

HTML, which stands for Hyper Text Markup Language is a text and image formatting markup language employed by web browsers to format web pages. It was first proposed by Tim Berners-Lee [1, 16]. It has become exponentially more popular since then, expanding beyond a small group of computer-science visionaries to the personal and business sectors. Today, it's almost a household word. As the utilization of World Wide Web intensified, static HTML web pages were rendered inadequate considering the growing requirements of mankind [2]. Earlier, web servers used to employ the basic HTTP protocol. Once they received a client request, they would reply with a static document containing only HTML content. However, gradually massive content began to be required which had to be saved on the web server. This led in the consumption of heavy storage area at the server side for big applications thus culminating into the waste

R. Kannan and F. Andres (Eds.): ICDEM 2010, LNCS 6411, pp. 288–295, 2012.
© Springer-Verlag Berlin Heidelberg 2012

of resources at the server side [3]. As a remedial measure, dynamic web scripting languages were introduced. A dynamic web scripting languages is a language which reacts to a user's action.   They are used to embed interactivity to otherwise static Web pages. They can also automatically fill up parts of Web-based forms, among other uses. Science zine [4] described the capabilities of JavaScript, a popular Web scripting language: "Without any network transmission, an HTML page with embedded Java-Script can interpret the entered text and alert the user with a message dialog if the input is invalid. Or you can use JavaScript to perform an action (such as play an audio file, execute an Applet, or communicate with a plug-in) in response to the user opening or exiting a page."

One of the first dynamic scripting languages was Common Gateway Interface (CGI).   Using CGI the web programmers were able to produce scripts which were able to read input parameters and return an HTML page meeting specific user requirements) [5]. Development of CGI led to the hunt for more sophisticated and robust web scripting languages. PHP (Hypertext Preprocessor) followed the era of CGI. It is one of the most heavily used dynamic web scripting languages in the world. It is widely used to implement lightweight web applications and to access databases and other kinds of middleware. It was originally developed by Rasmus Lerdorf in 1995 [6]. It is open source software released under the PHP license. It can be easily embedded into an HTML source document. Then after, it can be interpreted by a web server with a PHP processor module generating the web document.

JavaServer Pages (JSP) is a technology which uses Java as supporting language. It aims at allowing programmers to utilize the vast capability of Java in building their web applications [9]. It by released by Sun Microsystem in 1999. It may be considered as a high-level abstraction of Java servlets. JSP pages are loaded in the server and operated from a Java server packet, often packaged as a .war or .ear file archive. It allows Java code and certain pre-defined actions to be intermixed with static web markup content, with the resulting page being compiled and executed on the server to deliver an HTML or XML document. The compiled pages and any dependent Java libraries use Java bytecode rather than a native software format, and must therefore be executed within a Java virtual machine (JVM) that integrates with the host operating system to provide an abstract platform-neutral environment.

ASP.NET is a web application framework designed by Microsoft to facilitate building web sites, web applications and web services. It follows a code behind model i.e. it deals with the dynamic program code by placing them in a separate file or in a separate tag [8]. Thus, it allows the designers and coders to work separately. It permits the programmers to build applications using an event-driven GUI model, rather than in conventional web-scripting environments like CGI, PHP, Python etc. The framework employs existing utilities such as JavaScript with internal components like "ViewState" to bring persistent state to the inherently stateless web environment. The ASP.NET in itself is not a pro-gramming language. It is built on a Common Language Runtime(CLR) allowing the programmers to choose any language form a wide pool of languages such as Python , VB.NET, C#.NET   J#, Delphi.NET, Chrome etc to code the web application under consideration. A complete list of languages allowed in ASP.NET is given on [10].

The table below depicts a brief comparison between PHP, ASP.NET and JSP based on some general parameters.

Table 1. A brief comparison between PHP, JSP and ASP.NET

Area	PHP	JSP	ASP.NET
Licensing cost	Free licensing	Free licensing	Costly Licensing
Platform(s)	Multiple	Multiple	Windows only
External Hosting	Widely available with zero cost	Not so available although free	Widely available although requires fee
Security	Very good	Good	Good
Scalability	Scales very well	Scales well when configured properly	Can be difficult to scale
Configuration flexibility	Extremely flexible	Moderately flexible	Not very flexible
Framework(s)	Many available	Standard framework	Standard framework

The table given below depicts sample codes of PHP, JSP and ASP.NET outputting Hello World!

Table 2. Examples of PHP, JSP and ASP.NET scripts with HTML

PHP Script	JSP Script	ASP.NET Script	HTML result
<html><body> <?php echo "Hello World!"; ?></body> </html>	<html><body> <%="Hello World!" %> </body> </html>	<html><body> <% Response.Write("Hello World!"); %></body> </html>	Hello World!

In this paper, we intend to study the impact of three different and famous web scripting languages viz. PHP, JSP, ASP.NET on the performance of a web server. Although a wide variety of languages can be used with ASP.NET, in our study, we have used C# along with it. We conduct experiments on some standard benchmarks using both built-in modules and self- written codes.

1.1   Client Server Architecture

Client–server model of computing is a sort of distributed application structure [7].It is used by almost all the web scripting languages. The languages discussed in this paper also use it. In this section we provide an overview of this architecture.

Client server architecture divides the workloads between different service stations known as servers, and service requesters, called clients. Generally, servers and clients communicate over a network; however, they may lie on the same system. Such systems in which servers and clients lie on the same machine are called virtual machine. A server machine is a host which is running one or more server programs sharing its resources with clients. A client shares none of its resources. However it can always request a server's content or service function. Clients, hence, initiate communications with servers. Fig. 1 depicts the Client –Server architecture over the World Wide Web.

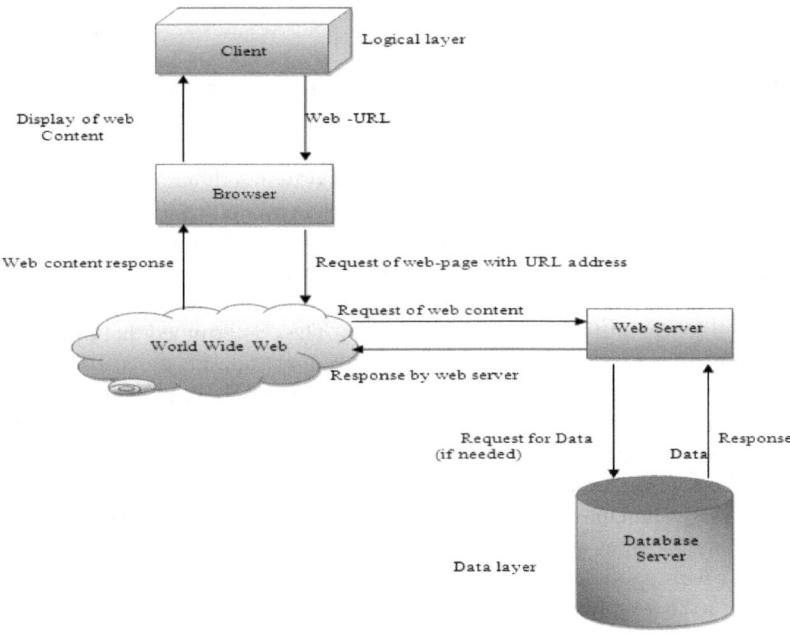

Fig. 1. Client Server Architecture

In our experiments, we have used the client- server architecture having both clients and servers residing on the same system. These types of systems are advantageous for debugging and testing purpose of web script language programming. While building any application, a programmer can test on his own computer whether the application is working as per his expectations or not. If not, he can change the application right on his computer. These tasks can be performed without the overhead of uploading the codes on any distant server time and again. Examples of such systems include LAMP, WAMP, and SAMP etc.

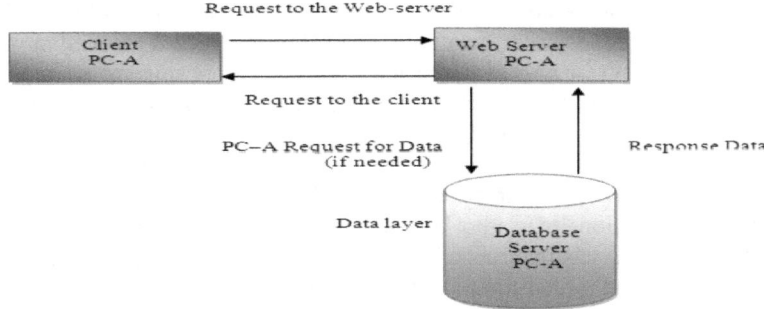

Fig. 2. Client and Server on the Single PC

2   Literature Survey

There has been a heavy research evaluating the performances of static and dynamic web contents. In paper [11], a sophisticated study was performed about the effect of dynamic contents on the performance of web servers. It was revealed that it is extremely slow to retrieve a web page when coupled with a dynamic scripting language, in this case Common Gateway Interface (CGI), than when it is a plain static web page.

In paper [12], the authors concluded that the personalization of web pages comes at a price. The processing required for dynamic web pages and the overhead arising out of the database access often result in a negative impact on the performance of the web server. The authors have quantified each of these effects. They determined that these effects as a whole diminish up to a factor of 8 the highest request rate bolstered by any user. The results obtained by them suggested that Java outperformed both PHP and Perl. They also inferred that web server performances under overload can be quite unpredictable. They also concluded that PHP, Perl and Jetty which are dynamic content generation technology are quite robust while some other technologies such as Resin are not.

In paper [13], Ramana studied the performances of MySQL and PHP components in the Linux environment using LAMP (Linux, Apache, MySQL, PHP) architecture. They built a web application with the help of LAMP and measured the performance with respect to the application. They quantified the improvement in performance that would increase if one was coded in C as against PHP. They also did some application level benchmarking comparative study on the performance of the application on Linux and Windows environments. They concluded that Apache outperforms Windows with IIS when the program was coded in PHP and the persistence was with MySQL. They also showed that Windows armed with Apache, PHP and MySQL falls in between.

Cecchet et al., in paper [14], compared three middleware architectures for generating dynamic web contents: PHP, Java servlets, and Enterprise Java Beans (EJB). They attached PHP to the Web server. They set the database interfaces in PHP to be adhoc and wrote it separately for each and every database. They determined that Java servlets execute independently rendering independence from any particular database. They achieved so doing all database operations using JDBC. EJB employed a component based approach which was platform-independent. It divided the business logic and the presentation logic in different tiers. Also the code for auction site using Java servlets was lengthier than that employing PHP implementation. The same holds for the online bookstore. They concluded that Java tools and safety properties associated with it did help in debugging, but it also required multiple re-casts posing many trade-offs between typed and untyped languages. Although EJB was determined to be quite easy to use, as it did not require written SQL queries, the implementation done by the authors required more lines of code in Java than in that required in servlets. It was due to the fact that they required many interfaces which were required to be implemented to structure the application logic into beans. PHP scripts were determined to be more efficient than Java servlets in terms of performance. However, PHP scripts were tied to the Web server and provided limited functionality and runtime support whereas Java servlets execute in a different process from the Web server. The authors used it to achieve better performance when web server is proved to be the bottleneck. The authors determined that servlets can be used to improve performance if there is database lock contention application. They also concluded that EJB offers the most flexible architecture. EJB offers many software engineering qualities such as modularity, portability, and maintainability. However it was determined that the EJB is less efficient than the Java servlets and PHP.

In paper [15], the authors presented three benchmarks for dynamic web sites with differing characteristics: an online bookstore, an auction site, and a bulletin board. They carried out bottleneck characterization of the benchmarks.

3   Experiments and Analysis

In order to compare the performances between PHP, JSP and ASP.NET, we have used the following versions of the languages under consideration. These are the latest versions of the above three languages.

- PHP 5.3.2
- JSP 2.1
- ASP.NET 4.0 (Microsoft .NET framework)

In order to carry out the experiments, we have used a machine possessing 1 GB main memory and a 1.83 GHz dual core processor with windows XP service pack 2 as the operating system. We used Apache 2.2.6, Apache Tomcat 6.0.26 and IIS 7.5 as the web servers.

We compared the three languages on the basis of the following four benchmarks,

- Finding the factorial of 100 (factorial benchmark).
- Determining whether a random word having 1 million characters is a palindrome or not (palindrome benchmark).
- Sorting a list of 1 million random integers using merge sort [17] (merge sort benchmark).
- Running Dijkstra's algorithm on a graph with 1000 nodes and 5000 edges [18] (Dijkstra benchmark).

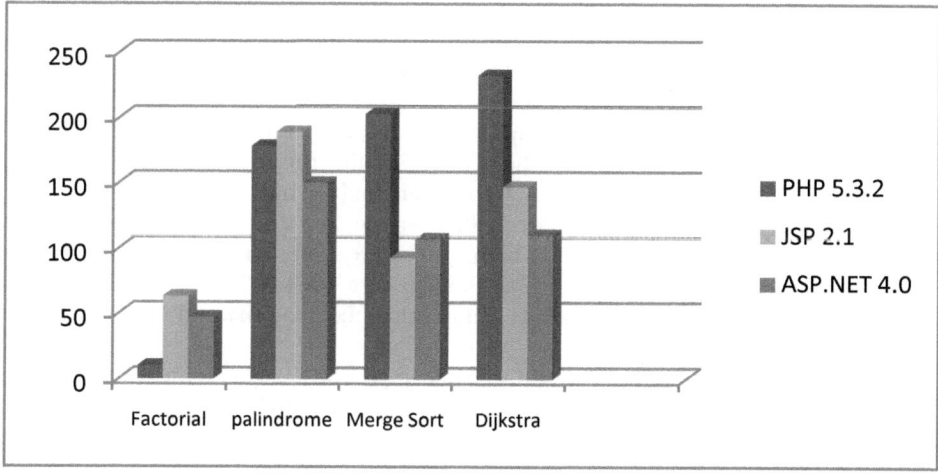

Fig. 3. Execution time using self- written codes

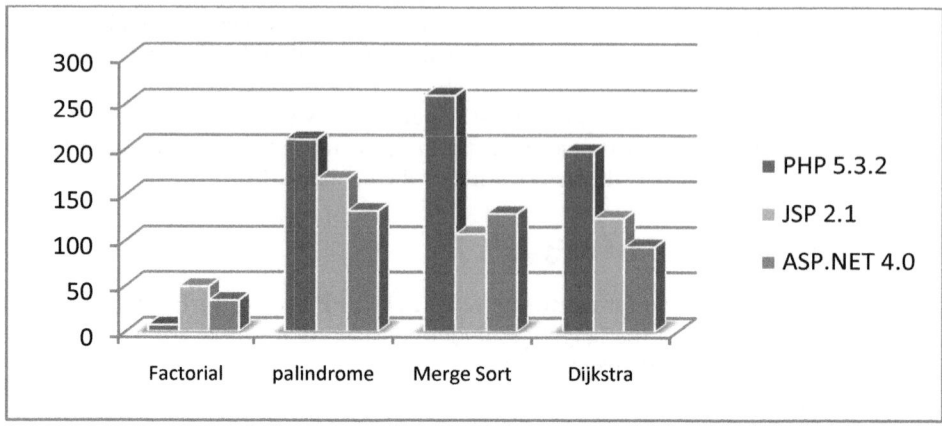

Fig. 4. Execution time using built-in modules

We conducted experiments on the above four benchmarks using the three languages under consideration. We used both self-written codes and built-in modules of the above four benchmarks in all the three languages. In ASP.NET we actually used C# since ASP.NET in itself is not a language rather it is a framework. We conducted 1000 tests on each benchmark with each language and calculated the total runtime of the execution.

Fig.3 depicts the total execution time of the three languages over 1000 tests on the four benchmarks using self-written codes. Similarly Fig. 4 depicts the total execution time of the three languages over 1000 tests on the four benchmarks using built-in modules.

4   Conclusions and Future Work

We carried out sophisticated experiments to ascertain the performances of three web scripting languages viz. PHP, JSP and ASP.NET. We have shown the results in Fig. 3 and Fig. 4. Fig. 3 depicts the experimental results for the self-written codes while the Fig. 4 depicts the experimental results for built-in modules. It can be easily concluded from the graphs that no language excels under all circumstances. If we consider numerical calculation, we can conclude that PHP works the best out of the three languages under consideration as shown by the actions of the three languages on factorial benchmark. It holds for both self-written codes and built-in modules. On the contrary, if we consider comparison based problems such merge sort, JSP comes out to the clear winner out of the three languages for both self- written and built-in modules. One can infer, in case of complex problems such as Dijkstra's algorithm and problems pertaining to string manipulations such as palindrome checking that ASP.NET performs stupendously.

In our experiments, we have used C# as the supporting language in ASP.NET .We know that we have a very large pool of languages available to be used as the supporting language with ASP.NET [10]. In future, experiments can be aimed at using different languages with ASP.NET.

References

1. Berners-Lee, T., Connolly, D.: Hypertext Markup Language – 2.0, RFC1866, MIT/W3C (1995)
2. Govindaraju, M., Slominski, A., Chiu, K., Liu, P., Engelen, R.V., Lewis, M.J.: Toward Characterizing the Performance of SOAP Toolkits. In: Proceedings of the 5th IEEE/ACM International Workshop on Grid Computing (2004)
3. Berners-Lee, T., Fielding, R.T., Nielsen, H.F.: Hypertext Transfer Protocol — HTTP/1.0, Internet RFC 1945 (1996)
4. Science zine, http://encyclozine.com/technology/computer/internet/web/JavaScript
5. Coar, K., Robinson, D.: The WWW Common Gateway Interface version 1.1, Internet draft (1999)
6. Lerdorf, R.: Programming PHP. O'Reilly Media, California (2002)
7. Berson, A.: Client/server architecture. McGraw-Hill Companies, New York (1992)
8. MacDonald, M.: ASP.NET: The Complete Reference. McGraw-Hill Companies, New York (2002)
9. Hanna, P.: JSP 2.0: The Complete Reference. McGraw-Hill Companies, New York (2003)
10. dotnetpowered Language List, http://www.dotnetpowered.com/languages.aspx
11. Yeager, N., McGrath, R.: Web Server Technology: The Advanced Guide for World Wide Web Information Providers. Morgan-Kaufmann Publishers, Inc., San Francisco (1996)
12. Titchkosky, L., Arlitt, M., Williamson, C.: A Performance Comparison of Dynamic Web Technologies. In: 11th IEEE/ACM International Symposium on Modeling, Analysis and Simulation of Computer Telecommunications Systems (2003)
13. Ramana, U., Prabhakar, T.: Some Experiments with the Performance of LAMP Architecture. In: Proceedings of the 2005 Fifth International Conference on Computer and Information Technology (2005)
14. Cecchet, E., Chanda, A., Elnikety, S., Marguerite, J., Zwaenepoel, W.: Performance Comparison of Middleware Architectures for Generating Dynamic Web Content. In: Endler, M., Schmidt, D.C. (eds.) Middleware 2003. LNCS, vol. 2672, pp. 242–267. Springer, Heidelberg (2003)
15. Amza, C., et al.: Specification and implementation of dynamic Web site benchmarks. In: Proceedings of the 5th IEEE Workshop on Workload Characterization (2002)
16. Berners-Lee, T.: Information Management: A Proposal, CERN (1990)
17. Dijkastra, E.J.: A note on two problems in connection with graphs. Numerische Mathematic, pp. 269–271(1959)
18. Knuth, D.E.: Sorting by Merging. The Art of Computer Programming. Addison-Wesley, Massachusetts (1998)

Masquerader Classification System with Linux Command Sequences Using Machine Learning Algorithms

T. Subbulakshmi, S. Mercy Shalinie, and A. Ramamoorthi

Department of Computer Science and Engineering,
Thiagarajar College of Engineering, Madurai
{subbulakshmitce,shalinie_m}@yahoo.com
armoorthi@gmail.com

Abstract. Intrusion Detection System plays a major role in today's security infrastructure. Both insider and outsider threats could be addressed by intrusion detection systems where the other components fail to do so. Firewalls can address only outsider threats where the log files manipulation can address only insider threats. The objective of this research paper is to apply the classifiers for UNIX User data and find the best algorithm. From the available UNIX User data all 9100 instances are taken. The classification rate and the false positive rate are used as the performance criteria with 3 fold cross validation. It is found that ZeroR is giving high performance with low false alarm rate and high classification rate. Real time data in truncated and enriched formats are also applied to finalize the best algorithm under each category of classifier. Here 6824 instances are used. BayesNet and REPTree are found to be the best performing algorithms.

Keywords: False positives, Intrusion Detection, Cross Validation, Insider and Outsider Threats.

1 Introduction

The security of computer network plays a major role in modern computer systems. In order to enforce high protection levels, a number of software tools are currently available. A few systems are aimed to detect the intruder who eludes the "first line" protection. However completely removing security checks as they appear, at present, are unrealistic. We can now try to detect intrusion attempts so that action may be taken to repair the damage later. There are many categories of network intrusions.

Examples include SMTP (Send Mail) attacks, guessing passwords, IP Spoofing, buffer overflow attacks, multi scan attacks, Denial of Service such as ping-of- death, SYN flood, etc,. Intrusion Detection is the act of detecting actions that attempt to compromise the confidentiality, integrity or availability of the resource. Intrusion detection System (IDS) inspects all inbound and outbound network traffic. When intrusive activity occurs, IDS let you know about that by making an alarm. It can generate false positives or false negatives.

R. Kannan and F. Andres (Eds.): ICDEM 2010, LNCS 6411, pp. 296–302, 2012.
© Springer-Verlag Berlin Heidelberg 2012

False positive occurs when an alarm is generated for a normal activity. False negative occurs when no alarm is there for an abnormal activity. Misuse detection is different from anomaly detection under IDS categories. In misuse detection it analyzes the information that it gathers and then it compares to large databases of attack signatures. In anomaly detection it monitors network segments to compare their state to normal baseline and look for anomalies. Misuse Detection is a particularly difficult problem because the extensive vulnerabilities of computer systems and the creativity of attackers. Pattern matching systems such as rule-based expert systems, transition analysis and genetic algorithms (GA) are the direct and some what efficient ways to implement misused detection. Inductive sequential patterns, artificial neural networks (ANN) and statistical methods and data mining techniques are used for anomaly detection.

This paper applies each of the machine learning algorithms under each classifier category by using the weka tool which is freely available on different sets of data. There it applies each of the machine learning algorithms under different classifier categories on the Unix User data and Real time data. The performance of each machine learning algorithm is evaluated on each dataset.

The criteria for performance evaluation that we have taken mainly are the classification rate, false positive rate alone. Based on their values under each category of classifiers the best performing algorithm is only taken into consideration. The value of classification performance for that best under each of the classifier category in Weka is only tabulated for each subset of records out of the dataset that we are using here.

2 Related Work

Intrusion detection Technology is an effective approach to dealing with network security. Misuse Detection uses well defined patterns of the attack that exploit weaknesses in system and application software to identify intrusions. These patterns are encoded in advance and used to detect intrusions normally.

An approach that uses the representation of a bag of system calls [Honavar, Dae-Ki Kang and Doug Fuller, 2005] in system call sequence is proposed. It has been shown by them that this representation us very suitable for well known attacks and trivially modified attacks. If the attacker is known of IDS the approach will fail as they mentioned in the paper.

Genetic algorithm is used for anomaly detection [Zhou Jian, Haruhiko Shirai, Isamu Takahashi, Jousuke Kuroiwa,Tomohiro Odaka and Hisakazu Ogura,2007a] by using Schonlau dataset and a hybrid command sequence model from historical session data is trained and the model is used as a criterion for verifying observed behavior.

An SCS model is constructed from historical session profile data of individual users. If the observed session contains the command sequence regardless of the location in that session it is labeled as legal. It could not fit to the situation where command combinations are involved. HCS model as an improvement of SCS model could describe multiple command sequence fragments and discrete commands in a single session so that it could recognize non sequential patterns. Training is done to find the optimal combinations of commands.

A command table is constructed and indexed by a numeric value for each command. The search operation is demonstrated and each gene in chromosome is encoded with the index and then decoded as a solution of HCS model. Then GA processing is done which involves an initialization and an evolution. The evolution includes fitness calculation, selection, cross over and mutation. The dataset is divided into 150 sessions with 100 commands for each session.

The experiments are done for 13 users over three months where for first 7 users 529 sessions used as training data and 521 sessions used as testing data and 465 sessions used as independent test data totaling 1515 sessions. These demonstrated that detection rate is more than 90\% against other statistical methods and 10\% higher than other command sequence model. The efficiency value is better and it gains the best cost with an FRR of 33.9\%.

The experiment is done by using p0f tool. 3-fold cross validation is applied for validating the results against one class SVM using supervised and unsupervised learning methods which are also then described. For one class SVM 94.65\% performance is attained as best using RBF kernel. Snort and Bro are the tools used for testing NIDS in real time.

Experiments show that 89.61\% detection rate with 14.19\% false alarm rate is achieved using K-gram kernel and 97.40\%, 23.77\% with string kernel respectively. When the k-parameter is 4 or more the string and K-gram kernels show bad performance. The K-gram and RBF kernel also have shown lower correlation coefficient of 0.59. Sequence based kernels are slightly better than the RBF kernels with same frequency of false alarms.

A Rule based approach for masquerade detection [Zhou Jian, Haruhiko Shirai, Isamu Takahashi, Jousuke Kuroiwa, Tomohiro Odaka, and Hisakazu Ogura, 2007b] is examined by using the common dataset of UNIX commands. It compares n-grams of command sequence using a technique known as boosting of decision stumps. Decision stump is the simplest form of decision tree which makes a decision by checking the presence and absence of a specified n-gram command sequence and rule based approach generates rules that are easier to interpret. It has a single decision node and two prediction values.

3   Dataset Used

The UNIX User dataset is used in our paper which contains two input attributes and one output attribute. The history and session are the two input attributes. The history attribute is numeric and the session attribute is nominal. History attribute specifies the line number with respect to the class attribute. The session attribute contains enriched command line argument given by the user in a UNIX terminal.

The dataset contains 9100 instances whereas an instance will be classified as it belongs to any one of the nine users based on the two input attributes. User0(562), User1(488), User2(755), User3(484), User4(911), User5(546), User6(2425), User7(1339), User8(1590), User9 (2345)are the possible values of the output attribute.

Then Real time data from a RedHat Linux Server involving seven Red Hat Linux Users has been used in our paper. The data has two attributes namely the line number and the enriched command line data. Based on the command line each instances are assumed as it is given by the masquerader or a normal user. Instances are categorized into two main categories. The records are manually assigned as a Masquerader such that if the record has a particular command it belongs to Masquerader category. The records are manually assigned as a Masquerader such that if the record has a particular command it belongs to Normal or Non-Masquerader category. We have used two different types of features in our Experiment. UNIX User Data contains all the three features and for Real time Data we used two features. 9,100 records of UNIX User Data are used for training of Machine Learning Algorithms.We are using 6824 records for testing the Machine Learning Algorithms as given in the table 2 below. The testing Data is used in both truncated and enriched formats. The Number of records U0 (978), U1 (736), U2 (1640), U3 (955), U4 (805), U5 (805), U6 (905).

4 System Model

In this paper the Detection System is modeled using the UNIX User dataset. This system model is developed with the objective of classifying the intrusions correctly with minimal false alarms. The system model is depicted in Fig. 1.

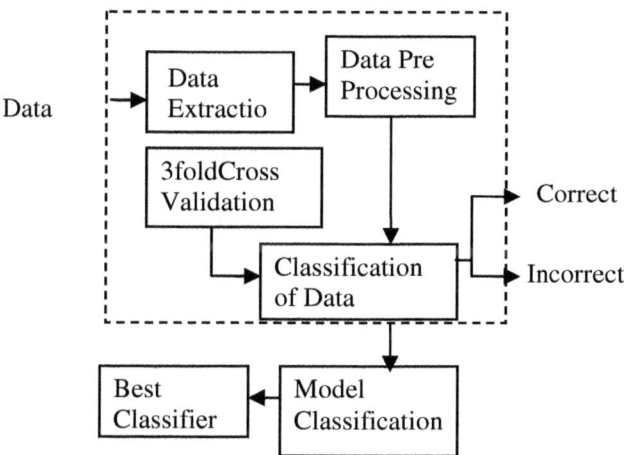

Fig. 1. Masquerader Detection System Architecture

4.1 Dataset

Here the UNIX User dataset is used which has 9100 instances involving 3 attributes. From the Real time dataset all instances are applied totaling 1376 instances.

4.2 Data Extraction

From the UNIX User dataset all instances involving all attributes are extracted. From the Real time command files all records are used.

4.3 Data Pre-processing

The extracted data is pre-processed such that it can be accepted as input to the classifier. The input files are prepared for both the sets of random collection. Every attribute is defined using it's data type and values for the attributes is also specified. The final input files are now ready to be fed as input to the classifier. For UNIX User data the files are converted into CSV or arff files For Real time data the files are separately maintained for enriched and truncated command line formats.

4.4 3fold Cross Validation

3-fold cross validation is done for each datasets where the instances are divided into so many numbers of samples and 3 samples are used for testing and the remaining samples are used for training the respective classifiers.

4.5 Classification of Misuse Data

The input files are given to the classifier with all the attributes one by one. The classifier is chosen from the category of classifiers. The type of cross validation is specified and the dependent class is selected. The classifier evaluation options like output model, output class-stats, output entropy evaluation measures, output confusion matrix, output predictions, store predictions for visualization and cost sensitive evaluation are given. There exist 2 kinds of instances. Actually the instance is said to be correctly classified if its class category is same as what is predicted by the classification algorithm. An instance is called an incorrectly classified instance if it is predicted as it belongs to some other class by the classification algorithm.

Then the classifier starts classifying the data and displays the result. The final classification will give the number of records that are correctly classified and the number of records that are incorrectly classified. The error values are displayed. The confusion matrix is also drawn. The performance measures Precision, Recall and F-Measure are calculated from the results.

4.6 Model Evaluation

Here the built model is evaluated. In this stage several options are available in weka. The model alone can be displayed. For each class too it can be shown. Entropy evaluation measures can be seen. Confusion matrix can be generated. Predictions can be stored. These predictions may be used in visualization. Cost sensitive evaluation can be made. Predictions can be made available for display. For cost sensitive evaluation random seed has to be set and for detailed evaluation cost matrix editor can be tuned.

4.7 Best Classifier

The classification algorithms that are applicable on both of these subsets under each classifier category are evaluated. The per-class stats and the entropy evaluation measures related to each algorithm on each subset of the data are noted down. Based on these measures the best performing algorithm under each classifier category is tabulated. Classification rate, False Positive Rate and Time to build the model are mainly used as the performance measures for comparisons.

5 Results and Comparison

With respect to the Classification Rate (CR) and False Positive Rate (FPR) we have found that ZeroR of Rules category is the best performing algorithm than the other best performing classifier algorithms in their respective categories. The VFI is the best under Miscellaneous and User Classifier is the best under trees category and CVParameter Selection is the best under Meta category.

Table 1. given below provides the algorithms that are best performing under each classifier category for enriched command line formatted real time data. Here the OneR algorithm under Rules category of classifier is the best performing one when compared to all other category of algorithms. When considering False Positive Rate(FPR) alone OneR is well by gaining lesser value near to zero and when considering Classification Rate(CR) Random Tree is the best performing one with a value near to 100%.

Table 1. Performance Results for UNIX User Data

S.No	Classifier	CR	FPR	Duration	Precision	Recall	FMeasure
1	CVParameter Selection	26.64	0.266	0.06	0.071	0.112	0.266
2	ZeroR	50.85	0.045	0	0.071	0.112	0.266
3	VFI	26.64	0.266	0	0.68	0.541	0.509
4	User Classifier	26.64	0.266	0.61	0.071	0.112	0.266

Table 2 given below lists the results about the high performance algorithms under each of the classifier category that are applied on truncated real time data. Here also OneR is found to be the best performing algorithm overall. When considering Classification Rate (CR) alone Bayes Net of Bayes category is found as best. When False Positive Rate (FPR) alone is considered, RBF Network of Functions category is found to be the best performing one.

Table 2. Performance Results For Enriched Real Time Data

S.No	Classifier	CR	FPR	Duration	Precision	Recall	F Measure
1	OneR	93.09	0.269	0	0.92	0.931	0.921
2	Hyper Pipes	92.65	0.299	0	0.917	0.927	0.899
3	IBK	93.07	0.270	0	0.92	0.931	0.921
4	HNB	93.06	0.275	0.61	0.92	0.931	0.921
5	Random Tree	93.08	0.279	0.06	0.92	0.931	0.921
6	Bagging	93.01	0.289	0.17	0.92	0.93	0.921
7	SMO	92.15	0.372	24.38	0.918	0.993	0.954

Table 3 given below lists the other performance values of the best performing algorithms under each classifier category.

Table 3. Performance Results for Truncated Real Time Data

S.No	Classifier	CR	FPR	Duration	Precision	Recall	FMeasure
1	OneR	93.65	0.236	0.6	0.945	0.979	0.962
2	Hyper Pipes	93.01	0.348	0	0.922	0.998	0.959
3	IBK	93.65	0.236	0.37	0.945	0.979	0.962
4	Bayes Net	93.73	0.277	0	0.937	0.990	0.963
5	Random Committee	93.65	0.236	0.16	0.945	0979	0.962
6	REPTree	93.73	0.288	0	0.947	0.980	0.963
7	RBFNetwork	93.44	0.225	12.46	0.947	0.974	0.96

6 Conclusion and Future Work

In our experiment we have evaluated the performance of all machine learning algorithms and compared the results using UNIX User dataset and Real time data in enriched and truncated formats. In future by using weka tool we will test the real time data for each of the algorithm and note down the performance values such as Classification rate, False Positive Rate, and Cost to build the model. Thereby we will find which algorithm is best performing in real time networked and clustered environment.

References

1. Kang, D.-K., Fuller, D., Honavar, V.: Learning Classifiers For Misuse And Anomaly DetectionUsing A Bag of System Calls Representation. In: Proc. IEEE Workshop on Information Assurance and Security (IAW 2005). United States Military Academy, West Point (2005)
2. Jian, Z., Shirai, H., Takahashi, I., Kuroiwa, J., Odaka, T., Ogura, H.: Hybrid Command Sequence Model for Anomaly Detection. In: Zhou, Z.-H., Li, H., Yang, Q. (eds.) PAKDD 2007. LNCS (LNAI), vol. 4426, pp. 108–118. Springer, Heidelberg (2007a)
3. Shon, T., Moon, J.: A hybrid machine learning approach to network anomaly detection. Information Sciences International Journal 177(18), 3799–3821 (2007)
4. Seo, J., Cha, S.: Masquerade Detection based on SVM and Sequence-based User Commands Profile. In: ACM Symposium on Information, Computer and Communications Security, March 20-22 (2007)
5. Jian, Z., Shirai, H., Takahashi, I., Kuroiwa, J., Odaka, T., Ogura, H.: Masquerade detection by boosting decision stumps using UNIX commands. Elsevier Journal on Computers and Security 26(4) (June 2007b)

Parsing Operations Based Approach towards Phishing Attacks

Gaurav Kumar Tak and Shashikala Tapaswi

ABV- Indian Institute of Information Technology and Management
Gwalior (M.P.), India
gauravtakswm@gmail.com, stapaswi@hotmail.com

Abstract. Currently, web attacks are so popular attacks under cyber crime category. Generally phishing attacks, SSL attacks and some other hacking attacks are kept into this category. Security against these attacks is the major issue of internet security.

This paper presents an new approach of parsing operation analysis of web URLs to provide the security against web attacks. This methodology is based on various parsing operations which use many techniques to detect the phishing attacks as well as other web attacks. This approach is completely based on the browser operation and also affects the speed of browsing. This approach also includes some DB-generated query operation, detection operation of the URL details and etc. Using proposed methodology, a new browser easily detects the phishing attacks, SSL attacks, and some other hacking attacks. With the use of this browser approach, we can easily achieve 98.14% security against phishing as well as web attacks.

Keywords: Parsing, Phishing, URL, Web attacks.

1 Introduction

In Current scenario, cyber crime is a popular and major issue over the internet. These crimes can easily be defined as immoral actions that include illegal access of data, illegal interception of data, eavesdropping of unauthorized data over an information technology infrastructure , data interference(which includes unauthorized damaging, deletion, deterioration, alteration or suppression of computer data),Unethical access of web services , Disturbance of social-peace, systems interference (interfering with the functioning of a computer system by inputting, transferring, destroying, removing, deteriorating, altering or suppressing computer data), misuse of devices, forgery (ID theft), and electronic fraud[1,4].

Cyber crime issues have become high-profile, particularly those surrounding hacking, copyright infringement, child pornography and child grooming.

In the field of internet security, phishing is the most popular web attack. Phishing can be defined as the criminally fraudulent process of attempting to acquire sensitive user information(such as usernames, passwords) and other confidential information(like security key and credit card or debit card details , master card details) by masquerading as a trustworthy entity in an electronic communication.

R. Kannan and F. Andres (Eds.): ICDEM 2010, LNCS 6411, pp. 303–308, 2012.
© Springer-Verlag Berlin Heidelberg 2012

Communications purporting to be from popular social web sites, auction sites, online payment Gateway or IT administrators are commonly used to lure the unsuspecting public. Phishing attacks are typically carried out by e-mail or instant messaging and they often direct users to enter details at a fake website whose look and feel are almost identical to the legitimate one. Even when using server authentication, they may require tremendous skill to detect that the website is fake. Phishing is an example of social engineering techniques used to fool users, and exploit the poor usability of current web security technologies, to break the security system of many web services, to access many authorized information unethically [8].

In this document, we are proposing the new technique for stopping phishing attacks by introducing the concept of parsing the web-URL before visiting the URL(Uniform Resource Locator) .Multi parsers are used for multiple operations, to detect the phishing attacks. Here in this methodology the browser will be more participating in the process of detecting the phishing attacks.

2 Related Work

Many techniques and algorithms had been developed and implemented for prevention of phishing and to secure the thefts of confidential information (usernames, passwords, security key, credit card /debit card/master card details).But there are also some issues are remaining on this matter.

Many techniques and schemes are proposed to provide a secure environment for e-banking services, e-commerce services and payment gateway services and to block the sniffing, eavesdropping etc. So that transmission of the confidential information will be preserved and unauthorized personnel can't access that information.

But day by day, phishing attacks are increasing. While most phishing attacks target the financial transaction website (Banking site, e-commerce, e-shopping website, payment gateway websites), more and more phishing incidents targeting online game operators and large ISPs (internet service provider) have also been discovered.

Many approaches (e.g. toolbars) have been proposed to prevent phishing attacks. The anti-phishing toolbars is also so common but not a user friendly approach out of them. It is based on web browser plug-ins that warns browsers when they visit any suspected phishing site. Commonly, anti-phishing tools use two major approaches for mitigating phishing sites. The first approach is based on heuristics to check the host name and the URL for common spoofing techniques. The second method lists out some blacklist phishing URLs. The heuristics approach is not 100% accurate since it produces low false negatives (FN), i.e. a phishing site is mistakenly judged as legitimate, which implies they do not correctly identify all phishing sites. The heuristics often produce high false positives (FP), i.e. incorrectly identifying a legitimate site as fraudulent. Blacklists have a high level of accuracy because they are constructed by paid experts who verify a reported URL and add it to the blacklists if it is considered as a phishing website [1, 4, 8].

Detection and identification of phishing websites in real-time, particularly for e-banking /payment gateway website, is really a complex and dynamic problem involving many factors and criteria. Many methods like improving site authenticity, one time password, having separate login and transaction password, personalized e-mail communication, user education about phishing are being implemented to prevent phishing attacks, but they don't provide high security.

3 Proposed Methodology

Proposed browser based methodology against phishing attacks is based on some facts of domains ,like most of time phishing websites are new registered domains and they have some identical portion of the real website domain. Here we propose query based analyzer approach against phishing attacks.

Our methodology uses some knowledge base which contains the information about previous blacklisted web domain for the particular user. Using the some previous attacks, detection of phishing attack is also performed.

In proposed methodology web-URL is parsed into various parsers to detect the phishing attacks. Proposed browser based approach, follow the few steps which are as follows:

1. Initially web URL is parsed into parser-A. During the parsing operation, if parser-A find 4 or more dots (.) letters in the web URL then it generates a pop-up alert box for the URL address, because URL can be a phishing website URL.

    This parsing step is based on the fact, that phishing attackers use the some fraction of the actual URL to generate the phishing URL with the combination of some dots (.) letters, but this is not always true for each phishing website. So proposed browser methodology also follow some other steps to detect the phishing attacks and provide a secure platform for the transmission of information and confidential data over the internet.

    Like URL *http://www.firstgenericbank.com.account-updateinfo.com/*, this URL contains 4 dots in itself and it is also phishing URL of First Generic Bank.

2. After completing the parser- A operation, URL is parsed into parser-B. This parser is used to get the other details of the URL (like year of domain registration, rating of the domain, popularity of the domain etc.).Using those details parser-B declares the URL is phishing website URL or actual website URL.

    Like Internet Explorer 7.0 browser also use the site rating to detect the phishing websites, but many times it is not user friendly and not able to detect all attacks.

3. After successful completion of above 2 steps, URL enters into parser-C. Operation of parser-C is db-generated query operation. Parser-C uses the fact that the web-URL is already visited by that specific user then it will be maintained in the history database of web browser of that user. During the parsing operation, it generates a query to find the trusted zone status of that particular URL. If the URL is already present in trusted zone for that user, then it will declare the URL as a safe and secure URL otherwise it will declare the URL as first visited URL.

This trusted zone db of the URLs can be different for the different user. So this db is completely dependent upon the website status which is already specified by the particular user.

4. After the finishing the above 3 operations ;URL enters into parser-D and parser-D is more analytical parser which analyze the URL and also title-tag content of the URL and finds other URLs whose pattern are like the analyzed URL, Compare all URLs using the URL details(like year of domain registration, rating of the domain ,popularity of the domain etc.) and display the results on the browser screen before redirecting to the web page. Parser-D also uses some information which is already analyzed with the help of parser-B.

Mozilla Firefox 3.6.4 use some fraction of step 4, it displays the URLs which is already visited by the user when the user enter some keywords of a URL. Firefox use some pattern matching approach for the previously visited URLs and new URL.

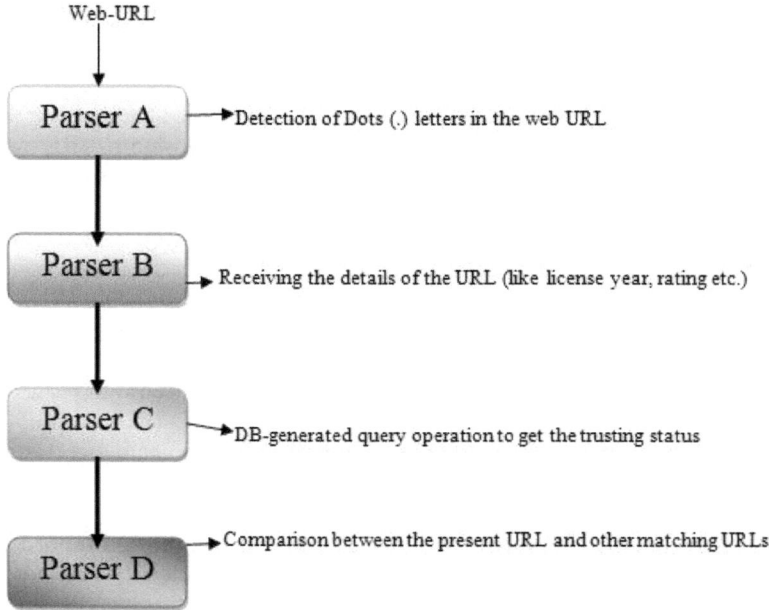

Fig. 1. Diagrammatic Representation of Parsing Operation of the URL

4   Implementation and Results

We have implemented the proposed methodology with the help of Java programming, Java network APIs, and using some web scripts languages and analyzed the results using the history of URLs of the Mozilla Firefox URL. Proposed methodology also uses the crawling step to analyze the URL over World Wide Web. We can implement this methodology with some new add-ons to install in present web browsers (like other Firefox add-ons).

We have analyzed the URL visited with the help of browser. The proposed methodology provides 98.14 % security against phishing attacks and some hacking attacks. We have not implemented our proposed methodology for during Dec, 2009 and Jan, 2010 but implemented during Feb, 2010 to April, 2010.

The following table data represents the recorded activities of the Web URLs in the other browser and in the new 'AP -beta version 1.0 browser' towards the phishing attacks and some hacking attacks.

Table 1. URL and some Web Attacks Analysis

Month	Dec,09	Jan,10	Feb,10	Mar,10	Apr,10
No. of URLs visited	897	901	813	1072	1193
Phishing Attacks	17	13	11	14	16
Detected phishing attacks with the browser	13	10	11	13	15
SSL Attacks	83	72	93	103	107
Detected SSL attacks with the browser	63	59	92	101	106
Some other Hacking attacks	6	9	7	13	12
Detected Hacking attacks with the browser	3	7	7	12	12

5   Conclusion and Limitation

Our proposed methodology is inspired by a problem with a large number of Phishing, SSL and other web attacks, we have encountered. We have recorded the web URLs activities of with the usage of proposed methodology and without usage of proposed methodology over 5 months. From data, we have analyzed the attacks and detected attacks over the time. The experiment results provide the complete scenario of the problem and security over the web. Our system indicated that the 98.14% security over the browsing. Table 1 represents the recorded data over the 5 months time period.

Limitations of the proposed method are that due to various parsing operations, its time complexity and space complexity is higher. So many times, it increases the browsing time of web browser. Due to slower speed of browsing, generally web users avoid this type of higher web security.

Acknowlegdement. The authors would like to thank ABV-Indian Institute of Information Technology and Management, Gwalior for the support provided for this work.

References

1. Ollmann, G.: The Phishing Guide Understanding & Preventing Phishing Attacks, NGS Software Insight Security Research
2. Aburrous, M., Hossain, M.A., Dahal, K., Thabatah, F.: Modelling Intelligent Phishing Detection System for E-banking Using Fuzzy Data Mining. In: 2009 International Conference on CyberWorlds, CW, pp. 265–272 (2009)
3. Abu-Nimeh, S., Nair, S.: Bypassing Security Toolbars and Phishing Filters via DNS Poisoning. In: Global Telecommunications Conference, IEEE GLOBECOM 2008, November 30-December 4, pp. 1–6. IEEE (2008)
4. Yu, W.D., Nargundkar, S., Tiruthani, N.: A phishing vulnerability analysis of web based systems. In: IEEE Symposium on Computers and Communications, ISCC 2008, July 6-9, pp. 326–331 (2008)
5. Alnajim, A., Munro, M.: An Anti-Phishing Approach that Uses Training Intervention for Phishing Websites Detection. In: Proceedings of the 2009 Sixth International Conference on Information Technology: New Generations (ITNG 2009), pp. 405–410. IEEE Computer Society, Washington, DC (2009),
   http://dx.doi.org/10.1109/ITNG.2009.109
6. Chen, J., Guo, C.: Online Detection and Prevention of Phishing Attacks. In: Proc. Chinacom 2006 (2006)
7. Beginning PHP5, Apache, and MySQL Web Development by Elizabeth Naramore, Jason Gerner, Yann Le Scouarnec, Jeremy Stolz, Michael K. Glass ISBN: 9780764579660
8. Sophos White Paper, Phishing and the threat to corporate networks (2005)
9. PHP, AJAX, MySql and JavaScript Tutorials, http://www.w3schools.com/
10. Prentice Hall - Deitel - Java How to Program, 4th edn., Java_2_Complete_Reference_5E, Java - How To Program, 6th edn.
11. von Ahn, L., Blum, M., Hopper, N.J., Langford, J.: CAPTCHA: Using Hard AI Problems for Security. In: Biham, E. (ed.) EUROCRYPT 2003. LNCS, vol. 2656, pp. 294–311. Springer, Heidelberg (2003)
12. Gedam, D.N.: RSA Based Confidentiality And Integrity Enhancements in SCOSTA-CL, A Thesis report, Department of Computer Science and Engineering, Indian Institute of Technology, Kanpur, India (July 2009)

Efficient Mining of Frequent Items Coupled with Weight and /or Support over Progressive Databases

B.N. Keshavamurthy, Mitesh Sharma, and Durga Toshniwal

Department of Electronics and Computer Engineering,
Indian Institute of Technology,
Roorkee,
Uttarakhand, India
{kesavdec,mitusuec,durgafec}@iitr.ernet.in

Abstract. In recent times, mining of frequent pattern in progressive databases is a very attractive area of research. In real world applications such as market basket analysis of retail-shop where the items are associated static attribute weight, which reflects each item has different importance and dynamic attribute support, which represents the frequency of an item. The mining of items which is having both static and dynamic attributes reveals an important knowledge than the traditional patterns. We use two notions in the process of mapping input items to general tree structure. One, the product of dynamic attribute value support and static attribute weight should be greater than user defined threshold. Second, the dynamic attribute value support should be greater than user defined threshold. Our proposed approach uses sliding window and apriori's antimonotone principle in mining the items associated weight and/or support over progressive databases.

Keywords: progressive databases, frequent item, supported item, weighted item.

1 Introduction

In recent years, due to the advancement of computing storage technology, digital data can be easily collected. It is very difficult to analyze the entire data manually. Thus a lot of works is going on for mining and analyzing such data using data mining techniques.

Of the various techniques of data mining analysis, sequential pattern analysis is one of the active areas of research work. Data sequence is a list of transactions, where each transaction contains a set of literals called items. Given a specified minimum support threshold, the sequential pattern mining finds all the subsequences in the sequence of databases. The sequential pattern mining was first addressed by Agarwal and Srikanth [1]. In general sequential pattern mining can be classified into three classes. (i) Apriori based horizontal partitioning methods [2], (ii) Apriori based vertical partitioning methods [3] and (iii) Projection based pattern algorithms [4], [5], [6], [7].

On the other hand in many domains, the content of the databases are uploaded incrementally. In order to get all the sequential patterns, the mining algorithms has to run whenever database changes because some data sequences which are not frequent

R. Kannan and F. Andres (Eds.): ICDEM 2010, LNCS 6411, pp. 309–316, 2012.
© Springer-Verlag Berlin Heidelberg 2012

in old database may become an frequent in updated database. Thus key concepts of incremental sequential pattern mining algorithms along with support and weight were introduced [8], [9], [10].

Both mining of frequent items on sequential and incremental data sets have been studied extensively. However, progressive sequential databases have posed new challenges because its inherent character such as it should not only add new items to the existing database but also removes the obsolete items from the database. The initial study on progressive sequential pattern mining was given by Jen W. et al. [11].

The rest of the paper is organized as follows: Section 2 contains problem definition followed by proposed systems. Section 3 presents representation technique for mining of frequency coupled weighted frequent items over data streams. Section 4 includes conclusion and references.

2 Proposed Work

2.1 Problem Statement

There are many research papers which have been discussed the progressive databases but the existing proposals do not efficiently extract the important hidden knowledge such as items coupled with static attribute weight and dynamic attribute support over progressive databases. So we map input items to general tree structure with two notions: one, the product of dynamic attribute value support and static attribute weight should be greater than user defined threshold. Second, the dynamic attribute value support should be greater than user defined threshold. Then mine frequent items from resulting tree. We have used sliding window concept to give more importance to the recent items than older items and apriori's antimonotone principle to prune the tree.

2.2 Proposed Issues

The general tree structure is used to solve the proposed issues. The construction of the tree is described as follows: The header–table is maintained to keep information about the present focus of the sliding window. The entry of header-table includes item-name, frequency or support and weight for each item. However, each node in a tree only maintains item-name and item batch number. The following two notions are used to decide whether the item is frequent is or not.

2.2.1 Item Dynamic Attribute Value Support and Static Attribute Value Weight, Are Considered for Deciding Frequentness of Item

We have considered the progressive database of Fig.1where we are operating the transactions in batch wise over a sliding window technique. Each batch has two transactions and the window size is three and the initial assumptions of weights for different items are given in weight-table.

In order to build the tree, the position of a node is decided first. This is decided based on the product of item dynamic attribute value support and static attribute weight. The node corresponding of item(s) which is (are) having higher value will be near the root and lower valued node will be far from the root. It helps even unnecessary growing of tree by growing the tree until items value satisfy user threshold.

To decide upon the priority over the items, Let us consider example of Fig. 2(a), in batch-1 the initial order of the items is < a, e, d, g, f, b, c, h >, which is only by consider the static attribute weights but after considering both dynamic attribute support and its static attribute weigh (i.e., <a:4.2,g:1.14, c:1,e:1, d:0.4, f:0.31, b:0.3, h:0.2>) its order is <a, g, c, e, d, f, b, h >. Similarly in other cases, the order of the items may or may not be same as its prior assumed weights, when we consider both support and weight for each batch or window. Fig.2a shows the tree construction for tree after inserting items of batch-1. Fig. 2b shows the tree after insertion batch-2 items, where as Fig.2c gives the resulting tree after insertion of batch-3 which is nothing but the window-1 final tree.

When the window slides from window-1 to window-2, it removes the items of batch-1 and adds the items of batch-4. Window-2 focuses items of batch-2 to batch-4. The Fig.3 gives the resulting trees. When the window slides from window-1 to window-2, it removes the items of batch-1 and adds the items of batch-4. Window-2 focuses items of batch-2 to batch-4. The resulting trees are given in Fig.3 and all the necessary tables are associated as follows:

Fig. 1. Example of transaction database, items coupled with support

Table 1. Header Table 1 (Batch-1)   **Table 2.** Header Table 2 (Batch-1 to Batch-2)

Item	Support	Weight	Node Priority
h	1	0.2	0.2
c	4	0.25	1.0
b	1	0.3	0.3
f	1	0.31	0.31
g	3	0.38	1.14
d	1	0.4	0.4
e	2	0.5	1.0
A	6	0.7	4.2

Item	Support	Weight	Node Priority
h	3	0.2	0.6
c	4	0.25	1.0
b	3	0.3	0.9
f	3	0.31	0.91
g	5	0.38	1.9
d	3	0.4	1.2
e	4	0.5	2.0
a	7	0.7	4.9

Table 3. Header Table 3 (Batch-1to Batch-3)   **Table 4.** Header Table 3 (Batch-2 to Batch-4)

Item	Support	Weight	Node Priority
a	10	0.7	7.0
c	5	0.25	1.25
g	6	0.38	2.88
e	6	0.5	3.0
d	6	0.4	2.4
f	3	0.31	0.93
b	6	0.3	1.8
h	3	0.2	0.6

Item	Support	Weight	Node Priority
h	2	0.2	0.4
c	3	0.25	0.75
b	6	0.3	1.8
f	2	0.31	0.62
g	5	0.38	1.90
d	5	0.4	2.0
e	4	0.5	2.0
a	7	0.7	4.9

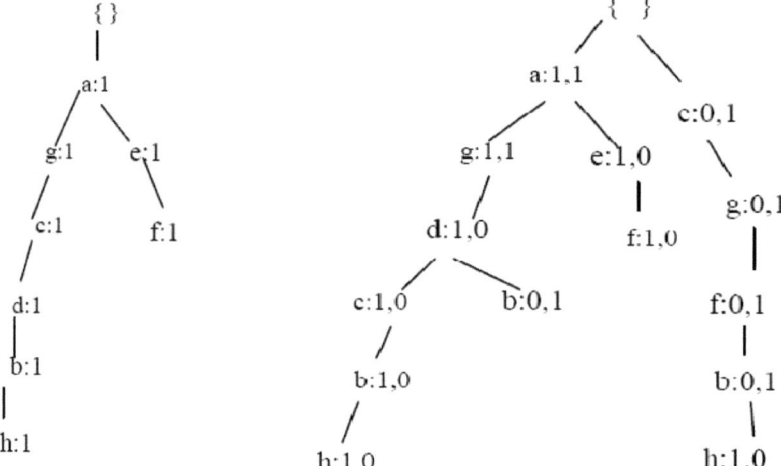

Fig. 2a. After inserting items of batch-1   **Fig. 2b.** After inserting items of batch-1 to batch-2

2.2.2 Item Dynamic Attribute Value Support Is Considered for Deciding Frequentness of Item

Unlike considering both support and weight to decide the priority of an item in section 2.2.1, here we only consider the dynamic attribute of an item to decide its significance. In the context of finding out items which were sold more frequent in real world application such as market basket analysis we may happen to apply this concept.

To decide upon the priority over the items, for example of Fig. 4a, in batch-1 we order the items by considering dynamic attribute support and its order is < a, c, g, e, d, f, b, h >. Fig.4b shows the resulting tree after batch-2 items insertion. Fig. 4c gives the tree after insertion batch-3 and which is the complete tree for sliding window window-1. When we slice the window from window-1 to window-2, it removes the obsolete batch batch-1 and adds new batch batch-4 and the resulting tree is given below in Fig. 5 and all the necessary tables are associated as follows:

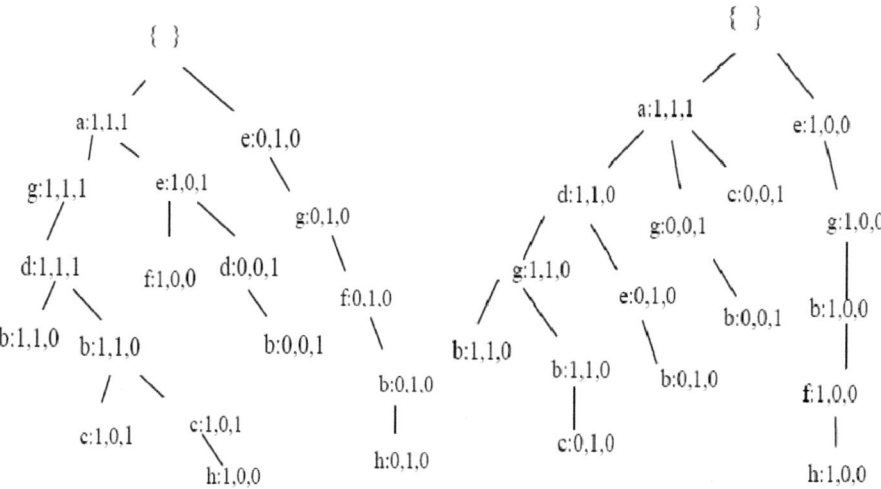

Fig. 2c. Tree construction for window-1 after inserting items of batch-1 to batch-3

Fig. 3. Tree construction for window-2 after inserting items of batch-2 to batch-4

Table 5. Header Table 5 (Batch-1)

Item	Support	Node Priority
a	6	6.0
c	4	4.0
g	3	3.0
e	2	2.0
d	1	10
f	1	1.0
b	1	1.0
h	1	1.0

Table 6. Header Tables 6 (Batch-1 to Batch-2)

Item	Support	Node Priority
a	7	7.0
g	5	5.0
c	4	4.0
e	4	4.0
b	3	3.0
d	3	3.0
f	3	3.0
h	3	3.0

Table 7. Header Table 7 (Batch-1 to Batch-3)

Item	Support	Node Priority
a	10	10.0
d	6	6.0
e	6	6.0
g	6	6.0
b	6	6.0
c	5	5.0
f	3	3.0
h	3	3.0

Table 8. Header Table 8 (Batch-2 to Batch-4)

Item	Support	Node Priority
a	7	7.0
b	6	6.0
d	5	5.0
g	5	5.0
e	4	4.0
c	3	3.0
f	2	2.0
h	2	2.0

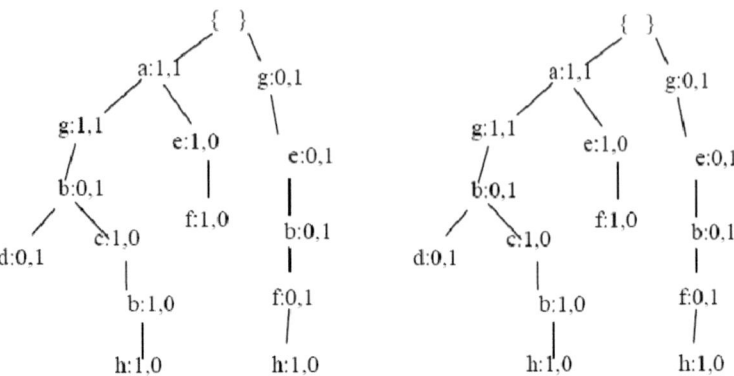

Fig. 4a. After inserting items of batch-1   **Fig. 4b.** After inserting items of batch-1 to batch-2

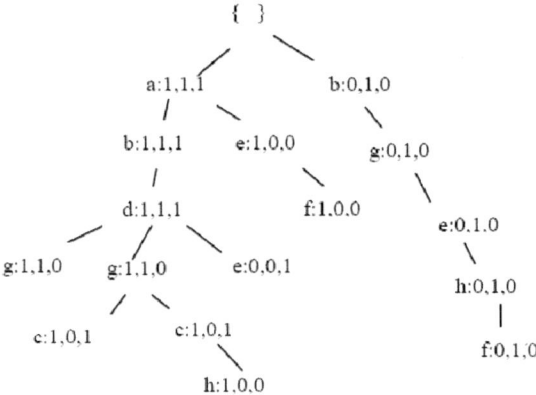

Fig. 4c. Tree construction for window-1 after inserting items of batch-1 to batch-3

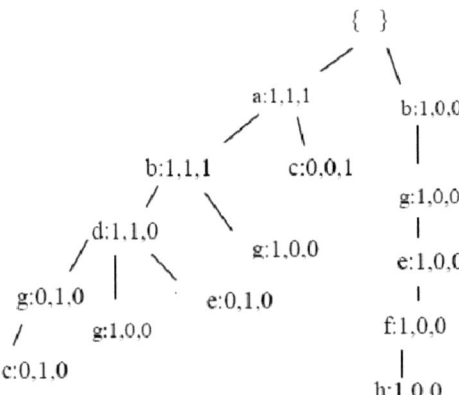

Fig. 5. Tree construction after inserting items of batch-2 to batch-4

3 Mining Process

Mining of the frequent patterns from input items mapped to tree data structure is one of the key operations in the process of extraction of knowledge from the data streams. We have been using breadth first search algorithm to mine the tree and apriori's antimonotone principle is use to prune the tree. We start mining process with the node(s) immediate to the root node. let us consider one of the node and check its corresponding value from the header table that whether product value of support and weight is greater than threshold, then the we call that node considered as frequent and proceed to the   child of it but in case, if the node is not frequent then the children cannot be frequent according to apriori's antimonotone principle so we prune the further nodes of that branch and this will continue for entire tree.

4 Conclusion

In this paper, we proposed a novel approach to mine the frequent items coupled with weight and/ or support which is a very important issue in the real world applications such as market basket analysis of retail-shop. Here we map the input items to general tree structure. In the present work, to decide about whether the item is frequent or not, we compare the user threshold value with item value (i.e., product of item support and its weight). If the item value is greater than or equal to threshold then the item is frequent else it is infrequent. It is working well with the tested data in future; we extend our work with real world dataset.

References

1. Manku, G., Motwani, R.: Approximate frequency counts over data streams. In: 28th International Conference on Very Large Data Bases, pp. 346–357 (2002)
2. Charikar, M., Chen, K., Farach-Colton, M.: Finding Frequent Items in Data Streams. In: Widmayer, P., Triguero, F., Morales, R., Hennessy, M., Eidenbenz, S., Conejo, R. (eds.) ICALP 2002. LNCS, vol. 2380, pp. 693–703. Springer, Heidelberg (2002)
3. Chang, J.H., Lee, W.S.: Finding recent frequent itemsets adaptively over online data streams. In: 2003 Int'l Conf. Knowledge Discovery and Data Mining, pp. 487–492 (2003)
4. Giannella, C., Han, J., Robertson, F., Liu, C.: Mining frequent itemsets over arbitrary time intervals in data streams, Technical Report, 587, Indiana University (2003)
5. Chi, Y., Wang, H., Yu, P.S., Muntz, R.R.: Moment: Maintaining Closed frequent itemsets over a stream sliding window. Int'l. J. Knowledge Information System 10(3), 265–294 (2006)
6. Tsai, P.S.M., Chen, Y.-M.: Mining frequent itemsets for streams over weighted sliding windows. Int'l J. Expert Systems with Applications 36(9), 11617–11625 (2009)
7. Ahmed, C.F., Tanbeer, S.K., Jeong, B.-S.: Efficient mining of weighted frequent pattern over data streams. In: 11th IEEE Int'l. Conf. on High Performance Computing and Communications, pp. 400–4006 (2009)
8. Agarwal, R., Srikanth, R.: Fast algorithms for mining association rules. In: 20th Int'l. Conf. on Very large databases, pp. 487–499 (1994)

9. Yun, U., Leggett, J.J.: WLP Miner: Weighted frequent itemset mining with a weight range and a minimum weight. In: 5th SIAM Int'l. Conf. on Data Mining, pp. 636–640 (2005)
10. Yun, U.: Efficient mining of weighted interesting patterns with a strong weight and/or support affinity. J. Information Sciences 177, 3477–3499 (2007)
11. Huang, J.-W., Tseng, C.-Y., Ou, J.-C., Chen, M.-S.: A General Model for Progressive Sequential Pattern Mining with Progressive Databases. IEEE Transaction on Knowledge and Data Engineering 20(9), 1153–1167 (2008)

Formal Development of Byzantine Immune Total Order Broadcast System Using Event-B

Raghuraj Suryavanshi and Divakar Yadav

Institute of Engineering and Technology
U P Technical University
Lucknow-226021 UP, India
{suryavanshi.cse,divakar.yadav}@ietlucknow.edu

Abstract. A reliable broadcast eventually delivers messages to all participating sites. A total order broadcast is a stronger notion of a reliable broadcast that deliver messages to all processes in a same delivery order. A formal rigorous reasoning is required to precisely understand behaviour of such techniques and an assurance is required to understand how they achieve the objectives. Event-B is a formal technique used for specifying and reasoning about complex systems. In this technique, a system is developed incrementally by adding more details in refinement to obtain more concrete specifications. In this paper, we present a formal development of Byzantine immune total order broadcast system using Event-B. We outline an abstract model specifying total order broadcast using fixed sequencer and introduce more details at refinement level for moving sequencer and detection of Byzantine sequencer.

Keywords: Total order broadcast, sequencer, Byzantine, Event-B.

1 Introduction

A distributed system is a collection of distinct sites that are spatially separated and cooperate with each other towards the completion of a distributed computation [1]. In these systems, there does not exist a common global clock or shared memory, so the up-to-date knowledge about the system is not known to any site or process. These systems communicate with each other through message passing system where the messages are delivered after arbitrary time delays [1]. This problem can be solved by group communication or broadcast primitives that provide ordering guarantees on the delivery of messages. It plays major role in replication where same copy of database is kept across several sites. There are several approaches for managing the replicas using group communication primitives [2,3,4,5,6]. A total order broadcast is one such primitives which ensures that a message is delivered to the different recipient sites in the same order. We have used sequencer based algorithm [7] in which a specific process is elected as a sequencer and becomes responsible for building a total order.

In this paper, we develop a formal model of Byzantine immune total order broadcast system using Event-B. Event-B is formal technique for the development of models of distributed systems. In the abstract model, we have considered fixed sequencer for building a total order delivery of messages. The refinement of abstract

R. Kannan and F. Andres (Eds.): ICDEM 2010, LNCS 6411, pp. 317–324, 2012.
© Springer-Verlag Berlin Heidelberg 2012

model involves the notion of moving sequencer and detection of a Byzantine sequencer.

The remainder of this paper is organized as follows: Section-2 describes the Event-B Section-3 gives an informal description of a Byzantine immune total order broadcast system, Section-4 presents an abstract B model of total order broadcast system having fixed sequencer, Section-5 presents refinement of abstract model containing the moving sequencer also detection and removal of Byzantine sequencer and Section-6 concludes the paper.

2   Event-B and the Rodin Platform

Event-B [8,9,10,11] is an event driven approach used to develop formal models of distributed systems through a series of refinement steps. This formal approach supports a step-wise development from initial abstract specifications to a detailed design of a system in the refinement steps. Through refinement we verify that design of a system conforms to the abstract specifications. An event is made up of three elements namely, its name, guards and the actions. The guards are necessary conditions for the event to occur. An event known as initialization event has no guard and it outline initial state of the system. This helps us to model the system such that new details are added at each refinement state to obtain more concrete specifications. Some frequently used B notations are given in table1.

The Rodin platform [10,11] is an open extensible tool for specification and verification of Event-B. It contains modelling element like event, variables, invariants and components like context and machines. It is embedded by various plug-ins such as proof-obligation generator, model-checkers, provers, UML transformers, etc.

3   An Informal Description of a Byzantine Immune Total Order Broadcast System

The algorithms for building a total order can broadly be classified as sequencer based algorithms, token based algorithms, communication history based algorithms and the destination agreement algorithms [7,12]. We have considered sequencer based algorithm where a specific site is elected as a sequencer and becomes responsible for building a total order. In the abstract model, we have used fixed sequencer approach where broadcasting site first send its message to a designated site, called sequencer. Upon receiving the message, the sequencer assigns it a sequence number and sends its sequence number to all destinations. Each site delivers a message according to the sequence number assigned by the sequencer site. In the refinement model, the concept of moving sequencer is introduced where the role of sequencer is moved from one site to another for load balancing and it also detects and removes the Byzantine sequencer. The sequencer is Byzantine if either the destination site receives two different messages with the same sequence number or a message having higher sequence number is delivered before a message having lower sequence number.

Table 1. Some frequently used B Notations

B Symbol	Description	B Symbol	Description
$\nrightarrow$	partial function	$\rightarrow$	total function
$\lhd\!\!\!-$	relational override operator	$\mathbb{P}$	power set
$\mathbb{P}_1$	non empty power set	$\mapsto$	mapping
$\lhd$	domain restriction	$\times$	Cartesian product

MACHINE Total m
VARIABLES   sender, totalorder, tdeliver
INVARIANTS
  Inv1: sender $\in$ MESSAGE$\nrightarrow$SITE   *Inv3:* tdeliver $\in$ SITE$\leftrightarrow$MESSAGE
  Inv2:   totalorder $\in$ MESSAGE$\leftrightarrow$MESSAGE
INITIALISATION $\triangleq$
BEGIN
  Act1: sender $:=$ ∅ *Act2:* totalorder $:=$ ∅   *Act3:* tdeliver $:=$ ∅
END

Fig. 1. Machine variables, invariants and initialization of abstract model

Broadcast $\triangleq$
ANY ss, mm
WHERE
  Grd1: ss $\in$ SITE   *Grd2:* mm $\in$ MESSAGE   *Grd3:* mm $\notin$ dom(sender)
THEN
  Act1:   sender $:=$ sender $\cup$ {mm $\mapsto$ ss}

Fig. 2. A specification of Broadcast event

4   Abstract Model

In the abstract model, fixed sequencer is used to ensure total order delivery of messages to participating sites. The SITE and MESSAGE are defined as carrier sets, each representing a set of sites and messages. The variable *sender* is defined as partial function from MESSAGE to SITE (see Fig. 1). The mapping $(m \mapsto s) \in$ *sender* indicates that a message m has been sent from a site s. The variable *totalorder* is defined as:

$$\text{totalorder} \in \text{MESSAGE} \leftrightarrow \text{MESSAGE}$$

A mapping $(m1 \mapsto m2) \in$ *totalorder* indicate that message *m1 is totally order before m2*. The variable *tdeliver* represents that a message is delivered to a site in total order. A mapping $(s \mapsto m) \in$ *tdeliver* represent that a site *s* has delivered *m* following a total order.

Order ≙
ANY ss, mm
WHERE
    Grd1: ss ∈ SITE   *Grd2:* mm ∈ MESSAGE
    Grd3: mm ∈ dom(sender)   *Grd4:* ss = sequencer
    Grd5: (sequencer↦mm)∉tdeliver
THEN
    Act1: tdeliver ≔ tdeliver ∪ {ss↦mm}
    Act2: totalorder ≔ totalorder ∪ (tdeliver[{sequencer}]×{mm})

Fig. 3. A specification of Order event

ToDeliver ≙
ANY ss, mm
WHERE
    Grd1: ss ∈ SITE   *Grd2:* mm ∈ MESSAGE   *Grd3:* ss≠sequencer
    Grd4: mm ∈ dom(sender)   *Grd5:* mm ∈ ran(tdeliver)
    Grd6: ss↦mm ∉tdeliver
    Grd7: ∀m·(m ∈ MESSAGE ∧ (m↦mm) ∈ totalorder⇒(ss↦m) ∈ tdeliver)
THEN
    Act1: tdeliver ≔ tdeliver ∪ {ss↦mm}

Fig. 4. A specification of ToDeliver event

Broadcasting a Message (Broadcast Event)
The specifications of the event Broadcast are given in Fig. 2. As outlined in the specification a site *ss* broadcast a message *mm*. The guard *Grd3* of this event ensures that a message has not been previously sent by the sender.

Ordering of Messages (Order Event)
The Order event, given in Fig. 3 models the ordering on messages that were sent before. The *Grd3* specifies that a message *mm* is a valid message that has been sent from any site. After receiving the messages the sequencer builds the total order and broadcast the messages to all sites. The guard *Grd5* specifies that this message has not been delivered to a sequencer. The actions of this event construct a total order on a message and it is delivered to a sequencer.

Total Order Delivery (ToDeliver Event)
The event ToDeliver (see Fig. 4) models the delivery of message *mm* to site *ss* following the total order. The *Grd 5* ensures that it has been delivered to a sequencer site and it also implies that the total order on the message *mm* has also been constructed.

5 Refinement Model

In the refinement model, the notion of moving sequencer is introduced. A notion of token is used to mark a site as a sequencer. A site having a token assumes the role of sequencer and becomes responsible for building a total order on the messages. If the sequencer is Byzantine then delivery order of messages will not be same all sites. The detection of Byzantine is carried out in two cases: either the destination site receives two different messages with the same sequence number or a message having a higher sequence number is delivered before a message having lower sequence number. This is modeled as :

$$sequenceno(mm) < sequenceno(m)\ \wedge\ m \mapsto mm \in totalorder$$

It shows the Byzantine failure of the sequencer because the message *m* whose sequence no. is larger than the message *mm* is delivered before the message *mm* at the destination site. Refinement model of total order broadcat is given in Fig. 5. We introduce new machine variables *sequenceno, movingseq, counter, sitefaultstatus, sitestatus and token* to specify concrete state. The SITEFAULTSTATUS is defined as enumerated set containing the element NONFAULTY, FAULTY, BYZA_DETECT. The SITESTATUS set contains the element PREPARE and SEQUENCER. The TOKEN is also enumerated set and contain the element, ENABLE, DESABLE. The variable *sequenceno* represents the sequence no. of a message. Variable *movingseq* represents a set of sites which are newly admitted in the system. The variable *sitestatus* maps each of the admitted site (from movingseq) to SITESTATUS. The variable *token* maps each of the sites from *movingseq* to TOKEN. The variable *sitefaultstatus* gives the information about fault status of the site and map each admitted site to SITEFAULTSTATUS.

Site_admit Event
A new site is admitted in the system if it does not already exist in the system(see *Grd2* of Fig. 6). This event add a newly admitted site and assign the *sitefaultstatus* as NONFAULTY and *sitestatus* as a PREPARE.

Selection of the Sequencer (Active_Token Event)
This event models the selection of a sequencer (see Fig. 7). At a time only one site can worked as sequencer. The token field of all other sites should be disabled (see *Grd 6*). It enables the token field of a sequencer.

We introduce new variables *sequenceno* and *counter* used in the Order and ToDeliver event. The variable *sequenceno* is defined as: $sequenceno \in MESSAGE \twoheadrightarrow Natural$ and it is used to assign the sequence number to the messages. The variable *counter* is defined as: $counter \in Natural$ and it is initialized with zero and incremented by one each time a message is sent out by the sequencer site.

Detection of Byzantine Sequencer (Byzantine_Checker1 Event)
Sequencer site is Byzantine if the delivery order of the messages at all the destinations are not same. This event detects the Byzantine sequencer if the destination site receives two different messages with the same sequence number (see *Grd7* of Fig. 8).

MACHINE
    overldm
REFINES   **Total m**
VARIABLES
    sender, totalorder, tdeliver, sequenceno, counter, movingseq, token, sitefaultstatus, sitestatus
INVARIANTS
    Inv1:   sequenceno $\in$ MESSAGE $\nrightarrow \mathbb{N}$ *Inv2:* counter $\in \mathbb{N}$
    Inv3: movingseq $\in \mathbb{P}$(SITE)   *Inv4:* token $\in$ movingseq$\rightarrow$TOKEN
    Inv5: sitestatus $\in$ movingseq$\rightarrow$SITESTATUS
    Inv6: sitefaultstatus $\in$ movingseq$\rightarrow$SITEFAULTSTATUS
INITIALISATION $\triangleq$
BEGIN
    Act1: sender $:= \varnothing$ *Act2:* totalorder $:= \varnothing$ *Act3:* tdeliver $:= \varnothing$
    Act4: sequenceno $:= \varnothing$ *Act5:* counter $:= 0$ *Act6:* movingseq $:= \varnothing$
    Act7: sitestatus $:= \varnothing$ *Act8:* sitefaultstatus $:= \varnothing$ *Act9:* token $:= \varnothing$
END

Fig. 5. Machine variables, invariants and initialization of refinement model

Site_Admit $\triangleq$
ANY ss
WHERE
    Grd1: ss $\in$ SITE   *Grd2:* ss $\notin$ movingseq
THEN
    Act1: movingseq $:=$movingseq $\cup$ {ss}
    Act2: sitefaultstatus(ss) $:=$NONFAULTY
    Act3: token(ss) $:=$DESABLE   *Act4:* sitestatus(ss) $:=$PREPARE
END

Fig. 6. specification of site_admit event

Active_token $\triangleq$
ANY ss
WHERE
    Grd1: ss $\in$ SITE   *Grd2:* ss$\in$ movingseq
    Grd3: sitefaultstatus(ss)=NONFAULTY
    Grd4: token(ss) = DESABLE   *Grd5:* sitestatus(ss)=PREPARE
    Grd6: $\forall$s·(s$\in$SITE $\wedge$ s$\in$ movingseq $\wedge$ token(s) =DESABLE)
THEN
    Act1: token(ss) $:=$ENABLE   *Act2:* sitestatus(ss) $:=$SEQUENCER
END

Fig. 7. specification of Active_token event

Byzantine_Checker1 ≜
ANY ss, mm
WHERE
  Grd1: ss∈movingseq   *Grd2:* ss ∈ SITE
  Grd3: sitestatus(ss) ≠ SEQUENCER *Grd4:* mm∈MESSAGE
  Grd5: ss↦mm ∈ tdeliver   *Grd6:* mm∈ ran(tdeliver)
  Grd7: ∃m·(m∈MESSAGE ∧ m∈dom(sequenceno) ∧mm∈dom(sequenceno)∧
      m↦mm∈totalorder∧ sequenceno(m)=sequenceno(mm))
THEN
  Act1: sitefaultstatus(ss)≔BYZA_DETECT
END

Fig. 8. A specification of Byzantine_checker1 event

Byzantine_Checker2 ≜
ANY ss, mm
WHERE
  Grd1: ss∈movingseq   *Grd2:* ss ∈ SITE
  Grd3: sitestatus(ss)≠ SEQUENCER *Grd4:* mm∈MESSAGE
  Grd5: ss↦mm ∈ tdeliver   *Grd6:* mm∈ ran(tdeliver)
  Grd7: ∃m·(m∈MESSAGE ∧ m∈dom(sequenceno) ∧mm∈dom(sequenceno)∧
      m↦mm∈totalorder∧sequenceno(mm)<sequenceno(m))
THEN
  Act1: sitefaultstatus(ss)≔BYZA_DETECT
END

Fig. 9. A specification of Byzantine_checker2 event

Detection of Byzantine Sequencer (Byzantine_Checker2 Event)
This event (see Fig. 9) detects that sequencer is faulty if at the destination site a message having higher sequence no. is delivered before the delivery of lower sequence no. This is ensured by the *Grd.7*.

Removal of Token from Faulty Sequencer (Desable _Token Event)
If any destination site detect that sequencer is Byzantine then the token field of the sequencer is disabled {token(ss) ≔ DESABLE } and assign the status as a faulty {sitefaultstatus(ss) ≔ FAULTY}.

Removal of Faultysite (Remove_Faultysite Event)
If the sequencer is detected as a faulty site its token is disabled and it is removed from the system {movingseq ≔ movingseq\{ss}} .

6 Conclusions

In this paper, we have presented a formal analysis of Byzantine immune total order broadcast system using Event-B on *Rodin platform*. In the abstract model, notion of fixed sequencer is used for constructing the total order on messages. In the refinement, ordering on messages is obtained using a notion of moving sequencer. In this refinement, we also outline the mechanism to identify whether a sequencer is Byzantine.

The sequencer is Byzantine if the delivery order of the messages will not be same at all the sites. It may occur if the destination site receives two different messages with the same sequence number or a message having higher sequence number is delivered before a message having a lower sequence number. After detecting the sequencer as a Byzantine it is removed from the system. This work is carried out on Rodin platform which generates the proof obligations. These proofs are discharged automatically by the prover of the tool.

References

1. Singhal, M., Shivratri, N.G.: Advanced Concepts in Operating Systems. Tata McGraw-Hill Book Company, India (2001)
2. Pedone, F., Guerraoui, R., Schiper, A.: The Database State Machine Approach. Distributed and Parallel Databases 14(1), 71–98 (2003)
3. Agrawal, D., Alonso, G., Abbadi, A., Stanoi, I.: Exploiting Atomic Broadcast in Replicated Databases (extended abstract). In: Lengauer, C., Griebl, M., Gorlatch, S. (eds.) Euro-Par 1997. LNCS, vol. 1300, pp. 496–503. Springer, Heidelberg (1997)
4. Holliday, J.: Replicated Database Recovery Using Multicast Communication. In: NCA 2001: IEEE International Symposium on Network Computing and Applications, Cambridge, MA, USA, October 8-10, pp. 104–107. IEEE Computer Society (2001)
5. Schiper, N., Schmidt, R., Pedone, F.: Optimistic Algorithms for Partial Database Replication. In: Shvartsman, A. (ed.) OPODIS 2006. LNCS, vol. 4305, pp. 81–93. Springer, Heidelberg (2006)
6. Stanoi, I., Agrawal, D., Abbadi, A.: Using Broadcast Primitives in Replicated Databases. In: Proc. of 18th IEEE Int. Conf. on Distributed Computing System, ICDCS 1998, pp. 148–155. IEEE Computer Society (1998)
7. Défago, X., Schiper, A., Urbán, P.: Total Order Broadcast and Multicast Algorithms: Taxonomy and Survey. ACM Computing Surveys 36(4), 372–421 (2004)
8. Yadav, D., Butler, M.: Application of Event B to Global Causal Ordering for Fault Tolerant Transactions. In: REFT 2005: Workshop on Rigorous Engineering of Fault Tolerant Systems, Newcastle upon Tyne, pp. 93–103 (2005)
9. Butler, M., Yadav, D.: An Incremental Development of the Mondex System in Event-B. Formal Aspects of Computing 20(1), 61–77 (2008)
10. Metayer, C., Abrial, J.R., Voison, L.: Event-B language. Technical Report, Deliverables 3.2, EU Project IST-511599-RODIN (2005),
    http://rodin.cs.ncl.ac.uk/deliverables/D7.pdf
11. Abrial, J.R.: A System Development Process with Event-B and the Rodin Platform. In: Butler, M., Hinchey, M., Larrondo-Petrie, M.M. (eds.) ICFEM 2007. LNCS, vol. 4789, pp. 1–3. Springer, Heidelberg (2007)
12. Birman, K.P., Schiper, A., Stephenson, P.: Lightweight Causal and Atomic Group Multicast. ACM Trans. on Computer Systems 9(3), 272–314 (1991)

Analyzing Data Flow in Trustworthy Electronic Payment Systems Using Event-B

Girish Chandra and Divakar Yadav

Institute of Engineering and Technology
U.P. Technical University
Lucknow-226021, UP, India
girish.chandraa@gmail.com,divakar.yadav@ietlucknow.edu

Abstract. Modern days scientific and commercial applications are fairly large and complex and its reliance on large-scale communication, distributed computing infrastructure and complex software system is growing. Electronic payment systems are at the core of many such financially critical software systems. Any failure in such applications may end up in financial losses and loss of trust of users. It is required that these systems exhibit trustworthy behavior and must be able to tolerate failures or attacks. Trustworthiness is now being addressed as an important issue in development of future software systems. In this paper we outline application of formal methods to ensure trustworthiness of electronic payment systems. B specifications of DigiCash payment system are presented. We have used ProB Model checker and animator for temporal model check and constraint based checking, discover errors due to invariant violation and deadlocks, thereby, validating the specifications.

Keywords: Electronic Payment System, Formal Methods, Model Checking, Event-B.

1   Introduction

Modern days scientific and commercial applications reliance on large-scale communication, distributed computing infrastructure and complex software system is growing, as a result failures of such application may be disastrous [3,7]. Therefore, it is required that these systems exhibit trustworthy behavior and must be able to tolerate failures or attacks. Trustworthiness is already an issue in development of business and safety critical system. Traditionally, performance, cost and functional requirements of the system has been dominant issue during software development process while the issue of user confidence or trustworthiness of the software systems has been ignored [4]. Trustworthiness is now being addressed as an important issue in development of future software systems [4,7] . The Trustworthiness of software defined by the National Institute of Standards and Technology (NIST) quoted in [4] as *software that can and must be trusted to work dependably in some critical functions and failure to do so may have catastrophic results, such as, serious injury, loss of life or property, business failure or breach of security.*

R. Kannan and F. Andres (Eds.): ICDEM 2010, LNCS 6411, pp. 325–332, 2012.
© Springer-Verlag Berlin Heidelberg 2012

Electronic payment systems with high assurance are required to satisfy a set of critical properties that include security properties, safety properties and fault-tolerance. The existing work on the development of formal specifications and verification of critical properties in such system is still in its infancy. Recently, it has been argued that a systematic approach toward development of models of such business critical system is required; that captures anomalies and ambiguities at an early stage of development and effectively validates the requirement of such system. Attempts have been used to model electronic payment system using various formal tools and techniques and related tools viz., FDR, NRL protocol analyzer, I/O Automata, KIV, ASM, HOL, Isabelle, B-Method, Z, Z/Eves, OMT, SPIN, NuSMV, CTL, AVISPA, CPALES, Alloy etc [8].

In this paper, we provide rigorous analysis of data flow among various entities and investigate the issue of trustworthiness in context of the electronic payment systems.

1.1   Modeling Approach

Event-B [5] is a formal technique that consists of describing rigorously the problem in an abstract model, introducing solutions or design details in the refinement steps to obtain more concrete specifications, and verifying that proposed solutions are correct. Event-B is a variant of B [1], designed for developing distributed systems. A system using this technique is modeled in terms of an abstract state space using variables with set theoretic types and operators that modify state variables. In Event-B, operations are referred to as events which occur spontaneously rather then being invoked. The events are guarded by predicates and these guards may be strengthened at each refinement step. The invariants state properties that must be *satisfied* by the variables and *maintained* by the activation of the events. We have used the ProB [2] model checker and animator for B specifications. The ProB tool supports automatic consistency checking of B machines via model checking. It allows fully automatic animation of B specifications, and can be used to systematically check a specification for errors.

Application of Event-B can be found in Mondex electronic purse system [6], formal development of total order broadcast [11], development of a train system [10], verification of one copy equivalence criterion in a distributed database system [9] and verification of liveness properties in distributed systems [12].

1.2   B Notations

The B notations are based on set theoretic notations and frequently used notations in our models are explained here. Let A and B be two sets, then the relational constructor ($\leftrightarrow$) defines the set of relations between A and B as :

$$A \leftrightarrow B = \mathbb{P}(A \times B)$$

where $\times$ is cartesian product of A and B. A mapping of element $a \in A$ and $b \in B$ in a relation $R \in A \leftrightarrow B$ is written as $a \mapsto b$.

The *domain* of a relation $R \in A \leftrightarrow B$ is the set of elements of A that R relates to some elements in B defined as :

$$dom(R) = \{a \mid a \in A \land \exists b.(b \in B \land a \mapsto b \in R)\}$$

Similarly, the *range* of relation $R \in A \leftrightarrow B$ is defined as set of elements in B related to some element in A defined as :

$$ran(R) = \{b \mid b \in B \land \exists a.(a \in A \land a \mapsto b \in R)\}$$

The *relational image* R[U] where U⊆A is defined as:

$$R[U] = \{b \mid a \mapsto b \in R \land a \in U\}$$

The *relational inverse* (R^{-1}) of a relation R is defined as :

$$R^{-1} = \{b \mapsto a \mid a \mapsto b \in R\}$$

If $R_0 \in A \leftrightarrow B$ and $R_1 \in A \leftrightarrow B$ are relations defined on set A and B, the *relational over-ride* operator $(R_0 \Leftarrow R_1)$ replaces mappings in relation R_0 by those in relation R_1.

$$R_0 \Leftarrow R_1 = (dom(R_1) \triangleleft R_0) \cup R_1$$

2   Event-B Model of DigiCash

As outlined in Fig. 1, a customer may submit a request for withdrawl or deposit of electronic coins to a bank. The requested bank, upon verifying the credit of the customer, pays electronic token to the customer. Similarly, a customer may deposit the unused electronic coin to the bank. The customer may spend the electronic coins to shop goods and services with a merchant. A merchant allows the customer to buy goods or services based on customer credit and the amount; and receive electronic coins. At a later stage, merchants produces electronic coins to the bank for validation.

The initial part of abstract model of DigiCash payment system as B Machine is given in Fig. 2. The *BANK, CUSTOMER, MERCHANT* and *ITEM* are modelled as deferred sets and they defines the types for the model. The *withdrawcoin* and *depositcoin* are declared as abstract variables and defined as invariant *I-1* and *I-2* using total functions. A mapping $(bb \mapsto amt) \in withdrawcoin(cc)$ indicates a customer cc withdrawn electronic coin worth amt from a bank bb. Similarly a mapping $(bb \mapsto amt) \in depositcoin(cc)$ indicates a customer cc deposits electronic coin worth amt to a bank bb. The set variable *customerbal* maps a customer to a set of natural numbers. A mapping $(cc \mapsto amt) \in customerbal$ indicate that a customer cc has balance amt to his credit. A customer may buy goods or services from a merchant upon payment of electronic coins. The goods and services are modeled as items. The abstract variable *itempurchased*, defined as invariant *I-4*, contains the mappings related to customer, merchant

328 G. Chandra and D. Yadav

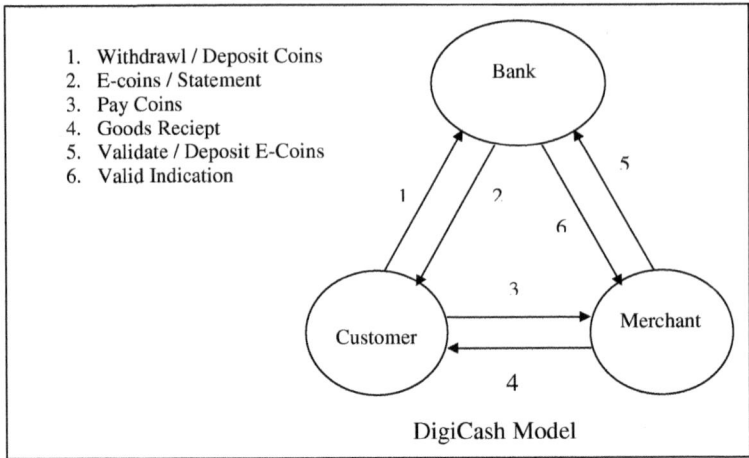

Fig. 1. Data Flow in Electronic Payment Systems

MACHINE

DigiCash

SETS

BANK;CUSTOMER;MERCHANT;ITEM
VARIABLES
withdrawcoin, depositcoin, customerbal,
itempurchased,, unvalidatedtoken, validatedtoken,
customercrdok, customercrdnotok
INVARIANT

I-1: $withdrawcoin \in CUSTOMER \rightarrow (BANK \rightarrow \mathbb{N})$

I-2: $\wedge\, depositcoin \in CUSTOMER \rightarrow (BANK \rightarrow \mathbb{N})$

I-3: $\wedge\;\; customerbal \in CUSTOMER \rightarrow \mathbb{N}$

I-4: $\wedge\, itempurchased \in CUSTOMER \leftrightarrow (MERCHANT \leftrightarrow ITEM)$

I-5: $\wedge\;\; unvalidatedtoken \in MERCHANT \rightarrow (CUSTOMER \rightarrow \mathbb{N})$

I-6: $\wedge\, validatedtoken \in MERCHANT \rightarrow (CUSTOMER \rightarrow \mathbb{N})$

I-7: $\wedge\, customercrdok \subseteq CUSTOMER$

I-8: $\wedge\;\; customercrdnotok \subseteq CUSTOMER$

I-9: $\wedge\;\; customercrdok \cap customercrdnotok = \varnothing$

Fig. 2. Initial Part of the Machine

and items. A mapping $(mm \mapsto it) \in itempurchased(cc)$ indicates that a customer *cc* purchased *it* item (goods or services) from a merchant *mm*. Similarly, variable *unvalidatedtoken* and *validatedtoken* are used to model the amount of unvalidated and validated tokens received from customers. The unvalidated tokens received from the customers in exchange of goods or services are validated by the bank. A variable *customercrdok* is used as a global abstract variable to indicate if a customers credit is OK. For a given customer cc, if $cc \in customercr$-dok then customer credit is considered OK, else if, $cc \in customercrdnotok$ then a customer can neither withdraw coins from a bank nor can he shop from a merchant. For each customer cc, either cc credit is ok or cc credit is not ok. This property is shown as invariant as *I-9*.

INITIALISATION
  withdrawcoin := CUSTOMER x {BANK x {0}}
‖ *depositcoin* := CUSTOMER x {BANK x {0}}
‖ *customerbal* := CUSTOMER x {0}
‖ *itempurchased* := ∅
‖ *unvalidatedtoken* := MERCHANT x {CUSTOMER x {0}}
‖ *validatedtoken* := MERCHANT x {CUSTOMER x {0}}
‖ *customercrdok* := *CUSTOMER*
‖ *customercrdnotok* := ∅

Fig. 3. Initialization

The initial state of DigiCash machine is obtained by initialization of variables outlined in Fig. 3. The initial values of variables *withdrawcoin* and *depositcoin* indicate that all customers have withdrawn or deposited electronic coins worth zero value with all banks. Customer balance of all customers are set to zero initially. All customers are said to have OK credit and assumed to have purchased no item from any merchant. Also, all merchants initially have zero value of unvalidated and validated coins received from customers.

The events of the DigiCash B machines are outlined in Fig. 4 and 5. The event *WithdrawCoin* models the event of withdrawing electronic coins from a bank. The guard $cc \in customercrdok$ ensures that only a customer cc whose credit is OK can withdraw coins from a bank bb. On occurrence of this event, the variable withdrawcoin is updated as below :

$$withdrawcoin(cc) := withdrawcoin(cc) \triangleleft$$
$$\{bb \mapsto withdrawcoin(cc)(bb) + amt\} \qquad (1)$$

As shown at (1), *withdrwawcoin* is updated using function override operator[1] such that values of the coins received by a customer cc from a bank bb in the past is added to the value of new coins received from bank bb. *withdrawcoin(cc)(bb)* represents total values of coins received by a customer cc from a bank bb.

The event *DepositCoin* models the event of depositing electronic coins by a customer cc to a bank bb as below.

$$depositcoin(cc) := depositcoin(cc) \triangleleft$$
$$\{bb \mapsto depositcoin(cc)(bb) + amt\} \qquad (2)$$

The event *SuccessfulPurchase* models the event of purchasing an item it worth amt coins from a merchant mm by a customer cc.

---

[1] (f ⊲ g) represents function f overridden by g.

WithdrawCoin (*cc∈ CUSTOMER,bb∈BANK, amt∈ ℕ1*) ≙
WHEN *cc ∈ customercrdok*
THEN *withdrawcoin(cc) := withdrawcoin(cc) ◁*
  {bb ↦ withdrawcoin(cc)(bb) + amt}
  ‖ *customerbal(cc) := customerbal (cc) + amt*
END;

DepositCoin (*cc∈CUSTOMER ,bb∈BANK, amt∈ ℕ1*) ≙
WHEN *customerbal(cc) ≥ amt*
THEN *depositcoin (cc) := depositcoin (cc) ◁*
  {bb ↦ depositcoin (cc) (bb) + amt}
  ‖ *customerbal(cc) := customerbal (cc) - amt*
END;

SuccessfulPurchase (*cc∈CUSTOMER,mm ∈MERCHANT,*
  it ∈ ITEM, amt ∈ ℕ1) ≙
WHEN *customerbal(cc) ≥ amt ∧ cc ∈ customercrdok*
THEN *itempurchased := itempurchased ∪{cc↦{mm↦ it}}*
  ‖ *customerbal(cc) := customerbal (cc) - amt*
  ‖ *unvalidatedtoken(mm) := unvalidatedtoken(mm) ◁*
  {cc ↦ unvalidatedtoken(mm)(cc) + amt}
END;

Fig. 4. Events-I

ValidateToken (*cc∈CUSTOMER,mm∈MERCHANT, bb∈ BANK)* ≙
WHEN *unvalidatedtoken(mm)* (cc) ∈ ℕ1
THEN *validatedtoken(mm) := validatedtoken(mm) ◁*
  {cc ↦ unvalidatedtoken(mm)(cc) + validatedtoken(mm)(cc)}
  ‖ *unvalidatedtoken(mm) := unvalidatedtoken(mm) ◁ {cc ↦ 0}*
END;

FailedValidation (*cc∈CUSTOMER ,mm ∈MERCHANT,bb∈BANK)*≙
WHEN *unvalidatedtoken(mm)* (cc) ∈ ℕ1
THEN *customercrdok := customercrdok − {cc}*
  ‖ *customercrdnotok := customercrdnotok ∪ {cc}*
END;

GetCredit (*cc ∈ CUSTOMER , bb ∈ BANK)* ≙
WHEN *cc ∈ customercrdnotok*
THEN *customercrdok := customercrdok ∪{cc}*
  ‖ *customercrdnotok := customercrdnotok - {cc}*

END;

Fig. 5. Events-II

The events *ValidateToken* and *FailedValidation* shown in the Fig. 5 models the events of validation of coins/token received by a merchant *mm* from a customer *cc* from a bank *mm*. The *ValidateToken* represents the successful validation of coins by a bank. The guard of this event indicate that this event can be activated only when a merchant have unvalidated coins/token having worth more than zero. Note that $\mathbb{N}1 = \mathbb{N} - 1$, where $\mathbb{N}$ is a set of natural numbers. As a outcome of occurrence of this event, the varibales validatedtoken and unvalidatedtokens are also updated as shown in Fig. 5. In the event of attempting validation of coins/token, a bank may refuse to validate the tokens presented by a merchant. The event *FailedValidation* represents an unsuccessful validation of the coins/token received by a merchant *mm* from a customer *cc* from a bank *mm*. As a consequence of occurrence of this event, the credit of customer is set as shown at (3).

$$customercrdok := customercrdok - \{cc\} \parallel$$
$$customercrdnotok := customercrdnotok \cup \{cc\} \tag{3}$$

A customer whose credit is not OK cannot buy goods or services from a merchant, also these customers may not withdraw coins from a bank. These conditions are included as a guard in the events *WithdrawCoin* and *SuccessfulPurchase* shown in the Fig. 4. Such customers may request the bank for upholding their status so that they can continue buying goods and services. The event *GetCredit* outlined in the Fig. 5 models an event of changing the status of a customer as shown below at (4).

$$customercrdok := customercrdok \cup \{cc\} \parallel$$
$$customercrdnotok := customercrdnotok - \{cc\} \tag{4}$$

The specifications of DigiCash model are model checked using ProB [2] model checker and animator. No deadlock or invariant violation was found to have occurred. However, in the model presented here, invariant conditions are rather weak. It is our understanding that stronger invariant that ensures critical properties to be satisfied by an electronic payment system, be expressed in the model.

3   Conclusions

The electronic payment systems are the crucial component of business critical systems. Formal analysis of critical properties is required to enhance trustworthiness of system that will help achieve clear specifications and proof of correctness of the system. Such analysis is likely to give a clear insight into the system and help to develop the understanding of limit of system within which it can be used.

In this paper we outlined our approach to formal development of electronic payment systems using Event-B formal technique. Abstract B specifications of DigiCash system were model checked using ProB model checker and animator tool. This tool supports automatic consistency checking of B machines via model checking. It allows fully automatic animation of B specifications, and can be used to systematically check a specification for errors. During exhaustive model checking no deadlock or invariant violation was found to have occurred. In the future work we plan to strengthen the invariant conditions and add more concrete design details in the refinement steps.

References

1. Abrial, J.R.: The B-Book: Assigning Programs to Meanings. Cambridge University Press (1996)
2. Leuschel, M., Butler, M.: ProB: A Model Checker for B. In: Araki, K., Gnesi, S., Mandrioli, D. (eds.) FME 2003. LNCS, vol. 2805, pp. 855–874. Springer, Heidelberg (2003)
3. Hasselbring, W., Reussner, R.: Toward Trustworthy Software Systems. Computer 39(4), 91–92 (2006)
4. Bernstein, L.: Trustworthy Software Systems. SIGSOFT Software Engineering Notes 30(1), 4–5 (2005)
5. Metayer, C., Abrial, J.R., Voison, L.: Event-B Language. Technical Report, Deliverable 3.2, EU Project IST-511599-RODIN (2005),
   `http://rodin.cs.ncl.ac.uk/deliverables/D7.pdf`
6. Butler, M., Yadav, D.: An Incremental Development of the Mondex System in Event-B. Formal Aspects of Computing 20(1), 61–77 (2008)
7. Achatz, R., et al.: The Software and Services Challenge. Technical Report, Contribution to the preperation of the Technology Pillar on "Software, Grids, Security and Dependability" in the 7th Framework Programme of EU (2006)
8. Heitmeyer, C.: Managing Complexity in Software Development with Formally Based Tools. In: Filipe, J.K., Poernomo, I., Reussner, R., Shukla, S. (eds.) FESCA 2004. Electronic Notes in Theoretical Computer Science, vol. 108, pp. 11–19 (2004)
9. Yadav, D., Butler, M.: Rigorous Design of Fault-Tolerant Transactions for Replicated Database Systems Using Event B. In: Butler, M., Jones, C.B., Romanovsky, A., Troubitsyna, E. (eds.) Rigorous Development of Complex Fault-Tolerant Systems. LNCS, vol. 4157, pp. 343–363. Springer, Heidelberg (2006)
10. Abrial, J.R.: Train Systems. In: Butler, M., Jones, C.B., Romanovsky, A., Troubitsyna, E. (eds.) Rigorous Development of Complex Fault-Tolerant Systems. LNCS, vol. 4157, pp. 1–36. Springer, Heidelberg (2006)
11. Yadav, D., Butler, M.: Formal Development of a Total Order Broadcast for Distributed Transactions Using Event-B. In: Butler, M., Jones, C.B., Romanovsky, A., Troubitsyna, E. (eds.) Methods, Models and Tools for Fault Tolerance. LNCS, vol. 5454, pp. 152–176. Springer, Heidelberg (2009)
12. Yadav, D., Butler, M.: Verification of Liveness Properties in Distributed Systems. In: Ranka, S., Aluru, S., Buyya, R., Chung, Y.-C., Dua, S., Grama, A., Gupta, S.K.S., Kumar, R., Phoha, V.V. (eds.) IC3 2009. CCIS, vol. 40, pp. 625–636. Springer, Heidelberg (2009)

Attribute -TID Method for Discovering Sequence of Attributes

Preetham Kumar[1] and V.S. Ananthanarayana[2]

[1] Department of Information and Communication Technology
Manipal Institute of Technology, Manipal, India
`preetham.kumar@manipal.edu`
[2] Department of Information Technology
National Institute of Technology Karnataka, Surathkal, India
`ananthvs1967@gmail.com`

Abstract. The abstraction based algorithms read databases in sequential order and then construct abstraction of the database in memory. Given any database with n attributes, it is possible to read the same in n! ways. These different n! ways lead to abstractions of different sizes. In this paper, for a given a set of transactions D, we find the sequence or order of the attributes in which the database is read, a representation which is compact than PC-tree, can be obtained in the memory.

Keywords: Attributes, Compact, Heads, Links, Sequence.

1 Introduction

Given any database with n attributes, it is possible to read the same in n! ways. It was found that the total memory space occupied was different for different ways of reading the database, when we constructed the existing most efficient, compact and complete representation of the database called Pattern Count tree [3]. Therefore, for a given database with n attributes, if we construct Pattern Count Tree based abstractions by reading the database in all n! ways, it is possible to find the abstraction which is more compact.

Finding the best sequence of attributes for a dataset by checking for all the possible combinations is an exhaustive and time consuming process. As the value of n, i.e. the number of attributes in the database becomes very large, this approach of checking for all combinations becomes prohibitive. Therefore, to find an abstraction which is more compact is an issue.This motivated us to come up with a novel approach that eliminates the need to iteratively construct the tree for all combinations of attributes, in order to find the best attribute order.

In order to achieve this, we have developed a method called RON's [7] mesh. This technique involves constructing mesh which include several links. If the database is very large then the process of constructing RON's mesh becomes tedious and it is very difficult to manage the links in RON's mesh. Hence to obtain all necessary information that we get from RON's mesh method, we gave a method which uses an Attribute -TID tree.

R. Kannan and F. Andres (Eds.): ICDEM 2010, LNCS 6411, pp. 333–340, 2012.
© Springer-Verlag Berlin Heidelberg 2012

2   Generation of Attribute -TID Tree

2.1   Structure of Attribute -TID Tree

The Attribute -TID Tree has two different nodes and is shown in Figure 1.

1. The first type of node shown in Figure 1(a), labeled attribute contains an attribute name and two pointers, one pointing to the nodes containing transaction ids and attribute values, and another is a child pointer pointing to the next attribute. This node represents the head of that particular branch.
2. The second type of node shown in Figure 1(b) has 2 parts. The first part labeled TID represents a transaction number or id and the second part of which is labeled Value, indicates attribute value in that transaction. This node has only one pointer pointing to the next object having this particular attribute.

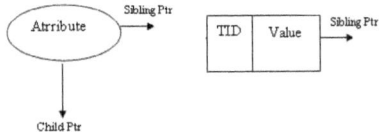

Fig. 1. (a) Attribute Node (b) TID Node in a Attribute -TID Tree

---

Algorithm 1. Construction of Attribute -TID Tree

Input: The database D
Output: Attribute -TID Tree
Method:
for each attribute with value v in a transaction t ∈ D **do**
    create a node labeled v and add it to the respective attribute node
end for

2.2   Defining Matrix and Determining the Sequence of the Attributes

If the number of attributes in the database is n, then take a matrix Mat of size n* n. Order[n], represents an array of size n for storing the order of attributes. node_min = Mat[i][i], where i corresponds to ith attribute having the least number of nodes under it.

r_min=Row_min(k)=min(Mat[i][j]), where i=k, and j is such that it is not equal to k and not already considered in Order[n].

Attr_order[n] : contains the final order of the attributes to be considered
node_span denotes the possible number of nodes at a given level in the tree.

Algorithm 2. For finding the sequence of attributes using Attribute -TID Tree

---

Input: Attribute -TID Tree
Output: A Matrix Mat of order n*n
Method:
for $(i = 0, j = 0; i \leq n, j \leq n)$ **do**
  if (i==j) **then**
    if every node under attribute i has distinct values **then**
      Mat[i][j] = number of nodes under the attribute number i.
      //Mat[i][i] stores the number of nodes under attribute Ai.
    else
      Mat[i][j]= number of nodes under the attribute number i with distinct values
    else
      Mat[i][j]= max(number of nodes under the attribute(Mat[i][i], Mat[i][i]))
    end if
  end if
end for
//**Finding the sequence of the attributes**
find node_min and r_min by scanning the matrix diagonally
Assume node_min row is i and r_min(i)=j
repeat
  if $(j! = i \wedge j \not\subset \text{Order})$ **then**
    t_count= t_count + node_span
    Order[attr_count]=j
    increment attr_count by 1
    min_links (j,Order[], attr_count,node_span,t_count)
  end if
until attr_count is equal to n
Procedure min_links(attribte number i, Order[n],attr_ count, node_span,
t_count)
if (attr_count==n) **then**
  if $t\_count <$ Final_tcount $\vee$ Attr_order[] $\in \emptyset$ **then**
    Update Final_tcount to t_count
    Update Attr_order[] with entries in Order[]
  end if
end if

---

attr_count : the number of attributes already considered for the sequence in Order[] and is initialized to zero.

t_count : denoting likely number of nodes to occur in a tree constructed for a sequence.

Final_tcount : the t_count value associated with sequence in Attr_order[].

3   Illustration

To compute the order of the attributes, we first fill all the entries of the matrix Mat of order n by scanning the Attribute -TID tree. The number of nodes under each attribute will be the respective diagonal entries. i.e Mat[i][i] = {number of nodes under attribute node Ai}. While discovering the number of nodes under any attribute, if there exists same values for two or more nodes under any attribute Ai, we just consider it as one node in order to fill the matrix, since same value is repeated in different transactions.

The other entries of the matrix such as Mat[i][j] represents the association between the attribute Ai and Aj and is obtained as follows:

Mat[i][j] = max(Mat[i][i], Mat[j][j]) (In RON's mesh this value corresponds to number of links between Ai and Aj.)

Then, we scan the matrix Mat diagonally to get the column (or attribute) under which the least number of nodes present. This attribute is the first attribute to be considered in the sequence of the attributes.

Illustration

Consider the sample database given in Table 1 which has 3 attributes and 3 tuples. The Attribute -TID Tree corresponding to Table 1 is given in Figure 2.

Table 1. Sample Database for determining the optimal order of attributes

TID	A1	A2	A3
T1	3	2	1
T2	6	2	1
T3	2	2	4

It follows from Figure 2 that there exist 3 nodes under A1 with different Values, and 3 nodes with the same Value for A2, and 2 nodes with the same Value and a node with different Value for A3. Association among the attributes is represented in the matrix defined by Table 2.

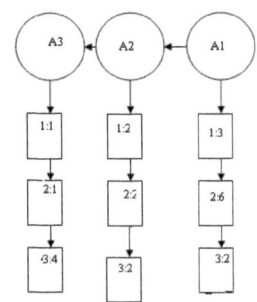

Fig. 2. Attribute -TID Tree

Table 2. Matrix for Figure 2

Attributes	A1	A2	A3
A1	3	3	3
A2	3	1	2
A3	3	2	2

Finding the sequence

It can be observed that the row number as well as the column number in the matrix denotes the header number (attribute number).

After scanning the matrix diagonally, we get node_min = 1 and corresponding value of i as 2. thus, i=2; t_count = 1; node_span=1. attr_count=1. So, Order[1] = 2.

One thing to be noted is that, once an attribute number is considered, i.e. header number in the array Order[], then the column number corresponding to that header number should not be considered for finding the row_min value in the specified row, besides the exclusion of the position in the row, where row number and column number are the same as that position stores the node number, not the number of links.

A call to function min_links gives the following results.

Since i=2, we go to 2nd row of the matrix and to get minimum available row_min value in the 2nd row i.e. row_min = 2, corresponding to i=3. Hence, i=3, Order[2] = 3, attr_count =1+1=2; node_span = 2, t_count = 1+2 = 3.

A call to function min_links gives the following results.

Since i=3, we go to 3rd row of the matrix and to get minimum available row_min value in the 3rd row i.e. row_min = 3, corresponding to i=1. Hence, i=1, Order[3] = 1, attr_count =2+1=3; node_span = 3, t_count = 3+3 = 6.

The final sequence obtained is: $2 \rightarrow 3 \rightarrow 1$

Testing the validity of the sequence by actually constructing the abstraction based on this sequence, we find that this abstraction is more compact than tree based abstraction called PC -tree. The algorithm works best for the n-attributed database that has many tuples that have same value under respective attributes.

4   Experimental Results

In order to test the algorithm we used two different types of data sets. We first applied this algorithm to SPECTF Heart Data[UCI Machine Learning Repository], that contained 45 attributes and had 187 tuples i.e n= 45 and Tn=187.

The best sequence of attributes obtained is as follows:
0(36)-31(126)-32(133)-34(138)-21(141)-12(145)-17(136)-18(144)-7(152)-9(148)-10(151)-4(143)-3(150)-8(151)-14(147)-13(151)-22(153)-5(152)-33(155)-27(154)-2(164)-30(148)-29(155)-1(161)-37(152)-38(159)-15(156)-20(159)-6(159)-16(160)-36(160)-25(175)-40(171)-41(161)-43(164)-44(165)-42(166)-26(167)-24(159)-23(168)-39(171).

The values in bracket along with the attribute numbers in the sequence denote the total number of nodes formed in RON's mesh. The results of the experiment are shown in Table 3.

Table 3. Experimental Results obtained with SPECTF Heart Data

Avg. Time taken to construct a tree for any sequence in seconds	1.2 sec
Total time taken to find the order of the attributes using iterative method	(45!)*1.2 secs
Time taken to find the order of the attributes using RON's mesh	4.3 sec
Time taken to find the order of the attributes using Attribute -TID Tree method	4.4 sec
Total number of nodes in the PC -tree (Sequential order)	7729 nodes
Total number of nodes in the PC -tree by reading the database in the order found by Attribute -TID Tree method	6651 nodes
Saving in nodes	1078 nodes
Total time taken by this method	4.4+1.2 = 5.6 secs

It is found that the sequence leading to compact abstraction leads to a saving of 1078 nodes (space), as compared to a tree constructed using the serial order of attributes (no sorting of elements required in this case).

In the experiment conducted above it has been observed that Attribute-TID tree method requires slightly more time than RON's mesh. As the number of transactions increases then number of links also increases in RON's mesh and time required to construct RON's mesh also increases. We have conducted experiment for the data sets generated by IBM synthetic data set generator and having transactions 5K, 10K, 15K, and 20K. The Table 4 and Figure 3 give this comparison. We found that Attribute -TID tree method is time efficient than RON's mesh[7].

The above algorithm is also compared with PC-tree for the data sets generated by IBM synthetic data set generator. These data sets have transactions 5K, 10K, 15K, 20K, 25K and 50K. The tree is first constructed by reading the database in

Table 4. Execution time in seconds for RON's mesh and Attribute -TID Tree

Data Sets in K	RON's Mesh	Attribute -TID Tree Method
5	62	65
10	125	109
15	186	168
20	248	205

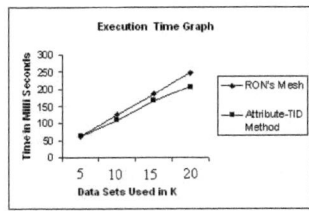

Fig. 3. Execution Graph

sequential order and then in the order of the attributes found by using Attribute
-TID tree method.

Table 5 gives the time required for the construction of PC -Tree after finding
the sequence of the attributes using Attribute -TID tree method. It is found that
in PC -Tree around 11% of saving of space is achieved for the above data sets.
The storage graph corresponding to these data sets is given in Figure 4.

We observe from the above experiments that by reading the database in the
order discovered from Attribute -TID Tree method, creates a compact abstraction. If an attribute has the same value for several tuples then only one node is
going to be constructed for that value of an attribute. Therefore, a lot of saving
of space can be achieved using this method.

Table 5. Experimental Results obtained with IBM Synthetic Data

Data Sets Used in K	Time in sec- onds	PC-Tree obtained by Sequential Reading in Bytes($\times 10^5$)	PC-Tree After Using the or- der found by Attribute -TID Tree method in Bytes($\times 10^5$)
5K	23	1.651	1.402
10K	35	3.18	2.827
15K	47	4.7	3.948
20K	76	6.2	5.619
25K	89	7.65	6.588
50K	178	14.52	11.829

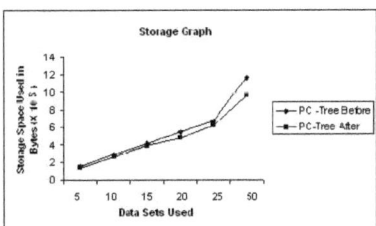

Fig. 4. Storage Space Used by PC-Tree Before and After Finding Order of the Attributes by Attribute -TID tree method

5   Conclusion

This paper explained the method for determining the order of attributes. If the database is read in this order, a compact abstraction of the database than PC - Tree can be constructed in the memory. Further we found that this abstraction is time efficient than RON's mesh. Even though a lot of saving of space is achieved with this method, we require some amount of time to discover order of attributes by Attribute -TID Tree method. Hence a method has to be developed to achieve efficiency in this regard.

References

1. Agrawal, R., Imielinski, T., Swami, A.: Mining Association Rules between Sets of Items in Massive Databases. In: Proceedings of the ACM-SIGMOD International Conference on Management of Data, Washington, D.C, pp. 207–216 (1993)
2. Agrawal, R., Srikant, R.: Fast algorithms for Mining association rules. In: Proceedings of the 20th VLDB Conference, pp. 487–499 (1994)
3. Ananthanarayana, V.S., Subramanian, D.K., Murty, M.N.: Scalable, Distributed and Dynamic Mining of Association Rules. In: Valero, M., Prasanna, V.K., Vajapeyam, S. (eds.) HiPC 2000. LNCS, vol. 1970, pp. 559–566. Springer, Heidelberg (2000)
4. Han, J., Pei, J., Yin, Y.: Mining Frequent Patterns without Candidate Generation. In: Proceedings of ACM-SIGMOD International Conference Management of Data, Dallas, TX, pp. 1–12 (2000)
5. Han, J., Kamber, M.: Data Mining Concepts and Techniques. Morgan Kaufmann Publishers, San Franscisco (2008)
6. Han, J., Jian, P., Mao, R.: Mining Frequent Patterns without Candidate Generation: A Frequent Pattern Tree Approach. Data Mining and Knowledge Discovery, 53–87 (2004)
7. Kumar, R., Kumar, P., Ananthanarayana, V.S.: Finding the Boundaries of Attributes Domains for Quantitative Association Rules using Abstraction - A Dynamic Approach. In: Proceedings of the 7th WSEAS International Conference on Applied Computer Science, Venice, Italy, pp. 52–58 (2007)

Author Index

GPSR Compliance

*The European Union's (EU) General Product Safety Regulation (GPSR)
is a set of rules that requires consumer products to be safe and our
obligations to ensure this.*

*If you have any concerns about our products, you can contact us on
ProductSafety@springernature.com*

In case Publisher is established outside the EU, the EU authorized
representative is:

Springer Nature Customer Service Center GmbH
Europaplatz 3
69115 Heidelberg, Germany

Batch number: 09474011

Printed by Printforce, the Netherlands